When Michelangelo Was Modern

Studies in the History of Collecting & Art Markets

VOLUME 14

The titles published in this series are listed at *brill.com/hcam*

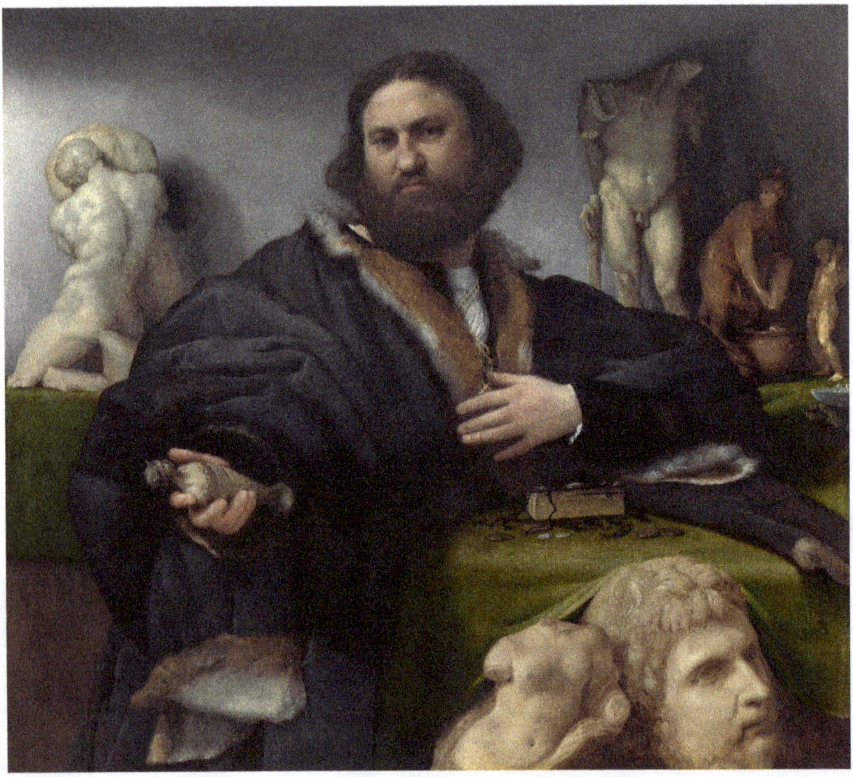

FRONTISPIECE Lorenzo Lotto (1488–1545). *Andrea Odoni*, 1527. Oil on canvas, 104.3 × 116.8 cm (41 × 46 in.)

ROYAL COLLECTIONS (HAMPTON COURT), GREAT BRITAIN

When Michelangelo Was Modern

Collecting, Patronage and the Art Market in Italy, 1450–1650

Edited by

Inge Reist

BRILL

LEIDEN | BOSTON

Cover illustration: Titian (1490–1576). *Jacopo Strada*. 1567–68. Oil on canvas 125 × 95 cm (49 × 37 in.). Vienna, Kunsthistorisches Museum

Published in association with The Frick Collection.

This book evolved from a symposium "When Michelangelo was Modern: The Art Market and Collecting in Italy, 1450–1650," organized by the Center for the History of Collecting, that was held at The Frick Collection on April 12 and 13, 2019. Both the book and the symposium were made possible through the generous support of the Robert H. Smith Family Foundation.

The Library of Congress Cataloging-in-Publication Data is available online at https://catalog.loc.gov

Typeface for the Latin, Greek, and Cyrillic scripts: "Brill". See and download: brill.com/brill-typeface.

ISSN 2352-0485
ISBN 978-90-04-46042-3 (hardback)
ISBN 978-90-04-51393-8 (e-book)

This book is printed on acid-free paper and produced in a sustainable manner.

Contents

Foreword

Since its foundation in 2007, the Center for the History of Collecting at The Frick Collection and Frick Art Reference Library has been committed to expanding the literature in this important and growing branch of the fields of art and cultural history.[1] This volume is the Center's most recent of several publications that have responded to the call from the Robert H. Smith Family Foundation to address subjects related to the collecting of art created during the Renaissance and Baroque eras. The first two focus on American collectors of works of long-dead artists of the Italian Renaissance and Baroque, while a third presents sculpture collections and patrons over the course of several centuries.

As the final volume of this quartet of Smith Foundation-sponsored publications, this book dials back the timeline of collecting during the Renaissance to encourage readers to contemplate the collecting culture, patronage, and art market of the fifteenth, sixteenth, and seventeenth centuries as though in real time—"when Michelangelo was modern." In doing so, the authors of the

---

1 To date, the Center has published ten books dedicated to a broad range of topics in the field, most have concentrated on collecting paintings of a particular period—the Italian Renaissance or the Dutch Golden Age, for example—while others focus on collecting the works of a particular artist and yet others have addressed broad, general topics such as women art collectors and Anglo-American patterns of collecting. The titles of these publications are *Power Underestimated: American Women Art Collectors*, eds., Inge Reist and Rosella Mamoli Zorzi (Venice: Marsilio, 2011); *British Models of Collecting and the American Response: Reflections Across the Pond*, ed. Inge Reist (Farnham and Burlington, VT: Ashgate, 2014); *Collecting Spanish Art: Spain's Golden Age and America's Gilded Age*, and *El Greco Comes to America: The Discovery of a Modern Old Master*, both eds., Inge Reist and José Luis Colomer (New York and Madrid: The Frick Collection and Centro Europa de Estudios Hispanica and Center for Spain in America, 2012 and 2017, respectively); five volumes of the series The Frick Collection Studies in the History of Collecting in America published by The Frick Collection, New York, and Pennsylvania University Press, University Park: *Holland's Golden Age in America: Collecting the Art of Rembrandt, Vermeer, and Hals*, ed. Esmée Quodbach (2014); *A Market for Merchant Princes: Collecting Italian Renaissance Paintings in America*, ed. Inge Reist (2015); *Buying Baroque: Italian Seventeenth Century Paintings Come To America*, ed. Edgar Peters Bowron (2017); *The Americas Revealed: Collecting Colonial and Modern Latin American Art in the United States*, ed. Edward J. Sullivan (2018); *America and the Art of Flanders*, ed. Esmée Quodbach (2020), and *Sculpture Collections in Europe and the United States 1500–1930: Variety and Ambiguity*, eds. Malcolm Baker and Inge Reist (Leiden and Boston: Brill, 2021). Most recently The Frick Collection, Centro de de Estudios Europa, and Center for Spain in America published a volume in honor of the Center for the History of Collecting's founding director: *What's Mine is Yours: Private Collectors and Public Patronage in the United States: Essays in Honor of Inge Reist*, edited by Esmée Quodbach (2021).

book's eleven chapters deepen our understanding of the modus operandi of the art market, including the commercial activities of artists as agents. The role of men and women of letters as well as courtesans is also highlighted, as they, too, served as agents and influenced shifts in taste.

In addition to presenting the activities of now-famous artists from the point of view of their contemporaries, these essays also make a profound contribution to the fields of art and cultural history by bringing to light much archival material. This kind of research has been at the heart of the Center's mission since its beginnings, as it has hosted symposia that air new research through primary documents, sponsored nearly one hundred fellowships, compiled a significant library of oral histories (a program coordinated with the Archives of American Art through the generosity of Barbara Fleischman), and created the uniquely valuable *Archives Directory for the History of Collecting in America* (https://research.frick.org/directory?_ga=2.261559949.1054247395.1613169979-1752025825.1571844301).

All of the Center's publications have their origins in symposia. These exceptionally successful events have appealed to audiences of specialists and the curious public alike as they have also introduced seasoned scholars to up-and-coming young professionals. Most significantly, the symposia have brought together scholars who may not have previously viewed their art historical areas of expertise through the lens of collecting, thus prompting lively exchanges as they viewed their favored category of art in the broader context of cultural history. The symposia are all available for viewing on the website of The Frick Collection (https://www.frick.org/center/symposia) and offer the added advantage of showing each slide show with the many images the authors brought together to support their texts, not all of which could be included in this volume.

As with any publication, many individuals and organizations deserve acknowledgement and thanks. Director Emerita Anne Litle Poulet was instrumental in garnering the support of the Robert H. Smith Family Foundation and we owe a great debt both to her and the Foundation. The Frick's current Anna-Maria and Stephen Kellen Director Ian Wardropper carried forward Anne Poulet's support of the Center as an active member of its Advisory Committee. The arrangements of the symposium that gave rise to this publication, from the selection of speakers to the logistics of the event, were flawlessly overseen by the Center's current and former staff: Center Director Emerita Inge Reist and the Center's two Assistant Directors Esmée Quodbach and Samantha Deutch as well as Margaret Laster, who conferred regularly with Louisa Wood Ruby, Head of Research at the Frick Art Reference Library, and

Ellen Prokop, Associate Head of Research at the Library. Inge then took up the baton and embarked on the long, often time-consuming journey of editing this volume with continuing institutional support from the Frick and conferring often with her counterparts at Brill, Liesbeth Hugenholtz and Christian Huemer, the Editor in Chief of Brill's series Studies in the History of Collecting & Art Markets, to whom we also owe our thanks. Last but certainly not least, we are deeply grateful to the chapter authors of this volume, each of whom was willing to spend time outside of demanding professional commitments, to contribute to this book, confident that it will take its place as a meaningful contribution to the burgeoning field of the History of Collecting.

Stephen Bury
Andrew W. Mellon Chief Librarian
Frick Art Reference Library

Figures

Contributors

Saida Bondini
is a Ph.D. candidate at the Courtauld Institute of Art, London and the University of Lausanne, Switzerland. Her current research, titled *Urban and Social Spaces. Art, Architecture, and Family Patronage in Bologna (1470–1520)* explores the interplay between artistic production, social relationships and the urban fabric of Bologna between the late fifteenth and early sixteenth centuries. Her broader research interests include artistic geography, social and artistic mobility, and the patronage of lay confraternities. Bondini has held fellowships and internships at The Metropolitan Museum of Art (Robert Lehman Collection), the Musée de l'Elysée in Lausanne, and the J. Paul Getty Museum (Paintings Department). Between 2017 and 2018, she was a Teaching Assistant in the Renaissance Department at the Courtauld Institute, where she is currently Associate Lecturer in Early Modern Italian Art.

Patrizia Cavazzini
is Research Fellow at the British School at Rome, advisor to the American Academy in Rome, member of the scientific committee of the Galleria Borghese, member of the Comité International d'Histoire de l'Art. She received her Ph.D. from Columbia University in 1996, where she studied with Joseph Connors, David Freedberg and Keith Christiansen. Her dissertation, published with the title *Palazzo Lancellotti ai Coronari*, won the Saibene prize of the Longhi foundation. Cavazzini is the author of *Painting as Business in Seventeenth-century Rome*, (Penn State University Press 2008) which explores the functioning of the art-market and the diffusion of collecting in the middle-class. The volume won the Choice award as "outstanding academic title" in 2009. In addition, she has published many articles on the art trade in Rome, including "Nicolas Poussin, Cassiano dal Pozzo, and the Roman Art Market" in *The Burlington Magazine*. Cavazzini has worked on the display and reception of pictures in Baroque Rome, in particular for the volume *Display of Art in the Roman Palace*, edited by Gail Feigenbaum. On this topic she has published an essay titled "On Painted Portraiture in XVII Century Rome: Theory, Practice and Appreciation," in the *Römisches Jahrbuch der Bibliotheca Hertziana*. She is now investigating the appreciation of Renaissance masterpieces in Baroque Rome. Her interest in collecting has also resulted in new discoveries on paintings by Raphael. For various exhibitions she has contributed essays on the biographies of Caravaggesque painters, their education, their environment, and the relationship between their life and work. Her essay on Artemisia Gentileschi

has been reprinted in *Italian Baroque Art*, an anthology in the Blackwell series aimed at highlighting the key debates in the field. Cavazzini is part of the international project *Pictor. Le mètier de peintre en Europe à la Renaissance*, which examines the painter's profession in the sixteenth-century in Western Europe.

Leah R. Clark

is Director of Studies for History of Art in the Department for Continuing Education at the University of Oxford and a fellow at Kellogg College. She holds a B.A. from the University of British Columbia, a M.A. from the Courtauld Institute of Art, and a Ph.D. from McGill University. Her research explores the roles objects play in creating networks in the fifteenth century through their exchange, collection, and replication. She is author of *Collecting Art in the Italian Renaissance Court: Objects and Exchanges* (Cambridge University Press, 2018), *Courtly Mediators: Transcultural Objects between Renaissance Italy and the Islamic World* (Cambridge University Press, forthcoming 2023), and co-editor (with Kathleen Christian) of a textbook on the global *Renaissance, European Art and the Wider World 1350–1550* (Manchester University Press, 2017) and *Courtly Mediators: Transcultural Objects between Renaissance Italy and the Islamic World* (Cambridge University Press, forthcoming 2023). Her research has appeared in a number of publications from book chapters in edited volumes to articles in a range of journals, including the *Journal of the History of Collections*. She has received awards and fellowships from a variety of institutions including the Social Sciences and Humanities Research Council of Canada, the Italian Government, the Arts and Humanities Research Council UK, and the British Academy.

Hannah Joy Friedman

is a postdoctoral researcher at the University of Zurich with broad research interests in the art of the early modern period, including art in Iberia and its global empire; the relationship between artistic theory and practice; prints and drawings; court culture and dissimulation; practices of collecting and displaying art; and art's capacity to shape knowledge and to function as evidence. She holds degrees in the history of art from Williams College (M.A. 2008) and from the Johns Hopkins University (Ph.D. 2016), and has also taught art history at Oberlin College, the University of Colorado in Boulder, and Columbia University. Her research has garnered fellowships from several institutions, including the Samuel H. Kress Foundation, the Charles Singleton Center for the Study of Premodern Europe at Johns Hopkins, and the Center for Advanced

Study in the Visual Arts at the National Gallery of Art, Washington, DC. She is currently at work on two books on the art of the Valencian-born painter, etcher, and draftsman Jusepe de Ribera (1591–1652).

Frances Gage
is associate professor of art history at Buffalo State, SUNY. She is a historian of sixteenth- and seventeenth-century Italian art and criticism, collecting, intellectual culture and medicine. She is the author of the book *Painting as Medicine in Early Modern Rome: Giulio Mancini and the Efficacy of Art* (2016) as well as numerous articles and essays. These have appeared in the journals *The Burlington Magazine, Intellectual History Review, Nuncius, Renaissance Studies* and *Renaissance Quarterly*. She is a contributor to *Conserving Health in Early Modern Culture*, edited by Sandra Cavallo and Tessa Storey, *Caravaggio: Reflections and Refractions*, edited by Lorenzo Pericolo and David Stone, *The Display of Art in the Roman Palace, 1550–1750* edited by Gail Feigenbaum with Francesco Freddolini, *Collecting Religious Art in Italy*, edited by Gail Feigenbaum and Sibylle Ebert-Schifferer and *The Academia Seminars*, edited by Peter Lukehart. In 2016, she co-curated with Dr. Cristina Neilson the exhibition *A Picture of Health: Art and the Mechanisms of Healing* at the Allen Memorial Art Museum at Oberlin College. Her work has been supported by many organizations including the American Philosophical Society, the Center for Advanced Study in the Visual Arts, the Folger Shakespeare Library, the NEH, the Newberry Library, the Renaissance Society of America and the Samuel H. Kress Foundation.

Chriscinda Henry
is Associate Professor of Art History at McGill University in Montréal, where she holds a Social Sciences and Humanities Research Council of Canada (SSHRC), Insight Grant for the project "Picturing Places, Networks, and Knowledge: Images in Early Modern Friendship Albums" (2019–24). She received her Ph.D from the University of Chicago and has held postdoctoral fellowships at the Yale University Humanities Center and The Harvard Center for Italian Renaissance Studies, Villa I Tatti. Prior to arriving at McGill she was Visiting Assistant Professor of Renaissance and Baroque Art at Oberlin College and Conservatory. Her research focuses on the relationship between secular art and social life in Renaissance Europe, and her first book on this subject, *Playful Pictures: Art, Leisure, and Entertainment in the Venetian Renaissance Home*, was published by the Pennsylvania State University Press in 2021.

Frederick Ilchman
is the Mrs. Russell W. Baker Curator of Paintings and Chair, Art of Europe, at the Museum of Fine Arts, Boston. He holds a B.A. from Princeton and a Ph.D. from Columbia. A specialist in the art of the Italian Renaissance, Frederick joined the MFA in 2001. His exhibitions for Boston include *Titian, Tintoretto, Veronese: Rivals in Renaissance Venice* (2009), organized with the Musée du Louvre, and *Casanova's Europe: Art, Pleasure, and Power in the 18th Century* (2018). Outside of Boston, he was part of the curatorial team for the exhibition *Tintoretto* (2007) at the Museo Nacional del Prado in Madrid, and co-curated *Paolo Veronese: A Master and His Workshop in Renaissance Venice* (2012) at the Ringling Museum in Sarasota. In 2018–19, he co-curated *Tintoretto: Artist of Renaissance Venice* at the Palazzo Ducale in Venice and the National Gallery of Art, Washington, DC. Frederick was one of four curators for an exhibition in 2021, also at the Palazzo Ducale, celebrating the 1600th anniversary of the city's legendary founding, *Venetia 1600: Nascite e Rinascite*. In 2005, he joined the board of directors of Save Venice Inc., the largest non-profit organization devoted to preserving the art and architecture of Venice. He became Chairman of the Board in 2016.

John Marciari
is the Charles W. Engelhard Curator, Head of the Department of Drawings and Prints, and Curatorial Chair at the Morgan Library & Museum, New York. A specialist in Italian and Spanish art of the fifteenth through and eighteenth centuries, his recent publications include the exhibition catalogues *Architecture, Theatre, and Fantasy: Bibiena Drawings from the Jules Fisher Collection; Guercino: Virtuoso Draftsman*; *Drawing in Tintoretto's Venice*; and *Italian Renaissance Drawings at the Morgan Library and Museum*; as well as the short monograph *Art of Renaissance Rome: Artists and Patrons in the Eternal City*. He has also written essays, entries, and reviews in a range of exhibition catalogues and scholarly journals on topics including Paolo Veronese, Federico Barocci, Caravaggio, and Diego Velázquez. He received his Ph.D. from Yale University and he is a Fellow of the American Academy in Rome. In connection with his position at the Morgan Library & Museum, Marciari is also the head of the Morgan Drawing Institute, a research center focused on the study of drawings from all periods, and he serves on the editorial board of the journal *Master Drawings*. His current projects include a book on the drawings of Giovanni Battista Piranesi.

Fausto Nicolai
earned his Ph.D. in Art History from the University of Tuscia-Viterbo (in 2008), after which he focused his studies on the development of visual arts in Rome and central Italy between the 16th and 17th centuries, with a particular interest in patronage and collecting practices, both in the secular and ecclesiastical environments. He has published articles on this subject in academic and international journals such as *The Burlington Magazine, Paragone, Prospettiva.* In 2008, Nicolai published his Ph. D. dissertation (*Mecenati a confronto. Committenza, collezionismo e mercato dell'arte nella Roma del primo Seicento. Le famiglie massimo, Altemps, Naro e Colonna,* Rome 2009), which illustrates through a comparative analysis the relationship between patronage and the rise of the art market in early seventeenth century Rome. After teaching for five years the History of Early Modern art at University of Cassino, he was appointed curator of the Frederick Mason Perkins Archive in Assisi in 2013. As a result of his research in that archive, he began to focus his scholarship on the American collecting of Early Renaissance Italian painting. Nicolai was awarded fellowships by the Center for The History of Collecting (The Frick Collection in New York, 2013 and 2015) and by the Metropolitan Museum of Art (2016–2018) to expand on that research. After publishing two articles (*Journal of History of Collections*, 2015 and 2019) he is currently preparing a book on Frederick Mason Perkins and the American art market of Italian Primitive painting in the early 20th century.

Inge Reist
is the Director Emerita of the Center for the History of Collecting, which she established at The Frick Collection and Frick Art Reference Library in 2007. Prior to that, she was the Chief of Research Collections and Programs and Head of the Photo Archive at the Frick. In 2013, she was the founding president of PHAROS—An International Consortium of Photo Archives. Holding a Ph.D. in Art History from Columbia University, specializing in Italian Renaissance and Baroque art, she has published widely in that field in major journals and exhibition catalogues that include *The Art Bulletin* and *Gazette des Beaux Arts*, as well as *Blackwell Companion to Renaissance and Baroque Art*. She has edited or co-edited six of the ten publications of the Center for the History of Collecting and has contributed chapters to several volumes focused the history of collecting published by the Getty Research Institute, most significantly, *Provenance: An Alternate History of Art* co-edited with Gail Feigenbaum. From 2005 to 2011 Inge was Chairman of the Association of Research Institutes in Art

History. Since retiring after thirty-seven years at the Frick, she remains active in the field having presented papers at conferences at Brandeis University, the New Orleans Museum of Art, and the Gulbenkian Foundation in Lisbon, as well as The Frick Collection.

Stephen K. Scher
earned his B.A. from Yale University in 1956, his M.A. from the Institute of Fine Arts of New York University in 1961, and Ph.D. in art history from Yale in 1966. From 1961 to 1974, he taught at Brown University serving as Art Department chair from 1972. In 1969 he organized the Rhode Island School of Design museum exhibition and accompanying catalogue *The Renaissance of the Twelfth Century*. In 1974 until his retirement in 2004, Scher was President and CEO of Scher Chemicals, Inc., a manufacturer of specialty organic chemicals, but throughout that time he continued to actively contribute to art research and serve as guest curator, catalogue author, and lender for numerous exhibitions: *The Currency of Fame: Portrait Medals of the Renaissance* (1994, The Frick Collection, The National Gallery of Art, and National Gallery of Scotland); *The Proud Republic: Dutch Medals of the Golden Age* (1997, The Frick Collection). For the Metropolitan Museum of Art, Scher contributed to *Byzantium: Faith and Power* (2004); *Set in Stone: The Face in Medieval Sculpture* (2006); *The Art of Illumination: The Limbourg Brothers and the* Belles Heures *of Jean de France, Duc de Berry* (2010); *The Portrait in Renaissance Italy from Masaccio to Bellini* (2011). Dr. Scher is a member of four visiting committees at the Metropolitan Museum of Art: Medeval; European Sculpture and Decorative Arts; Paper Conservation; and Object Conservation and is a member of the Visiting Committee for Collections at The Frick Collection. He is a member of the Yale Library Associate Trustees and serves. on the Board of Visitors of the Tyler School of Art at Temple University. Dr. Scher has lectured and published extensively on medieval and Renaissance art. His own collecting activities have focused on commemorative, especially Renaissance, portrait medals. He is donating the bulk of this collection to The Frick Collection, where he helped organize an exhibition of highlights from the collection, entitled *The Pursuit of Immortality: Masterpieces From The Scher Collection of Portrait Medals*. The Frick has also published a catalogue of the entire collection. Dr. Scher received the Yale Medal in November 2015, the British Art Medal Society's President's Medal in October, 2018, and the Iris Award from the Bard Graduate Center in April 2021.

INTRODUCTION

Shaping the Splendor of Italian Renaissance Art through Collecting and Patronage

Inge Reist

For many, consideration of art patronage and collecting during the Renaissance and Baroque periods, brings to mind the provinces of princes, popes, and prelates—Lorenzo de' Medici (1449–1492) and Federico Gonzaga (1500–1540), Popes Julius II (1443–1513) and Urban VIII (1568–1644) or Cardinals Giulio de' Medici (1478–1534) and Scipione Borghese (1577–1633), just to name a few. But, in reality, the cast of characters that shaped the art collecting landscape of the late fifteenth, sixteenth, and seventeenth centuries was remarkably varied, calling on a broad range of talented personalities that included middlemen and connoisseurs from all walks of life, social strata, and professions. As a consequence, we discover that each in his or her own way contributed to a fascinating moment in the history of collecting and patronage, when the *modus operandi* of the art market, more or less as we know it today, began to take shape.[1] In Richard Goldthwaite's analysis of the shifting economic circumstances in Renaissance Italy, increased consumerism and the concomitant demand and market for works of art went hand in hand with the status seeking of collectors, patrons and artists alike, as taste came to establish social credentials.[2]

1 The literature on the art market in Italy during the sixteenth and seventeenth centuries has expanded considerably in recent years, notably with studies that introduce economists' methods of analysis such as game theory as well as more conventional evaluations of supply and demand. See for example Nelson and Zeckhauser, *The Patron's Payoff* and numerous contributions to the volume edited by Fantoni, Matthew, and Matthews-Grieco, *The Art Market in Italy* especially Goldthwaite's contribution "Economic Parameters," which problematizes issues surrounding the production and consumption of art as economic activity, taking into account supply, demand, subcontracting, and developing demand among specific audiences and consumers. Goldthwaite's earlier publication *Wealth and the Demand for Art* (1993) focuses more sweepingly on the developing consumerism within Italian Renaissance society as well as the "producers' strategies" that artists adopted to create demand. O'Malley's *The Business of Art* offers detailed analyses of contracts during the Renaissance and in doing so sheds valuable light on workshop practices and the expectations held by both the artists and the patrons. Throughout this volume, the authors address how the market was impacted by shifting taste, even as their primary focus is on collecting and patronage rather than data-driven analyses of art market economics.

2 Goldthwaite, *Wealth and the Demand for Art*, 245–249.

 DOI:10.1163/9789004513938_002

Modern authors, rightly point to Giorgio Vasari's *Lives of the Artists* (1550; 1568) as the most consequential, if not also the first publication to comment on the economic concerns of artists and how they adopted strategies that aimed at developing a demand for their art. As Philip Sohm observes, "Vasari delved first into ways that economics permeated artists' lives: how money established social status and drove art marketing, how it shaped the material conditions of living, and (most fundamentally) how it affected artistic practice, consumption and perception." For their part, Nelson and Zeckhauser cite the preface to Vasari's third book in which he states that higher prices could incentivize artists to deliver higher quality works, thus signaling to patrons that paying more could reap rewards.[3]

This volume brings to life many of this varied cast of personalities active in the production and consumption of works of art, some of whom are profiled in this introduction. Many were indeed kings, princes, and prelates, but others were artists, who at times supplemented their incomes to serve as dealers, advisers, or experts called in for contract mediation, while still others were merchants, diplomats, or men and women of letters. By presenting case studies of collecting and patronage the chapters that follow illuminate many of the subtle distinctions between art collectors' roles as patrons of untested artists on the one hand, and collectors of recognized artists—both contemporary and of earlier generations—on the other hand. More often than not, intermediaries and the artists themselves were involved in cultivating new markets, for drawings or forgeries, for example, in match-making artists and patrons, or in finalizing contracts and debating pricing issues.

The title of this book "When Michelangelo Was Modern" suggests a strong focus on collectors of contemporary art in Italy—risk-takers who were willing, through their patronage, to support and promote untested artists of their own time, unable to know the heights those artists' reputations would achieve in later decades and centuries. However, the reality is that the nature of Renaissance and seventeenth-century culture, with its emphasis on celebrating the classical past, meant that collecting antiquities went hand in hand with taking a chance on a young artist; and the nature of commerce and diplomacy during the Renaissance meant that the developing art market was international in its reach, leading to the spread of Italian culture to all of the major courts and cultural centers of Europe.[4] A glorious example of this may still be

3 Sohm, "Introduction," 30, and Nelson and Zeckhauser, *The Patron's Payoff*, 25–26.

4 Among others, Goldthwaite observes that the collecting impulse, as influenced by humanist writings that celebrated ancient Roman culture, led to the formation of major collections of antiquities throughout Italy (see Goldthwaite, *Wealth and the Demand for Art*, 247).

seen and appreciated at The Frick Collection, where two magisterial allegories by Paolo Veronese (1528–1588) hang. These pictures were offered by the artist/dealer Jacopo Strada (1507–1588; cover image) to Duke Albrecht v of Bavaria (1528–1579) but were ultimately sold by Strada to the Habsburg Holy Roman Emperor Maximilian II (1527–1576) and inherited by his successor Rudolf II (1552–1612) to be housed with his vast collection in Prague.[5]

Evidence of how collecting antiquities went hand in hand with acquiring works by young artists lies in the famous story of Michelangelo's (1475–1564) early sale of a sculpture of a sleeping Cupid to Cardinal Raffaele Riario (1461–1521) through the dealer Baldassare del Milanese.[6] The oft-told tale recounts how the twenty-year-old sculptor, knowing the preference collectors had for antique statuary, was encouraged by his patron Lorenzo di Pierfrancesco de' Medici (1463–1503) to bury his sculpture, carved in a manner imitative of the ancients, with the intention of then roughing it up to give it the appearance of having been unearthed after centuries in the ground. In the near term, the trick failed, because Cardinal Riario demanded his money back once he learned of the deception; but in the longer term, the ploy did much to boost the young sculptor's reputation in Rome and did nothing at all to damage the reputation of the work itself, which was subsequently acquired by Cesare Borgia (1475–1507) who in turn gave it to his sister Lucrezia Borgia's (1480–1519) sister in law Isabella d'Este (1474–1539).[7] Stephen Scher elaborates on this story and much else about Isabella's exceptional collection in his chapter in this volume, while Hannah Friedman's essay examines the new "economy of taste" that was spawned by copies, fakes, and forgeries of ancient and modern works. Significantly, apparently undeterred by the ruse, Cardinal Riario went on to commission Michelangelo to carve a more than life-size statue of Bacchus (Museo Nazionale del Bargello, Florence), which he also ended up rejecting likely due to its drunken imbalance. Nonetheless, the *Bacchus* soon found a good home in the collection of Jacopo Galli, where Maarten van Heemskerck

5 Xavier Salomon convincingly asserts that the two allegories, long assumed to have been sold directly to Rudolf II, were, in fact offered to Albrecht and subsequently sold to Maximilian. See Salomon, *Veronese's Allegories*, 20–21 and Salomon, *Veronese*, 174–178.

6 The story of Michelangelo's Cupid being passed off as an ancient statue originates with the artist's contemporary biographers Vasari (*Life of Michelangelo*, 49–52) and Condivi (*Vita di Michelagnolo*, 33–34). For a detailed investigation of the commission and disappearance of Michelangelo's Cupid, see Norton, "The Lost Sleeping Cupid," and also Hirst, *Young Michelangelo*, 13–28, and Stephen K. Scher's chapter in this volume.

7 Norton, "The Lost Sleeping Cupid," 251–252.

(1498–1574) recorded it ca. 1533–36, displayed among the many antiquities Galli kept in his courtyard in Rome.[8]

1 Two Venetian Collectors

Two descriptions of collections in Venice, one from the sixteenth century and one from the seventeenth, convey the essence of the collecting taste of the times.[9] The first dates to Marcantonio Michiel's (ca. 1484–1552) visit in 1532 to the collection of the Venetian merchant Andrea Odoni (1488–1545):

> In the court downstairs.... The marble figure of a woman entirely draped, headless and handless, is antique and it used to be in the studio of Tullio Lombardo, who reproduced it several times in his many works.... The many other marble heads and figures, mutilated and shattered, are antique.... The nude marble figure of a man, represented in the act of walking, handless and headless near the door, is antique.[10]

But of greater interest to us are the rooms in the floor above where, in addition to ancient statuary and natural curiosities typical of the components of *Kunstkammern* of princes and scholars, Odoni displayed elements of books of hours, small bronzes by modern masters, and paintings by the most highly-regarded artists of the day.

> In the little study upstairs. The porphyry cup was made by Piero Maria Fiorentino, and is the one which formerly belonged to Francesco Zio [an uncle whose collection Odoni inherited]. The inlaid crystal cup was made by Cristoforo Romano, and formerly belonged to Francesco Zio. The cup of petrified root was made by Vittore di Arcangeli. The four headings of the small Book of Hours ... were painted by Giacometto. The David at the beginning of the other small Book of Hours was painted by Benedetto Bordone. The five small vases of gems and gold are modern and formerly

8 Lieberman, "Michelangelo's 'Bacchus'," 65–74. The Galli courtyard was an especially suitable location for the statue in light of its self-conscious inspiration from and rivalry of ancient statuary. See Freedman, "Michelangelo's Reflections on Bacchus," 121–135, especially 121–125, and Hannah Friedman's essay in this volume.

9 The most extensive study of collecting in Venice is Hochmann, Lauber, and Mason, *Il collezionismo d'arte, Cinquecento*, and, Borean and Mason, *Il collezionismo d'arte, Seicento*; for collecting antiquities, see also Damen, "Shopping for *cose antiche*."

10 Michiel, *Anonimo: Notes on Pictures*, 96–97.

> belonged to Francesco Zio, as well as the porcelain vases and plates, the antique vases and medals, and the animals, that is to say, the petrified crabs, fishes and snakes, a dried chameleon, some small rare lizards, crocodiles and quaint fishes.... In the room upstairs. The oil picture with two half-length figures of a girl and an old woman behind her is by Jacopo Palma. The portrait of Messer Andrea himself, in oil, half-length, represented looking at some antique marble fragments, was painted by Lorenzo Lotto. The picture representing Our Lady with the Divine Infant, St. John as a child, and a female saint in a landscape is by Titian. The chests in the same room, the bedstead and the doors, were painted by Stefano, a pupil of Titian's. The large figure of a woman, nude lying down painted on the back of the bed is by Gerolamo Savoldo of Brescia.[11]

Michiel thus makes clear that Odoni's taste ran the gamut from antique statuary of the kind Lotto (ca. 1580–1556). artfully placed in his 1527 portrait of the collector (frontispiece) to modern paintings datable to the 1520s by Titian (1488/90–1576), Palma Vecchio (ca. 1480–1528), and Girolamo Savoldo (ca. 1480–ca. 1548) to small bronze statuettes, crystal vases, cameos, and shells, and quasi-scientific objects of interest such as petrified crabs. Intriguingly, Odoni displayed his prized contemporary works, including the portrait by Lotto, in his bedroom which may seem odd to twenty-first-century connoisseurs, but this is, in fact, in keeping with a long-standing practice in Italy to concentrate precious domestic furnishings in a multi-use chamber that served as bedroom, study and reception area. Only with the expansion of consumption during the sixteenth century did domestic spaces become more specialized in function and décor.[12] In Odoni's time, a typical Venetian house had the bedroom / study / reception room on the main floor of a residence, the *piano nobile*, while the areas of the ground floor, the *androne*, were generally used for commercial purposes and were, as Michiel describes, filled with fragments of ancient statuary and modern copies. Moreover, as Andrew Martin observed, Odoni may well have taken his cue from the first-century writing of Pliny the

---

11 Ibid., 97–99. See also Rosella Lauber "Andrea Odoni," in Hochmann, Lauber, and Mason, *Il collezionismo d'arte, Cinquecento*, 298–300 for a brief, but impressively detailed biography of Odoni, that, in addition to Michiel, cites Pietro Aretino's praise of Odoni in a letter of 30 August 1538, Vasari's observations published in his *Vita* of Girolamo da Treviso, and work Odoni inherited from Francesco Zio. The most recent and extensive study on Odoni is Schmitter, *The Art Collector*.

12 For elaboration on how the functions of interior spaces changed as the acquisition of more domestic furnishings increased, and as the collecting of antiquities accelerated, see Goldthwaite, *Wealth and the Demand for Art*, 232–237.

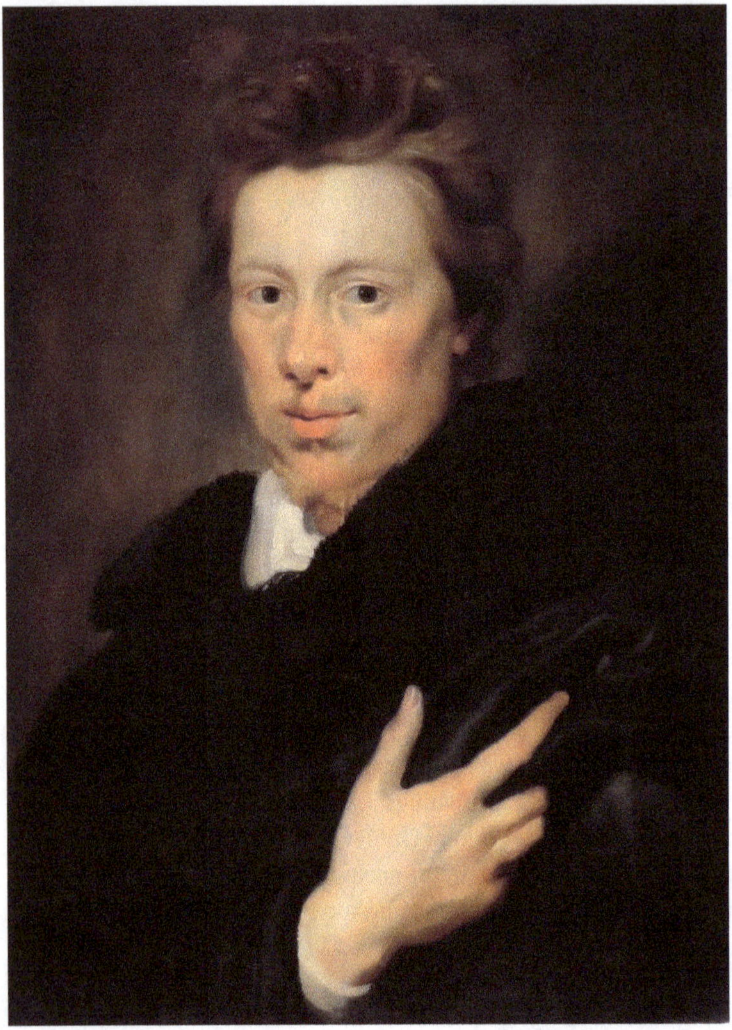

FIGURE 0.1 Peter Paul Rubens (1577–1640), *Daniel Nijs*, 1612–13. Oil on panel, 65.4 × 48.3 cm (25 ¾ × 19 in.)
DAYTON ART INSTITUTE, DAYTON, OHIO

Elder in his *Historiae Naturalis* who also places art that the collector especially valued in his bedroom.[13]

An interesting foil to Odoni is the collector Daniel Nijs (1572–1647; fig. 0.1), whom the seventeenth-century chronicler of Venice Marco Boschini lauded as

13 Martin, "'Amica e un albergo'," 162.

"one of the foremost traders of the city and a great connoisseur of pictures"[14] and who eventually gained notoriety for brokering what was understood even in its own time as the sale of the century of Federigo Gonzaga's collection in Mantua to King Charles I of England.[15] Nijs's life was essentially that of a Flemish expatriate merchant in Venice which brought him considerable success, as the seventeenth-century architect and author Vincenzo Scamozzi (1548–1616) noted in his 1615 publication *L'idea dell' architettura*. Scamozzi positions his description of Nijs's collection in the section of his book dedicated to the new trend for displaying private art collections in rooms called *gallerie* designed specifically for that purpose.

> Signor Daniel Nijs, honored Flemish merchant, moved by his generous mind and provoked by the virtuosity of the aforesaid [collectors], has himself also adorned his *portico* and another room with objects with which later to embellish his own homeland … Here are found perhaps 40 statues of various sizes and almost 80 carved heads, a large number of which come from the collection of the illustrious signor Simon Zeno; and not a few torsos and bas-reliefs. There are also around 60 paintings, a number of which belonged to the Excellent Coradino, and 20 portraits by the hands of the most celebrated artists of all times up to the present day. Furthermore he owns an ebony archive [or cabinet] completely decorated on the inside as well as on the outside, where there are many small delicate pictures along with some singular miniatures. Inside are kept portraits of princes, woodcuts, niello and enamel objects, engravings, and all the drawings by Albrecht Dürer and Lucas van Leyden, in addition to a great number of drawings by the hands of the most celebrated masters as well as all types of seashells. The value of this archive is estimated to be as high as 10,000 scudi.[16]

---

14 Anderson, *The Flemish Merchant of Venice*, 54.

15 Ibid., 115–143, provides an exceptionally detailed account of Nijs's role as a broker for the sale. For Nijs's activities as a merchant and his relations with agents and diplomats from England and the Low Countries, see the biography by Maartje van Gelder, "Daniel Nijs," in Borean and Mason, *Il collezionismo d'arte, Seicento*, 295.

16 Scamozzi, *L'idea dell'architettura*, Part 1, Book 3, chapter 19, 306: "Il signor Danielle Nis honorato Mercante Fiamengo, mosso dal suo generoso animo, & incitato dalle virtù de' soddetti hà ancor esso ornato un suo Portico, e stanza per dover poi in breve adornarne la sua propria Patria, e que' Paesi di là, ove si ritrova havere forsi 40 statue di varie grandezze, e presso 80 teste di rilievo: buona parte de' quali furono del Ciarissimo Signor Simon Zeno, e non pochi torsi, e bassi rilievi: e circa 60 quadri, parte de' quali furono dell'Eccellentissimo Corradino: e 20 teste di mano de' più celebri Pittori, che siano stati fino à questi tempi. In oltre hà un' & anco alcune miniature singolari: e là dentro si

Worth noting is that when Nijs declared bankruptcy, his cabinet was the possession he held to the bitter end during the liquidation of his assets.[17]

Others who waxed eloquent about Nijs's discerning taste were the poet-humanist Giulio Cesare Gigli (ca. 1570–ca. 1640) and Constantijn Huygens (1596–1687), the Dutch poet and writer who later served as secretary to Princes Frederick Henry and William II of Orange. In 1620, Huygens described the collection this way when he accompanied the Ambassador of the United Provinces of the Netherlands to Venice:

> July the 1st … After dinner Monsieur the Ambassador was taken to see the admirable collection of the gentleman Daniel Nijs … who, after an infinity of paintings and ancient statues, showed us a small, ebony table-shaped cabinet within which were so many rare paintings, medals, shells and similar curiosities that one would need three days to examine, let alone describe everything. The collection's value is estimated at 16,000 ducats. Among the statues in his house is a real antique Julius Caesar, which we were assured came from the temple at Ephesus.[18]

Significantly, in both the Scamozzi and Huygens descriptions, matters of provenance and monetary value are apparently deserving of comment, as the writers attached value both to past ownership and to the material worth of the work of art itself. Regrettably, Nijs's greatest triumph, brokering the extraordinary sale of the Gonzaga collection to Charles I, proved to be his economic downfall not least because the King defaulted on payment. In the end, Nijs had creditors across Europe from England to Transylvania.[19]

---

conservano retratti de Prencipi e lavori di Cavo & à Niello e Smalti, Intagli di Bullino: e tutti li Disegni di Alberto Durero, e Luca d'Olanda, e gran numero fatti à mano de' più celebri maestri: oltre a' Bovoli di Mare d'ogni sorte; onde si stima questo Archivo ascender al valore di dieci mila scudi." Translation by Anderson *The Flemish Merchant of Venice*, 60–61, who also discusses Scamozzi's remarks on the gallerie of other Venetian collectors, see 58–61.

17 Anderson, "Merchants as Collectors," 158 and, for the most detailed account of the contents of the cabinet and its eventual sale, see Idem., "Daniel Nijs's Cabinet," 172–176, especially 175. An additional note in the context of this essay is that Nijs was likely in possession of the Michelangelo Cupid that had made its way into the Gonzaga collection and it, too, was among the last items he relinquished from his warehouse. See Norton, "The Lost Sleeping Cupid," 253.

18 For comments on Gigli's praise of Nijs's collecting prowess, see Anderson, *The Flemish Merchant of Venice*, 63–65, citing Gigli, *La pittura trionfante*, 29–31; and for the visit of the Dutch ambassador, see Huygens, *Journaal van de Reis*, 150, as cited by Anderson, *The Flemish Merchant of Venice*, 69–70 and note 70.

19 Anderson, "Merchants as Collectors," 158.

Certainly, these Art Merchants of Venice had great advantages as collectors, given the almost frenzied commercial activity of the lagoon city, as trade with the East and along the Silk Route attracted opportunistic foreigners from other countries and other Italian city states. Frederick Ilchman's essay in this volume examines Venetian collections in greater depth.

2 The Changing Status of the Artist

The last years of the fifteenth and the sixteenth century saw a re-fashioning of the art collecting climate all across Italy and the simultaneous elevation of the status of the artist, the agent, and the collector above the dominant view during the Middle Ages that viewed art as a commodity and the artist as craftsman. Essential to understanding the factors that resulted in that societal realignment is a brief review of the activities of artists and patrons during the preceding century.

According to Volker Reinhardt, among others, writing in 1998 for the anthology *Art Markets in Early Modern Europe*, mid-fifteenth century art-making depended largely on the guild system, or its equivalent art associations, and family workshops.[20] The case of Neri di Bicci (1419–1491) in Florence is probably typical and exceptionally well documented in his workshop diaries—his *Ricordanze*—which note all of his commissions over twenty-seven years beginning in 1453, the year after his father's death when he took over the workshop.[21] At the age of fifteen, as a third-generation painter working in the shop his father had inherited from his grandfather, Neri joined the Confraternity of St. Luke, which eventually would become Florence's official guild. The *Ricordanze* of this popular artist make clear that commissions came to him from people in all professions—tailors, bakers, cobblers, as well as members of the upper classes and their widows—and from the records we deduce that these patrons aimed primarily to decorate domestic interiors or, even more often, to adorn family chapels and funerary monuments, not so much to commission and own art for its own sake. As Megan Holmes has observed, Neri's clients constituted "a

20 Reinhardt, "The Roman Art Market," 81.

21 The activities of Neri di Bicci's shop are outlined and documented above all by Holmes, "Neri di Bicci," 213–223, in which the artist's workshop practices are analyzed in detail, including his subcontracting to specialized craftsmen (gilders, framemakers, etc.) and his calculated incorporation of new trends in artistic style while maintaining a predominantly conservative approach that appealed to his middle-class clientele. See also O'Malley, *The Business of* Art, who focuses most particularly on the artist's contracts, and Prieto Gilday, "The Women Patrons," 51–75.

new constellation of consumers within the art market that emerged in the second half of the fifteenth century as the number and variety of consumer goods rose throughout Europe in tandem with an increase in the spending power of the middle and upper ranks in society. Neri di Bicci's finely wrought, moderately priced, richly ornamented tabernacles and small altarpieces, apparently appealed to artisans—with their high regard for craft and their interest in economizing—and to the *nouveau riche* who were defining and realizing themselves through their material consumption."[22]

As Reinhardt observes, this would change dramatically during the last years of the fifteenth century when what he calls the "individualization process" took hold.[23] The shift meant that individuals commissioned major works of art to enhance their own prestige and in doing so they exercised greater "client control." The result was a dramatic increase in patronage in city-states such as Urbino, Mantua, and Ferrara, where art became a vehicle for magnifying political power and dominance, and the display of art, often in galleries dedicated to that purpose, as Scamozzi described, would reflect dynastic stability. Important to emphasize is that this represents the intersection of collecting and patronage, that is, it entails the direct support of contemporary artists through commissions and has little if anything to do with collecting art of the past, even as amassing a collection of ancient statuary, coins, and cameos, could also do much to enhance the potent image and prestige of a ruler.[24] The Medici were the most obvious examples of this but by no means the only ones as the Montefeltro and della Rovere families followed suit in Urbino, and the Este and Gonzaga families did the same in Ferrara and Mantua. A somewhat different kind of patronage emerged in Bologna, as Saida Bondini explores in her essay, where the patronage of an increasingly powerful urban elite paralleled the established role of the leading family of the city, the Bentivoglio.

Cosimo de' Medici (1389–1464) is said to have remarked, "For fifty years I've done nothing but earn money and spend money, and I have realized that it is much sweeter to spend it than to earn it."[25] And, corroborating this, his grand-

---

22 Holmes, "Neri di Bicci," 218.

23 Reinhardt, "The Roman Art Market," 81. See also Prieto-Gilday, 58–62 who references Guido Guerzoni's detailed analysis of four categories of employment that artists enjoyed, with varying degrees of security and social recognition, at the several courts of the Este family for the period from 1471 to 1560 in "The Italian Renaissance Courts' Demand," a study replete with statistics about payments and duration of service.

24 For an in-depth exploration of the interplay between patrons, artists, and their intended audiences that takes into account various economic theories, including game-theory, see Nelson and Zeckhauser, *The Patron's Payoff*, especially 17–35.

25 Davis and Lindsmith, *Renaissance People*, 40.

son Lorenzo il Magnifico claimed Cosimo had spent more than 600,000 florins on art, architecture and civic monuments such as the expansion, reconstruction, and Fra Angelico's (1395–1455) decoration of the Dominican convent of San Marco.[26]

For the Church, too, using art as visual propaganda became the new normal, in Reinhardt's opinion, beginning during the reign of Pope Nicholas v (1397–1455) who saw to the expansion and beautification of the Vatican Palace with the tower and chapel that bears his name, also frescoed by Fra Angelico.[27] Certainly, as the reformation gathered steam and the Catholic Church Triumphant retaliated, art became the most powerful instrument for galvanizing the allegiance of the faithful and spreading Catholic doctrine in enormous, newly built and lavishly decorated preaching churches that sprouted all over Italy and the Catholic world.

With the sixteenth century, the top-flight artists came to be revered and enjoyed a greatly elevated social standing, Michelangelo "Il Divino" being the prime example of this. With regard to Giovanni Bellini (ca. 1430–1516), whose work Isabella d'Este was desperate to acquire, the Marchioness's agent Pietro Bembo (1470–1547) explained that the painter (brother-in-law of her court artist Andrea Mantegna [ca. 1430–1506]) "does not like to be given many written details, which cramp his style, his way of working as he says is always to wander at will in his pictures, so that they can satisfy himself as well as the beholder."[28] Eventually, Isabella was able to acquire a small *Nativity* by Bellini to be hung in her bedroom, a picture which to this day is regrettably unidentified.[29]

Such self-assurance and acknowledgement of the elevated status of first-rate artists is nicely summed up by the Portuguese humanist Francisco de Holanda, writing in his 1538 *Diálogos em Roma*: "As for me, I give the highest price for the work done by a great painter, even if he has spent little time over it.... I value very little that which an unskilled painter has painted in many

---

26 Ibid., 40. See also Nelson and Zeckhauser, *The Patron's Payoff*, 56–57 for references to Cosimo's contemporaries and Cosimo himself regarding his expenditures on architecture and his awareness that what could be viewed as generous support of civic institutions by some, notably Timoteo Maffei, could also be judged as excessively self-indulgent. Nelson and Zeckhauser point out that years after Cosimo's death, both Niccolò Machiavelli and Giorgio Vasari asserted that the patron was acutely aware of the envy that lavish project could provoke.

27 Reinhardt, "The Roman Art Market," 82, asserts that Nicholas V's patronage of Fra Angelico marks a turning point in the Church using art for propagandistic purposes.

28 Gilbert, "What Did the Renaissance Patron Buy?" 417.

29 Letters between Isabella and her agent-intermediaries with Bellini concerning the *Nativity* were published by Fletcher, "Isabella d'Este and Bellini's 'Presepio'," especially 708 on her plan to hang the painting in her bedroom.

years of work, however much they call him a painter." Holanda comments as well on the generous remuneration Italian painters tended to receive: "One great reason one can paint only in Italy and nowhere else consists in the salaries and prices painters receive here."[30] Indeed, as the century progressed, more and more artists received salaries as part of a noble household, which did not, however, preclude their accepting outside commissions, and this would only accelerate during the seventeenth century. Frances Gage's chapter elaborates on the issues of pricing and the celebrity of artists, specifically Giovanni Lanfranco (1582–1647), in the last essay of this volume.

3 Humanist Collectors and Patrons: Three Case Studies

Recognizing that the shift to what became a modern art market with active agents and middlemen was fueled by patrons wanting to enhance their power and image, with the result that the status of the artist came to be recognized as socially and intellectually consequential, a closer examination of a few examples is warranted. An obvious place to begin is with men and women of letters such as the humanist writers Pietro Aretino (1492–1556), Veronica Gambara (1485–1550), and Francesco Barberini's multi-talented secretary and art patron Cassiano dal Pozzo (1588–1657), all of whom enriched the intellectual lives of artists as well as kings, courtiers, diplomats, prelates and fellow writers and critics. Of equal interest are the roles played by merchant-advisors such as Battista della Palla, the principal agent for King Francis I of France (1494–1547), as well as artist/dealers such as Jacopo Strada, Vincenzo and Pietro Stampa, Nicolas Regneri, and Paolo del Sera, all of whom will be examined in detail below.

3.1 *Pietro Aretino*

Pietro Aretino (fig. 0.2) was not to the manor born: His father was a shoemaker who abandoned his family early on yet with the help of noble patrons and through the sheer force of his talents as an author, playwright, satirist and occasional blackmailer, he cut a powerful figure in the cultural and political life of Rome, Ferrara and Venice during the first half of the sixteenth

30 Holanda, *Diálogos em Roma*, 107, as cited by Philip Sohm, "Introduction," 2–3. See also Nelson and Zeckhauser, *The Patron's Payoff*, 174–175, who note that decades earlier, during the 1490s, Andrea Mantegna was receiving an annual salary of 180 ducats, as well as accommodation, and other material benefits for himself and his family, an amount more than double the salary of another court painter and that of the chancery secretary.

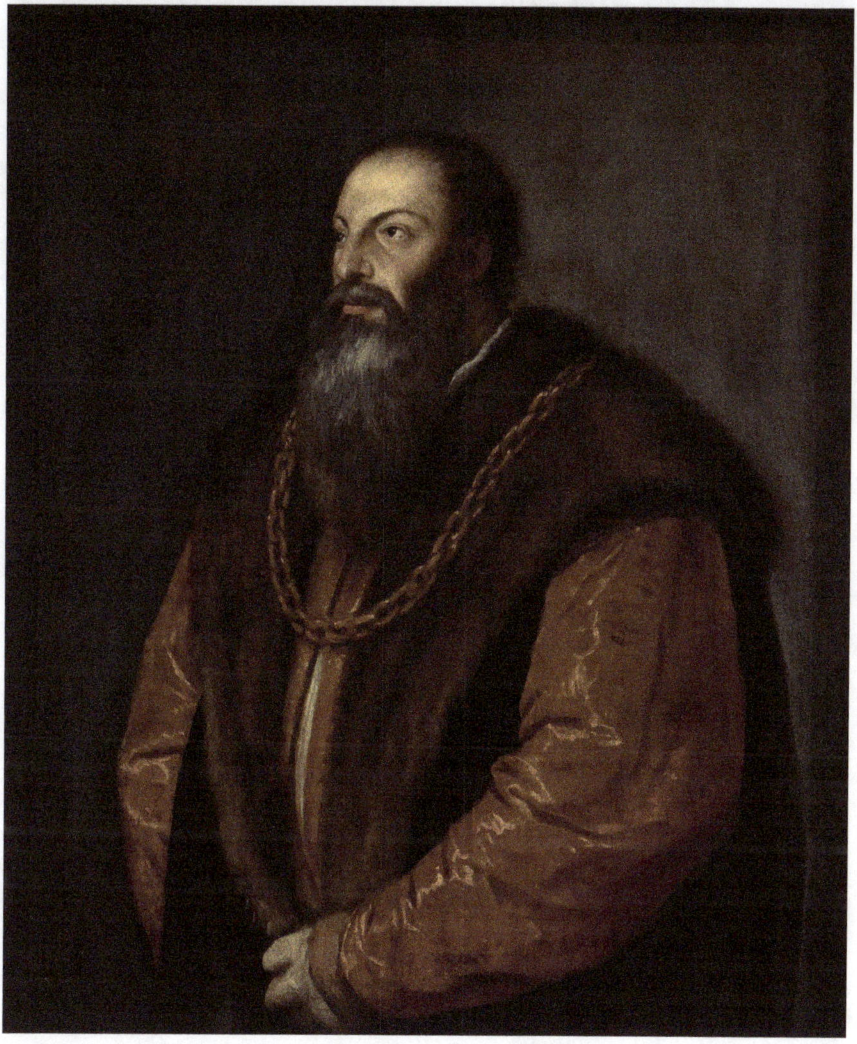

FIGURE 0.2 Titian (1490–1576), *Pietro Aretino*, ca. 1537. Oil on canvas, 101.9 × 85.7 cm (40 1/8 × 33 ¾ in.)
THE FRICK COLLECTION, NEW YORK

century.[31] Thanks to his mother's long-standing relationship with the nobleman Luigi Bacci, Pietro was raised in a sophisticated atmosphere that well prepared him for his years in Rome, first as the protégé of the wealthy banker

31 The literature on Aretino is vast and tends to focus on his literary career and role in Venetian Humanist circles. His relationships with contemporary artists is examined in depth by Palladino, "Pietro Aretino." See also Aretino, *Lettere*.

and great patron of Raphael (1483–1520), Agostino Chigi (1466–1520) and then the pope himself, Leo X (1475–1521), and the papal nephew Cardinal Giulio de' Medici, later Pope Clement VII. Having earned the moniker "The Scourge of Princes"[32] Aretino at times found himself on the move to escape death threats issued by his literary victims; but by 1527, after the Sack of Rome by Emperor Charles V (1500–1558), he settled in Venice and there at least part of his activity was devoted to developing a somewhat surprisingly nurturing climate for contemporary artists. Viewing his collection as something of a teaching tool, he opened it up to artists for study and was even known to have made introductions for them to see the antiquities collection of his archrival in Padua Pietro Bembo.[33] Aretino gladly received paintings as gifts from artists, knowing as they did, that he would find opportunities to promote their work to his wealthy patrons.

On a deeper intellectual level of support for young artists, it is interesting to note, as Lora Palladino has, that Aretino's commissions of religious works closely aligned with his own writings: For example, Titian's *Ecce Homo* likely relates to Aretino's *The Passion of Christ*, and Jacopo Sansovino's (1486–1570) bas-relief of the Madonna and Child is a rejoinder to Aretino's *Life of the Virgin*, while Sansovino's statue of Saint Catherine relates to Aretino's *Lives of the Saints*, published in 1540.[34]

Aretino's early patronage of Jacopo Tintoretto (1518–1594) signifies the writer's engagement with young talent: in 1545, he commissioned the mythological paintings *Apollo and Marsyas* (Wadsworth Atheneum, Hartford) and *Mercury and Argus* (unlocated).[35] And just three years later, Aretino wrote high praise of the painting that launched Tintoretto's public career *The Miracle of the Slave* (Gallerie dell'Accademia, Venice), painted for the confraternity, or Scuola, of S. Marco:

> … [T]here is no one so poorly acquainted with the art of design that he would not be amazed at the relief of the figure which, lying wholly naked

32 The moniker was assigned to Aretino by Ariosto in the 46th canto, stanza 14 of his epic poem *Orlando furioso* (See https://it.wikisource.org/wiki/Orlando_furioso_(1928)/Canto_46 [consulted August 2021]).

33 Aretino's personal collection is addressed in Palladino, "Pietro Aretino," 319–325, and for his role as a mentor, 322–323.

34 Ibid., 324–325.

35 I am grateful to Frederick Ilchman for calling my attention to the fact that the pair of canvases acquired by Aretino is not connected to the Ovidian subjects Tintoretto painted on panel for Vettor Pisani at San Paternian, commissioned 1541–2 and now in the Galleria Estense in Modena.

> on the ground, is offered up to cruel martyrdom. His colors are flesh, his contours rounded, and his body alive, so I swear, by the affection that I have for you, that the mien, airs, and looks of the crowd which surround it so greatly resemble the impressions which the crowd within the picture make that the spectacle appears to be real, not feigned. But despite all this, do not become arrogant, because that would amount to a refusal to advance to a higher level of perfection.[36]

Worth noting is that, in contrast to his advice to the young artist, Aretino himself had no issue with displaying his own arrogance with a self-congratulatory note at the beginning of his praise of Tintoretto's work: "Now that public acclaim confirms the praise I already awarded the great *historia* dedicated to the Scuola of S. Marco, I rejoice no less in my own judgment, which is very precocious, than I do in your art, which is so surpassing."[37]

There's no question that Aretino's admiration for Titian was both deeply felt and well-known to his contemporaries. This is evidenced in the humanist writer Ludovico Dolce's (1508–1568) 1557 publication *Dialogue on Painting* called *Aretino* which features Aretino as the character defending the Venetian style of painting championed by Titian and concludes with a praising biography of the artist himself.[38] Yet Aretino wasn't beneath criticizing the leading painter of his day: When he first saw the portrait of himself, now in the Pitti Palace, he remarked critically that it appeared "more sketched than finished," although it has been proposed that here Aretino may have been thinking strategically, because the portrait was intended as a gift to the Grand Duke of Tuscany Cosimo de' Medici (1519–1574), whose court artists at the time adhered to the much more polished, highly finished painting style of Agnolo Bronzino (1503–1572). Aretino's comment may, therefore, have been issued to stave off potential criticism from the Florentines.[39]

More typically, Aretino was instrumental in brokering Titian's commission to paint the portrait of the French King Francis I, a picture that would eventually become the King's image for the ages. The portrait, dating to 1539, most likely depends on the artist's reinterpretation of a medal struck in 1537 designed by Benvenuto Cellini (1500–1571) during his trip to the French court.

36 Palladino, "Pietro Artetino," 348–349. Palladino provides both the original Italian and her translation of the quotation.

37 Ibid., 348.

38 Dolce, *Dialogo della pittvra*; for Aretino's and Titian's mutual recognition of the benefits of collaboration to garner patronage, and the eight sonnets by Aretino in praise of Titian, see Palladino "Pietro Aretino," 270–271.

39 Palladino "Pietro Aretino," 339–340.

Characteristically strategic in his use of flattery, Aretino accompanied the shipment of the portrait along with Titian's version of Mary Magdalene now in Bordeaux with these words: "Here, most saintly King [are] the two works, one magnifying the honor of men, the other magnifying the glory of God."[40] This action, together with other demonstrations of interest and support of contemporary artists, thus leads to the conclusion that even as Pietro Aretino was the scourge of Princes, in his dealings with artists, he showed a supportive, more human side.

3.2 *Veronica Gambara*

In sharp contrast to the acerbic literary life of Pietro Aretino is another sixteenth-century humanist patron, in this case a woman of great sophistication. Veronica Gambara from Correggio was born into a prominent family with a long lineage of female intellectuals including Emilia Pia da Montefeltro, the principal exemplar of female virtue in Baldassare Castiglione's renowned book *The Courtier*. Gambara made the most of the humanist education she acquired side by side with her brothers, as she also flexed her talent as a poet to promote the arts and establish her court at Correggio as an essential destination for artists and men of letters.[41] By the age of seventeen, her literary mentor became the eminent neo-Petrarchan scholar Pietro Bembo, which may account for Aretino dubbing his rival's protégée "A Laureated Harlot"[42] After her husband's death in 1518, Gambara proved to be an accomplished stateswoman: she managed the *condottiere* for more than thirty years; forged alliances first

40 Scailliérez, *François Ier et ses artistes*, 50, who quotes Aretino's letter in French: "Voici, très saint Roi, les deux oeuvres (…) l'une magnifie l'honneur des hommes et l'autre magnifie la gloire de Dieu" citing Janet Cox Rearick, *La collection de François Ier* (exh. cat., Musée du Louvre; Paris: Réunion des Musées Nationaux), 10. See also Adhémar, "Aretino: Artistic Adviser," 315, who does not, however identify the religious painting as the *Magdalene* in Bordeaux.

41 Despite Gambara's reputation among contemporaries and the survival of some 50 poems she wrote on subjects ranging from love to politics and at least 137 letters, the literature on her is not as extensive as her talent would suggest. Useful biographical material is included in McIver, "Two Emilian Noblewomen," 159–176; Moody, "Under the Sign of Dido: Veronica Gambara (1485–1550), Life, Letters, and Poetry," April 2004 (http://www.jimandellen.org/gambara.biography.html [page last updated 19 April 2004]); Poss, "A Renaissance Gentildonna," 47–66, where many of Gambara's 50 poems are published and analyzed. That Gambara was held in exceptionally high regard within the pantheon of women *letterate* is evidenced by Ariosto's passage in *Orlando furioso*, Canto 46, 3–4 cited by McIver, "Two Emilan Noblewomen," 160.

42 Stortoni, *Women Poets of the Renaissance*, 23–5. Poss publishes translations of a selection of Gambara's poetry based on Chaippetti, ed., *Rime e lettere*; See also Finzi, *Umanità di Veronica Gambara*.

with Francis I, whom she had met and very much impressed in 1515, initiating a lifelong correspondence with the French monarch, and then later entered into an even more advantageous alliance with Emperor Charles V, whom she received at her court in 1530, honoring him with verses she had composed for the occasion.[43] Adding to her literary and political achievements, is her lasting contribution to the visual arts, resting above all on her unwavering support of Antonio Allegri, better known as Correggio (1489–1534).

Gambara assuredly regarded Correggio as a personal friend. This is attested by her comment to Isabella d'Este referencing "our master Antonio Allegri" and numerous legal documents for which Gambara asked the artist to serve as a witness.[44] Not surprisingly, then, she took a pro-active approach to securing commissions for Correggio. Some of the pictures he produced specifically for her are today only known from descriptions—most especially the panel paintings that hung in her garden pavilion or *casino*, described by Luigi di San Giusto as "marvels of art"—but we now know that she played an instrumental role negotiating through her friend Scipione Montino della Rosa (ca. 1475–1550) the commissions for several of Correggio's masterpieces in Parma, including the glorious frescoed cupola of San Giovanni Evangelista.[45] Moreover, Katharine McIver has convincingly proposed that Gambara also played a role in securing for Correggio other commissions from her friends and correspondents, including the *Noli Me Tangere* (Museo del Prado, Madrid) painted for Agostino Ercolani, as well as Federigo Gonzaga's paintings of *Leda* (Gemäldegalerie, Berlin) and *Danae* (Galleria Borghese, Rome).[46]

3.3 *Cassiano dal Pozzo*

A third scholar-patron, in this case one active during the Baroque era, who deserves special examination is Cassiano dal Pozzo.[47] Born into a noble family in Turin, Cassiano was raised in Florence and educated at the University of Pisa. Interested in science as well as the arts—a friend and correspondent with Galileo in fact—Cassiano moved to Rome in 1612 and soon became an

43 The alliance Gambara formed with Charles V resulted in treaties guaranteeing Imperial protection for Correggio and financial backing for the construction of improved fortifications. See Stortoni, *Women Poets*, 24.

44 The comment was penned in a letter dated September 3, 1528 and the artist served as a witness to the marriage settlement of Gambara's son Ippolito in 1534; see McIver "Two Emilian Noblewomen," 162 and Poss "Veronica Gambara," 49.

45 McIver, "Two Emilian Noblewomen," 162–163.

46 Ibid.

47 Cassiano da Pozzo is the subject of numerous scholarly publications. Noteworthy among them is the series *The Paper Museum of Cassiano dal Pozzo*. The extent of the project is thoughtfully reviewed in *The Burlington Magazine*, 523, 544, 553.

essential member of the intellectual elite of the city. There, one of the leading patrons of the arts and the Medici Grand Duke's representative in Rome Cardinal Francesco Maria del Monte (1549–1627) ensured that Cassiano would meet, among others, Cardinal Maffeo Barberini (later Pope Urban VIII), and his nephew Francesco Barberini (1597–1679), whose household dal Pozzo joined as secretary in 1623. With Francesco—a fellow member of the scientific association the Accademia dei Lincei—Cassiano traveled on diplomatic missions to France and Spain, where he saw and recorded the royal collections on display, most enduringly that of Francis I.

Though best known as a passionate classicist, Cassiano, like Aretino, encouraged the artists of his own time many of whom also enjoyed Barberini patronage.[48] His exhaustive studies of the art and culture of ancient Rome were enhanced by commissions to contemporary artists to produce drawings after ancient statuary and frescoes such as the *Aldobrandini Wedding* (Museo Vaticano) for his so-called *Cartacheum* or "Paper Museum."[49] Cassiano also supported local and foreign artists through major commissions, the most spectacular of which is undoubtedly Nicolas Poussin's exceptional set of the Seven Sacraments, completed in 1642.[50]

Cassiano was one of several writers to leave us a record of the French royal collection, largely formed by Francis I, a great Italophile and Leonardo da Vinci's last patron. Although Cassiano wrote in detail about copies ordered by Francis's heir, Henry IV (1553–1610) after some of the masterpieces hung in the bathroom at Fontainebleau were showing signs of deterioration due to

48 Among the contemporary artists recorded in his collection are Pietro da Cortona, Simon Vouet and Caravaggio. See Green, *Poussin Paints the Sacraments*, 31.

49 Whitehouse, *Ancient Mosaics and Wallpaintings*, 44–55, on "The surviving Dal Pozzo drawings of mosaics and Wall Paintings," and 59–60 for Giulio Mancini's list of surviving ancient wall paintings.

50 For citations to the plethora of literature on Cassiano's patronage of Poussin, see Standring, "Some Pictures by Poussin," 608, note 1; for Cassiano's personal support of Poussin during the artist's first years in Rome, see Cavazzini, "Nicolas Poussin," 808–814; and for an in-depth study of Poussin's sacraments, painted for Cassiano, see Green, *Poussin Paints the Sacraments*, who discusses (53–63) the arrangement of the seven pictures in the patron's house, all hung in one room, along with a copy of the *Aldobrandini Wedding*. Green points out (31) that Cassiano's collection display was "intended to encompass the full range of Plinian knowledge of everything in the world" and that his "museum scheme was new, replacing the heterogenous collections of the sixteenth-century *Wunderkammern* with scientific display." Patrizia Cavazzini's chapter in this volume offers helpful context for Cassiano's patronage of foreign artists, as she focuses on his and other Roman collectors' support of Poussin and Valentin de Boulogne.

humidity, he did not, unfortunately, leave an object-by-object record of precisely which pictures had entered the collection under Francis.[51]

4 Agents and Artists as Middlemen

4.1 *Italian Agents for King Francis I*

More about the formation of Francis I's apparently insatiable appetite for Italian painting comes to light by tracing the work of his agents Giovanni Battista Puccini, Tommaso Sartini, and Battista della Palla (1489–1532).[52] Not surprisingly, Francis did come by some of his greatest masterpieces the easy way, as diplomatic gifts presented by Pope Leo X and others in powerful positions. These include works by Raphael (*St. Michael*, and *The Holy Family of Francis I*) and likely a *Visitation* by Sebastiano del Piombo (1485–1547), commissioned by the Venetian Cardinal Marco Cornaro (1482–1524) as a present for the French Queen in anticipation of the birth of the Dauphin.[53] Leah Clark's chapter that follows examines in greater detail the role intermediaries played in brokering gifts and exchanges. Gifts, aside, however, the negotiations carried out by Francis's Italian agents are more challenging and more relevant to an examination of the *modus operandi* of the art market.

Early on in his collecting career, Francis seems to have held special admiration for artists active in Florence during the first decades of the century, Andrea del Sarto (1486–1530) and Fra Bartolomeo (1472–1517) figuring prominently among them, the former having spent several months in France in the service of the King from May to September of 1518. In 1516, Giovanni Battista Puccini sent Francis del Sarto's *Dead Christ Mourned* (known today only though Agostino Veneziano's engraving) and *Virgin and Child with St. Elizabeth*; while in 1532, the merchant Tommaso Sartini sent the king a *St Sebastian* (today unlocated) and probably also *The Incarnation of Christ* by Fra Bartolomeo, both acquired by Sartini directly from the artist at the convent of S. Marco in Florence.[54] But

51 Scailliérez, *François Ier et ses artistes*, 14, note 25, citing Müntz, *La Renaissance en Italie*.

52 A helpful summary of the formation of Francis's collection is Scaillierez *François I et ses artistes* 20–30, 106–109, 117, especially 23–28 for the king's relationships with Italian agents.

53 Unless otherwise noted, all extant paintings in Francis's collection are now in the Musée du Louvre, Paris.

54 Although unlocated, the composition of the *St. Sebastian* that Sartini puchased for 20 gold florins and then sold to Francis for 300 gold scudi is known from a copy in Fiesole attributed to the little-known artist Ezechia da Vezzano that was identified by Cox Rearick, "Fra Bartolomeo's *St Mark*." See also Cornelison, "Relocating Fra Bartolomeo," 311–334.

FIGURE 0.3 Andrea del Sarto (1486–1530), *The Sacrifice of Isaac*, 1527. Oil on panel, 213 × 84 cm (84 × 63 in.) GEMÄLDEGALERIE ALTE MEISTER, STAATLICHE KUNSTSAMMLUNGEN, DRESDEN

the agent who was by far the most active in expanding Francis' collection was Battista della Palla. Through him, the king acquired literally dozens of pictures as della Palla came to be recognized as the connoisseur who had developed a sixth sense of what his patron would like.[55] Notable among the paintings and sculptures acquired or commissioned for Fontainebleau through his agency are Andrea del Sarto's *Charity* (National Gallery of Art, Washington) and *Sacrifice of Isaac* (Dresden, Gemäldegalerie; fig. 0.3); Jacopo Pontormo's (1494–1557)

55 Della Palla's life and career is examined in depth by Elam, "Art in the Service of Liberty," 33–109. See also Cox Rearick, "The Collection of Francis I," 83–88, and Goldthwaite, "The Painting Industry," 292, who underscores della Palla's role in promoting an international secondary market for Italian paintings.

Raising of Lazarus (lost or unlocated);[56] probably a lost statue of Hercules by Michelangelo; and Baccio Bandinelli's (1488–1560) *Mercury* (also lost).[57]

Further galvanizing the role of the Italians in France was the School of Fontainebleau and other Italian artists who physically went to France to work for the king: Rosso Fiorentino (1495–1540) (arriving in 1530, recommended by Aretino); Francesco Primaticcio (1504–1570), invited two years later; Niccolò dell'Abbate (1512–1571); and Benvenuto Cellini, just to name a few. From time to time, these, too, were pressed into service as art agents for the King, as Primaticcio was on two occasions when he was sent to Rome to scour the Eternal City for antiquities in 1540 and 1546.[58] Thus we find that border-crossings were basically irrelevant when it came to art collecting at this time, when patronage and agency were understood to function on an international stage.

4.2 *Jacopo Strada*

Jacopo Strada, from whom the Emperor acquired The Frick Collection's *Allegories* by Veronese, continued to work successfully on the international stage.[59] As an artist who had trained in the studio of Giulio Romano (1499–1546) in Mantua, he staged festivals and produced extraordinary designs for metalwork; but he also served as a dealer in antiquities for most of his career, initially in Nuremburg, and later for the Augsburg branch of the wealthy banking dynasty of Hans (or Johann) Jacob Fugger (1516–1575). In Munich, Strada designed the *Antiquarium* for Duke Albrecht of Bavaria who bought heavily from the artist-agent to fill his *Kunstkammer* there. Most significantly, Albrecht was likely instrumental in obtaining for Strada the appointment in 1563 to be the Habsburg Court Antiquary for the Duke's brother-in-law

56 Ibid.,62–63. Although commissioned for Francis through della Palla, neither *The Charity* nor *The Sacrifice of Isaac* was ever delivered to Fontainebleau; following the artist's death, his widow sold the former to Niccolò Antinori and the latter to the widow of Filippo Strozzi, after which it entered the Uffizi in 1633, to be acquired in 1649 by Francesco I d'Este, whose descendant Francesco III eventually ceded much of his collection to Augustus III of Saxony whose collection formed much of the core of Dresden's Gemäldegalerie. For a brief mention and a proposed dating of *The Raising of Lazarus*, likely painted c.1529 for Francis, see Beuzelin, "Jacopo Pontormo," 93.

57 For details regarding the acquisition of Bandinelli's *Mercury* and Michelangelo's *Hercules*, see Elam "Battista della Palla," 57–61.

58 Scaillieriz, *François I et ses artistes*, 28–30.

59 The most comprehensive biography of Strada is Jansen, *Jacopo Strada*. His life and career are neatly summarized by Salomon, *Veronese's Allegories*, 21–23. For his metalwork designs, see Lawrence, *Jacopo Strada*.

Maximilian II (1527–1576) in Vienna.[60] As he continued to work for all members of the Habsburg dynasty, Strada frequently went to Italy on their behalf on the one hand to acquire antiquities for Albrecht—for example from the collection of Pietro Loredan (1482–1570) and from the heirs of Pietro Bembo—and on the other hand to acquire contemporary works for Rudolf, regularly acting as an intermediary between the Imperial court and artists such as Titian and the sculptor Alessandro Vittoria (1525–1608).[61] For the most part, however, Strada seems to have built up his stock by buying from existing collections rather than directly from the artists, thus fueling a burgeoning secondary market similar to what we know today.[62] As court antiquary from 1564, Strada assumed curatorial responsibilities for the Imperial collections until 1579, when he passed the title over to his son Ottavio (1550–1607), while still remaining a member of the Imperial court household. Knighted in 1573 and being married into aristocracy (Baroness Ottilie Schenk von Rosberg), Strada had successfully positioned himself within the highest social stratum of the court. An avid collector himself, Strada ensured that he lived in a style comparable to his patrons, having constructed a grand mansion in Vienna to house his "Musaeum" that comprised his vast library of more than 3000 volumes, numerous drawings by followers of Raphael such as Giulio Romano and Perino del Vaga, coins and medals, paintings and antiquities.[63] However, his sale of the Frick Veroneses notwithstanding, after Rudolf moved his court to Prague, Strada's activities as an agent began to wane, despite the fact that his granddaughter Anna Maria Strada (also known as Katerina Stradová, 1579–1629) was the Emperor's mistress, said to have borne him six children. Thus, with his activities as an agent diminished, Strada dedicated much of his time during his later years, to his life's work, compiling drawings by contemporary artists of the ancient and modern monuments of Rome.[64]

60 Lawrence, *Strada*, 14.

61 Jansen, "Jacopo Strada," *Grove Art Online, Oxford Art Online*: oxfordartonline.com.db29.linccweb.org/subscriber/article/grove/art. Other Habsburg rulers who employed Strada included the Bohemian Vilém Rožmberk, for whom he prepared manuscripts and may have purchased works of art, and the Moravian nobleman Jan Šembera Černohorský z Boskovice (1543–1597), for whom he supervised some decorations in the 'Imperial Room' of his manor house at Bučovice (near Brno).

62 Salomon, *Veronese's Allegories*, 21–22, traces a number of the collections Strada tried to or was successful in acquiring. With respect to Strada's acquisitions of collections of drawings, see Marciari's chapter in this volume.

63 Jansen, *Oxford Art Online*.

64 Jansen, *Oxford Art Online*, and Idem., *Jacopo Strada*, 21–22.

5 Collecting and Patronage during the Seventeenth Century

Throughout the later sixteenth and seventeenth centuries the kind of noble and regal patronage we saw with Veronica Gambara and Francis I continued, even as the "individualization process" gained momentum. Young artists sought and enjoyed sponsorship from aristocratic families as, for instance, Giuseppe Cesari (1568–1640) was favored by the Aldobrandini pope Clement VIII (1536–1605), who gave the artist a knighthood as the Cavaliere d'Arpino and steered dozens of commissions his way; and Guido Reni (1575–1642) enjoyed the support of the Borghese, as did Gianlorenzo Bernini (1598–1680).[65]

Perhaps the best-known example of this aspect of patronage is the support the young Caravaggio (Michelangelo Merisi, 1571–1610) received from Cardinal Francesco Maria del Monte. Too often, del Monte's exceptionally generous and nurturing patronage has been viewed askance, probably because of his pro-French political stance that earned him defamatory rumors about his lifestyle from the pro-Spanish factions in Rome who sought to undermine any prospect he may have had of ascending to the papacy.[66] When we review the facts, however, it is hard to envision a more supportive patron of the arts and sciences. Caravaggio was the greatest beneficiary of the Cardinal's largesse, as he was given residency in Del Monte's Palazzo Madama (now the Italian Senate) from 1596/7 until 1600, during which time he is recorded to have painted vast numbers of his highly individualized genre scenes and depictions of saints (fig. 0.4). Moreover, Del Monte secured Caravaggio's first major public commission—the Contarelli Chapel in San Luigi dei Francesi and made a gift of the artist's *Medusa* to the Grand Duke of Tuscany.[67] Not only did Del Monte's patronage elevate Caravaggio's own reputation, but it sowed the seed for something of an

---

65 For elaboration on the importance of a powerful patron for a young artist, see Reinhardt, "The Roman Art Market," 87–90, and Spear, "Rome: Setting the Stage," 70, 77–78.

66 Roccasecca, "Bourbon del Monte, Francesco Maria," *Grove Art Online, Oxford Art Online* (published online 2003) oxfordartonline.com.db29.linccweb.org/subscriber/article/grove/art.

67 Ibid. Early sources, together with a 1627 inventory of del Monte's pictures, confirm that among the commissions Caravaggio executed for del Monte that survive today were *The Musicians* (Metropolitan Museum of Art, New York); *The Fortune Teller* (Musei Capitolini, Rome); *The Cardsharps* (Kimbell Museum, Fort Worth); *St. Francis of Assisi in Ecstacy* (Wadsworth Atheneum, Hartford); *St Catherine of Alexandria* (Museo Nacional Thyssen-Bornemisza, Madrid) and, though originally commissioned by Ciriaco Mattei, the *St. John the Baptist* (generally accepted as the version in the Musei Capitolini, Rome, which corresponds to the painting listed in the del Monte inventory of 1627); see Pritchard, "Caravaggio's Capitoline *St John*," 35–36 and notes 7 and 9. See also Friedlaender, *Caravaggio Studies*, 169–170 (cat. 20), and Posèq, "Caravaggio and the Antique," 155–156.

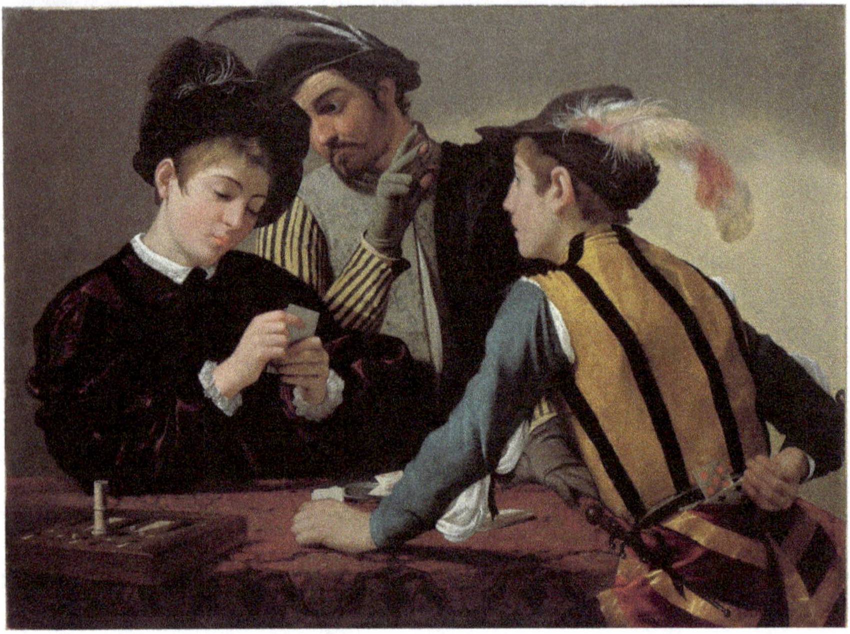

FIGURE 0.4 Caravaggio (1571–1610), *The Cardsharps*, 1594. Oil on canvas, 94.2 × 37 cm (37 × 51.5 in.)
KIMBELL ART MUSEUM, FORT WORTH

art market phenomenon in the production and sales of Caravaggesque paintings, as Fausto Nicolai explains in his chapter on Giovan Angelo Altemps and Prospero Orsi.

Caravaggio was far from the only young artist del Monte promoted. By the time he died in 1626, the Cardinal's collection contained nearly 700 paintings, a large proportion of which were the work of contemporary artists such as Agostino and Annibale Carracci, Cavaliere d'Arpino, Guido Reni, Jusepe Ribera, Guercino, Carlo Saraceni, Adam Elsheimer Giovanni Battista Caracciolo, Scipione Pulzone, Giovanni Baglione, Antiveduto Gramatica, Alessandro Turchi, and Girolamo Muziano. Toward the end of his life, del Monte became an avid promoter of the classicizing painter Andrea Sacchi (1599–1661), though sadly the fresco cycle of the *Seasons* that Sacchi painted for him no longer survives.[68]

There were occasions when artists who enjoyed support from one noble patron initially, were able to "trade up" as their reputations rose. This was the case for Pietro da Cortona (1596–1669), who arrived in Rome from his native

68 Ibid.

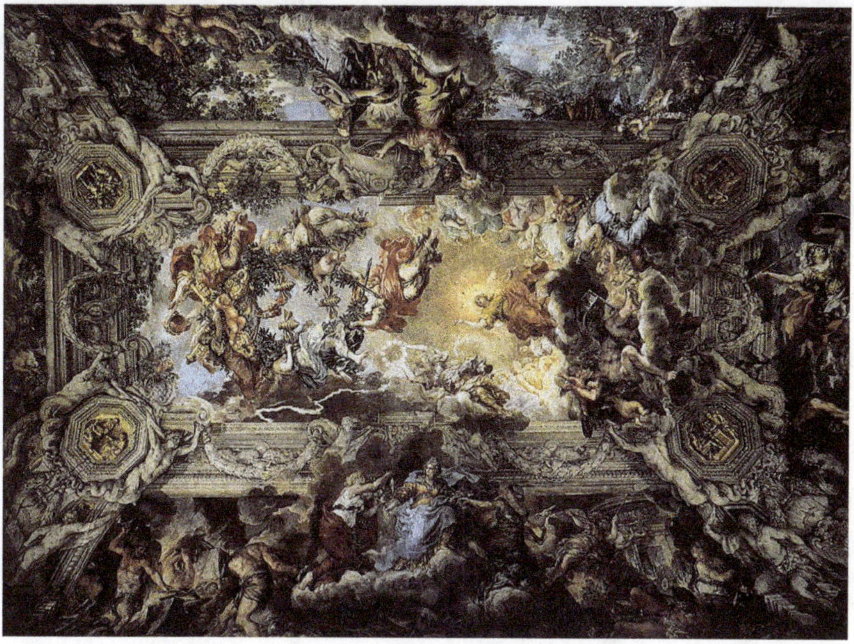

FIGURE 0.5 Pietro da Cortona (1596–1669), *Allegory of Divine Providence* 1633–39. Fresco
PALAZZO BARBERINI, ROME

Tuscany with the sponsorship of the Sacchetti family, but then, as his star rose, was able to better position himself as the favorite painter of the ruling papal family, the Barberini, for whom he painted what has long been recognized as the most celebrated ceiling fresco of the high baroque in Rome, *The Allegory of Divine Providence* (1633–39; fig. 0.5) for the Palazzo Barberini. In Cortona's case, as he enjoyed a reputation and level of prosperity second only to Bernini's, there was no such thing as an exclusive commitment to a patron (in fact there rarely was) as he gladly took on commissions as demanding and rewarding as the Planetary Rooms of the Pitti Palace for the Medici Grand Duke, and even in the case of that enormous commission, he frequently absented himself from Florence to take on additional work in Rome.[69]

Returning to the individualization process of the role art played in society and in the economy: With the elevated status and the high demand for both religious and secular art that prevailed through most of the seventeenth

69 Fumagalli, "Florence," 189; and for further discussion of Pietro da Cortona's sharp business practices, see Spear "Rome: Setting the Stage," 50–51, 54–55, 62; and Reinhardt, "The Roman Art Market," 88. The fundamental study of the Planetary Rooms remains Campbell, *Pietro da Cortona at the Pitti Palace*.

century, artists could expect to receive gifts in addition to monetary compensation. For example, upon completion of his works for the Co-Cathedral of St. John, Caravaggio famously received from the Knights of Malta not only a knighthood but a gold chain and two slaves, while Pietro da Cortona pointedly declined any gifts that might reduce his bill of 7,900 scudi for thirty-two cartoons for St. Peter's, commenting that "Whence the petitioner [Cortona], who does not ask for any gift, as is done by others, but only suitable payment for his labors …" and, indeed, in 1668 he was paid the outstanding balance owed him.[70]

6 Agents for the Secondary Market

Running parallel to direct patron-artist relationships, and further evidence of how individualized the roles artists played with respect to the market had become, are cases of artists who brokered deals independently and catered to the secondary market. This practice became increasingly robust as patrons sought out works by famous artists of earlier generations such as Raphael, Bellini, or Titian, and as foreign buyers were ever more eager to own Italian pictures. Two cases of this kind of independent dealing are Niccolò Renieri (born Nicolas Régnier, 1591–1667) and Paolo del Sera (1617–1672). Renieri (fig. 0.6), an artist trained in Rome among the followers of Caravaggio, painted all his life but derived his income principally as an art agent, particularly from sales to a British clientele, typified by the ambassador to Venice Basil Feilding, 2nd Earl of Denbigh (ca. 1608–1675) who himself served as a procurer of Italian paintings and sculptures for his brother-in-law the Duke of Hamilton as well as for King Charles I.[71]

70 The gifts to Caravaggio are mentioned by Bellori, *Vite de' pittori*, (Rome, 1672) and published in translation by Friedlaender, *Caravaggio Studies*, 245–54, the gifts noted on 250–251: "In addition to honoring Caravaggio with the Cross of Malta, our Grand Master gave him a precious chain of gold and two slaves along with other signs of his esteem and satisfaction with his work." Cortona's disinterest in a gift and focus on full payment is noted by Spear, "Rome: Setting the Stage," 61–63, citing Anna Lo Bianco (ed.), *Pietro da Cortona, 1597–1669* (exh. cat.) Palazzo Venezia, Rome. Milan: Electa 1997, Regesto, 488. Cortona's petition for full payment is quoted in translation and analyzed by Spear "Rome: Setting the Stage," 50–52.

71 For Renieri's career as an artist, with reference to his role as an agent for Feilding and, by extention, the Duke of Hamilton, see Fantelli, "Nicolò Renieri 'pittor fiamengo'," especially 84; and Schütz, "The Collection of Archduke Leopold William," who remarks on eighteen pictures Feilding acquired for the Duke of Hamilton which were shipped to London in 1637. See also Shakeshaft, "'To Much Bewiched'," especially 124, n. 9 citing Ellis Waterhouse,

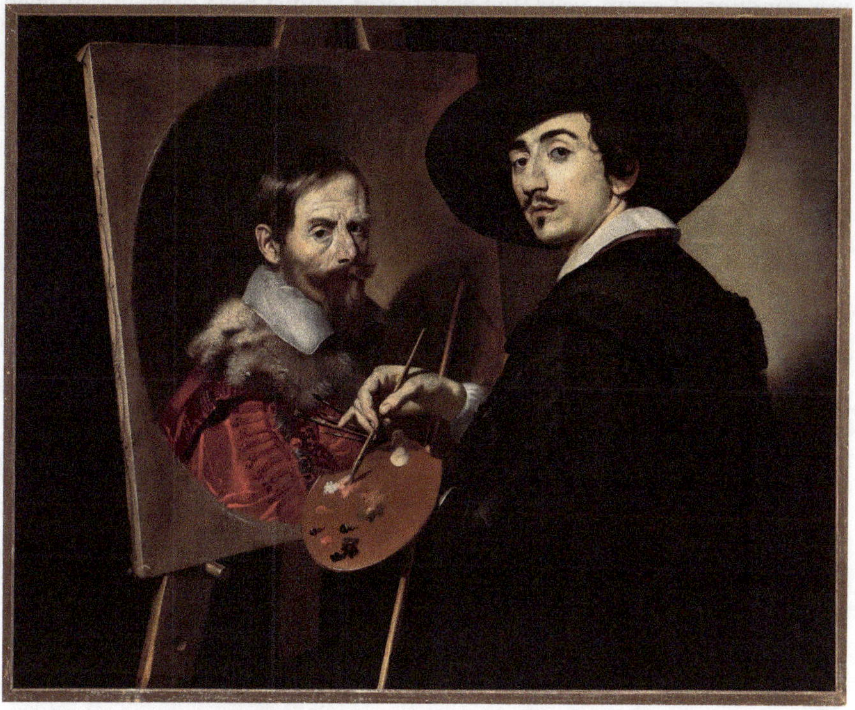

FIGURE 0.6 Nicolas Regnier (1591–1667), *Self Portrait*, ca. 1620–1625. Oil on canvas, 111 × 138 cm (43 11/16 × 54 5/16 in.)
FOGG ART MUSEUM CAMBRIDGE, MA

Paolo del Sera was a collector himself, but actively sold works on the secondary market, concentrating on works by artists of the Venetian golden age, and brokering the sales of whole collections whose owners found themselves in economic distress. A case in point is Sera's sale of Veronese's *Christ and the Centurion* (Nelson-Atkins Museum of Art, Kansas City) on behalf of the financially troubled Grimani-Calergi family.[72] He also acted as the agent for Leopoldo de' Medici and was a member of the Medici household for thirty years, starting in 1632. Collector that he was, Sera was always ready to sell anything he owned as he would also forego a purchase to conserve his cash liquidity, as he remarked to the Medici duke concerning a Tintoretto that he

"Paintings from Venice for Seventeenth Century England," *Italian* Studies 7 (1952): 1–23, who published documentation of Renieri's sale of thirty-two pictures to Feilding for 1820 ducats. Renieri's activities as an art dealer are alluded to by Sohm, "Venice," 232 (his appraisal of the Widman collection), 234 (his idea to hold an art lottery in Venice in 1666).

72 For Paolo del Sera, see Zarrillo, "Complementary Activities," 129–140, and for the *Centurion*, 133.

was handling, "I assure your Highness that if I didn't have such a great need of cash for my business, I should wish to buy it as an investment."[73] Indeed, true to his word, in 1654 Sera sold his entire personal collection to Leopoldo and his brother. Sera's actions provide what may be viewed as definitive proof of the complete commodification of art as we know it today and the basis on which the modern art market would develop and hone its *modus operandi* in the decades that followed, with power-wielding middlemen and the expansion of the secondary market through the agency of dealers and public auctioneers.

7 Conclusion

This introduction serves only to outline the very rich topic that is the focus of this volume. The chapters that follow expand on several of the points addressed here, while others introduce new personalities, as Chriscinda Henry does in profiling the courtesan-collector Elisabetta Condulmer, while still others trace the shift in collecting attitudes toward a special category of collecting, as John Marciari meticulously marks the growth in connoisseurship of drawings as independent works of art, not simply practical components of the creative process. Together, all of the essays in this volume offer an opportunity to look at famous works of art that may be exceptionally familiar in art-historical terms but less so as markers of the socio-economic shifting sands during a particular cultural moment. At the same time, each chapter is intended to deepen our appreciation of the role patrons and the art market played in promoting and galvanizing the reputations of young artists as they also defined what it meant to be a collector when Michelangelo was modern.

Bibliography

Adhémar, Jean. "Aretino: Artistic Adviser to Francis I." *Journal of the Warburg and Courtauld Institutes* 17, no. 3/4 (1954): 311–318.

Anderson, Christina M. "Daniel Nijs's Cabinet and Its Sale to Lord Arundel in 1636." *The Burlington Magazine* 154, no. 1308 (March 2012): 172–176.

Anderson, Christina M. *The Flemish Merchant of Venice: Daniel Nijs and the Sale of the Gonzaga Art Collection*. New Haven and London: Yale University Press, 2015.

73 Ibid., 134.

Anderson, Christina M. "Merchants as Collectors and Art Dealers: The Cases of Daniel Nijs and Carlo Hellemans, Flemish Merchants in Venice." In *Early Modern Merchants as Collectors*, edited by Christina M. Anderson, 156–166. London: Routledge, 2017.

Aretino, Pietro. *Lettere sull'arte*, edited by Carlo Cordié, Fidenzio Pertile, Ettore Camesasca. Vite, lettere, testimonianze di artisti italiani, 3 vols. Milan: Edizioni del Milione, 1957–59.

Ariosto, Ludovico. *Orlando furioso* (https://it.wikisource.org/wiki/Orlando_furioso_(1928)/Canto_46 [consulted November 2020]).

Beuzelin, Cécile. "Jacopo Pontormo: A Scholarly Craftsman." In *The Artist as Reader: On Education and Non-Education of Early Modern Artists*, edited by Heiko Damm, Michael Thimann, Claus Zittel, 71–104. Leiden: Brill, 2012.

Borean, Linda, and Stefania Mason. *Il collezionisma d'arte a Venezia* [1]. *Il Seicento*. Venice: Marsilio, 2007.

[Burlington Magazine]. "Editorial: The Cassiano dal Pozzo Project." *The Burlington Magazine* 131, no. 1037 (August 1989): 523, 544, 553.

Campbell, Malcolm. *Pietro da Cortona at the Pitti Palace. A Study of the Planetary Rooms and Related Projects*. Princeton: Princeton University Press, 1977.

Cavazzini, Patrizia. "Nicolas Poussin, Cassiano da Pozzo, and the Roman Art Market in the 1620s." *The Burlington Magazine* 155, no. 1329 (December 2013): 808–814.

Condivi Ascanio. *Vita di Michelagnolo Buonarroti*, edited by Emma Spina Barelli. Milan: Rizzoli, 1964.

Cornelison, Sally J. "Relocating Fra Bartolomeo at San Marco." *Renaissance Studies* 23, no. 3 (June 2009): 311–334.

Cox-Rearick, Janet. *The Collection of Francis I: Royal Treasures*. New York: H. N. Abrams, and Antwerp: Fonds Mercator Paris: 1996.

Cox Rearick, Janet. "Fra Bartolomeo's *St Mark Evangelist* and *St Sebastian with an Angel*." *Mitteilungen des Kunsthistorishen Institutes in Florenz* 18 (1974): 329–54.

Damen, Giadda. "Shopping for *Cose Antiche* in Late Sixteenth-Century Venice." In *Reflections on Renaissance Venice: A Celebration of Patricia Fortini Brown*, edited by Mary E. Frank and Blake de Maria, 133–141.

Davis, Robert C., and Beth Lindsmith. *Renaissance People: Lives that Shaped the Modern Age*. Los Angeles: J. Paul Getty Museum, 2011.

Dolce, Lodovico. *Dialogo della pittvra di m. Lodovico Dolce, intitolato l'Aretino: nel quale si ragiona della dignità di essa pittura, e di tutte le parti necessarie, che a perfetto pittore si acconuengono: con esempi di pittori antichi, & moderni: e nel fine si fa mentione delle uirtù e delle opere del Diuin Titiano*. Venice: Gabriel Giolito de' Ferrari, 1557.

Elam, Caroline. "Art in the Service of Liberty: Battista della Palla, Art Agent for Francis I." *I Tatti Studies* 5 (1993): 33–109.

Fantelli, Pier Luigi. "Nicolò Renieri 'pittor fiamengo'." *Saggi e Memorie di storia dell'arte* 9 (1974): 77–115, 173–197.

Finzi, Riccardo. *Umanità di Veronica Gambara: Commemorazione pronunciata a Correggio, nel 4 centenario della morte della poetessa, il 28 maggio 1950*. 2nd rev. ed. Reggio Emilia: Tipolitogr. Emiliana, 1969.

Fletcher, J. M. "Isabella d'Este and Giovanni Bellini's 'Presepio'." *The Burlington Magazine* 113, no. 825 (December 1971): 703–713.

Freedman, Luba. "Michelangelo's Reflections on Bacchus." *Artibus et Historiae* 24, no. 47 (2003): 121–135.

Friedlaender, Walter. *Caravaggio Studies*. Princeton: Princeton University Press, 1955.

Fumagalli, Elena. "Florence." In Spear and Sohm, *Painting for Profit*, 173–204.

Gambara, Veronica. *Rime e lettere di Veronica Gambara*, edited by Pia Mestica Chaippetti. Florence: De Barbera, 1879.

Gigli, Giulio Cesare. *La pittura trionfante* (1615), edited by Barbara Agosti and Silvia Ginzburg. Porretta Terme: I Quaderni del Battello Ebbro, 1996.

Gilbert, Creighton. "What Did the Renaissance Patron Buy?" *Renaissance Quarterly* 51, no. 2 (Summer, 1998): 392–450.

Goldthwaite, Richard A. *Wealth and the Demand for Art in Italy 1300–1600*. Baltimore and London: Johns Hopkins University Press, 1993.

Goldthwaite, Richard A. "Economic Parameters of the Italian Art Market (15th to 17th Centuries)." In *The Art Market in Italy, 15th–17th Centuries (Il mercato dell'arte in Italia, secc. XV–XVII)*, edited by Marcello Fantoni, Louisa C. Matthew, and Sara F. Matthews-Grieco, 213–223. Ferrara: ISR and Modena: Franco Cosimo Panini, 2003.

Goldthwaite, Richard A. "The Painting Industry in Early Modern Italy." In Spear and Sohm, *Painting for Profit*, 275–301.

Green, Tony. *Nicolas Poussin Paints the Seven Sacraments Twice: An interpretation of Figures, Symbols, and Hieroglyphs, Together with a Running Commentary on the Paintings, the Drawing and the Artist's Letters*. Somerset: Paravail, 2000.

Guerzoni, Guido. "The Italian Renaissance Courts' Demand for the Arts: The Case of d'Este of Ferrara (1471–1560)." In *Art Markets in Europe, 1400–1800*, edited by Michael North and David Ormrod, 61–80. Aldershot, Brookfield, Singapore, and Sydney: Ashgate, 1998.

Hirst, Michael. *The Young Michelangelo: The Artist in Rome 1496–1501*. London: National Gallery Publications, 1994.

Hochmann, Michel, Rosella Lauber, and Stefania Mason. *Il collezionismo d'arte a Venezia*[1]. *Dalle origini al Cinquecento*. Venice: Marsilio, 2008.

Holanda, Francisco de. *Diálogos em Roma, 1538*. Heidelberg: Universitätsverlag C. Winter, 1998.

Holmes, Megan. "Neri di Bicci and the Commodification of Artistic Values in Florentine Painting (1450–1500)." In *The Art Market in Italy, 15th–17th Centuries (Il mercato dell'arte in Italia, secc. XV–XVII*), edited by Marcello Fantoni, Louisa C. Matthew, and Sara F. Matthews-Grieco, 213–223. Ferrara: ISR and Modena: Franco Cosimo Panini, 2003.

Huygens, Constantijn. *Journaal van de Reis naar Venetië* (1620), edited and translated by Frans Blom. Amsterdam: Prometheus/Bert Bakker, 2003.

Jansen, Dirk Jacob. *Jacopo Strada and Cultural Patronage at the Imperial Court*. Leiden: Brill, 2018.

Jansen, Dirk J. "Jacopo Strada." *Grove Art Online, Oxford Art Online*: oxfordartonline .com.db29.linccweb.org/subscriber/article/grove/art, accessed August 2021.

Lawrence, Sarah. *Jacopo Strada (1510–1588), Mannerist Splendor: Extravagant Designs for a Royal Table*. San Francisco: Serge Sorokko Gallery, 2007.

Lieberman, Ralph. "Regarding Michelangelo's 'Bacchus'." *Artibus et Historiae* 22, no. 43 (2001): 65–74.

Martin, Andrew John. "'Amica e un albergo di virtuosi': La casa e la collezione di Andrea Odoni." *Venezia cinquecento: Studi di storia dell'arte e della cultura* 10, no. 19 (2000): 153–170.

McIver, Katherine A. "Two Emilian Noblewomen and Patronage Networks in the Cinquecento." In *Beyond Isabella: Secular Women Patrons of Art in Renaissance Italy*, edited by Sheryl E. Reiss and David G. Wilkins, 159–176. Sixteenth Century Essays & Studies, 54. Kirksville, Missouri: Truman State University Press, 2002.

Michiel, Marcantonio. *The Anonimo: Notes on Pictures and Works of Art in Italy Made by an Anonymous Writer in the Sixteenth Century*, translated by Paolo Mussi and edited by George C. Williamson. London: G. Bell and Sons, 1903.

Moody, Ellen. "Under the Sign of Dido: Veronica Gambara (1485–1550), Life, Letters, and Poetry." (http://www.jimandellen.org/gambara.biography.html [page last updated 19 April 2004]).

Müntz, Eugène. *La Renaissance en Italie et en France à l'époque de Charles VIII*. Paris: Mesnil, 1885.

Nelson, Jonathan K., and Richard J. Zeckhauser. *The Patron's Payoff: Conspicuous Commissions in Italian Renaissance Art*. Princeton and Oxford: Princeton University Press, 2008.

Norton, Paul F. "The Lost Sleeping Cupid of Michelangelo." *Art Bulletin* 39, no. 4 (December, 1957): 251–257.

O'Malley, Michelle. *The Business of Art: Contracts and the Commissioning Process in Renaissance Italy*. New Haven and London: Yale University Press, 2005.

Palladino, Lora Anne. "Pietro Aretino: Orator and Art Theorist." Ph. D. dissertation, Yale University, 1981.

The Paper Museum of Cassiano dal Pozzo. London: Harvey Miller, and Turnhout: Brepols, 1998–2019.

Posèq, Avigdor W. G. "Caravaggio and the Antique." *Artibus et Historiae* 11, no. 21 (1990): 147–167.

Poss, Richard. "A Renaissance Gentildonna, Veronica Gambara." In *Women Writers of the Renaissance and Reformation*, edited by Katherine M. Wilson, 47–66. Athens, Georgia: University of Georgia Press, 1987.

Prieto Gilday, Rosi. "The Women Patrons of Neri di Bicci." In *Beyond Isabella: Secular Women Patrons of Art in Renaissance Italy*, edited by Sheryl E. Reiss and David G. Wilkins, 51–75. Sixteenth Century Essays & Studies, 54. Kirksville, Missouri: Truman State University Press, 2002.

Pritchard, Shannon. "Caravaggio's Capitoline *St John*: An Emblematic Image of Divine Love." *Athanor* (Florida State University Museum of Fine Arts Publishing) 23 (2005): 35–41.

Reinhardt, Volker. "The Roman Art Market in the Sixteenth and Seventeenth Centuries." In *Art Markets in Europe 1400–1800*, edited by Michael North and David Ormrod, 81–92. Aldershot, Brookfield, Singapore, Sydney: Ashgate, 1998.

Roccasecca, Pietro. "Bourbon del Monte, Francesco Maria." *Grove Art Online, Oxford Art Online* (published online 2003) oxfordartonline.com.db29.linccweb.org/subscriber/article/grove/art, accessed August 2021.

Salomon, Xavier F. *Veronese's Allegories: Virtue, Love, and Exploration in Renaissance Venice* (exh. cat.). New York: The Frick Collection, 2006.

Salomon, Xavier F. *Veronese*. London: National Gallery Company, 2014.

Scailliérez, Cécile. *François Ier et ses artistes dans les collections du Louvre*. Monographies des musées de France. Paris: Réunion des musées nationaux, 1992.

Scamozzi, Vincenzo. *L'idea dell'architettura universale* [1615]. Venice: Girolamo Albrizzi, 1714.

Schmitter, Monika Anne. *The Art Collector in Early Modern Italy: Andrea Odoni and His Venetian Palace*. Cambridge and New York: Cambridge University Press, 2021.

Schütz, Karl. "The Collection of Archduke Leopold William." In *Documentation—Exhibitions: 1648—War and Peace in Europe. Essay Volumes*, vol. 2: *Art and Culture*. https://www.lwl.org/westfaelischer-friede-download/wfe-t/wfe-txt2-17.htm.

Sohm, Philip. "Introduction." In Spear and Sohm, *Painting for Profit*, 1–32.

Sohm, Philip. "Venice." In Spear and Sohm, *Painting for Profit*, 205–253.

Spear, Richard E. "Rome: Setting the Stage." In Spear and Sohm, *Painting for Profit*. 33–114.

Spear, Richard E., and Philip Sohm, eds. *Painting for Profit: The Economic Lives of Seventeenth-Century Italian Painters*. New Haven and London: Yale Univeristy Press 2010.

Standring, Timothy J. "Some Pictures by Poussin in the Dal Pozzo Collection: Three New Inventories." *The Burlington Magazine* 130, no. 1025 (August 1988): 608–626.

Stortoni, Laura A. *Women Poets of the Italian Renaissance: Courtly Ladies and Courtesans*. New York: Italica Press, 1997.

Vasari, Giorgio. *The Life of Michelangelo*. Translated from the 1568 Milanese edition by A. B. Hinds, with introduction by David Hemsoll. London: Pallas Athene, 2006.

Whitehouse, Helen. *Ancient Mosaics and Wallpaintings. Series A. Antiquities and Architecture.* Part I. *The Paper Museum of Cassiano dal Pozzo, A Catalogue Raisonné. Drawing and Prints in the Royal Library at Windsor Castle, The British Museum, The Institut de France and Other Collections*, general editors Francis Haskell and Jennifer Montague. London: Harvey Miller Publishers ([Imprint of Brépols, Turnhout] 2001).

Zarrillo, Taryn Marie. "Complementary Activities: Marco Boschini, Paolo del Sera and Niccolò Renieri as Merchants, Collectors and Painters in Seicento Venice." In *Early Modern Merchants as Collectors*, edited by Chrisitna M. Anderson, 129–140. London and New York: Routledge, 2019.

CHAPTER 1

Merchant-Banker, Diplomat, Courtier or Agent? Intermediaries and Collecting Art in the Renaissance Courts

Leah R. Clark

> And I send you a strand of amber with some animals inside which I know your Ladyship will like, but it is not for sale. It belongs to someone who values it greatly because they appreciate rare things, but I had them lend it to me so you could see it.
>
> LORENZO DA PAVIA to ISABELLA D'ESTE, 14 February 1500[1]

Isabella d'Este (1474–1539), the Marchioness of Mantua and the famous Renaissance collector, acquired access to knowledge about art objects through intermediaries, as is demonstrated by the loaning of carved amber by her agent Lorenzo da Pavia (?–1517). Central to Renaissance collecting practices was the knowledge of objects (such as their quality and materials) as was the network at the collector's disposal. Isabella was not permitted to buy this particular amber strand but her collecting acumen was enhanced by her interaction with it, which highlights an important component of collecting: the value of having physical access to objects at a time when the rarity of mechanical reproduction of images did not allow for the frequent visual circulation of commodities. By being shown this treasure, Isabella was partaking in a knowledge exchange that provided her with a reference point to gauge other objects against, while in turn, Lorenzo's access to such objects equipped him with knowledge to convey to prospective clients. It was through the close engagement with objects, often through opportunities to see others' collections during state visits or through the loaning of artefacts, that elites and their agents came to acquire

1 Quoted and translated by Welch, *Shopping in the Renaissance*: 265, and 357, n. 71. For the first general studies on merchants in the early modern period see le Goff, *Marchands et banquiers*; Yver, *Le commerce*.

 | DOI:10.1163/9789004513938_003

knowledge about the qualities and values of things. This physical relationship to and engagement with material things also reveals the forms of knowledge that were at stake in commissioning, acquiring, and collecting objects at this time.

Objects collected in the Italian Renaissance courts included traditional art historical media—colossal sculpture and painting—as well as material culture—gems, jewels, books, and furniture. Distinctions between these types of objects belong to modern categorizations; those who attended court in the Renaissance would likely have valued a small gem over a painting for instance, pointing to the risk of anachronisms when applying our modern categories and object hierarchies to things of the past. Those who facilitated the circulation of goods required that their roles were multifaceted and malleable to the needs of their patrons or clients—whether an agent such as Lorenzo da Pavia whose main business was a musical instrument maker or a merchant-banker such as Lorenzo de' Medici (1449–92), who also served as diplomat and de facto ruler of Florence. This adaptability was particularly important during a time when new global markets were opening up, introducing diverse goods and requiring new sets of expertise.

1 A World of Wonders

Writing from Venice in the early sixteenth century, Roberto Macigni the Ferrarese ambassador reported enthusiastically to Cardinal Ippolito d'Este (1479–1520; brother of Isabella d'Este), on the galleys coming and going and the merchandise on offer.[2] From Alexandria, Cairo and Beirut to Turkey and Cyprus, there were exotic animals as well as textiles, ivory, spices, gems and much more on offer. Manufactured closer to home, the Este also sought glassworks from the shops in Murano, which were used to store the spices and medicines acquired from the East. These more "foreign" objects were indeed part of the wide range of objects on display in *studioli* or collecting spaces (fig. 1.1), as well as those scattered around the palace to observe, use, and admire, as the numerous Este inventories in the archives attest.[3] What they point to is the immense range and network of the circulation of goods, in which numerous individuals were involved. The antiquities and paintings we so often associate with Renaissance collecting could often be displayed as an ensemble with Chinese

2 Archivio di Stato di Modena (hereafter ASMO) Ambasciatori Venezia 13.

3 See for example the various inventories under Guardaroba or Amministrazione dei Principi, ASMO.

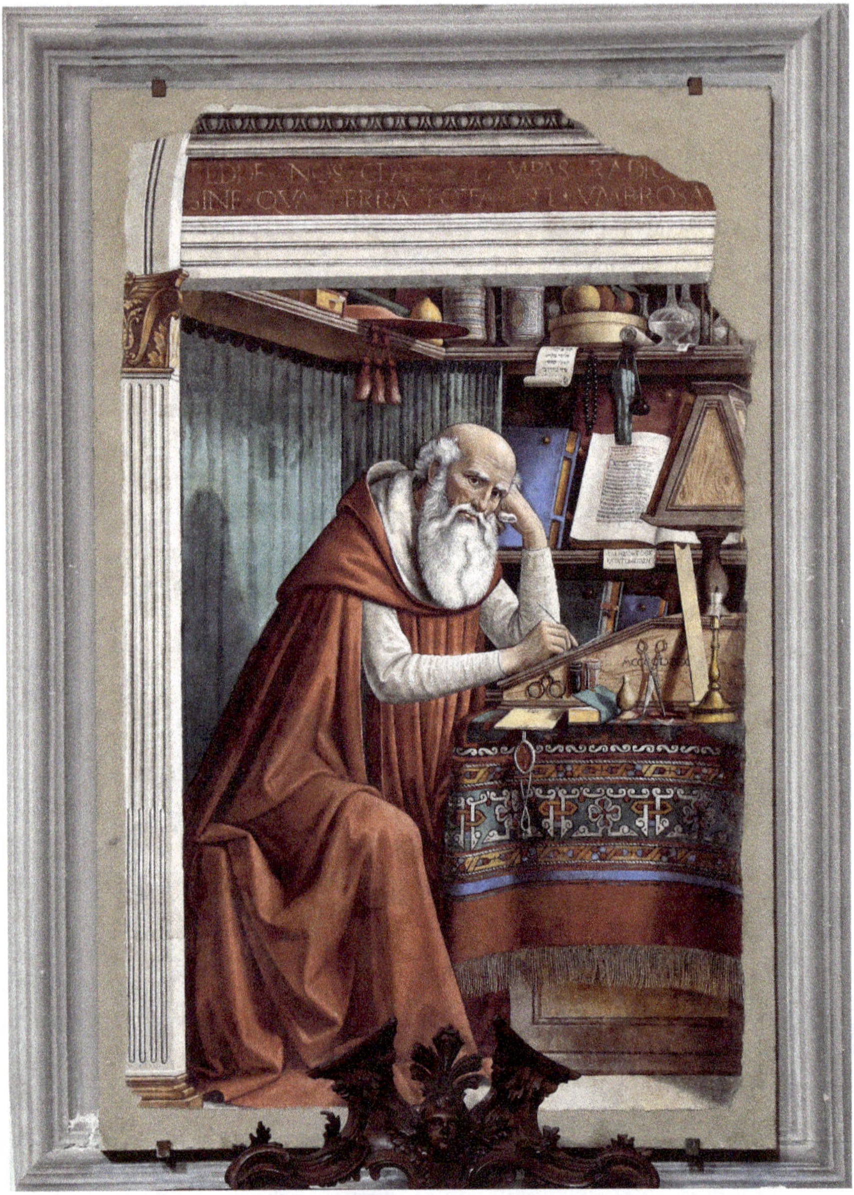

FIGURE 1.1 Domenico Ghirlandaio (1448–1494), *St Jerome in his Study*, 1480. Fresco, 184 × 119 cm. (72 × 47 in.)
CHURCH OF OGNISSANTI, FLORENCE, GETTY IMAGES

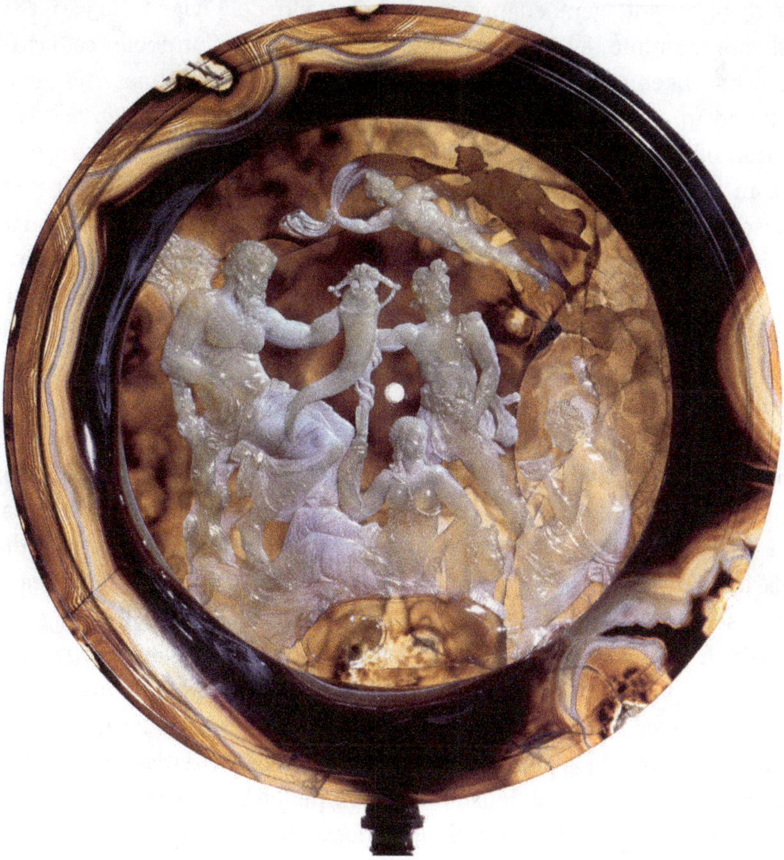

FIGURE 1.2 *Tazza Farnese*, c.200–150 BC, sardonyx agate, 20 cm wide. Museo Archeologico Nazionale, Naples
PHOTO: ARCHIVIO DELL'ARTE/LUCIANO PEDICINI

porcelain and Syrian metalwork. The acquisition of these goods involved intermediaries that included Florentine, Venetian, Catalan, and Genoese merchant-bankers that worked both in Italy and abroad, connecting vast global networks.

The ambitions of those who bought and traded goods also point to the risks in doing so, the Medici, the famous Florentine merchant-banking family, being a prime example. On 19 November 1495, the Medici were expelled from Florence, as their attempts to take over and rule republican Florence didn't go according to plan. Many of their possessions including the *Tazza Farnese* (fig. 1.2) were handed over to their business associate Lorenzo Tornabuoni (1465–97) in Rome, as were many other of the family's highly prized collectibles.[4] Earlier,

4 I use "collectibles" here as a term meaning an item that was meant to enhance a collection, but unlike modern collectibles, as this chapter argues, Renaissance collectibles were less static and more prone to dispersion.

the goldsmiths and gem engravers Michelangelo de Viviano (1459–1528), Salvestrino d'Antonio del Lavacchio and Giovanni delle Corniuole (ca. 1470–ca. 1516) had been given the task of appraising these hardstones and gems sequestered from the famous Medici collections, including the *Tazza*.[5] The evaluation of the precious hardstone was specifically sought by experts well trained in the material value and authenticity of gems and jewels, but they were also probably chosen because of Medici partisanship. Despite Lorenzo de' Medici's well-known and highly prized skills in diplomacy and politics, the Medici family's rise to power was unstable, and they were expelled from the city that they had hoped to rule. The *Tazza Farnese* reflects the instability of the political and economic power of those who owned it and encapsulates many of the concerns that this study addresses.

The *Tazza* was (and is) a complex object—an ancient hardstone from Egypt, which was carefully crafted to manipulate the best qualities of its material. Its cultural, aesthetic, and monetary value was embedded in its uniqueness, its age, its craftsmanship, its survival, and its connection to illustrious individuals. Its fairly large size and the fact that it was carved on both sides, meant that it posed challenges as well as possibilities for display as well as engagement. Worth a large sum of money, it could be used as collateral, but once in an owner's possession, it was shown off to visitors as a highly prized collectible, connected to knowledge, rather than economics. The dispersal of the Medici collections in 1495 points to the very paradox of these treasures and the tensions inherent in the relationship between people's possessions and their identities. Indeed, it demonstrates that the decades spent acquiring, choosing, negotiating, and manoeuvring objects to be housed in the Medici collections could all be lost with a single blow of expulsion.

The *Tazza Farnese* has a particularly fascinating biography, revealing the large networks at play in the circulation of art across space and time. In 1239 the *Tazza* belonged to Frederick II of Naples (1194–1250), but by the early fifteenth century, it had ended up in Persia, where it was drawn by Mohammed al-Khayyam either in Samarkand or Herat.[6] It has been suggested that the owner at that time was the Aqqoyunlu ruler, Uzun Hasan (1425–78) in Tabriz or, if not him, one of his immediate predecessors. In the mid fifteenth century, Alfonso I d'Aragona (1394–1458), King of Naples is recorded purchasing the *Tazza* from either a Genoese or Venetian merchant. How it ended back in Italy is unknown; it may have been through the Venetian route, or through direct exchanges with the Ottoman Empire. The object was then recorded in 1465 in the inventory of the Venetian Ludovico Trevisan (1401–65), the Chamberlain of

5 Fusco and Corti, *Lorenzo de' Medici*, 165–66 and see Docs 269–71. Also see Clark, *Collecting Art in the Italian Renaissance*.

6 Gennaioli, ed. *Pregio e bellezza*.

the Apostolic Camera in Rome. Pope Paul II (1417–71) acquired it from Trevisan and then in 1471 Lorenzo de' Medici obtained the precious item when he oversaw Pope Paul II's estate. Lorenzo's acquisition underlines how a merchant banking family sought to buy their power and prestige, through access to and exchange of such objects and the formation of their own collections.[7]

The varying evaluation of the *Tazza Farnese* also provides an indication of the constantly shifting value of things (and the pitfalls of historical records). Frederick II is recorded paying 1230 in Neapolitan gold currency for it, while Alfonso I d'Aragona is said to have paid 1000 or 2000 ducats for it. In a letter from 1480, when owned by Lorenzo, it was valued at 4,000 ducats but in his 1492 inventory, it was appraised at 10,000 ducats. However, it was given a low value when it was evaluated by the aforementioned goldsmiths and gem dealers when taken from the Medici in 1495. Finally, in the 1537 inventory of Duke Alessandro de' Medici (1510/11–1537), it was noted that Alfonso had paid 12,000 ducats for it, Lorenzo had bought it for 3,000 and it was valued at 2,000.[8]

The variations in price not only reflect variations in the market, but also political and social motivations. The evaluators of the Medici goods when the family was exiled were likely providing a low appraisal so that the Medici could later reclaim the items at a low cost. At other times, the prices of works were inflated to demonstrate the power and prestige of the owner or as attempts to outbid or scare off other potential buyers. This relates to what I have termed "object knowledge," an individual's ability to appraise not only the object but also the information he or she was receiving about it: knowledge of the stories around such objects, knowledge of other types of objects in the same category; and knowledge about who might want to purchase such an object or would be willing to enter into competition with others to buy it.[9] This knowledge was essential for intermediaries and was often conveyed by agents but it was also a collector's task to assess the validity of this information.

2 Merchant-Bankers and the Circulation of Objects

Merchant-bankers facilitated the circulation of goods, as collections of their clients were often fluid, changing with the vagaries of wealth and power, and thus savvy merchant-bankers were frequently in a good position to acquire these goods for themselves. Would the acquisition of a new gem put one into too much debt and lead to notoriety, or would its acquisition and consequent

7 Belozerskaya, *Medusa's Gaze*; Rogers, "The Gorgeous East," 73; Lentz and Lowry, *Timur and the Princely Vision*, 221 (cat. 150).

8 Fusco and Corti, *Lorenzo de' Medici*, 203.

9 See Clark, *Collecting Art in the Italian Renaissance*.

display build up one's reputation? Would one's careful selection of objects for a collection end up being dispersed at one's death and result in the loss of not only the collection but also one's identity? Would the loaning of a significant amount of money to an important ruler prove useful in a merchant-banker's future rise to power or come in handy when he was in trouble with the law, or would this sum never be repaid and result in his financial ruin? Would an art object given as a diplomatic gift achieve the necessary political results one was looking for? The answers were not usually straightforward, but often had ripple effects that became more embroiled according to the layers of exchange over time.

The literature on early modern merchant-bankers has generally followed two trajectories. One side of the scholarship has been largely focused on economics, providing a quantitative analysis of items, prices, supply, and demand.[10] The other trajectory has focused on the cultural pursuits of merchant families, such as the famous Florentine merchant-banking houses of the Medici or Strozzi, examining artistic patronage and its cultural products in terms of family chapels and palaces.[11] Less attention has been paid to the heterogeneous identities of merchant-bankers, not only as intermediaries in the circulation of goods, but as collectors, ambassadors, negotiators, and pawnbrokers. Working across Italy and further afield in Europe, merchants navigated diverse forms of government, resulting in a paradoxical status often performing the role of "courtiers" abroad and republican citizens at home. Most importantly, what has been largely neglected is how their negotiation of these roles (their function as "double agents")[12] was intricately connected to the movement of objects, which created a web of connections, obligations, and associations. Starting with the objects and the practices of exchange can reveal interconnections across boundaries and geographic spaces, an approach that moves away from the traditional focus of select sites such as Republican Florence or a specific courtly setting and also opens up the potential to look beyond Europe.

10 The literature is large, but for good introductions to the subject see Cassandro, "Affari e uomini d'affari"; de Roover, *The Rise and Decline of the Medici Bank*; Jacoviello, "Affari di Medici e Strozzi"; Petralia, *Banchieri e famiglie mercantili*; Silvestri, "Sull'attività bancaria napoletana"; Sposato, "Attività commerciali degli Aragonesi"; Tognetti, "Uno scambio diseguale"; Dauverd, *Imperial Ambition*. Earlier general studies on merchants in the Medieval period and Renaissance include le Goff, *Marchandset banquiers*; Yver, *Le commerce*.

11 Sale, "The Strozzi Chapel"; Borsook, "Documenti relativi alle Capelle"; Kent, "Più superba de quella de Lorenzo"; Goldthwaite, *Private Wealth*, 31–73. Two recent exhibitions have attempted to bring together the artistic and social concerns of merchant-bankers and the related material culture: *Denaro e Bellezza*, eds. Sebregondi and Parks; *The Splendour of the Medici*, eds. Bietti, Giusti, and Sframeli.

12 Keblusek, "Introduction."

The term "merchant-banker" is usually used to reference individuals who were involved in trade, but also in transactions dealing with large quantities of money. In the period itself, "mercante" was often applied to those who were involved in transactions that we would associate today with banking.[13] Many firms acted in the capacity as merchants and sometimes this was their primary business, whereby credit, pawning, and loans were secondary, and often linked to their business transactions in goods. Merchant-bankers could often serve in diplomatic roles too. Indeed, their multiple roles points to the fluidity of such categories at a time when some have argued the "new diplomacy" had begun to stabilize those very roles, as evidenced in the position of the resident ambassador, for example.[14] Lorenzo de' Medici is a particularly extreme case as the head of a merchant-banking family who hoped that their mercantile ambitions would eventually be superseded by their political ambitions, exchanging economic value for prestige, virtue and knowledge.

Banking and trade in the fifteenth century relied on a credit system involving pawning, pledging, and gifting, and many transactions were conducted with a promise to pay, or with a credit secured with one's belongings.[15] Acquiring goods, then, often involved the exchanging of one item for another, and introduced different objects to different individuals on a regular basis. Fifteenth-century merchant-bankers often lent large sums of money to court rulers and this was not usually only for financial gain (if at all) but for the possible privileges it could provide. There was, however, always an element of risk in these ventures, both for the lender and the borrower.

Recent studies on consumption practices and the early modern economy have proliferated in recent years, no doubt influenced by contemporary economic predicaments and globalization. Work by Lisa Jardine and Evelyn Welch, for example, has broadened our understanding of the social components of consumerism, looking at what it meant to shop and purchase objects in the early modern period.[16] Similar studies have pinpointed the accumulation of

---

13 Lane and Mueller, *Money and Banking*, 69; de Roover, *Business, Banking, and Economic Thought*, 210.

14 For the seminal text on the new diplomacy see Mattingly, *Renaissance Diplomacy*. For recent scholarship which has largely questioned the traditional view, see Thomson, "For a Comparative History"; Watkins, "Toward a New Diplomatic History"; Um and Clark, *Art of Embassy*; Clark, *Collecting Art in the Italian Renaissance*, 22–56.

15 Welch, *Shopping in the Renaissance*.

16 Welch, *Shopping in the Renaissance*; Jardine, *Worldly Goods*. Jardine's work is useful conceptually, but has been criticized for its historical inaccuracies; for a review see Martines, "Review Essay." On the second hand market, Matchette, "Credit and Credibility." Other studies include Armstrong, I. Elbl, and M. Elbl, eds., *Money, Markets and Trade*; Subrahmanyam, ed. *Merchant Networks*; Fantoni, Matthew, and Matthews-Grieco, eds.,

goods in the Renaissance as the beginning of the history of consumerism and materialism, and have gone so far as celebrating this period as the birth of modern capitalism.[17] More recent interests in gifting practices have provided an alternative approach, underlining the role of the gift as a binding force, in contrast to an individualistic economy.[18] However, late fifteenth-century consumption practices have to be studied on their own terms, functioning within a dual economy of gifts and commerce. In the fifteenth century, these two systems sometimes worked together, sometimes came up against each other in conflict, but undoubtedly influenced each other.[19] Possessions were often transient and status and reputation depended on one's ability to negotiate the circulation of one's goods, through the careful balance of pawning, credit, and gifting.[20]

Records of pawned jewels and gems reveal their mobility and underline that it was a common practice amongst the elite. In September 1487, pawned jewels from the Aragonese at the Neapolitan court were sent from Florence with Francesco Valori (1439–1498), ambassador of Florence, to Naples for the Strozzi Bank. The list of jewels included a large ruby, an emerald, a brooch, among others. In the same delivery, it is recorded that a separate small wooden box containing *Il Davit*—the famous jewel then belonging to King Ferrante d'Aragona of Naples (1424–94), described as a pendant *balassio* set in gold with pearls and placed on a gold chain—was consigned back to the court in December 1487.[21] *Il Davit* had actually been in the possession of merchant-banker Filippo Strozzi (1428–1491) as a pawned object for three years, and one wonders who may have seen or had access to the jewel while it was in Florence. Lorenzo de' Medici, for example, smuggled out of Rome a strongbox of gems that had belonged to Francesco Gonzaga, Marquess of Mantua (1466–1519). The gems were being held by creditors there after Francesco's death, and were not yet for sale, which points to the multiple ways, at times ruthless and illegal, that collectors as well as others interacted with these possessions.[22] Loans and pawning were also

---

The Art Market In Italy; Smith and Findlen, eds., *Merchants and Marvels*; Muldrew, *The Economy of Obligation*; Nelson, and Zeckhauser, *The Patron's Payoff.*

17 Mukerji, *From Graven Images*; Goldthwaite, "The Empire of Things"; Goldthwaite, *Wealth and the Demand*; Goldthwaite, "The Economy of Renaissance Italy."

18 The literature on early modern gifting is extensive, introductions to the subject include Clark, *Collecting Art in the Italian Renaissance*, 22–56; Um and Clark, *Art of Embassy*; Cutler, "Gifts and Gift Exchange"; Cutler, "Significant Gifts"; Groebner, *Liquid Assets*; Heal, *The Power of Gifts*.

19 For an innovative study which looks at these two systems together, although for a later period, see Fontaine, *The Moral Economy.*

20 Clark, "Transient Possessions."

21 Griffi, *Banchieri e gioielli*, 20–21. Archivio di Stato di Firenze, Carteggio Strozziane (hereafter ASF CS) 47, 99.

22 Brown, Fusco, and Corti, "Lorenzo de' Medici," 92–3.

clearly linked to trade relations, and merchants would often receive concessions on customs duties as payment. In 1475 the Strozzi Company sold a *balassio*, which was set with three large pearls, two diamonds and an emerald to the king for 700 ducats in exchange for extracting an equivalent sum in salt out of Puglia.[23] Similarly in 1477 King Ferrante d'Aragona (1424–1494) offered to waive the customs dues in the exportation of foodstuffs from his kingdom, in order to meet the 964 ducats he owed to the Medici bank in Naples.[24]

The Florentine merchant-banking company of the Strozzi provides an illuminating case of overlapping social, political, and economic ties. The economic dependencies of these banks' clients were often intricately bound up with political motivations. Within these relations, objects could often cause or become the site of tension and conflict, while they were also the locations of contact within these larger networks. Filippo Strozzi became one of the main bankers serving the Neapolitan crown in the second half of the fifteenth century. The Strozzi family had been exiled from Florence in the 1430s due to anti-Medicean sentiment stemming from one branch of the family. In 1447 Filippo Strozzi (1428–1491) moved to Naples from Spain where he had been working and this was a start of a fruitful relationship for Filippo. Not only did Filippo's business in Naples—the establishment of a bank and *fondaco*—earn great revenues, but he was also granted the title of councilor of state. Moreover, it was Ferrante who negotiated Filippo's repatriation to Florence, by writing to Lorenzo de' Medici. In September 1466, the exile ban on the Strozzi was lifted and in November Filippo returned to Florence. Although Filippo was now based in Florence, he still carried out commissions and loans for the Neapolitan crown and remained heavily involved with the Aragonese, traveling down to Naples throughout the 1470s. Ironically, Filippo, once an exiled Florentine, was given the role of intermediary between Florence and Naples following the Pazzi Conspiracy (1478) and he was asked to accompany Lorenzo de' Medici to Naples in 1478, underlining his dual political and economic roles.[25]

As a banker, Filippo Strozzi provided quick capital for the crown, furnished loans, and supplied credit for pawns and bills of exchange for larger payments. In his capacity as a merchant, Filippo purchased various luxury objects in Florence and shipped them to the Neapolitan court and he also arranged for Florentine artists to travel to Naples and work there. For example, throughout his life, Filippo was an important contact for books shipped from Florence to

23 Jacoviello, "Affari di Medici e Strozzi," 180.

24 Abulafia, "The Crown and the Economy," 136.

25 Pontieri, "La dinastia Aragonese," 288; Goldthwaite, *Private Wealth*, 56–7; Clark, *Collecting Art in the Italian Renaissance*, 59–108.

Naples. While Naples had a set of resident court humanists, scribes, and illuminators and there are frequent payments to these individuals in the accounts, the Neapolitan court still sought to purchase and commission books outside of Naples, notably from Florence.[26] Merchant-bankers were not merely pawns or disinterested intermediaries for the flow of material goods, they also contributed to the taste for and knowledge of these items, as they actively purchased many for themselves. Thus, while living between Florence and Naples, within a span of twenty years, Filippo went from Florentine exile to political representative, and performed the numerous roles of banker, lender, councilor, tastemaker, and ambassador.

In 1473, Filippo recorded sending numerous gifts to "friends" in Naples including a large *lettuccio* (daybed) made by Benedetto da Maiano (1442–97) given to King Ferrante. The list of gifts appears in one of Filippo Strozzi's account books, which records credits and debits, as well as more personal notes and details, similar to the personal observations found in Florentine *ricordanze*.[27] Particularly striking is the way he characterizes the gifts' recipients as "amicj di casa" articulating these are friends of the Strozzi family, rather than business relations. Filippo might have been deliberately referencing Cicero's discussion of liberality, where the great orator mentions the role of *amici* and *nostros* (clients) as recipients of gifts, noting how their sons and grandsons would keep alive the memory of the gift.[28] *Ricordanze*, while taking the form of a personal diary, were of course more public in their style of rhetoric, written with the assumption that they would be passed on and read by future generations.[29] Calling the King of Naples a friend certainly speaks to social aspirations, but such an assertion also points to the multifaceted roles Filippo performed and suggests a dual identity—a sense of belonging as a member of the Neapolitan court (one might even say a form of courtier), even though he had returned to Florence and was now a citizen of that republic.

The act of giving, however, is never disinterested and Filippo's attention to the gifts among "friends" underlines an inherent contradiction in gift-giving: gifts as "freely given" with lack of "self-interest" as a sign of friendship and

---

26 Barone, "Le Cedole di Tesoreria," 230.

27 ASF, CS, V, 22, 95R–95V. The gifts are recorded as bought between 24 November 1472 and 3 June 1473. The list comprises various court individuals from the king to the king's secretaries. For partial transcriptions see del Treppo, "Le avventure storiografiche," 510–13; Sale, "Strozzi Chapel," 514–6, Appendix A. IV.4. Also see further discussion in Clark, *Collecting Art in the Italian Renaissance*, 59–108.

28 Guerzoni, "Liberalitas, Magnificentia, Splendor," 348.

29 Rubin, "Domenico Ghirlandaio."

gifts as "deeply imbued with agendas of hierarchy and reciprocity."[30] Filippo Strozzi's involvement in numerous political negotiations between Florence and Naples certainly indicates a political and diplomatic framework for the gifts. The list reveals an incredibly wide range of individuals—the king and his children, as well as humanists, advisors, secretaries, and merchants. The gifts were well chosen for the recipients, such as the antique marble busts and a painting by Rogier van der Weyden (c.1399–1464) for the councilor to the King, Diomede Carafa (?1406–87) who was a well-known collector of antiquities and art. The variety of individuals bestowed with offerings suggests that such a list does not solely speak to diplomacy, but rather, to the overlapping spheres of economics, politics, and social prestige.

The obligation of the gift is part of a series of exchanges, where gifts and counter-gifts are both material and immaterial, and in some instances, the rewards are undetermined, stored up as favors that might be tapped into when necessary in navigating the stormy waters of fifteenth-century diplomacy. Gifts in the form of paintings, sometimes portraits, as Anthony Colantuono has articulated could also serve as "mute diplomats," informing political negotiations when words failed.[31] More "neutral" commercial transactions such as pawns or loans, could also operate similarly. As mentioned, a merchant-banker such as Lorenzo de' Medici provided bills of exchange, pawns, loans, and "commodities" to the princely elite, but he was also heavily involved in political negotiations and gift exchanges. Even as objects were used to solidify alliances, pay for wars, create ties of indebtedness and obligation, and operate as signs of virtue or magnificence, they were also the sites of political tensions, instigators of financial ruin, and indicators of betrayal. As is evident in the example of Lorenzo da Pavia that opens this chapter, sometimes objects changed hands with no monetary gain: they may be borrowed or loaned in an economy of knowledge, where access to objects might determine future purchases. As this study has demonstrated, many individuals associated with the trade in art objects could be considered "double agents," a term coined by Keblusek and Noldus referring to the multiple roles that early modern agents could perform, such as merchants, artists, collectors, and diplomats, sometimes simultaneously.[32] The term "negozio" often used in diplomatic correspondence, conveys the multiple duties such double agents took on, which ranged from acquiring goods, commissioning artists, and purchasing works

30 Hilsdale, *Byzantine Art and Diplomacy*, 13.
31 Colantuono, "The Mute Diplomat," 51–76.
32 Keblusek and Noldus, *Double Agents*.

of art or books, to negotiating secret political agreements, signing trade deals, and issuing military commands.[33]

Bibliography

Abulafia, David. "The Crown and the Economy under Ferrante I of Naples (1458–94)." In *City and Countryside in Late Medieval and Renaissance Italy. Essays Presented to Philip Jones*, edited by Trevor Dean and Chris Wickham, 125–46. London and Ronceverte: The Hambledon Press, 1990.

Armstrong, Lawrin, Ivana Elbl, and Martin M. Elbl, eds. *Money, Markets and Trade in Late Medieval Europe. Essays in Honour of John H. A. Munro*. Boston and Leiden: Koninklijke Brill, 2007.

Barone, Nicola. "Le Cedole di Tesoreria dell'Archivio di Stato di Napoli dal 1460 al 1504." *Archivio storico per le province napoletane* 9 (1884): 5–34, 205–348, 387–429, 601–37.

Belozerskaya, Marina. *Medusa's Gaze. The Extraordinary Journey of the Tazza Farnese*. Oxford: Oxford University Press, 2012.

Borsook, Eve. "Documenti relativi alle Capelle di Lecceto e delle Selve di Filippo Strozzi." *Antichità Viva* 9, no. 3 (1970): 3–20.

Brown, Clifford M., Laurie Fusco, and Gino Corti. "Lorenzo de' Medici and the Dispersal of the Antiquarian Collections of Cardinal Francesco Gonzaga." *Arte Lombarda* 90/91 (1989): 86–103.

Cassandro, Michele. "Affari e uomini d'affari fiorentini a Napoli sotto Ferrante I d'Aragona (1472–1495)." In *Studi di storia economica Toscana nel medioevo e nel rinascimento. In memoria di Federigo Melis*. Biblioteca del "Bollettino Storico Pisano," 103–23. Pisa: Pacini Editore, 1987.

Clark, Leah R. "Transient Possessions: Circulation, Replication, and Transmission of Gems and Jewels in Quattrocento Italy." *Journal of Early Modern History* 15, no. 3 (2011): 185–221.

Clark, Leah R. *Collecting Art in the Italian Renaissance Court: Objects and Exchanges*. Cambridge: Cambridge University Press, 2018.

Colantuono, Anthony. "The Mute Diplomat: Theorizing the Role of Images in Seventeenth-Century Political Negotiations." In *The Diplomacy of Art. Artistic Creation and Politics in Seicento Italy*, edited by Elizabeth Cropper, 51–76. Milan: Nuova Alfa Editoriale, 2000.

Cutler, Anthony. "Gifts and Gift Exchange as Aspects of the Byzantine, Arab, and Related Economies." *Dumbarton Oaks Papers* 55 (2001): 247–278.

33 Frigo, "Prudence and Experience," 21–22.

Cutler, Anthony. "Significant Gifts: Patterns of Exchange in Late Antique, Byzantine, and Early Islamic Diplomacy." *Journal of Medieval & Early Modern Studies* 38, no. 1 (2008): 79–101.

Dauverd, Céline. *Imperial Ambition in the Early Modern Mediterranean: Genoese Merchants and the Spanish Crown.* Cambridge: Cambridge University Press, 2015.

de Roover, Raymond. *The Rise and Decline of the Medici Bank. 1397–1494.* New York: W.W. Norton & Company Inc, 1966.

de Roover, Raymond. *Business, Banking, and Economic Thought in Late Medieval and Early Modern Europe. Selected Studies of Raymond de Roover*, edited by Julius Kirshner. Chicago and London: University of Chicago Press, 1974.

del Treppo, Mario. "Le avventure storiografiche della Tavola Strozzi." In *Fra storia e storiografia. Scritti in onore di Pasquale Villani*, edited by P. Marcy and A. Massafra, 483–515. Bologna: Società editrice il Mulino, 1994.

Denaro e Bellezza. I banchieri, Botticelli e il rogo delle vanità (exh. cat), edited by Ludovica Sebregondi and Tim Parks. Florence: Palazzo Strozzi, 2012.

Fantoni, Marcello, Louisa C. Matthew, and Sara F. Matthews-Grieco, eds. *The Art Market In Italy. 15th–17th Centuries/ Il mercato dell'arte in Italia secc. XV–XVII.* Ferrara: Franco Cosimo Panini Editore, 2003.

Fontaine, Laurence. *The Moral Economy: Poverty, Credit, and Trust in Early Modern Europe.* New York and Cambridge: Cambridge University Press, 2014.

Frigo, Daniela. "Prudence and Experience: Ambassadors and Political Culture in Early Modern Italy." *Journal of Medieval & Early Modern Studies* 38, no. 1 (2008): 15–34.

Fusco, Laurie, and Gino Corti. *Lorenzo de' Medici: Collector and Antiquarian.* Cambridge: Cambridge University Press, 2006.

Gennaioli, Riccardo, ed. *Pregio e bellezza. Cammei e intagli dei Medici.* Livorno: Sillabe, 2010.

Goldthwaite, Richard A. *Private Wealth in Renaissance Florence. A Study of Four Families.* Princeton: Princeton University Press, 1968.

Goldthwaite, Richard A. "The Economy of Renaissance Italy: The Preconditions for Luxury Consumption." *I Tatti Studies in the Italian Renaissance* 2 (1987): 15–39.

Goldthwaite, Richard A. "The Empire of Things: Consumer Demand in Renaissance Italy." In *Patronage, Art, and Society in Renaissance Italy*, edited by F. W. Kent and Patricia Simons, 153–75. Oxford: Oxford University Press, 1987.

Goldthwaite, Richard A. *Wealth and the Demand for Art in Italy 1300–1600.* Baltimore and London: The Johns Hopkins University Press, 1993.

Griffi, Filena Patroni. *Banchieri e gioielli alla corte aragonese di Napoli.* Naples: Francesco Giannini & Figli, 1984.

Groebner, Valentin. *Liquid Assets, Dangerous Gifts. Presents and Politics at the End of the Middle Ages.* Translated by Pamela E. Selwyn. Philadelphia: University of Pennsylvania Press, 2000.

Guerzoni, Guido. “Liberalitas, Magnificentia, Splendor: The Classic Origins of Italian Renaissance Lifestyles.” *History of Political Economy* 31 (1999): 332–378.

Heal, Felicity. *The Power of Gifts: Gift Exchange in Early Modern England*. Oxford: Oxford University Press, 2014.

Hilsdale, Cecily J. *Byzantine Art and Diplomacy in an Age of Decline*. New York: Cambridge University Press, 2014.

Jacoviello, Michele. “Affari di Medici e Strozzi nel regno di Napoli nella seconda metà del Quattrocento.” *Archivio storico italiano* 144 (1986): 169–96.

Jardine, Lisa. *Worldly Goods: A New History of the Renaissance*. London: Macmillan, 1996.

Jardine, Lisa, and Jerry Brotton. *Global Interests. Renaissance Art Between East and West*. Ithaca: Cornell University Press, 2000.

Keblusek, Marika. “Introduction: Double Agents in Early Modern Europe.” In *Double Agents: Cultural and Political Brokerage in Early Modern Europe*, edited by Marika Keblusek and Badeloch Noldus, 1–9. Leiden and Boston: Brill, 2011.

Keblusek, Marika, and Badeloch Noldus, eds. *Double Agents: Cultural and Political Brokerage in Early Modern Europe*. Leiden and Boston: Brill, 2011.

Kent, F. W. “‘Più superba de quella de Lorenzo’: Courtly and Family Interest in the Building of Filippo Strozzi’s Palace.” *Renaissance Quarterly* 30, no. 3 (1977): 311–23.

Lane, Frederic C., and Reinhold C. Mueller. *Money and Banking in Medieval and Renaissance Venice. Coins and Moneys of Account*. Vol. 1, Baltimore and London: The Johns Hopkins University Press, 1985.

le Goff, Jacques. *Marchands et banquiers du Moyen Age*. Paris: Presses universitaires de France, 1966.

Lentz, Thomas W., and Glenn Lowry. *Timur and the Princely Vision. Persian Art and Culture in the Fifteenth Century*. Los Angeles: Los Angeles County Museum of Art, 1989.

Mack, Rosamond E. *Bazaar to Piazza. Islamic Trade and Italian Art, 1300–1600*. Berkeley, Los Angeles and London: University of California Press, 2002.

Martines, Lauro. “Review Essay: The Renaissance and the Birth of Consumer Society.” *Renaissance Quarterly* 51 (1998): 193–203.

Matchette, Ann. “Credit and Credibility: Used Goods and Social Relations in Sixteenth-Century Florence.” In *The Material Renaissance*, edited by Michelle O’Malley and Evelyn S. Welch, 225–41. Manchester and New York: Manchester University Press, 2007.

Mattingly, Garrett. *Renaissance Diplomacy*. London: Butler and Tanner, 1963.

Mukerji, Chandra. *From Graven Images. Patterns of Modern Materialism*. New York: Columbia University Press, 1983.

Muldrew, Craig. *The Economy of Obligation. The Culture of Credit and Social Relations in Early Modern England*. New York: Saint Martin’s Press, 1998.

Nelson, Jonathan K., and Richard Zeckhauser, eds. *The Patron's Payoff: Conspicuous Commissions in Italian Renaissance Art*. Princeton: Princeton University Press, 2008.

Petralia, Giuseppe. *Banchieri e famiglie mercantili nel Mediterraneo aragonese. L'emigrazione dei pisani in Sicilia nel Quattrocento*. Pisa: Pacini Editore, 1989.

Pontieri, Ernesto. "La dinastia Aragonese di Napoli e la casa de' Medici in Firenze." *Archivio storico per le province napoletane* 26 (1940): 274–342.

Rogers, Michael J. "'The Gorgeous East': Trade and Tribute in the Islamic Empires." In *Circa 1492: Art in the Age of Exploration* (exh. cat.), edited by Jay A. Levenson, 69–74. Washington, New Haven and London: National Gallery of Art and Yale University Press, 1991.

Rubin, Patricia Lee. "Domenico Ghirlandaio and the Meaning of History in Fifteenth-Century Florence." In *Domenico Ghirlandaio 1449–1494. Atti del Convegno Internazionale Firenze, 16–19 ottobre 1994*, edited by Wolfram Prinz and Max Seidel, 97–117. Florence: Centro Di, 1996.

Sale, John Russell. "The Strozzi Chapel By Filippino Lippi in Santa Maria Novella." PhD Thesis, University of Pennsylvania, 1976.

Silvestri, Alfonso. "Sull'attività bancaria napoletana durante il periodo aragonese." *Bollettino dell'Archivio Storico Banco di Napoli* 6 (1953): 80–121.

Smith, Pamela H., and Paula Findlen, eds. *Merchants and Marvels. Commerce, Science, and Art in Early Modern Europe*. New York and London: Routledge, 2002.

The Splendour of the Medici: Art and Life in Renaissance Florence (exh. cat). Edited by Monica Bietti, Anna Maria Giusti, and Maria Sframeli. Budapest: Museum of Fine Arts, 2008.

Sposato, Pasquale. "Attività commerciali degli Aragonesi nella seconda metà del quattrocento." In *Studi in onore di Riccardo Filangieri*, 213–31. Naples: L'arte Tipografica, 1959.

Subrahmanyam, Sanjay, ed. *Merchant Networks in the Early Modern World*. Vol. 8. Aldershot: Variorum, 1996.

Thomson, Erik. "For a Comparative History Of Early Modern Diplomacy." *Scandinavian Journal of History* 31, no. 2 (2006): 151–172.

Tognetti, Sergio. "Uno scambio diseguale. Aspetti dei rapporti commerciali tra Firenze e Napoli nella seconda metà del Quattrocento." *Archivio storico italiano* 158 (2000): 461–90.

Um, Nancy, and Leah R. Clark, eds. *Special Issue: The Art of Embassy: Situating Objects and Images in the Early Modern Diplomatic Encounter. Journal of Early Modern History*. Vol. 20.1, 2016.

Watkins, John. "Toward a New Diplomatic History of Medieval and Early Modern Europe." *Journal of Medieval & Early Modern Studies* 38, no. 1 (2008): 1–14.

Welch, Evelyn S. *Shopping in the Renaissance: Consumer Cultures in Italy, 1400–1600*. New Haven and London: Yale University Press, 2005.

Yver, Georges. *Le commerce et les marchands dans l'Italie méridionale au XIII*[e] *et au XIV*[e] *siècle*. Paris: Albert Fontemoing Éditeur, 1903.

Zemon Davis, Natalie. *The Gift in Sixteenth-Century France*. Madison: The University of Wisconsin Press, 2000.

CHAPTER 2

Birth in Venice: The Origins of Art Collecting in the *Serenissima*

Frederick Ilchman

When museumgoers today approach a painting, among the first questions they ask is "Who painted it?" Happily, labels can tell us the name of the artist, or at least a best guess. "Who painted it?" was also a burning question in Venice five hundred years ago, when about half a century had passed since the creation of a picture today accepted as by Antonello da Messina (ca. 1430–1479)—enough time to cast doubt over its attribution (fig. 2.1).[1]

The small panel now in London's National Gallery, *Saint Jerome in His Study*, makes perfect sense to us as a work by Antonello da Messina of around 1475, painted during his sojourn in Venice. As early as the 1520s, however, the picture's authorship was unclear, as recorded in a manuscript compiled between 1521 and 1543 by Marcantonio Michiel (ca. 1484–1552), a Venetian noble and aspiring politician. Fascinated by art and art collections, he took detailed notes on what he had examined in private homes and public locations in seven cities in northern Italy, including eleven private collections in Venice. Michiel's comments are revolutionary in the amount of detail given to individual objects—especially the tantalizing descriptions of fourteen paintings supposedly by Giorgione (ca. 1478–1510)—and for the summaries of these collections. Michiel offers far more information than household inventories, which rarely supply an artist's name.[2] In many cases, Michiel specifies the painter or sculptor, describes the subject and relative size, and even sometimes notes the support of a painting (panel or canvas) or the medium of sculpture or decorative

1 Fundamental studies on collecting in Venice in this period include Hochmann, Lauber, and Mason, *Dalle origini al Cinquecento*; Borean and Mason, *Il Seicento*; and Aikema, Lauber, and Seidel, *Il collezionismo a Venezia*. For help on this essay, I am grateful to Inge Reist, Gabriele Matino, Leslie Contarini, Ella Mints, Cara Wolahan, and above all Catherine Lacroix. Monika Schmitter generously shared bibliography and expertise as well as an advance copy of her important book, *The Art Collector in Early Modern Italy: Andrea Odoni and his Venetian Palace*.

2 On Michiel and his *notizie* as well as comparisons to records of collections from later in the century, see Schmitter, "Display of Distinction," 27–37. For Venetian inventories, see Henry, "What Makes a Picture?"

 | DOI:10.1163/9789004513938_004

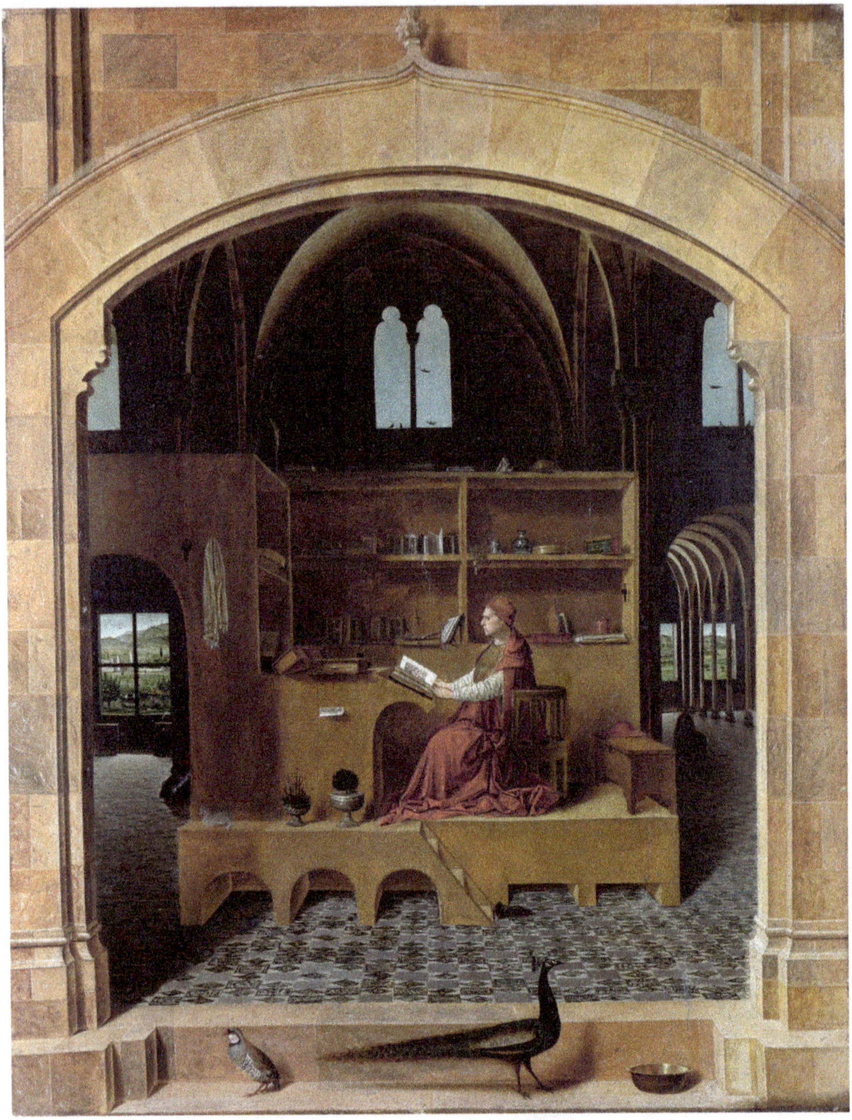

FIGURE 2.1 Antonello da Messina (ca. 1430–1479), *Saint Jerome in His Study*, ca. 1475. Oil on panel, 45.7 × 36.2 cm (18 × 14.3 in.)
NATIONAL GALLERY, LONDON

arts. Occasionally, he indicates provenance or suggests a work may be a copy. Even if many of the great public works of Renaissance art remain in Venice today, the contents of the innumerable private collections have largely been dispersed. Michiel's notes thus offer a precious window into these personal and family collections in the sixteenth century: homes full of classical statuary (often fragments), illuminated manuscripts, medals, drawings, prints, and of course many paintings.[3]

In 1529, Michiel took pains to describe the *Saint Jerome* in the collection of silk merchant Antonio Pasqualino.[4] The writer admits he is stumped by the identity of the artist, and records divergent opinions:

> Some believe that the little picture of St Jerome dressed as a cardinal reading in the study is by the hand of Antonello da Messina, but the majority with more justification attribute it to Giannes or Membling, an old Flemish painter, and so it shows that style, although the face is finished in the Italian way so that it seems to be by the hand of Jacometto. The buildings are in the Flemish style [*alla ponentina*]. The little landscape is lifelike [*naturale*], minute and highly finished, and one sees it outside a window and beyond the study door, and then it fades out [*fugge*], and the whole work is perfect for its subtlety, colouring, drawing, strength and relief. In it a peacock, quail, and a barber's basin are all represented. A small open letter is attached to the desk, which seems to contain the master's name, but, not withstanding, if one looks carefully at it from close up, it does not contain any letters but is all made up. Others believe that the figure has been repainted by Jacometto Veneziano.[5]

Michiel was an early example of what we call a connoisseur, someone who cultivated expertise and took delight in erudite conversations about art. His aesthetic judgment was lauded by none other than Pietro Aretino (1492–1556).[6] Like other sophisticated Venetians, Michiel admired Netherlandish paintings of the fifteenth century for their profusion of tiny details, including still life

3 On the antiquities market in Renaissance Venice, see Brown, "Le antichità," 309–337, and Damen, "Shopping for *Cose Antiche*."

4 The description is transcribed in Michiel, *Marcanton Michiel's Notizia*, 98–101. The manuscript was annotated over the years in different inks, obscuring Michiel's intentions. On this complexity, see Schmitter, "The Dating of Marcantonio Michiel," 564, n. 1. The enormous gothic Palazzo Pasqualini (now known as Palazzo Zaguri) in Campo San Maurizio was no longer Antonio's residence by the time of Michiel's visit; that probably took place in a home near San Moisè. See the entry by Lauber in Hochmann, Lauber, and Mason, *Dalle origini al Cinquecento*, 303–304, and Lauber, "Opera Perfettissima," 82–84.

5 Chambers and Pullan, *A Documentary History*, 427. Translation by Jennifer Fletcher. While capturing much nuance, this translation locates two sentences in different places in the passage compared with Frimmel's transcription. On the painting, see the entry in Lucco, *Antonello da Messina*, cat. 31.

6 Fletcher, "Michiel's Collection," 382. For Aretino as critic, patron, and broker, see the essay by Reist in this volume.

passages, convincing evocations of textures, careful play of light, and distant landscapes that recede into the mist. The technical mastery of these elements in the *Saint Jerome* suggested to him, and to the "majority" of people he consulted, that the artist must be Jan van Eyck (ca. 1390–1441) or Hans Memling (ca. 1430/1440–1494), or at least someone from the Low Countries. At the same time, the figure of Jerome, particularly the face, seemed more likely to be by an Italian artist. Michiel tries to solve his attribution dilemma with what is today a common way out—noting the compromised condition—and declares that the picture could well have been made in two campaigns, with the figure repainted by Jacometto Veneziano, a painter and miniaturist active from ca. 1472 until ca. 1497.[7]

Implicit in Michiel's attributional impasse and the length of his analysis is that the correct artist of the painting was not only worth knowing, but *essential* to know.[8] His manuscript suggests that a work of art derived much of its interest from the skill of its creator, who worked in what we now call a "signature style." In the absence of documents or signatures for this painting—one can imagine Michiel's frustration that the fictive paper label, or *cartellino*, on the side of the desk, does not contain actual words—the correct painter should be identifiable through visual comparisons. Although we might feel that Michiel is waffling here, he would probably insist that he was being thorough, giving an outstanding painting the attention it merited.

Despite his curiosity and abundant knowledge, Michiel never published his book nor may he have ever planned to do so.[9] His notes neglect his own collection at his home in Santa Marina. His mixed record as an art collector reflects this inconsistent ambition. He owned twenty paintings (including a Giorgione and a Giovanni Bellini [ca. 1430–1516]), nineteen bronzes, and five marble sculptures. While the number and range of works may initially impress, not all of the extant works do.[10] A few have been identified; the Bellini must be the beautiful *Pietà* now in the Gallerie dell'Accademia. Another is the more prosaic bronze ewer now in the Fitzwilliam Museum, Cambridge, with the inscription "M. Antonius Michiel had it made in the year 1548." We can be sure

7 Michiel is practically the only early source on Jacometto; see Pope-Hennessy, *Italian Paintings*, 240–243, Schmitter, "Display of Distinction," 104–109, Schmitter, *The Art Collector*, 147–150, and Serafini, "Jacometto Veneziano."

8 Many scholars have commented on Michiel's corrections to his manuscript, evidence he had revised his opinion or received additional information. See, for example, Schmitter, "Display of Distinction," 79–82.

9 Fletcher, "Michiel, 'che ha veduto assai,'" 603.

10 Fletcher, "Michiel: His Friends and Collection," 465. For the Bellini, the so-called *Donà dalle Rose Pietà*, see Moschini Marconi, *Opere d'Arte*, 75, and Tempestini, *Giovanni Bellini*, 166–170, 225.

that the permanent labeling on the vessel—crediting the patron and supplying provenance—reflected his own efforts in recording private collections, characteristic of the "collector mentality."[11] Such an inscription was surely intended to help future list makers, that is, future Michiels.

Michiel also commissioned an awkward marble sculpture of *Mercury* from Antonio Minelli (ca. 1465–ca. 1529), based on antique originals and complete with a circular horoscope set into a small altar. Now in the Victoria and Albert Museum, the sculpture bears a Latin text noting that the work was commissioned by Michiel and begun on 14 February 1527; and the horoscope for 15 June appears on the bronze disc (fig. 2.2).[12] If the sculpture advertises well the patron's erudition, it less successfully demonstrates his taste. While it is hard to interpret what the sculpture meant to Michiel, Jennifer Fletcher perceptively noted that this date happened to be in the month when he married, and that the god Mercury was a "useful symbol for a Venetian patrician simultaneously engaged in antiquity, diplomacy and business."[13] Michiel's *Mercury* thus seems to be an attempt to have it both ways: a work that looked antique and therefore emanated classical gravitas, but was also personalized for the owner. That is, it was intended to function as both collected and commissioned, a dual charge that perhaps explains its ungainliness. If we cannot particularly praise the art he owned, we should credit Michiel with one very distinguished collection: the notes he compiled on the collections of others.

How to describe Michiel's Venice? A useful starting point is the crowded urban setting seen in *The Miracle of the Cross at the Rialto Bridge* (ca. 1494–1496, Gallerie dell'Accademia; fig. 2.3).[14] Vittore Carpaccio (ca. 1465–ca. 1526) painted this mural for a public setting, the Scuola Grande di San Giovanni Evangelista. The ostensible subject—the exorcism of a possessed boy in the upper story of the loggia at left—is overwhelmed by visual information.[15] Carpaccio has populated his cityscape with a varied cast, including many merchants of Venice

11 "The permanent labeling of expensive objects is characteristic of the collector mentality, where a distinguished provenance in and of itself bestows value on the object." See Brown, *Private Lives*, 223–224, figs. 248, 249.

12 Pope-Hennessy, *Catalogue of Italian Sculpture*, II, 510–512; Fletcher, "Marcantonio Michiel's Collection," 383 n. 14; https://collections.vam.ac.uk/item/O18105/mercury-statuette-minelli-antonio/.

13 Fletcher, "Michiel: His Friends and Collection," 466. Brown, *Private Lives*, 223, assigns this sculpture to the category of "modern fakes, meant to fool no one."

14 On the painting, whose 2020–21 conservation treatment sponsored by Save Venice has revealed abundant detail within the teeming setting, see Matino and Brown, *Carpaccio in Venice*, 100–103.

15 Now known as the "eyewitness style," this mode reflected an ideal vision of Venetian ritual and the city's appearance, employing a plethora of detail to insist on the veracity of the miracle depicted. See Brown, *Venetian Narrative Painting*, 1–6, 125–132.

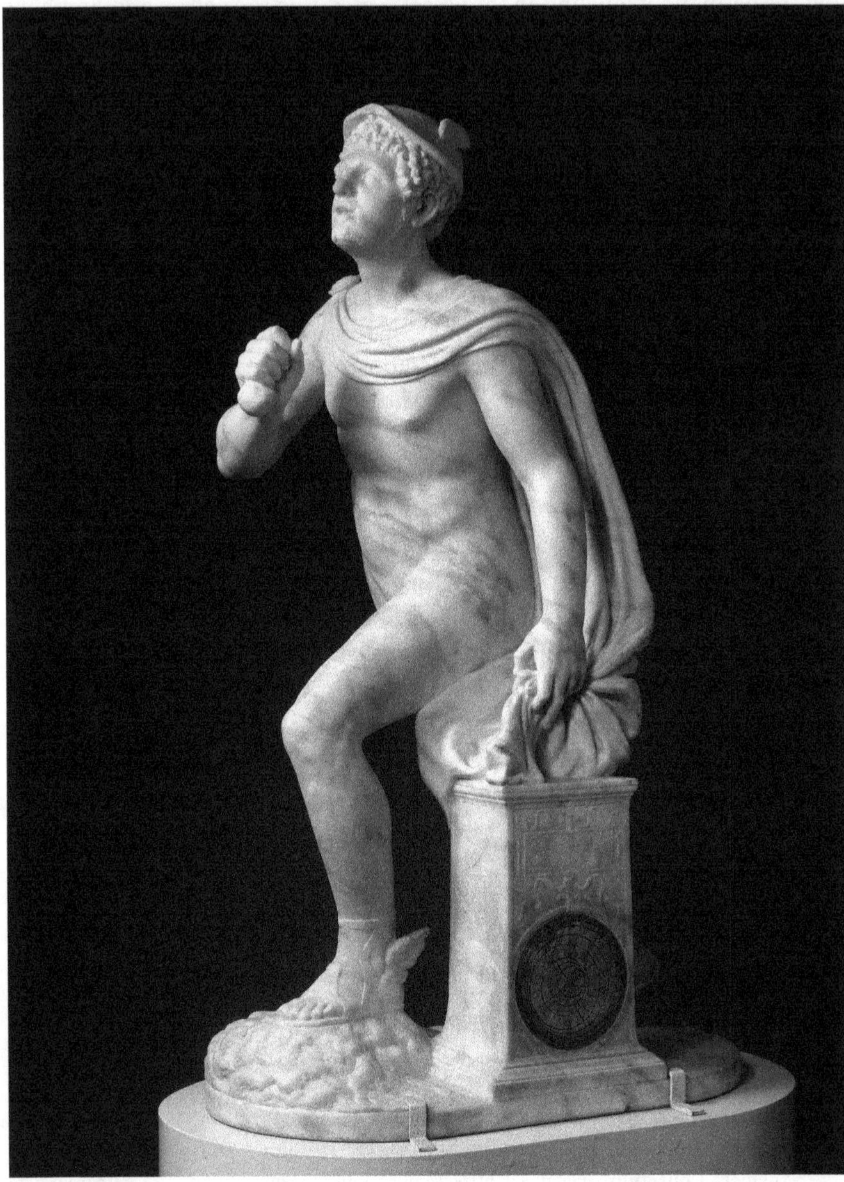

FIGURE 2.2 Antonio Minelli (ca. 1465–ca. 1529), *Mercury*, 1527. Marble inlaid with bronze, 77.5 × 26.5 × 44 cm (30.5 × 10.4 × 17.3 in.). Victoria and Albert Museum, London
PHOTO COURTESY OF VICTORIA AND ALBERT MUSEUM, LONDON

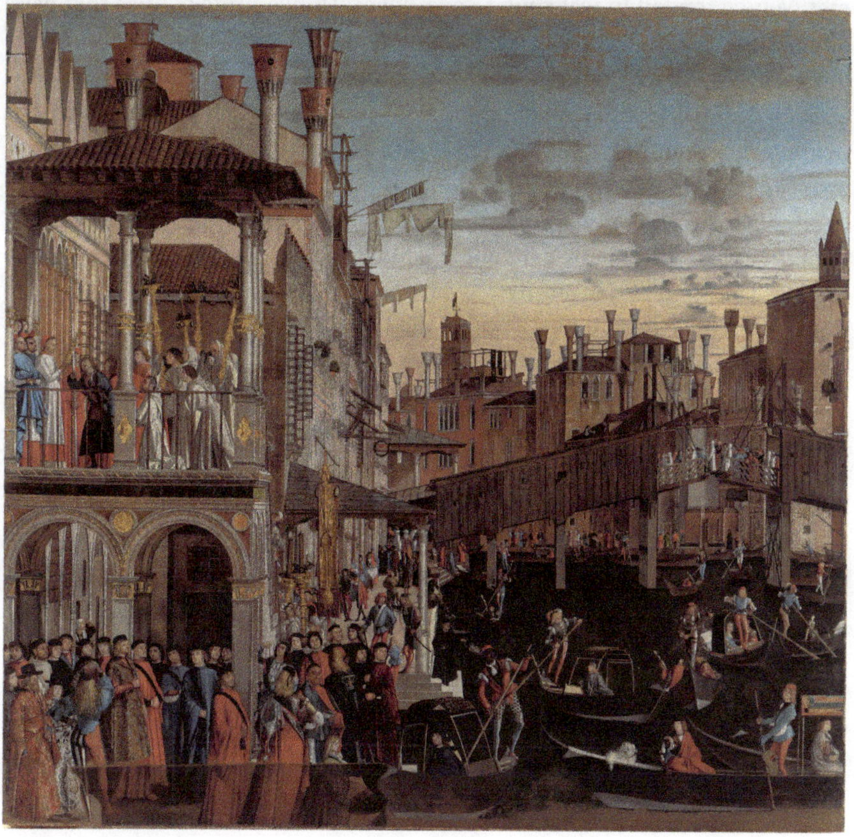

FIGURE 2.3 Vittore Carpaccio (ca. 1465–ca. 1526), *Miracle of the Cross at the Rialto Bridge*, ca. 1494–96. Tempera and oil on canvas, 371 × 392 cm (146 × 154 in.). Gallerie dell'Accademia, Venice
PHOTO BY MATTEO DE FINA, COURTESY OF SAVE VENICE

plying their trade on land and moving about town by boat. Fanciful chimney pots, church steeples, shop signs, and laundry out to dry punctuate the pink sky of the setting sun.

Carpaccio depicts a thriving city. Unlike that of Milan or Bologna, for example, Venice's government had been enviably stable for centuries, worthy of the sobriquet *La Serenissima Repubblica*. Political stability enabled commercial prosperity, and both conditions stimulated art collecting. In the sixteenth century, Venice had some 160,000 inhabitants, making it of one of the most populous cities in Europe, and arguably its most cosmopolitan and sophisticated. The diverse population included large groups of foreigners, either as permanent residents or in town on business. As a crossroads where different cultures met, Venice tended to welcome foreign ideas. Unlike principalities that were dominated by a ruling family, who would monopolize the best artists and dictate taste, Venice as a republic had a much broader power structure—and thus a much bigger potential clientele for art. It is not outlandish to imagine that nearly every adult depicted in Carpaccio's painting—prelates, businessmen, artisans, gondoliers, even perhaps the laborers carrying barrels on the quay—could have afforded a work of art, if only a religious print, map, or modest painting.[16] This enormous demand would have employed hundreds of craftsmen and printers. The very best artists of Carpaccio's generation, including Carpaccio himself, would have served the top clients.

A monumental work on paper makes clear the sophistication of both product and customer in this period: Jacopo de' Barbari's (ca. 1460/70–ca. 1516) woodcut *View of Venice*, dated 1500, printed on six large sheets of paper using six blocks and showing the city from the air (fig. 2.4).[17] Surveying the population, patricians constituted the top 5%; these men stocked the magistracies and councils that governed Venice. The next layer were *cittadini* or citizens (lawyers, doctors, notaries, civil servants, wholesale and international merchants), another 5–6%. The remaining 89–90% comprised *popoli* (shopkeepers, artisans, minor merchants, laborers), and also foreigners.[18] Copies of de' Barbari's view were priced at 3 ducats each, a substantial amount.[19] Yet many

16 Morse, "The Venetian *Portego*," concludes that "over 90 percent of Venetian households, from almost all social classes, owned at least one image or object of religious significance." 91, 104 n. 8. The most modest images were often called *anchone* ("icons"), printed devotional works sometimes colored by hand. In 1441 Venetian printers objected to *anchone*, both painted and printed, being brought into Venice from outside the city, evidently flooding the market. See P. Thornton, *The Italian Renaissance Interior*, 265.

17 For de' Barbari's woodcut, see Schulz, "Jacopo de' Barbari's View," and Howard, "Venice as a Dolphin."

18 For demographic and social structure in Venice in the context of collecting, see Henry, "What Makes a Picture?," and Schmitter, "Virtuous Riches," esp. 908–913. For *cittadini* as art collectors and patrons, see Schmitter, ibid., and De Maria, *Becoming Venetian*. For an in-depth discussion of *cittadini* within the social order and in period terminology, see Schmitter, *The Art Collector*, esp. 16–31.

19 For wages and prices, see Labalme and White, *Venice*, Cità Excelentissima, 541–543. For examples relating to artists, see Chambers and Pullan, *A Documentary History*: Lorenzo Lotto rented part of a house for 20 ducats a year (420); Lotto painted a family portrait for Zuan della Volta (National Gallery, London) for 20 ducats (ibid.); Lotto's apprentice was to earn 15 ducats over three years (439). Philip Sohm discusses the economic status of painters in Venice in the later sixteenth through mid-eighteenth centuries in Spear and Sohm, *Painting for Profit*, 205–253. Sohm surveys prices per painting for church and government commissions in terms of size and number of figures, prices for other commodities, taxes, income from copying and restoring paintings or working as an appraiser or dealer, and more.

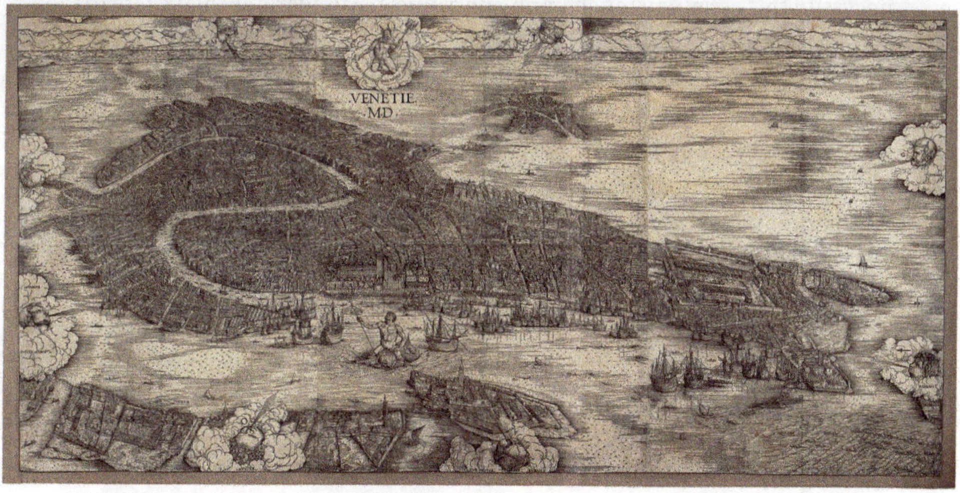

FIGURE 2.4 Jacopo de' Barbari (ca. 1460/70–ca. 1516), *View of Venice*, 1500. Woodcut, 132.72 × 277.5 cm (52.25 × 109.25 in.). Minneapolis Institute of Art, Minneapolis
PHOTO COURTESY OF MINNEAPOLIS INSTITUTE OF ART (MIA)

Venetians, at least those in more specialized occupations, could probably afford one.

Against this backdrop, something extraordinary happened in the history of art collecting. My assertion is that in the period covered by this volume, and particularly the first decades of the sixteenth century, Venice was the earliest place in Europe that could qualify as having an "art market" in the modern sense. There are numerous instances where Venice records the first example, or at least an early adoption, of many developments that we today consider essential to the activities of specialized art collecting and a burgeoning art trade. These include art connoisseurship as a specialized skill (as seen in Michiel); the invention of the oil-on-canvas easel painting and the related emergence of the gallery picture;[20] a new attention to the creation of household collections and special rooms for the display of art, which in turn encouraged artists who served this niche; a taste for contemporary art created elsewhere;[21] cultural patrimony policy to prevent export of national treasures; the illustrated collection catalogue, and more. These are a lot of firsts or early instances, so by

20 For the technological combination of oil on canvas and the emergence of the easel picture, see Ilchman, "Venetian Painting in an Age of Rivals," esp. 29–38, and "Prologue: The Transformation," esp. 90–91. For a Venetian subset of the gallery picture, see Schmitter, "The *Quadro da Portego*."

21 In Venice this especially applied to paintings by Netherlandish artists; see below.

necessity this essay will touch upon only some, particularly as they relate to the collecting and appreciation of paintings.

These sixteenth-century developments were connected to a fundamental shift in attitudes toward works of art, whereby the skill of the maker came to be regarded as equally or more important than the ostensible religious or didactic function of an image. This change began in Italian cities around 1500 and particularly embraced objects within private homes.[22] To put it another way, a picture that had been understood primarily as a *Saint Jerome* in earlier decades was now becoming appreciated first and foremost as an "Antonello." The shift—from the priorities of a notary compiling a household inventory to the priorities of a Michiel—is especially evident in Venice and during the lifetime of our trailblazing connoisseur.

In broad terms, this volume explores stories of objects, people, and spaces. These categories of Venetian objects, people, and spaces intersect in Antonello's *Saint Jerome*. This is a remarkable picture, described in detail by an early art historian who offered several plausible candidates for the painter. Inside the painting is a clue to the original settings of such small pictures: a *studiolo* or study. Just as Jerome sits at a specially constructed desk, raised off of the chilly floor by a wooden platform and surrounded by his books, so would a precious painting like Antonello's have been displayed in an enclosed space. These rooms were intentionally intimate and sequestered, where treasures could be kept securely and admired privately or with a close friend or two.

A *studiolo*, also called a *camerino* (little room), is the first of two key spaces within a Venetian home. Carpaccio's *Vision of Saint Augustine*, ca. 1502–3 (fig. 2.5) can help us visualize the differences in scale, privacy, and function between a multi-purpose *camera* and the smaller *studiolo* or *camerino*. In the painting, Augustine sits at his desk in a large Venetian *camera*, here set up as an office and strewn with books, small sculptures, and scientific instruments.[23] In the center of the back wall is a substantial altar, itself functioning as a cupboard, surmounted by a bronze of the Risen Christ. Of particular interest is the doorway at left, opening onto a *studiolo*. This intimate compartment afforded tranquility for reading and prayer, and presumably housed some of the most valuable volumes. Little rooms like Augustine's *studiolo* were derived from

22 See Motture and Syson, "Art in the *Casa*," 268–269, for the notion of the beginning around 1500 of the "age of art," an era that continues down to our time, building on earlier arguments by Hans Belting and Alexander Nagel.

23 The *studiolo*'s presence is often noted; see, for example, Schmitter, *The Art Collector*, 144. For Carpaccio's painting, see Matino and Brown, *Carpaccio in Venice*, 87–88. Many of the small objects around the desk, such as the shell, hourglass, astrolabes, and armillary sphere, all possessing important theological associations, are now much more legible following the conservation treatment sponsored by Save Venice and completed in December 2020.

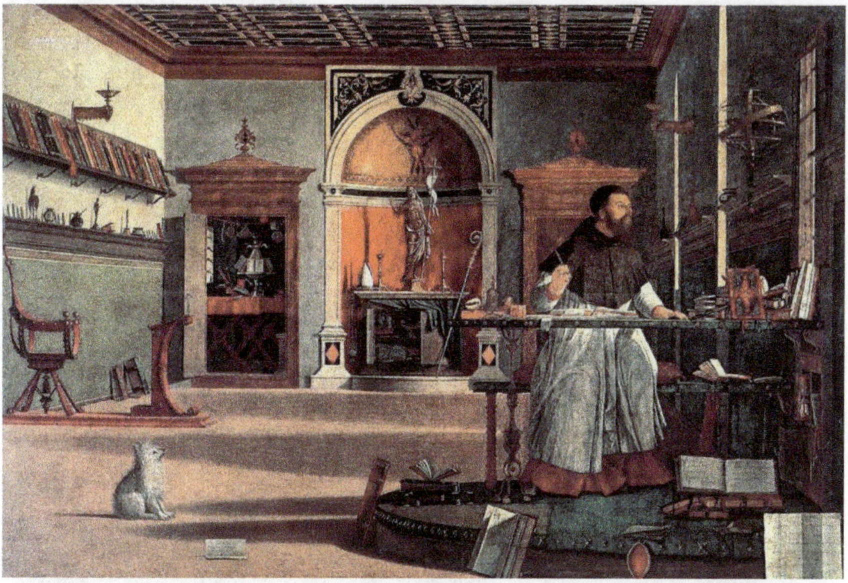

FIGURE 2.5 Vittore Carpaccio (ca. 1465–ca. 1526), *Vision of Saint Augustine*, ca. 1502–3. Tempera on canvas, 141 × 210 cm (56 × 83 in.). Scuola San Giorgio degli Schiavoni, Venice
PHOTO BY MATTEO DE FINA, COURTESY OF SAVE VENICE

monk's cells where the contemplative acts of reading and writing took place. In the fifteenth century, the *studiolo* arose from the merging of the cleric's cell with the secular treasury of a rich family's prized possessions.[24] Special shelving and cupboards, as we see in the Antonello and the Carpaccio, soon became *de rigueur*. Eventually, such a room full of treasures, when subjected to an organizing principle, would become a *wunderkammer* or *kunstkammer* (cabinet of curiosities or cabinet of art). At the final stage, ambitious versions of such rooms would eventually be called a "museum"—seat of the muses.[25]

A study could be carved out of a larger bedchamber, as seen in the drawing by Lorenzo Lotto (ca. 1480–1556), *An Ecclesiastic in his Study*, from the 1520s (fig. 2.6). As discussed by Elizabeth Currie, the presence of a bed for a nap "combined with the cluttered feel of so many belongings amassed together, produced a sense of comfort that, for some, was a vital characteristic of the ideal study."[26] This concept remains with us; surely we feel reassurance when surrounded by our books. In this particular study, we see medals, bells, candlesticks, scientific instruments, a variety of vessels, and paintings and sculptures.

24 P. Thornton, *The Italian Renaissance Interior*, 296. For *studioli*, see ibid., 296–298; D. Thornton, *The Scholar*, 8; Liebenwein, *Studiolo*; and Ruvoldt, "Sacred to Secular."

25 Findlen, "The Museum," and Hochmann, "Le collezioni veneziane nel Rinascimento."

26 Currie, *Inside the Renaissance House*.

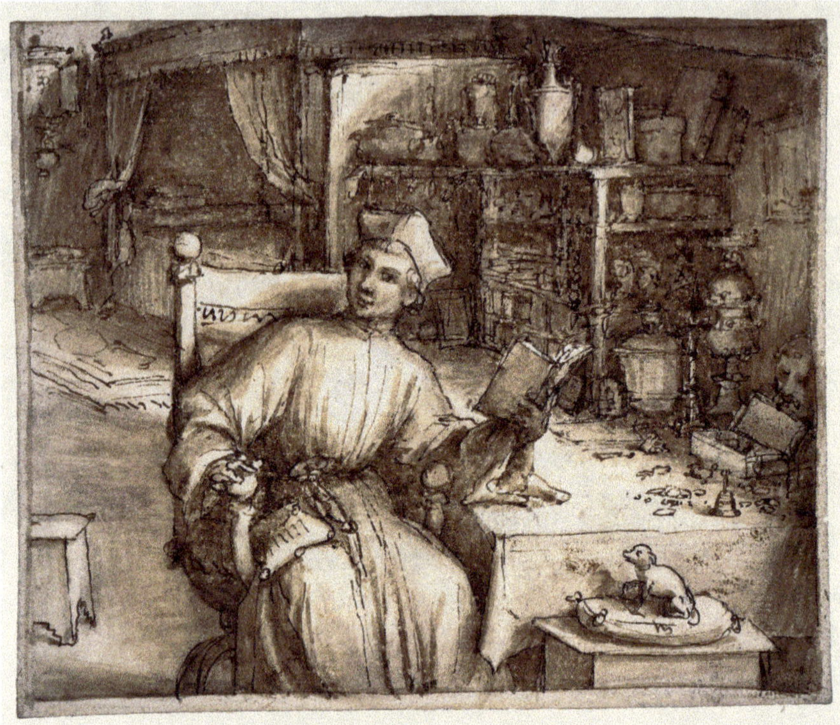

FIGURE 2.6 Lorenzo Lotto (ca. 1480–1556), *Ecclesiastic in His Study*, 1520s. Pen and brown ink, brown wash, over black chalk, 164 × 197 mm (6.5 × 7.8 in.). British Museum, London

This cheerful cleric clearly loves his possessions; they not only allow him to feel at home, they *define* home. At the same time, the plethora of objects has outgrown the space and makes it hard to rank their importance. Viewing this drawing, we wonder who is this man's best friend, the book in his hand or the dog on the foreground cushion? The Venetian *studiolo* of Andrea Odoni (1488–1545), as seen in Lotto's portrait (frontispiece), is similarly bestrewn.

To be sure, *studioli* were not unique to Venice and its territories; small rooms that functioned as offices and refuges for solitary contemplation and reading, as well as intimate conversation, were found in the homes of humanists and aristocrats across Italy.[27] In any case, it stands to reason that the existence of

27 See the discussion of study and *studiolo*, ibid. There are prominent examples of these spaces outside Venice. The Florentine Niccolò Machiavelli explained that when he returned home he would take off his street clothes and dress in special robes—better to be in dialogue with ancient authors—before spending hours in his *scrittoio* without ever becoming bored; cited in Ruvoldt, "Sacred to secular," 643. Also note the example of the care that Isabella d'Este took in arranging the antiquities she acquired for her *studiolo* in

studioli and *camerini*, as intimate spaces, would not only be logical places to display small works of art, but also spur the collection and creation of works specifically for such settings.

Venice was distinct in two aspects of collecting for these small rooms. The enormous market allowed some painters to focus solely on the very top echelon of private clientele, yet in a different way from a court artist serving a prince. These Venetian painters enjoyed substantial creative freedom. For the most part, Giorgione was able to forgo altarpiece and government commissions in order to concentrate on small-format easel pictures destined for the studies or bedrooms of connoisseurs, such as *The Tempest* (Gallerie dell'Accademia), noted by Michiel in the home of Gabriele Vendramin (1484–1552) in 1530.[28] Giorgione helped create a new category of poetic pictures, elusive in meaning. His clients knew of him by word of mouth. Isabella d'Este (1474–1539)—the same collector who resolved to obtain a painting by Leonardo da Vinci (1452–1519), regardless of subject—wrote a letter on October 25, 1510 to her agent in Venice, asking him to purchase a painting by Giorgione of "una nocte" ("night," perhaps a Nativity). The agent had to admit that although he had been able to track down two paintings that fit the description in private collections, neither owner wished to sell, even at high prices. Moreover, since Giorgione had recently died, nothing could be done.[29] Documents offer examples whereby even those who commissioned paintings might prioritize the artist over the subject matter. Venetian collectors in 1538, 1548, and 1552 commissioned pictures from Jacopo Bassano (ca. 1510–1592), allowing the artist to pick the subject; in other words, obtaining "a Bassano" was the primary goal.[30]

The second characteristic of Venetian collections was a strong predilection for Netherlandish paintings, which in their small scale and refinement were eminently suited for *studioli*. Michiel records works by Van Eyck, Rogier van der Weyden (ca. 1400–1464), Hieronymus Bosch (ca. 1450–1516), Memling, and many other northern painters.[31] One entry that can be linked with a

---

Mantua, making sure she had space to accommodate potential purchases. D. Thornton, *The Scholar*, 105. On Isabella as collector, see Scher in this volume.

28 Michiel, *Marcanton Michiel's Notizia*, 106. Summarizing the literature, including many interpretations for the painting, see Lauber in Dal Pozzolo and Puppi, *Giorgione*, cat. 46, 427–431; Dal Pozzolo, *Giorgione*, 238–251; Nichols, *Giorgione's Ambiguity*, 148–165. For Giorgione's career more generally, and especially a discussion of his patrons, see Anderson, *Giorgione*, 129–189.

29 Ilchman, "Prologue: The Transformation," 85.

30 Gilbert, "What did the Renaissance Patron Buy?," 433–434.

31 Within this large topic, see Campbell, "Notes on Netherlandish Pictures," Aikema and Brown, *Venice and the North*, particularly Aikema, "Lure of the North," 82–91, and Aikema, "Tesori ponentini."

surviving painting is Memling's diminutive *Diptych of Saint John and Saint Veronica*, ca. 1470–75. Michiel saw this in Padua in the home of Pietro Bembo (1470–1547), an eminent Venetian humanist, influential cleric, and eventual cardinal.[32] On August 31, 1502, Carlo Bembo, brother of Pietro, agreed to lend the diptych, now divided between the Alte Pinakothek, Munich, and the National Gallery of Art, Washington, and other paintings to Isabella d'Este in Mantua, in response to her request.[33] This episode illustrates how easily small works of art could be transported, influencing both collectors and fellow artists in a new location. The Memling also underscores the appeal of Netherlandish pictures in elevated Italian circles.

Unfortunately, Bembo's diptych is a rare surviving northern painting that can be linked to an early source. Most records are frustratingly vague. Inventories seldom named individual painters, though at least the school was often noted (e.g. "di stilo greco" or "alla grecha" for icons, and "fiamengo" or "alla fiandra" for Netherlandish). Most of the Northern pictures recorded in Venetian collections have disappeared, and only tantalizing references survive. For example, a watershed auction in 1506 of paintings from the collection of Michele Vianello included a picture attributed to Jan van Eyck of *The Submersion of Pharaoh's Army in the Red Sea* that Isabella d'Este coveted. Not bidding enough at the auction, she lost no time in securing the painting from the man who did; she paid the enormous price of 115 ducats, nearly forty times the cost of a de' Barbari *View*.[34] Admiring the art of other places and cultures—in addition to local artists—seems a reasonable criterion for an art collecting scene that resembles our own.

While the *studiolo* was a pan-Italian phenomenon, a second key space within Venetian homes—the *portego*—was much more specific to the *Serenissima*. Returning to Palazzo Pasqualini, the former home of the owner of Antonello's *Jerome*, the façade that dominates Campo San Maurizio is actually one of two main façades (fig. 2.7). A second façade overlooks the *fondamenta* (quay) and canal on the opposite side. Generally, the principal entrance of a substantial

32 Michiel, *Marcanton Michiel's Notizia*, 20. For Bembo as collector and cultural force, see Beltramini, Gasparotto, and Tura, *Pietro Bembo*. Ibid., 100–101 for the diptych. Also Nalezyty, *Pietro Bembo*.

33 Campbell, "Notes on Netherlandish Pictures," 471.

34 Isabella d'Este purchased the supposed Van Eyck from the winning bidder, Andrea Loredan, brother of the doge, for the price he had paid. Loredan must have relinquished the painting in order to put her in his debt. For the painting, see Brown and Lorenzoni, "An Art Auction," 25. For the discussion of the auction and its aftermath in terms of diplomacy and cultural politics, see Magno, *La Splendida*, 147–150.

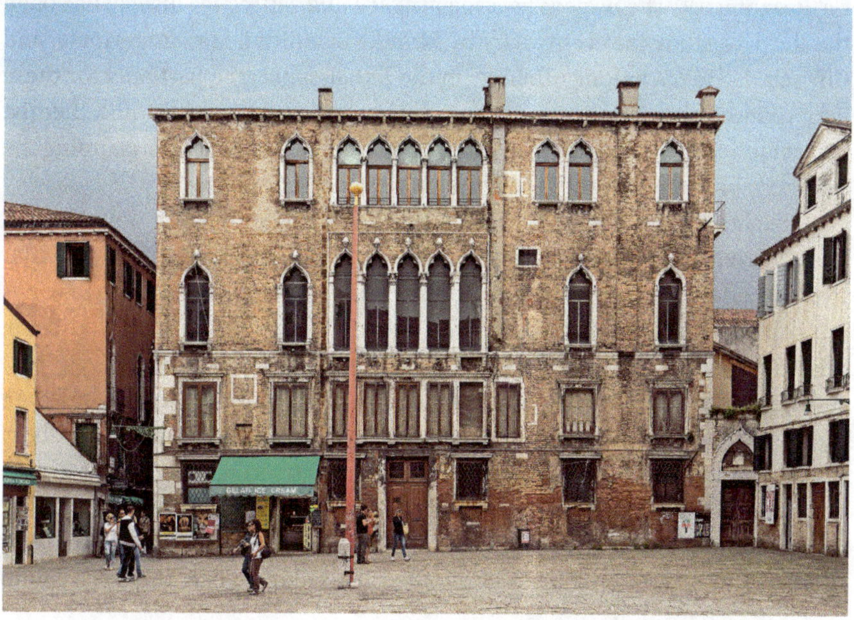

FIGURE 2.7 Façade of Palazzo Pasqualini, now Zaguri, Campo San Maurizio, Venice
PHOTO BY DIDIER DESCOUENS

home in Venice faced a canal, where the water entrance was. The fenestration indicates that this building is composed of four main floors. There is a ground floor, generally used for storage or rented out to shops. Above is a low-ceilinged story, called a *mezzanino* (mezzanine), containing offices and perhaps studies. Above that is a floor with much higher ceilings, the *piano nobile*, the principal floor of the building. It included a single large room to serve mostly as a corridor, as well as smaller rooms on either side for receiving guests, taking regular meals, and sleeping. Palazzo Pasqualini is tall enough that it has a second *piano nobile*, with a somewhat lower ceiling, under the roof.

Characteristically Venetian is how most of the windows are clustered together in the midpoint, along a vertical axis. Given the extreme urban density in Venice, central courtyards—so important for bringing light and air to interior rooms in Florentine or Roman palazzi—are very rare. Instead, the clustered windows on a Venetian façade were intended to illuminate a long and narrow room that runs the depth of the building. This long room was the *portego*, and a constant in Venetian architecture, whether the building was built ca. 1430 in the gothic style, as in the Ca' d'Oro, or constructed in the late seventeenth century and completed in the 1750s, as in the much larger

Ca' Rezzonico.[35] The *portego* as a social space and setting for display has been the focus of study in recent years by Monika Schmitter, Margaret Morse, and Chriscinda Henry, among others.[36] In the Renaissance, the partiality for these long rooms struck foreigners as typically Venetian; the architect and theorist Sebastiano Serlio (1475–ca. 1554) noted this tendency in the 1540s, claiming the existence of these long rooms as "the universal custom of the city."[37]

Consider a generic floor plan of a large Venetian house, with "four parallel load-bearing walls" separating the plan into "three axial spaces perpendicular to the façade."[38] The *portego* takes up the entire inner axis; the other two wings are composed of smaller rooms—the bed-chambers, sitting rooms, kitchen, and sometimes a study. In Venetian practice, the *portego* was mostly a passageway leading to more intimate spaces. It could be transformed, however, for receptions, performances, and banquets. Its size and long walls, with doors only along the two long sides, made it an obvious setting to place furniture, display arms and armor, and exhibit art, including maps, family portraits, and other paintings, particularly those on canvas.[39] The idea that specialized rooms should exhibit certain kinds of art was not limited to Venice. In Rome, Giulio

---

35 On the *portego* and its functions, see Brown, *Private Lives*, esp. 71–75, and Schulz, *The New Palaces*, 5–28, 39. For the *portego* of Andrea Odoni, its contents described in detail by Michiel, see Schmitter, *The Art Collector*, 111–140.

36 Schmitter, "The *Quadro da Portego*." See the generic floor plan in Morse, "The Venetian *Portego*," 89, part of a larger argument of how this room could function as a "spiritual environment," 90. Henry, "What Makes a Picture?," 253–254, reminds us that the term "quadri" could embrace "a broad range of framed and unframed art objects including miniature tapestries, wood and terracotta relief panels, even prints pasted directly on the wall."

37 Serlio, *On Architecture*, 106.

38 Morse, "The Venetian *Portego*," 92.

39 See Brown, "Behind the Walls" and *Private Lives*. Research by Genevieve Carlton of 531 Venetian inventories from the period 1530–1553 found a total of 115 maps versus 63 portraits, thus questioning the assumption that portraits dominated public rooms in Venetian homes. *Worldly Consumers*, 172 n. 77. Of course some of these maps may have been displayed in rooms other than the *portego*. Carlton's book on the Renaissance consumption of maps includes much on Venice, concluding that by decorating their homes with maps Venetians "were not only showing a concern for the outside world but also using maps to reinforce their public reputations." Ibid., 158. As is often cited, in 1568 Giorgio Vasari wrote in his *Life* of Giovanni Bellini how he admired the Venetian tradition of displaying prominently in homes portraits of ancestors, reviving an ancient custom. Vasari-Milanesi, *Vite de' più eccelenti pittori*, III, 168–169. In curating the exhibition *Tintoretto 1519–1594* at Venice's Palazzo Ducale (9 September 2018–6 January 2019), my co-curator and I attempted to recreate a *portego* decorated with family portraits. We turned a long and awkward space within the exhibition suite, the Sala dei Filosofi, into a *portego*, displaying thirteen individual portraits and two group portraits. For Tintoretto's portraits, see Echols and Ilchman, "Portraitist."

Mancini (1559–1630) authored a manuscript ca. 1621 on paintings connoisseurship. He advocated for the display of certain subjects in particular spaces in a home, with maps, for example, being appropriate in larger rooms where visitors could roam freely: "per i paesaggi e cosmografie si metteranno nelle gallerie e dove puol andar ognuno."[40]

As Schmitter has persuasively argued, these long and large Venetian rooms seem to have called for a new format of picture, the "quadro da portego," that is, a "portego painting." It has been observed that Venetian canvas pictures grew in size during the sixteenth century.[41] One explanation for this trend is the preponderance of large rooms (*porteghi*) where smaller paintings, such as those intended for smaller rooms, e.g. *camere* and *studioli*, were simply too little to make an impact. Large rooms inspired big paintings. Admittedly, "quadro da portego" is a rare term in surviving documents, but it is nevertheless a period term. There is, for example, the 1528 inventory of the studio contents of the painter Palma il Vecchio (ca. 1479–1528), where a picture is described as "one *portego* picture on wood … with Christ and the twelve apostles and two women, half-finished."[42] This matches a *Christ and the Woman of Canaan* (Gallerie dell'Accademia), started by Palma and completed by another painter.[43] This is a typical example of a *portego* picture, which might be defined as horizontal format with plenty of figures and narrative content. As confirmed by sixteenth-century inventories, certain subject matter predominates in these horizontal paintings.[44] Destined for public spaces within private homes, the pictures were typically religious or had religious overtones, reinforcing the piety or political alliances of the family. Thus a large battle scene, such as Jacopo Tintoretto's (ca. 1518–1594) *Conversion of Paul* (National Gallery of Art, Washington) would highlight the military character of the arms and armor often displayed in these

40 Mancini, *Considerazioni sulla pittura*, I, 143. Like Michiel before him, Mancini was absorbed with determining the author of a painting, and particularly concerned with distinguishing originals from copies or forgeries. His objective was to teach other amateurs to offer judgments on paintings, and to acquire and install them: "per i quali un huomo di diletto di simili studij possa con facilità dar giuditio delle pitture propostegli, saperle comprar, acquistar et collocarle…." Ibid., 5. For the circulation and meanings of maps and other printed images in Renaissance Venice, see Wilson, *The World in Venice*.

41 Lucco, cited in Schmitter, "The *Quadro da Portego*," 700. For another view on the steady increase in scale, see Ilchman, "Tintoretto: Pensare e Disegnare," esp. 49–56.

42 Schmitter, "The *Quadro da Portego*," 697–698, with other examples of *portego* used in inventories. For Palma's 1528 inventory, see Rylands, *Palma Vecchio*, 346–350, with the painting in question listed on 350, [8].

43 Ibid., A63.

44 Schmitter, "The *Quadro da Portego*," appendix, 744–6.

rooms.[45] A feast or dining picture, such as Veronese's (1528–1588) *Supper at Emmaus* (Louvre, Paris), would emphasize the occasional banqueting function of these rooms, and the abundance of portraits within the composition recalls the custom of displaying family portraits in the *portego*.[46]

In the case of Titian's (ca. 1488–1576) *Ecce Homo* (Kunsthistorisches Museum, Vienna), an imposing canvas (2.4 × 3.6 m) for the D'Anna (or De Hane) family from Brussels, a gripping crowd scene seems to refer to contemporary struggles between the Ottoman Turks and the Hapsburg empire.[47] Within the painting, a prominent diagonal staircase and platform allocates the figures to varying heights. As Schmitter concludes, "Titian has risen to the challenge of the *quadro da portego* problem—how to compose a long, large scene that maintains interest and draws the viewer's eye across space."[48] Moreover, the sky visible at top in these three paintings would have served to open up the room, making the space feel larger. The expected setting had thus determined not only the scale of each painting, but also something of its composition.

Fitting for a nation underpinned by capitalism, the government generally left art collectors alone. Sumptuary laws theoretically regulated interior decoration, but were clearly ineffective.[49] Starting in the sixteenth century, many foreign-born merchants made Venice the base of their art dealing activities. Some, like Jacopo Strada (1507–1588; cover image), lived elsewhere but insisted on staying in touch with Venetian collectors and artists to enable major transactions.[50] These businessmen enjoyed the relative freedom and ease of commerce in Venice, not to mention the enormous potential stock available from the city's private households.[51] Brokering the sale of these collections

---

45 Ibid., 716.

46 Ibid., 710–711; see also Penny, *Venice 1540–1600*, 229.

47 For Titian's painting and patrons and the role of Pietro Aretino, see De Maria, *Becoming Venetian*, 133–143.

48 Schmitter, "The *Quadro da Portego*," 741, building upon De Maria's analysis.

49 See Schmitter, "Virtuous Riches," 916, n. 36. In 1476, the expenses of outfitting a single room (paneling, gilding, or paintings) were limited to a maximum of 150 ducats. Political and military crises later led to restrictions on luxury objects: gold boxes, gilded mirrors, cushions of silk decorated with pearls, curtains of brocade or damask, silk hangings, gold or silver vessels. Gilbert, "Venice in the Crisis," 279. The 150 ducat cap, introduced in 1476, was affirmed in 1512. Brown, "Behind the Walls," 321–324.

50 On Strada, see the essay by Reist in this volume.

51 For Flemish dealers as collectors, see Anderson, "Merchants as Collectors," Reist in this volume, and Aikema, "Tesori ponentini." For Daniel Nijs as dealer, see Anderson, *The Flemish Merchant of Venice*. Sohm underscores the connections between publications on art and the art market itself when he observes that "the four major books on painters and painting written by Venetians in the seventeenth century were dedicated to art collectors or art dealers," *Painting for Profit*, 210.

was business as usual. The large paintings decorating Venice's monasteries and convents, however, began to be considered by the middle of the seventeenth century as national patrimony, not to be sold abroad. Impoverished and suppressed monasteries and convents were particularly vulnerable to the ready cash of foreign buyers. As discussed by Allison Sherman, the threat of export of Tintoretto's *Wedding Feast at Cana* from the refectory of the Crociferi as well as large paintings by Titian and Porta Salviati (1520–1575) from the monastery of Santo Spirito was too much for the Venetian government. In 1659 the Senate allocated these pictures to the sacristy of the newly constructed church of Santa Maria della Salute, "to be kept on behalf of the public."[52] Responding to the pleas of Venetian artists, government officials established an early public museum—a new kind of space for pictures—to retain sixteenth-century masterpieces and thus honor the golden age of Venetian painting.

Long before the creation of this picture gallery, some Venetian private collections allowed public access. The best-known collections were described in guidebooks and generally open to visitors who had letters of introduction or could bluff their way in.[53] One of the most impressive was that of Andrea Vendramin (ca. 1565–1629) at San Gregorio, lauded in 1615 by the architect Vincenzo Scamozzi (1548–1616). Two rooms were set aside to exhibit numerous works of classical art, many ancient medals, a *scrittoio* (writing desk) made of olivewood and ebony, and "perhaps 140 good paintings, large and small."[54] Andrea Vendramin's place in art history results from his decision in 1627 to put down on paper his encyclopedic collections, from minerals, gems, and other natural wonders to ancient ceramics and Egyptian rings and scarabs, as well as the usual ancient marbles, paintings, and medals.[55] While inventories

52 Sherman, "Titian and Tintoretto in the Sacristy"; the quotation is on 49. Long before the sacristy of the Salute became a home for paintings, the classical art collections of Cardinal Domenico Grimani (1461–1523) and his nephew Giovanni Grimani (1506–1593) were donated to the Venetian state and known as the "Statuario Pubblico."

53 See Brown, *Private Lives*, for Francesco Sansovino's list in his guidebook of top private collections of antiquities (234), and examples of Federico da Porto of Vicenza visiting the home of Marin Sanudo at San Giacomo dall'Orio in the early sixteenth century (222–223), and Fynes Moryson of Lincolnshire, England, who gained entry to Nicolo Vendramin's collection on the Giudecca in 1594 (240), despite "being altogether unknowne to him."

54 Scamozzi, *Idea dell'architettura*, III, 305. If Andrea's painting collection was notably large, Venetians at nearly all social levels steadily increased their holdings of pictures during the hundred years from the early sixteenth century to the early seventeenth. See the analysis of over a thousand inventories in Cecchini, "Collezionismo e mondo materiale," 173–176, 184–186.

55 Borenius, *The Picture Gallery of Andrea Vendramin*, and Borenius, "More about the Andrea Vendramin Collection"; for more recent analysis of Vendramin, see Brown, *Private Lives*, 235–240, and Halbertsma, *Scholars, Travellers and Trade*, 7.

and their concomitant brevity go back centuries, these manuscripts are special since they boast illustrations in brown ink and wash. These illustrations reveal many of the organizing principles that Vendramin employed, including a tall cabinet for rings, gems, and coins and an entire wall of shelving divided into dozens of compartments to hold antiquities such as lamps and vases. His rigorous standards of arrangement have left the cheerful clutter of Lotto's *Ecclesiastic in His Study* (fig. 2.7) far behind.[56] Individual objects, their storage, and the decoration of Vendramin's two rooms have merged, creating a whole more than the sum of its parts.

Vendramin listed his antiquities in six catalogues. Other catalogues described paintings, Venetian coins, books, manuscripts, and collections of natural history. Overall, only six volumes survive in libraries in London, Oxford, and Berlin. Many of the illustrations of paintings are captioned with the name of the artist; thus the volume in the British Library may be the earliest illustrated collection catalogue of paintings—a format still central to art history today.[57] Alas, only three of the paintings recorded in Andrea's catalogue can be identified with extant works. Nevertheless, the scale of his collection underscores a crucial fact. Even if some of the attributions seem optimistic to us, particularly the nine pictures assigned to Bellini and thirteen to Giorgione, Andrea Vendramin's catalogue of paintings—like so many inventories from the sixteenth and seventeenth centuries—is a sobering reminder of just how many works have disappeared over the generations. What has come down to us is a mere fraction of what was produced.

In conclusion, it appears that Venetians offer the first example, or a very early adoption, of many circumstances that we now deem central to specialized art collecting and a thriving art market. These include the development of art connoisseurship; a fashion for household collections which spurred acquisitions; specific spaces within the home for display; a taste for contemporary art created elsewhere; the invention of the oil-on-canvas easel painting and the related development of the gallery picture; cultural patrimony policy; and the illustrated collection catalogue.

That all these advances happened in the same city should not be a surprise. Venice's pioneering role in modern art collecting can be explained by the *Serenissima*'s combination of great size, wealth, and cosmopolitan nature, plus a particular social structure with an unusually large upper middle class. This huge market supported hundreds of artists and artisans, while Venice's

56 Brown, *Private Lives*, 235.

57 British Library, MSS Sloan 4004.

capitalist spirit encouraged competitive collecting. Akin to Silicon Valley in recent decades, where an astonishing number of tech inventors and entrepreneurs are concentrated in California's Bay Area, and therefore innovations foster further innovations, Venice in the Renaissance benefited from the sheer size and remarkable concentration of artistic objects, spaces, and people. Together, such factors deserve credit for this "birth in Venice."

Bibliography

Aikema, Bernard. "Tesori ponentini per la Serenissima: Il commercio d'arte fiamminga a Venezia e nel Veneto fra Quattro e Cinquecento." In *Tra committenza e collezionismo*, edited by Enrico Maria Dal Pozzolo and Leonida Tedoldi, 35–48. Vicenza: Terra Ferma, 2003.

Aikema, Bernard, and Beverly Louise Brown. *Renaissance Venice and the North: Crosscurrents in the Time of Bellini, Dürer, and Titian*. New York: Rizzoli, 2000.

Aikema, Bernard, Rosella Lauber, and Max Seidel, eds. *Il collezionismo a Venezia e nel Veneto ai tempi della Serenissima*. Venice: Marsilio, 2005.

Anderson, Christina M. *The Flemish Merchant of Venice: Daniel Nijs and the Sale of the Gonzaga Art Collection*. New Haven and London: Yale University Press, 2015.

Anderson, Christina M. "Merchants and Collectors and Art Dealers: The cases of Daniel Nijs and Carlo Hellemans, Flemish Merchants in Venice." In *Early Modern Merchants as Collectors*, edited by Christina M. Anderson, 156–166. London: Routledge, 2017.

Anderson, Jaynie. *Giorgione: The Painter of 'Poetic Brevity.'* Paris and New York: Flammarion, 1997.

Beltramini, Guido, Davide Gasparotto, and Adolfo Tura. *Pietro Bembo e l'invenzione del Rinascimento*. Venice: Marsilio, 2013.

Borean, Linda, and Stefania Mason. *Il collezionismo d'arte a Venezia. Il Seicento*. Venice: Marsilio, 2007.

Borenius, Tancred. "More about the Andrea Vendramin Collection." *The Burlington Magazine* 60, no. 348 (March 1932), 140–141, 144–145, 147.

Borenius, Tancred. *The Picture Gallery of Andrea Vendramin*. London: Medici Society, 1923.

Brown, Clifford M., and Anna Maria Lorenzoni. "An Art Auction in Venice in 1506." *L'Arte* 18–20 (1972): 121–136.

Brown, Patricia Fortini. "Behind the Walls: The Material Culture of Venetian Elites." In *Venice Reconsidered: The History and Civilization of an Italian City State, 1297–1797*, edited by John Martin and Dennis Romano, 295–338. Baltimore: Johns Hopkins University Press, 2000.

Brown, Patricia Fortini. "Le antichità." In *Commercio e cultura mercantile*. Vol. IV, *Il Rinascimento italiano e l'Europa*, edited by Franco Franceschi, Richard Goldthwaite, and Reinhold Mueller, 309–337, 717–723. Treviso: Angelo Colla Editore, 2007.

Brown, Patricia Fortini. *Private Lives in Renaissance Venice: Art, Architecture, and the Family*. New Haven and London: Yale University Press, 2004.

Brown, Patricia Fortini. *Venetian Narrative Painting in the Age of Carpaccio*. New Haven and London: Yale University Press, 1988.

Campbell, Lorne. "Notes on Netherlandish Pictures in the Veneto in the Fifteenth and Sixteenth Centuries." *The Burlington Magazine* 123 (August 1981): 467–473.

Carlton, Genevieve. *Worldly Consumers: The Demand for Maps in Renaissance Italy*. Chicago and London: University of Chicago Press, 2015.

Cecchini, Isabella. "Collezionismo e mondo materiale." In Hochmann, Lauber, and Mason, eds. *Il collezionismo d'arte a Venezia. Dalle origini al Cinquecento*, 164–191. Venice: Marsilio, 2008.

Chambers, David, and Brian Pullan. *Venice: A Documentary History: 1450–1630*. Toronto: University of Toronto Press, 2001.

Currie, Elizabeth. *Inside the Renaissance House*. London: V&A Publications, 2006.

Dal Pozzolo, Enrico Maria, and Lionello Puppi. *Giorgione*. Milan: Skira, 2009.

Dal Pozzolo, Enrico Maria. *Giorgione*. Milan: Motta, 2009.

Damen, Giada. "Shopping for *Cose Antiche* in Late-Sixteenth-Century Venice." In *Reflections on Renaissance Venice: A Celebration of Patricia Fortini Brown*, edited by Mary E. Frank and Blake de Maria, 133–141. Milan: 5 Continents, 2013.

De Maria, Blake. *Becoming Venetian: Immigrants and the Arts in Early Modern Venice*. New Haven and London: Yale University Press, 2010.

Echols, Robert, and Frederick Ilchman. "Portraitist." In *Tintoretto: Artist of Renaissance Venice*, edited by Robert Echols and Frederick Ilchman, 145–169. Washington: National Gallery of Art, 2018.

Findlen, Paula. "The Museum: Its Classical Etymology and Renaissance Genealogy." *Journal of the History of Collections* 1 (1989): 59–78.

Fletcher, Jennifer. "Marcantonio Michiel, 'che ha veduto assai'." *The Burlington Magazine* 123 (October 1981): 602–608.

Fletcher, Jennifer. "Marcantonio Michiel's Collection." *Journal of the Warburg and Courtauld Institutes* 36 (1973): 382–385.

Fletcher, Jennifer. "Marcantonio Michiel: His Friends and Collection." *The Burlington Magazine* 123 (August 1981): 453–467.

Gilbert, Creighton. "What did the Renaissance Patron Buy?" *Renaissance Quarterly* 51, no. 2 (Summer, 1998): 392–450.

Gilbert, Felix. "Venice in the Crisis of the League of Cambrai." In *Renaissance Venice*, edited by John Hale, 274–292. London: Faber and Faber, 1973.

Halbertsma, R. B. *Scholars, Travellers and Trade: The Pioneer Years of the National Museum of Antiquities in Leiden 1818–1840*. London and New York: Routledge, 2003.

Henry, Chriscinda. "What Makes a Picture? Evidence from Sixteenth-Century Venetian Property Inventories." *Journal of the History of Collections* 23, no. 2 (2011): 253–265.

Hochmann, Michel. "Le collezioni veneziane nel Rinascimento: Storia e storiografia." In *Il collezionismo d'arte a Venezia: Dalle origini al Cinquecento*, edited by Michel Hochmann, Rosella Lauber, and Stefania Mason, 2–39. Venice: Marsilio, 2008.

Hochmann, Michel, Rosella Lauber, and Stefania Mason, eds. *Il collezionismo d'arte a Venezia. Dalle origini al Cinquecento*. Venice: Marsilio, 2008.

Howard, Deborah. "Venice as a Dolphin: Further investigations into Jacopo de' Barbari's View." *Artibus et historiae* 35 (1997): 101–111.

Ilchman, Frederick. "Prologue: The Transformation of Venetian Painting around 1500." In *Titian, Tintoretto, Veronese: Rivals in Renaissance Venice*, edited by Frederick Ilchman, 85–91. Boston: Museum of Fine Arts, 2009.

Ilchman, Frederick. "Tintoretto: Pensare e disegnare in grande." *In Settimo e Ottavo Incontro in ricordo di Michelangelo Muraro*, edited by Giuseppina Menin Muraro e Daniela Puppulin, 49–75. Sossano Veneto: Biblioteca Comunale, 2000.

Ilchman, Frederick. "Venetian Painting in an Age of Rivals." In *Titian, Tintoretto, Veronese: Rivals in Renaissance Venice*, edited by Frederick Ilchman, 21–39. Boston: Museum of Fine Arts, 2009.

Labalme, Patricia H., and Laura Sanguinetti White, *Venice*, Cità Excelentissima*: Selections from the Renaissance Diaries of Marin Sanudo*. Baltimore: Johns Hopkins University Press, 2008.

Lauber, Rosella. "'Opera perfettissima.' Marcantonio Michiel e la *Notizia d'opere di disegno*." In *Il collezionismo a Venezia e nel Veneto ai tempi della Serenissma*, edited by Bernard Aikema, Rosella Lauber, and Max Seidel, 77–116. Venice: Marsilio, 2005.

Liebenwein, Wolfgang. *Studiolo, storia e tipologia di uno spazio culturale*, edited by Claudia Cieri Via. Ferrara: Panini, 2005.

Lucco, Mauro. *Antonello da Messina: L'opera completa*. Cinisello Balsamo, Milano: Silvana Editoriale, 2006.

Magno, Alessandro Marzo. *La Splendida. Venezia 1499–1509*. Bari-Rome: Editori Laterza, 2019.

Mancini, Giulio. *Considerazioni sulla pittura*. Rome: Accademia nazionale dei Lincei, 1956.

Matino, Gabriele, and Patricia Fortini Brown. *Carpaccio in Venice: A Guide*. Venice: Marsilio, 2020.

Michiel, Marcantonio. "Der Anonimo Morelliano (Marcanton Michiel's Notizia d'opere del disegno)," edited by Theodor Frimmel. *Quellenschriften Kunstgeschichte und Kunsttechnik* 1. Vienna: Carl Graeser, 1896.

Morse, Margaret A. "The Venetian *Portego*: Family Piety and Public Prestige." In *The Early Modern Italian Domestic Interior, 1400–1700: Objects, Spaces, Domesticities*, edited by Erin J. Campbell, Stephanie R. Miller, and Elizabeth Carroll Consavari, 89–106. Farnham: Ashgate, 2013.

Moschini Marconi, Sandra. *Gallerie dell'Accademia di Venezia. Opere d'Arte dei secoli XIV e XV*. Rome: Istituto poligrafico dello Stato, 1955.

Motture, Peta, and Luke Syson. "Art in the *Casa*." In *At Home in Renaissance Italy*, edited by Marta Ajmar-Wollheim and Flora Dennis, 268–283. London: V&A Publications, 2006.

Nalezyty, Susan. *Pietro Bembo and the Intellectual Pleasures of a Renaissance Writer and Art Collector*. New Haven and London: Yale University Press, 2017.

Nichols, Tom. *Giorgione's Ambiguity*. London: Reaktion, 2021.

Penny, Nicholas. *The Sixteenth Century Italian Paintings*. Vol. 2, *Venice, 1540–1600*. London: National Gallery, 2008.

Pope-Hennessy, John. *Catalogue of Italian Sculpture in the Victoria and Albert Museum*. 3 vols. London: Her Majesty's Stationery Office, 1964.

Pope-Hennessy, John. *The Robert Lehman Collection*. Vol. 1. *Italian Paintings*. New York: Metropolitan Museum of Art, 1987.

Ruvoldt, Maria. "Sacred to Secular, East to West: The Renaissance Study and Strategies of Display." *Renaissance Studies* 20, no. 5 (2006): 640–657.

Rylands, Philip. *Palma Vecchio*. Cambridge: Cambridge University Press, 1992.

Serafini, Alessandro. "Jacometto Veneziano." In *Dizionario Biografico degli Italiani*, 62. (2004) https://www.treccani.it/enciclopedia/jacometto-veneziano_%28Dizionario-Biografico%29/.

Scamozzi, Vincenzo. *Idea dell'architettura universale*. Venice: Presso Lavtore, 1615.

Schmitter, Monika. *The Art Collector in Early Modern Italy: Andrea Odoni and His Venetian Palace*. Cambridge: Cambridge University Press, 2021.

Schmitter, Monika. "The Dating of Marcantonio Michiel's 'Notizia' on Works of Art in Padua." *The Burlington Magazine* 145, no. 1205 (August 2003): 564–571.

Schmitter, Monika. "The Display of Distinction: Art Collecting and Social Status in Early Sixteenth-Century Venice." PhD diss. University of Michigan, 1997.

Schmitter, Monika. "The *Quadro da Portego* in Sixteenth-Century Venetian Art." *Renaissance Quarterly* 64, no. 3 (Fall, 2011): 693–751.

Schmitter, Monika. "'Virtuous Riches': The Bricolage of Cittadini Identities in Early-Sixteenth-Century Venice." *Renaissance Quarterly* 57, no. 3 (Autumn, 2004): 908–969.

Schulz, Juergen. *The New Palaces of Medieval Venice*. University Park: Penn State University Press, 2004.

Schulz, Juergen. "Jacopo de' Barbari's View of Venice: Map Making, City Views, and Moralized Geography before the Year 1500." *Art Bulletin* 60 (1978): 425–475.

Serlio, Sebastiano. *Sebastiano Serlio on Architecture*. Vol. 2, edited and translated by Vaughan Hart and Peter Hicks. New Haven and London: Yale University Press, 2001.

Sherman, Allison. "Titian and Tintoretto in the Sacristy of Santa Maria della Salute: A *Seicento Accademia* for Displaced Treasures of the Venetian *Cinquecento*." In *The Enduring Legacy of Venetian Renaissance Art*, edited by Andaleeb Badiee Banta, 41–60. London: Routledge, 2016.

Spear, Richard E., and Philip Sohm. *Painting for Profit: The Economic Lives of Seventeenth-Century Italian Painters*. New Haven and London: Yale University Press, 2010.

Tempestini, Anchise. *Giovanni Bellini*. New York: Abbeville, 1999.

Thornton, Dora. *The Scholar in His Study: Ownership and Experience in Renaissance Italy*. New Haven and London: Yale University Press, 1997.

Thornton, Peter. *The Italian Renaissance Interior, 1400–1600*. New York: Abrams, 1991.

Vasari, Giorgio. *Le vite de' più eccelenti pittori, scultori ed architettori* [1568], edited by Gaetano Milanesi. Florence: G.C. Sansoni, 1878–1885.

Wilson, Bronwen. *The World in Venice: Print, the City, and Early Modern Identity*. Toronto: University of Toronto Press, 2005.

CHAPTER 3

Courtesans as Collectors and Tastemakers in Renaissance Italy

Chriscinda Henry

In his *novella* on the famous Roman courtesan Imperia Cognati (1486–1512), Matteo Bandello (ca. 1480–1562) describes her sumptuously ornamented home as befitting a princess: "There were among other rooms a salon and a bedroom and a study, so luxuriously adorned, that there was nothing but velvets and brocades, and on the ground the finest carpets."[1] In the removed and intimate study where Imperia entertained her illustrious visitors—papal banker Agostino Chigi was her official protector from 1508—the walls were lined with thick, cut velvet hangings in ornately patterned gold brocade. Above the wall hangings stood a collection of the most beautiful vases in alabaster, porphyry, *serpentino* (a green marble), and many other kinds of precious stones, arranged on a "masterfully made" cornice shelf painted entirely in gold and ultramarine blue.[2] Below, finely engraved wooden chests and coffers lined the perimeter of the chamber. The centerpiece of the study was a small table, "the most beautiful in the world" according to Bandello, covered in green velvet.[3] On the table Imperia kept either a lute or cittern and books of music she used to entertain her visitors. Together, these furnished the material evidence of her *virtù* (virtue or talent) as a musician who could sight read and composed madrigals. Finally, Bandello notes that the room contained many richly adorned books in vulgar and Latin, which attested to Imperia's linguistic skill, erudition, and poetic talent.

---

1 Bandello, *Le novelle*, vol. 8, n. 42, 79: "Era tra l'altre cose una sala et una camera et un camerino, sì pomposamente adornate, che altro non v'era che velluti e broccati, e per terra finissimi tappetti." In typical Renaissance fashion, Imperia's *camerino*, or study, was attached to the *camera* (a multi-purpose bedroom), forming a suite removed from the more heavily trafficked areas of the home.

2 Ibid., n. 42, 79: "Eravi poi una cornice tutta messa a oro et azzurro oltramarino, maestrevolmente fatta, sovra la quale erano bellissimi vasi di varie e preziose materie formati, con pietre alabastrine, di porfido, di serpentine e di mille altre spezie."

3 Ibid., n. 42, 79: "Si vedeva poi nel mezzo un tavolino, il più bello del mondo, coverto di velluto verde."

 | DOI:10.1163/9789004513938_005

Bandello's detailed image of the courtesan's study as a treasury for precious objects, destination for convivial retreat, and site of informal literary and musical entertainment projects the cultivated, socially refined, and sumptuous ideal Imperia and other elite courtesans of the Renaissance embodied, forming what Cathy Santore has aptly coined "a portrait by property."[4] In another typical *novella* of the period the Sienese author Pietro Fortini (d. 1562) presents a young Roman courtesan bedecked in the richest clothes complete with "infinite gold trimmings," clusters of pearls, jewels, and gold chains, as virtually indistinguishable in her appearance from the room she adorns, whose furnishings include gilt leather wall hangings and exquisite paintings.[5] Throughout both the encomiastic and invective literature on Italian courtesans, the male author's description of the radiant, sensuous, and potent woman becomes conflated with her opulent surroundings. She consistently dazzles, and on occasion even intimidates and overwhelms, her male visitors and hopeful suitors. In fashioning her self-image and the domestic environment in which she practiced her profession, the courtesan walked a fine line between seeking to project the intellectual and social virtues of the chaste court ladies she emulated—elegance, wit in conversation, refined education, accomplishment in poetry and music—and displaying the seductive attributes and accouterments commensurate with the "paradise of Venus."[6]

However, this notion of the home as a self-portrait is complicated by issues of economic agency and personal freedom inherent to the courtesan's complex and often tenuous social position. The term *cortigiana onesta*, or honorable courtesan, first emerged in late fifteenth-century Rome, "where it was used to denote the prostitutes who were patronized by the elite, highly educated men employed at the papal court."[7] While exempt from living in brothels and public prostitution districts, members of this small caste of educated, accomplished women remained in most cases financially dependent on wealthy male patrons and clients, whether a single individual or network of *signori*.[8] These men enabled the courtesan's elevated, independent lifestyle, whether through

4 Santore, "Julia Lombardo," 44–83.

5 Fortini, *Novelle*, 1180–81.

6 Ugolini teases out tensions between the *cortigiano*, *donna di corte*, and *cortigiana* (courtier, court lady, and courtesan), *The Court and Its Critics*, 75–83. Fortini Brown, using a phrase from a period source, characterizes the courtesan's residence as a "paradise of Venus," *Private Lives*, 159–87.

7 Quaintance, *Textual Masculinity*, 17. See also Ugolini, *The Court and Its Critics*, 75–76.

8 One exception from the Roman context is the courtesan Fiammetta Cassini (d. 1512), who as a young woman was left a sizable estate by bequest from Cardinal Jacopo Ammannati Piccolomini, see Stollhans, "The Pious Act."

regular and sustained (sometimes contractually stipulated) material support, individual fee payments, or by engaging in the courtly pretext of gift exchange. As Tessa Storey has characterized the latter phenomenon, just as the courtesan "made a 'gift'" of her body, the man [was] "naturally obliged" (but also legally required) to "honour this gift with a counter-gift."[9]

To remain with the example of Imperia Cognati, Bandello prefaces his description of her splendid residence by introducing the wealthy Roman nobleman Angelo del Bufalo, her long-term lover and benefactor, "who kept her for many years under his power … in a most honorably furnished home."[10] According to Bandello, her luxurious home signaled first and foremost del Bufalo's liberality and gentility rather than Imperia's cultural and intellectual interests and discerning taste. The question thus becomes one of agency: to what extent was Imperia, as a "kept woman," responsible for the decoration of her own home? Exchanges between courtesans and their *signori* in contemporary poetry, songs, verse dialogues, and comedies present a clear answer to this question in repeatedly asserting that courtesans made specific material requests of the wealthy men who financed their sumptuous lifestyles. The most commonly solicited gifts mentioned in these sources include precious jewelry and perfume, furnishings and household items such as gilt mirrors, birdcages, and musical instruments, silk clothing and bed linens, pets, wine, and expensive foodstuffs.[11]

While such sources certainly exaggerate for literary effect, courtesans had to broadcast their taste for luxury and conspicuous consumption in order to be perceived as both successful in their profession and on par with the fashionable court ladies and urban noblewomen they imitated. Peter Thornton has further posited that courtesans, given their unique social freedoms and the premium they placed on standing out as erudite, fascinating, and stylish, had incentive to pursue novelty and take risks in their consumption habits rather than conform to the decorum and convention that bound other elite women of the Renaissance. He concludes it reasonable "to claim that it was in the rooms of the great courtesans that many new fashions in interior decoration were forged."[12] Evidence presented in this essay bolsters Thornton's hypothesis with regard to courtesans pushing the boundaries of taste appropriate to gender

9 Storey, *Carnal Commerce*, 71–72.

10 Bandello, *Le novelle*, n. 42, 78, "Egli [Angelo del Bufalo] molti anni in suo poter la [Imperia] tenne … E perciò che egli è molto liberale e cortese, tenne quella in una casa onoratissimamente apparata…."

11 For a particularly detailed list of a courtesan's gift requests see Verini, *Il vanto della cortigiana*, 355–61.

12 Thornton, *The Italian Renaissance Interior*, 355.

conventions in both their art collecting and domestic entertainment practices. The distinctly modern and cosmopolitan collection and display practice of the Venetian courtesan Elisabetta Condulmer examined here finds no point of comparison with other secular women patrons, who were primarily noblewomen and widows of independent financial means.[13] However, her collection does overlap with *avant garde* male collectors of the period, which should not prove surprising given the courtesan's unique position within Renaissance society and its homosocial networks. What proves more difficult to establish given the limited scope of available archival evidence is the courtesan's potential role as a tastemaker who influenced broader patterns of interior design.

1 The Evidence

Unfortunately, with regard to Imperia, beyond the fine furniture, precious vases, musical instruments, and books listed in his *novella*, Bandello does not mention the other, less expensive types of objects, such as paintings, that surely also ornamented her residence. She was after all a friend and model of Raphael, who purportedly painted her portrait as Venus and frescoed the façade of her home in Borgo, where she lived prior to the "little palace" provided by del Bufalo.[14] Thus, in order to test Thornton's hypothesis and recover the collecting habits of courtesans and their potential role as tastemakers, descriptions found in *novelle*, poetry, travelogs, letters, and other potentially fictionalized sources must be weighed against the archival evidence furnished by wills, household property inventories, and other documentary sources. These happen to survive in greater number and detail for Venice than for Rome. Following the Roman example, Venice facilitated the rise of an elite, independent courtesan class of prostitutes during the opening two decades of the sixteenth century by loosening government regulations. Until 1498 all Venetian prostitutes were officially restricted to the bordellos of the Castelletto area near the Rialto market, although frequent infractions occurred.[15] Shawn Keener has emphasized that "lifting the ban was a watershed, giving *meretrici* greater control over their lifestyle and clientele," not to mention accelerating

13 On the patronage, collecting, and domestic design habits of secular women patrons in Renaissance Italy other than courtesans, see Reiss and Wilkins, *Beyond Isabella*, and McIver, *Women, Art, and Architecture*.

14 Petrucci, "Cognati, Imperia," http://www.treccani.it/enciclopedia/imperia-cognati_(Dizionario-Biografico)/.

15 For a thorough history of Venetian prostitution see Scarabello, "Per una storia della prostituzione," 15–101.

their dispersal into other, more fashionable parts of the city where they took up independent residence.[16]

The Venetian patrician Marin Sanudo (1466–1536) first employs the term *cortesana* in his diaries to mark the death of the esteemed singer Lucia Trivixan in October 1514, who numbered among the first generation of prostitutes to benefit from the relaxed controls. Sanudo describes her as not only the consummate courtesan of her day in Venice, but also as the host of an informal domestic *ridotto*, a habitual salon-like gathering in her home, which was frequented by the most talented professional musicians of the city. The musicians' esteem for Trivixan as a colleague and *virtuosa* (a woman of exceptional talent, learning, and skill) was such that they planned and paid for a funeral service in her honor at the church of Santa Caterina.[17]

2 Courtesans in Venetian Property Inventories

Detailed archival records pertaining to two early-sixteenth century Venetian courtesans have thus far come to light. In an important article, Cathy Santore published the statement of assets Julia Lombardo filed just prior to her death in 1543, along with several detailed property inventories, which were taken in 1569 when her household remained largely intact in the possession of her sister Angelica.[18] Following this, Patricia Fortini Brown examined the tax declarations, will, and property inventory of Elisabetta Condulmer (d. 1538).[19] Condulmer and Lombardo numbered among the small fraction of Venetian prostitutes who were talented, ambitious, and successful enough to become known as honorable courtesans, or *somtuose meretrize* (sumptuous prostitutes), another term used by Sanudo, and considered as a kind of professional royalty.[20] According to Michel de Montaigne (1533–1592), the number of Venetian courtesans "living like princesses" had swelled to around 150 by the end of the 1570s.[21] This number would have been far lower in the 1520s and 30s when the phenomenon was at an earlier stage of its development.[22]

16 Keener, "Virtue, Illusion, *Venezianità*," 121.

17 Sanudo, *I Diarii* (*MCCCCXCVI–MDXXXIII*), vol. 19, col. 138 (16 October 1514).

18 Santore, "Julia Lombardo," 62–80.

19 Fortini Brown, *Private Lives*, 173–81.

20 Sanudo, *Diarii*, vol. 33, col. 233 (9 May 1522), uses the term "somtuosa meretrize" in referring to Julia Lombardo.

21 The *Catalogo di tutte le principal et più honorate Cortigiane di Venetia* (Venice, ca. 1565), lists 210 names, which is likely an exaggeration. Montaigne gives the somewhat lower number of 150, *Journal de voyage*, 73.

22 On the population of prostitutes in Venice in the early sixteenth century see Scarabello, "Per una storia della prostituzione," 53.

Based on overlapping mentions in diaries, letters, poetry, and other literary and documentary sources, there were likely around forty to sixty courtesans living in such luxurious and "noble" fashion during this earlier period, and these women would have been capable of amassing at least modest art collections through a combination of direct patronage (certainly the case with portraits), purchases on the open market, and gifts. Julia Lombardo proves exceptional even within this elite group of women, as one among a handful of the most internationally recognized Venetian courtesans of her day. She is one of the women mentioned in a satiric dialogue between a Venetian and a foreign visitor to the lagoon city, *La tariffa delle puttane di Venegia* (Venice, 1535), where she is described as "rich in gold and land." In 1531 the former French ambassador to Venice named her along with several other famous courtesans as the most perfect type of Venetian merchandise.[23] For her part, Condulmer enjoyed sufficient renown to be mentioned first among twenty-two professional colleagues, including Lombardo, in a satiric poem, *La vita rotta di Giacomina*, which was also published in Venice in the 1530s.[24]

The Venetian documents corroborate several key details from Bandello's *novella*, notably that courtesans possessed *studioli* filled with precious collectables and objects symbolic of intellectual cultivation and classical knowledge in the courtly-humanist tradition, and that they owned books and musical instruments for personal and professional use, including the hosting of *ridotti*. Julia Lombardo's study was a veritable treasure trove housing *all'antica* miniature sculptures in bronze and gold, jewel-encrusted boxes and figurines, and the ornamental crowns she would have worn when entertaining visitors. Like Imperia, her *studiolo* featured a cornice shelf studded with fifty glass and *reticello* vases, flasks, and goblets, along with vessels and dishes in porcelain and maiolica. The cornice also featured an assortment of books and a small portrait of Dante, which demonstrated her literary credentials.[25] However, unlike

23 *La tariffa delle puttane di Venegia*, ed. Danilo Romei, *Nuovo Rinascimento* database, http://www.nuovorinascimento.org/n-rinasc/ind_tit.htm, 24, v. 98, "De la lombarda, che d'oro e terreni ricca." The ex-ambassador made his comment naming Cornelia Griffo, Julia Lombardo, Biancha Saraton, Elena Ballarin, and other famous Venetian courtesans at a dinner party in Antwerp, which is recorded in a letter by Giovanni Francesco Mazzardo reprinted in Sanudo, *Diarii*, vol. 54, col. 421 (6 March 1531).

24 Condulmer appears in *La vita rotta di Giacomina* (v. 438–449), where she is introduced as "La Condolmera," and further identified as "Beta" (short for Elisabetta). Lombardo comes just after her at v. 458–465. Coletti has published this anonymously authored satiric lament against Venetian courtesans in the annex to his dissertation, "Liaisons vénales." Condulmer may also be the "Betta" named in v. 671 and v. 676 of *La tariffa*, who is later called "Lisabetta" in v. 707. Condulmer is the only courtesan with the first name Elisabetta I have found in contemporary literary texts.

25 Santore, "Julia Lombardo," 72–73.

Imperia, both Elisabetta and Julia enjoyed considerable financial independence, the former as both a renter and homeowner in Venice, and the latter as the renter of her urban apartment and owner of numerous agricultural properties on the mainland, from which she received substantial rents. Although it cannot be trusted as a reliable source, the *Vita rota di Giacomina* attributes Julia's wealth to a professional transition from courtesan to madam, or private brothel keeper, which, if true, would likely have occurred in the early 1530s.[26]

The archival documents pertaining to Condulmer and Lombardo also confirm some basic information already known about other distinguished courtesans of the Renaissance, for example, that well-known artists painted their portraits. Cornelia Griffo, who was, along with Lombardo, one of the principal courtesans of Venice in the early sixteenth-century, commissioned Lorenzo Lotto to paint her portrait in 1545, while Jacopo Tintoretto later painted Veronica Franco (1546–1591).[27] Giorgio Vasari claims that Raphael painted portraits of the Roman courtesan Beatrice Ferrarese (Beatrice de' Bonis) and "infinite" other women like her, including the artist's own mistress. Vasari also attributes a portrait of the talented Roman courtesan-singer Barbara Salutati (d. after 1544), who was the lover of Niccolò Macchiavelli, to the Florentine painter Domenico Puligo.[28] The formal portrait that scholars now associate with Vasari's account of "La Barbara" celebrates the virtue and beauty of its female subject through the two poetic love songs—one spiritual, one secular—that are legible on the pages of the musical partbook resting open between her hands. The partbook lays next to an open volume of poetry inscribed PETRARCHA (fig. 3.1).[29]

26 *La vita rotta*, v. 458–59: "Iulia Lombarda poi che di fat'escha / sol per tenere schola di bardasse" (Julia Lombarda who left [the profession] only to keep a 'school' of young male prostitutes). "Scola" or "scoleta" was the term used to denote illegal, home-based prostitution operations. On this see Coletti, "Liaisons vénales," annex, 94, n. 266.

27 Griffo's portrait commission at a price of 4 ducats, which she later cancelled, is recorded in one of Lotto's account books, *Il "libro di spese diverse,"* 36. Franco refers to her portrait painted by Jacopo Tintoretto in her *Lettere familiari a diversi* (Venice, 1580, modern edition, n. 21, 34–35). The portrait has often been associated with *A Portrait of a Lady* by Tintoretto or a close follower now in the Worcester Art Museum (1948.22). This portrait was inscribed "V. Franco" on the relining canvas at an unknown date.

28 Vasari, *Le Vite*, vol. 4, 365: "[Raphael] Ritrasse Beatrice Ferrarese et altre donne, e particularmente quella sua, et altre infinite." In the same volume, 465: "[Puligo] Ritrasse anco in un quadro la Barbara Fiorentina in quel tempo famosa, bellissima cortigiana e molto amata da molti, non meno che per la bellezza per le sue buone creanze, e particolarmente per essere bonissima musica e cantare divinamente."

29 On Puligo's portrait as Barbara Salutati see Mary Rogers, "Fashioning Identities," 91–103; Slim, "A Motet for Macchiavelli's Mistress," vol. 2, 457–72.

FIGURE 3.1
Domenico Puligo (1492–1527), *Portrait of a Woman with a Music Book* (*Barbara Salutati*), ca. 1523–25. Oil on panel, 100 × 80.5 cm (39.4 × 31.7 in.)
PRIVATE COLLECTION

While not described in terms of its visual details or attributed to a specific artist, the inventory of Elisabetta Condulmer's household property reveals that she displayed a large, framed portrait of herself with a protective curtain in the *portego*, the long, central reception chamber at the heart of the Venetian home.[30] Among the twenty-eight paintings on display in her apartment, Julia Lombardo hung a framed portrait of a woman with its cover in the principal bedroom, which Santore reasonably hypothesizes to have been her own portrait.[31] Writing at the turn of the seventeenth century, the English traveller Thomas Coryat confirmed that "the picture of the noble courtesan most exquisitely drawn" commonly greeted visitors upon their arrival from a prominent position in the *portego*.[32] Although it proves difficult to convincingly associate such cursory descriptions with surviving female portraits of the period, the textual evidence, to which more could be added, puts to rest the argument forwarded by several modern art historians that portraits of courtesans did not exist in the Renaissance.[33]

30 Archivio di Stato di Venezia (hereafter ASV), *Cancelleria Inferiore, miscellanea di notai diversi* (hereafter MND), b. 37, n. 28, inventory of Elisabetta Condulmer (13 September 1538): "nel portego: uno retrato grando di madona lisabeta condulmera cum suo Timpano."

31 Santore, "Julia Lombardo," 55, 62.

32 Thomas Coryat, *Crudities*, vol. 1, 403.

33 Charles Hope, Enrico Maria dal Pozzolo, and Augusto Gentili are scholars who reject the idea of courtesans as subjects for Renaissance paintings. For example, Gentili claims

Beyond these corroborations, the Venetian archival evidence, and in particular the inventory of Elisabetta Condulmer's movable property, goes further than other sources in revealing the courtesan's role as Renaissance tastemaker with regard to her habits of art collecting, interior decoration, domestic hospitality, and informal entertainment. Condulmer was a Venetian woman of impoverished noble birth whose life, *casa*, and possessions—including her impressive art collection—have been examined by Monika Schmitter and myself in addition to Fortini Brown.[34] Condulmer, daughter of the disgraced patrician Girolamo Condulmer and mother of seven children by three different men (none of them her husband), lived independently of her husband Gabriel de' Angeli in a well-appointed *piano nobile* apartment in the parish of San Felice in Cannaregio. Here she would have entertained her *signori*, fellow *virtuosi*, friends, and foreign visitors, in addition to managing her large family and household. Most notable among her long-term lovers was Gian Francesco Torresani (1498–1557/8), the successful editor who directed the publishing program of the Aldine press from 1517 to 1528. In addition to important editions of Latin and Greek texts, he published Baldassare Castiglione's best-selling conduct book, *The Courtier* (1528).[35] Condulmer referred to Torresani as "mio signor," they had three children together, and he kept significant personal property in her home, which suggests that he lived there on at least a part-time basis.[36] When she died in her thirties pregnant with her eighth child in September 1538, the notary Angelo da Canal drew up a detailed household inventory that reveals much about the way she lived, her artistic taste, and how she entertained guests in her home.

3 Musical Accomplishment

Elisabetta Condulmer owned four lutes, three of medium size and one large, which speaks to her musical practice of self-accompanied singing. To sing and

categorically, "there do not exist, in Venetian painting of the early *Cinquecento*, 'portraits of courtesans,'" "Amore e amorose," 95.

34 Schmitter discusses the paintings in Condulmer's *portego* in "The Quadro da Portego," 693–751. I examine the comic and carnivalesque art in her collection in light of contemporary entertainment practices, *Playful Pictures*.

35 Palau, "Gian Francesco," 28–44.

36 Gian Francesco Torresani's father Andrea had been Aldus Manutius' publishing partner and they shared a residence. Condulmer also had 2 children and a long-term liaison with the patrician Camillo Michiel. On these relationships see Fortini Brown, *Private Lives*, 174–81.

play an instrument, most commonly the lute or harpsichord, was an almost *de rigeur* accomplishment among Renaissance courtesans. The secular song repertoire favored by courtesans and *gentildonne* alike trafficked in Petrarchan themes of unrequited love centered on the female object of desire. This poetic music of love and longing, combined with the courtesan's physical allure and the luxurious setting of her home, were imagined to possess a formidable, even dangerous, seductive power. As Coryat satirically puts it in his *Crudities* of 1611, the noble Venetian courtesan, "will endeavour to enchant you partly with her melodious notes that she warbles out upon her lute."[37] Julia Lombardo's home contained only one green harpsichord in the second bedroom that featured the attached *studiolo*, and this suite may have been occupied by another courtesan.[38] Any other smaller, more portable instruments Julia may have owned, such as lutes or viols, would have been long gone—sold or discarded—by the time the inventories of her household were drawn up some twenty-six years following her death.

4 Festivity and Disguise

Condulmer also owned ten *volti da stravestir* (masks for disguise), seven of which were in satin, and three of which had beards.[39] Like other Venetians, courtesans commonly used the simple mask known as a *volto* (literally "face") or *larva*. For women this mask was a white or black oval that covered the eyes and nose or full face, which hid their features and allowed them to circulate anonymously in the city, whether during carnival or at other permitted times of year.[40] A 1610 engraving of *Masked Revelers in Venice during Carnival* by

37 Coryat, *Crudities*, vol. 1, 405.

38 Santore, "Julia Lombardo," 69: Nella camera verso Santa Caterina, "Uno Arpichordo verde." The bed in this room was identified by the servants of the Lombardo sisters as having belonged to Madonna Cecilia Colon[n]a, possibly another courtesan who shared Lombardo's three-bedroom apartment.

39 ASV, MND, b. 37, n. 28, inv. of Elisabetta Condulmer (13 September 1538): "Voltj rassi da stravestir. no. sette, Voltj con barba da stravestir. no. tre." On the *volto* mask type see Reato, *Le maschere veneziane*, 44–45.

40 In addition to carnival, masks were permitted during the Feast of the Sensa (May–June) and at other times, but courtesans, *bravi*, and others who wished to circulate unrecognized in the city appear to have worn them whenever it suited their purpose. Tommaso Garzoni, one of the first commentators to write at length about the Venetian habit of wearing masks in public, severely criticizes the practice in his *Piazza universale* (1585). He—like the Venetian government in its legislation—linked masking with prostitution, sedition, and violent crime, Reato, *Le maschere veneziane*, 7–19, 38–39.

Giacomo Franco shows a Venetian courtesan wearing the second type of mask, that with mustache and beard, in the foreground (fig. 3.2). Courtesans infamously also cross-dressed as a part of their sexual play with clients, as detailed by Pietro Aretino and others in their satiric accounts, and a bearded mask, like male undergarments, could potentially form part of such activity.

However, the number of masks Condulmer owned also suggests group sociability and festivity. Those with beards align with the topsy-turvy atmosphere and social role reversals of the carnival season, in which courtesans played a highly visible part. The masks could have been used for public carnival celebrations, private masquerade balls and parties, and domestic theatrical events in which courtesans may have participated as performers alongside their male companions and professional entertainers. From at least the first decade of the sixteenth century, the elite patrician youths who formed the festive brigades of the *Compagnie della calza* (Companies of the Hose), invited courtesans rather than their patrician female counterparts to their banquets and parties. These young men performed in *momarie* (masked pantomimes with music and dancing) and musical comedies alongside hired performers, and often everyone present, including the courtesans, wore costumes appropriate to the theme, dressing up as classical deities, shepherds, nymphs, peasants, and other characters.[41] Sanudo also notes that the *compagni* and other elite youths frequented the homes of courtesans, both individually and in small cliques. Raimondo Guarino terms this practice of young patricians socializing with prostitutes "a phenomenon of distinction and sophisticated transgression."[42]

With its impressive twenty-four chairs, long pinewood dining table, and three painted *portego* benches, the reception hall of Condulmer's home would have served as the site for large banquets and other forms of domestic hospitality and entertainment. The *portego* was the first room visitors entered upon climbing the stairs to the *piano nobile*, where privileged Venetian families lived, but was not normally a center of everyday domestic activity. Rather, as Patricia Fortini Brown has elucidated, "the function of the *portego* was, first and foremost, display," and for many elite Venetians around the turn of the sixteenth century the forms of this display shifted as the *portego* became primarily a locus for sociable recreation and entertainment—receptions, banquets, parties, balls, concerts—in lieu of the demonstration of family honor through the presentation of arms, armor, and ancestral portraits.[43]

41 The Council of Ten attempted to ban *Compagnie* parties to which prostitutes were invited, Sanudo, *Diarii*, vol. 15, col. 448 (12 January 1513). On the festive costumes worn at such parties see Newton, *The Dress of the Venetians*.

42 Guarino, *Teatro e mutamenti*, 153: "un fenomeno di distinzione e raffinata trasgressione."

43 Fortini Brown, "The Venetian Casa," 57. On the changing role of the *portego* in the early sixteenth century see Schmitter, "The Quadro da Portego," 701–4.

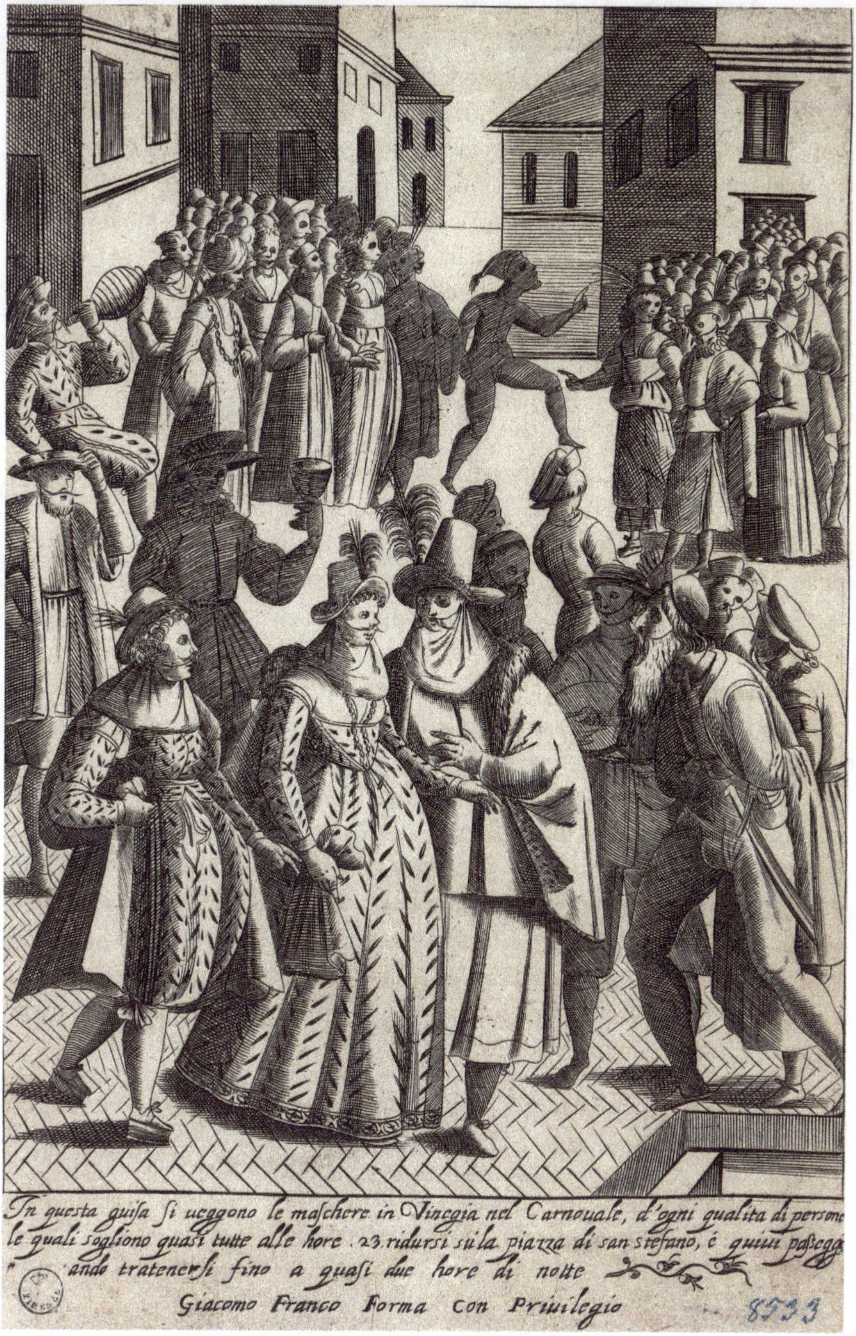

FIGURE 3.2 Giacomo Franco (1550–1620), *Masked Revelers in Venice during Carnival.* Engraving from *Habiti d'uomini e donne Venetiane con la processione…*, 1610, 251 × 157 mm Museo Correr, Venice
PHOTO: ART RESOURCE, NEW YORK

5 Art Collection and Display

As Cristina de Benedictis has noted, the *portego* also came to function as a veritable art gallery in the sixteenth century, and Condulmer's was no exception. Her *portego* contained a heterogeneous mix of sacred, secular, and mythological subject matter in addition to several portraits, and in total had ten paintings and eight drawings (or possibly prints) on the walls, many identified as foreign or Flemish in style. This bricolage display pattern was typical of the most "modern" and sophisticated Venetian collectors at the time, perhaps most famously the small, interconnected network of prominent men visited by the patrician connoisseur Marcantonio Michiel (1484–1552), who documented North Italian collections of art and antiquities in his *Notizia d'opere del disegno* (1521–43).[44]

Unlike these men, Condulmer displayed several pictures with comic "genre" subjects in her *portego*, which point to an unconventional, adventurous taste in art still rare for Venice at the time: "a portrait in the Flemish style of a tooth-puller," "a picture in the Flemish style of a man in a barrel," and "a picture of an old man with a birdcage."[45] As I have argued elsewhere, such carnivalesque subjects that mock human folly and vice—avarice, ignorance, drunkenness, lust—prove recognizable as figures or narrative vignettes drawn from the paintings and engravings of the Netherlandish artists Hieronymus Bosch, Quentin Massys, and Lucas van Leyden. The connection is most direct in the case of Lucas van Leyden's 1523 engraving *The Dentist*, which shows a cruel marketplace surgeon taking advantage of a gullible peasant with the aid of a cunning female assistant (fig. 3.3). Technically virtuosic and innovative from the standpoint of subject matter, prints like Van Leyden's circulated throughout Europe among collectors, artists, humanists, printers, and publishers. Here it is worth noting that Condulmer's *signore* Francesco Torresani, who had a humanist education and vast intellectual network, was a personal acquaintance of Erasmus, among his other notable international connections.[46]

44 Michiel, *Der Anonimo Morelliano*, trans. by Frimmel.

45 ASV, MND, b. 37, n. 28: "nel portego: uno retrato grando di madona lisabeta condulmera cum suo Timpano, uno mapamondo soazado meza, uno retrato di uno alla forestiera, *uno retrato de uno che cava denti alla fiandrese, uno quadro di uno homo in una bote alla fiandrese*, uno quadro de piramo et Tisbe, uno quadro de una dona et uno homo nudo, *uno quadro de uno vechio con una cheba*, uno quadro grando de la maddalena alla fiandrese, uno quadro grande de una dona nuda vien ligada ad uno albore, uno quadro con la madona et li tre maggi, otto quadreti de carte in colade soazadi [emphasis mine]."

46 Erasmus wrote his colloquy, *Opulentia sordida*, about the Torresani household in Venice where he was a guest for eight or nine months in 1508. In it he critiques Francesco and his

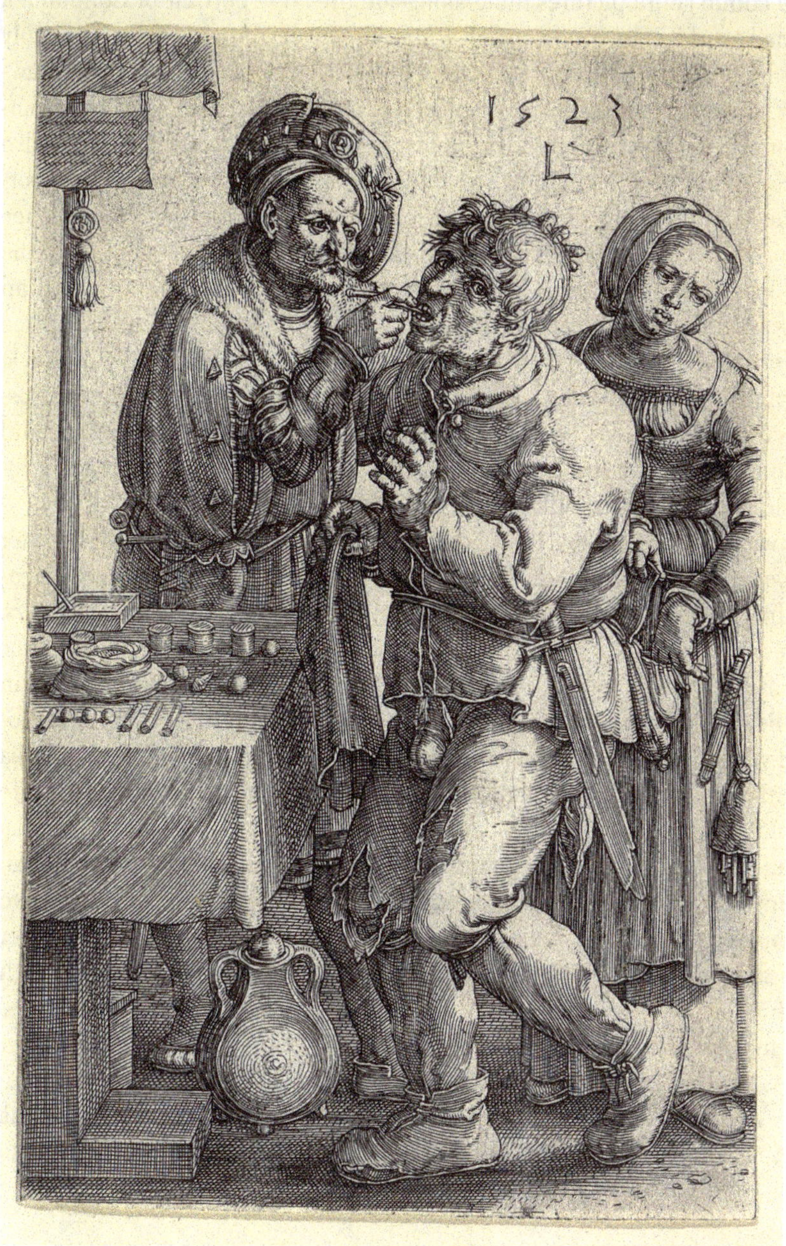

FIGURE 3.3 Lucas van Leyden (1494–1533), *The Dentist*, 1523. Engraving, 117 × 75 mm (4 5/8 × 2 15/16 in.). The Metropolitan Museum of Art, New York. Elisha Whittelsey Collection, Elisha Whittelsey Fund, 1960
PHOTO: METROPOLITAN MUSEUM OF ART, WWW.METMUSEUM.ORG

The comic genre pictures hung alongside the large portrait of Condulmer, a framed world map, a portrait of a man done "in a foreign style" (possibly Torresani?), a painting of the Adoration of the Magi, and a suite of eight drawings or prints pasted on paper and placed in metal frames, whose subject matter is unfortunately not given in the inventory. Beyond this, Condulmer also featured in her *portego* a group of paintings that must have spoken to important facets of her professional and personal identity, promoting an ambience of romance, drama, erudition, and devotion. These included a painting of the tragic lovers Pyramus and Thisbe, a painting of a woman and a nude man (likely an amorous subject), a large painting of a nude woman tied to a tree (Andromeda?), and a large painting of Mary Magdalene in the Flemish style (an appropriate choice given the Magdalene's status as patron saint of prostitutes). Jan van Scorel's *Mary Magdalene* of ca. 1530 provides a stunning and sensuous example of just how seamlessly the image of patron saint and contemporary courtesan could fuse (fig. 3.4).

By way of comparison, Julia Lombardo displayed eight paintings in her *portego*, and like Condulmer these included a variety of religious and secular subjects, several of which were likely mythological, although no portraits. Besides the ubiquitous icons of the Virgin Mary, Christ, and individual saints, she featured a large battle scene and a painting of *Lot and his Daughters*, an apt reflection on lust and corrupted morality that became more explicitly associated with prostitution in seventeenth-century Dutch painting.[47] As Monika Schmitter has shown, such ambitious, multi-figure narrative paintings were typical enough of the space to become known as "quadri da portego."[48] Like Condulmer, Lombardo owned both Flemish (or Flemish-style) and Italian paintings, although apparently no genre paintings or prints. She possessed two paintings of unidentified nude women, a large one in the *portego* and another in the second bedroom with the harpsichord and attached *studiolo*, both with gold frames. My survey of sixteenth-century Venetian property inventories confirms that such pictures most commonly depicted Venus, who among her various guises served as the guardian of prostitutes. Venus was followed in popularity at some remove by *Fortuna*, although nymphs and other mythological, historical, and biblical characters, such as Danaë, Cleopatra, and Lucretia, also

brother: "they lived high, whored, gambled and … sometimes lost sixty ducats a night at dice," *Collected Works of Erasmus*, vol. 1, 991.

47 For example, in one version of *The Prodigal Son with the Courtesans* (private collection), Frans Francken II (1581–1642) places a large painting of *Lot and his Daughters* on the wall of the brothel.

48 Schmitter, "The Quadro da Portego," 693–751.

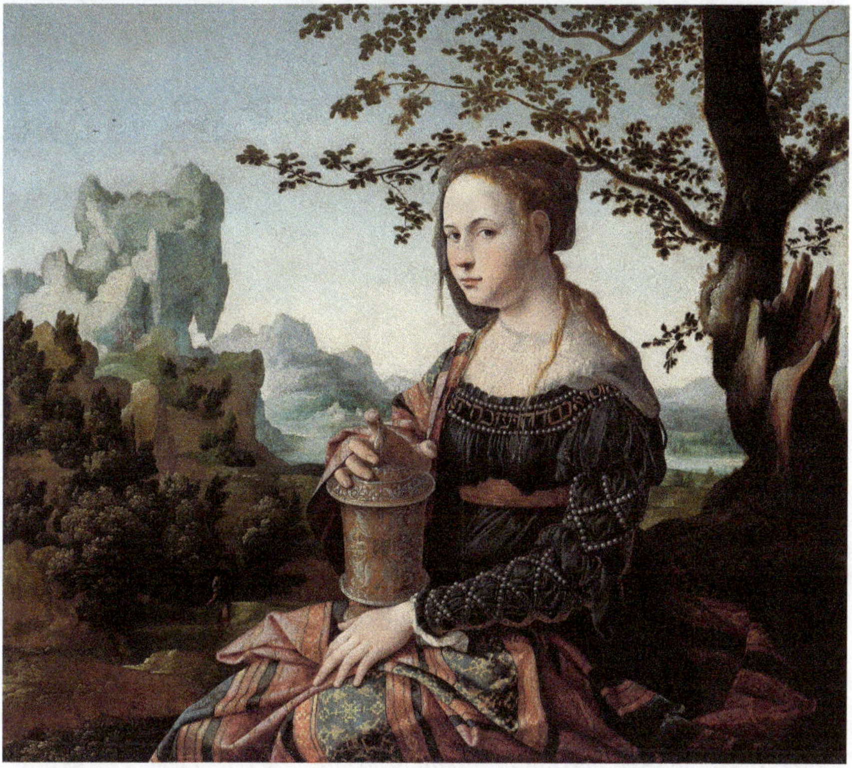

FIGURE 3.4 Jan van Scorel (1495–1562), *Mary Magdalene*, ca. 1530. Oil on panel, 66.3 × 76 cm (26 × 30 in.)
RIJKSMUSEUM, AMSTERDAM

crop up in the documents, as they of course do in extant paintings.[49] Jacopo Palma il Vecchio's *Venus in a Landscape* of ca. 1520 now in the Courtauld furnishes but one typical example of what such a "donna nuda" painting could have looked like (fig. 3.5).

Lombardo also owned a painting of a "man of arms" and another of a young knight, the first of which hung in the principal bedroom near her presumed portrait. The second painting hung alongside that of the nude woman in the secondary bedroom. Santore suggests that these paintings may have been actual portraits of Lombardo's *signori*, given as gifts to their favorite, however

49 For detailed information on the popularity of paintings of nude and semi-nude women in sixteenth-century Venice according to the evidence of property inventories see Henry, "Buffoons, Rustics, and Courtesans," Appendix 1, 306–8.

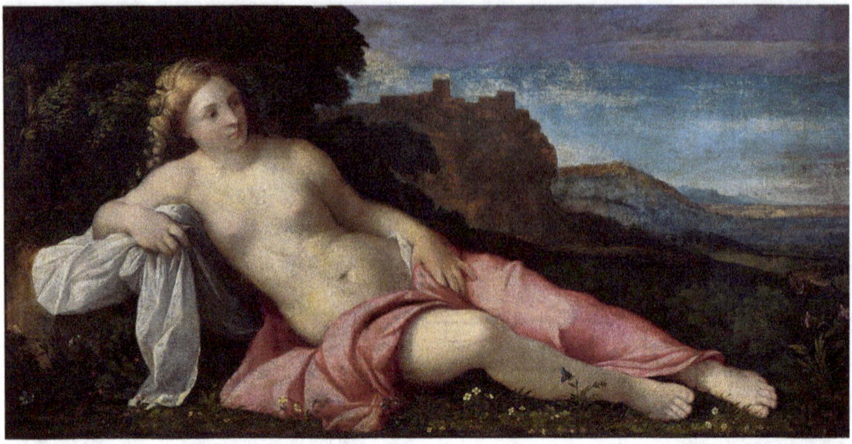

FIGURE 3.5 Jacopo Palma il Vecchio (1480–1528), *Venus in a Landscape*, Oil on canvas, ca. 1520, 77.5 × 152.7 cm
THE COURTAULD, LONDON (SAMUEL COURTAULD TRUST)

they were perhaps more likely invented images of *uomini armati*.[50] The subgenre of generic "portraiture" dedicated to noble knights, sometimes shown with their pages, proves somewhat similar in kind to the idealized *bella donna* imagery produced during the same period, as exemplified by Sebastiano del Piombo's smoldering *Portrait of a Man in Armor* of ca. 1512 (fig. 3.6). Santore hypothesizes, in part based on the visual evidence of a seventeenth-century satiric engraving of a Venetian courtesan's bedchamber, that paired paintings of nude women and armed men may have been popular among courtesans. In Lombardo's home these pairings in the bedrooms could have invoked the same dramatic and sensuous blend of courtly, chivalric, and mythological intrigue and romance as did the subjects favored by Condulmer in her *portego*.

While Santore's thesis seems plausible enough, it should be noted that the male collectors featured in Michiel's *Notizia* and in property inventories also favored such generic, idealized subjects, including armed men and nude women. These men, who were patrician, *cittadini*, and resident foreign merchants, highly placed ecclesiasts and government officials and bureaucrats, defined themselves in part through their private intellectual and cultural interests and sophisticated taste for both modern, international art and classical antiquities. Like courtesans, several of them—the patrician Gabriele Vendramin and *cittadini* Andrea Odoni and Francesco dalla Vedova—hosted

50 Santore, "Julia Lombardo," 55–56.

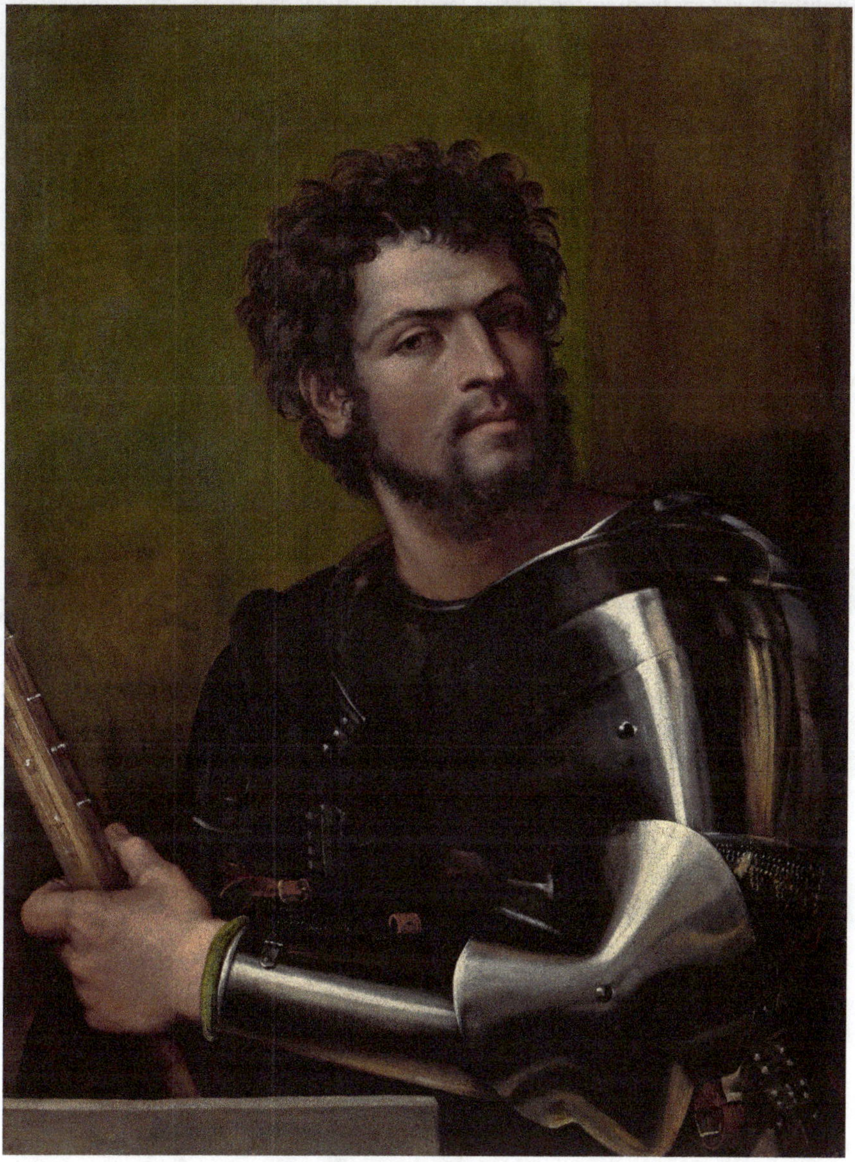

FIGURE 3.6 Sebastiano del Piombo (1485–1547), *Portrait of a Man in Armor*, ca. 1512. Oil on canvas, 87.7 × 66.7 cm (34 ½ × 26 ¼ in.)
WADSWORTH ATHENEUM MUSEUM OF ART, HARTFORD, CT., THE ELLA GALLUP SUMNER AND MARY CATLIN SUMNER COLLECTION FUND

domestic *ridotti* frequented by the leading *virtuosi* of Venice, including scholars, writers, musicians, artists, and potentially also courtesans. It should thus come as no surprise that Venetian courtesans, particularly one with a long-term attachment to an important editor-publisher, would assert themselves by collecting art in a manner similar to the highly placed, culturally engaged men in their direct and indirect social networks. As Guido Ruggiero has summarized, within these homosocial networks courtesans "demonstrated and even bestowed honor, status, and *virtù* with the help of their arts."[51] Beyond playing music, reciting poetry, and composing sonnets and madrigals, courtesans could deploy the collection of art and material culture as a crucial facet of their scrupulously orchestrated self-fashioning.

In conclusion, the contents of a courtesan's home open a window onto her multi-faceted identity and cultural and aesthetic values that reaches far beyond fulfilling a male fantasy of absolute *luxuria*, the conflation of lust and luxury, woman and object, set out in Fortini's *novella* and in the invective literature on Renaissance courtesans. In their *studioli*, Imperia Cognati and Julia Lombardo demonstrated a pronounced *all'antica* taste and cultivated their literary and musical credentials in much the same way as did Italian noblewomen such as Isabella d'Este, Veronica Gambara, Silvia Pallavicina, and others.[52] The contents of Elisabetta Condulmer's *portego* clearly demonstrate her role as the host of sizable banquets, parties, and diverse entertainments. Finally, the paintings owned by Lombardo and Condulmer demonstrate a unique cross-section of subjects that explore the moral valence of the temptress in biblical narratives, promote a sophisticated, virtuous form of feminine beauty and sensuality, foster an atmosphere of romantic drama steeped in classical myth and chivalric romance, and signal intellectual cultivation and sophisticated knowledge of the contemporary art scene.

51 Ruggiero, "Who's Afraid of Giuliana Napolitana?" 281.

52 For connections between art and music making in Isabella d'Este's *studiolo* see Shephard, "Isabella and the Decorum of Voice," in *Echoing Helicon*, 63–99, and for the *studioli* and literary and musical interests of Gambara, Pallavicina, and Barbara Pallavicina-Rangona, McIver, "Two Emilian Noblewomen" and "The Renaissance *Palazzo* Interior as a Private Voice for Women," in *Women, Art, and Architecture*, 107–36.

Bibliography

Primary Sources

Anonymous (Antonio Cavallino?). *La tariffa delle puttane di Venegia*, edited by Danilo Romei. *Nuovo Rinascimento* database, 2020. http://www.nuovorinascimento.org/n-rinasc/ind_tit.htm.

Anonymous. *Catalogo di tutte le principal et più honorate Cortigiane di Venetia* (Venice, ca. 1565). Codice Cicogna 2483. Museo Civico Correr, Venice.

Archivio di Stato di Venezia, Cancelleria Inferiore, miscellanea di notai diversi, inventari.

Bandello, Matteo. *Le novelle*. 9 volumes. Livorno: Gaetano Poggiali, 1791–1793.

Coryat, Thomas, and George Coryate. *Coryate's Crudities*. 2 vols. Glasgow: James MacLehose and Sons, 1905.

Erasmus, Desiderius. *Collected Works of Erasmus, Colloquies*, edited by Craig R. Thompson. 2 vols. Toronto: University of Toronto Press, 1997.

Fortini, Pietro. *Novella XI*, in *Raccolta di novellieri italiani*, Part 2, 1180–81. Florence: Tipografia Borghi e Compagni, 1834.

Franco, Veronica. *Lettere familiari a diversi*, edited by Benedetto Croce. Bari: Laterza, 1949.

Lotto, Lorenzo. *Il "libro di spese diverse" con aggiunla di lettere e d'altri documenti*, edited by Pietro Zampetti. Venezia–Roma, Istituto per la collaborazione culturale, 1969.

Michiel, Marcantonio. *Der Anonimo Morelliano* (*Marcantonio Michiel's Notizia d'Opere del Disegno*). *Text und Übersetzung*, translated and text by Theodor Frimmel. Vienna: Verlag Carl Graeser, 1896.

Montaigne, Michel de. *Journal de voyage en Italie par la Suisse et l'Allemagne en 1580 et 1581*, edited by Maurice Rat. Paris: Editions Garnier, 1955.

Sanudo, Marin. *I Diarii* (*MCCCCXCVI–MDXXXIII*), edited by Rinaldo Fulin, Federico Stefani et al., 58 volumes. (Venice: F. Visentini, 1879–1903).

Vasari, Giorgio. *Le Vite, Terza Parte*, volume 4. Florence: Gaetano Milanesi, 1879.

Secondary Sources

Aikema, Bernard. "Tesori ponentini per la Serenissima. Il commercio d'arte fiamminga a Venezia e nel Veneto fra Quattro e Cinquecento." In *Tra committenza e collezionismo Studi sul mercato dell'arte nell'Italia settentrionale durante l'età moderna*, edited by Enrico Maria dal Pozzolo and Leonida Tedoldi, 35–48. Vicenza: Terra Ferma, 2003.

Brown, Patricia Fortini. *Private Lives in Renaissance Venice: Art, Architecture, and the Family*. New Haven and London: Yale University Press, 2004.

Brown, Patricia Fortini. "The Venetian Casa: A Panoramic View." In *At Home in Renaissance Italy: Art and Life in the Italian House, 1400–1600*, exhibition catalogue, edited by Marta Ajmar-Wollheim and Flora Dennis, 50–65. London: Victoria & Albert Museum, 2006.

Coletti, Fabien. "Liaisons vénales et amours extra-conjugales à Venise au XVIe siècle: Réalités sociales et representations littéraires." PhD dissertation, University of Toulouse le Mirail–Toulouse II, 2016.

DePrano, Maria. "*Chi vuol esser lieto, sia*: Objects of Entertainment in the Tornabuoni Palace in Florence." In *The Early Modern Italian Domestic Interior, 1400–1700: Objects, Spaces, Domesticities*. Edited by Erin J. Campbell, Stephanie R. Miller, Elizabeth Carroll Consavari, 127–42. London and New York: Routledge, 2016.

Gentili, Augusto. "Amore e amorose persone: Tra miti ovidiani, allegorie musicali, celebrazioni matrimoniali." In *Tiziano: Amor Sacro, Amor Profano*, exhibition catalogue, Palazzo delle Esposizioni, Rome 82–105. Milan: Electa, 1995.

Graf, Arturo. *Attraverso il Cinquecento*. Turin: Ermanno Loescher, 1888.

Guarino, Raimondo. *Teatro e mutamenti Rinascimento e spettacolo a Venezia*. Bologna: Il Mulino, 1995.

Henry, Chriscinda. "Buffoons, Rustics, and Courtesans: Low Painting and Entertainment Culture in Renaissance Venice." PhD dissertation, The University of Chicago, 2009.

Henry, Chriscinda. *Playful Pictures: Art, Leisure, and Entertainment in the Venetian Renaissance Home*. University Park, PA: Pennsylvania State University Press, 2021.

Keener, Shawn. "Virtue, Illusion, *Venezianità*: Vocal Bravura and the Early *Cortigiana Onesta*." In *Musical Voices of Early Modern Women: Many-Headed Melodies*, edited by Thomasin LaMay, 119–33. Aldershot, UK and Burlington, VT: Ashgate, 2005.

McIver, Katherine A. *Women, Art, and Architecture in Northern Italy, 1520–1580: Negotiating Power*. Aldershot, UK and Burlington, VT: Ashgate, 2006.

Newton, Stella Mary. *The Dress of the Venetians 1495–1525*. Aldershot, UK: Scolar Press, 1988.

Palau, Annaclara Cataldi. "Gian Francesco Torresani of Asola and the Aldine Printing Press: A New Chapter in Intellectual and Printing History." *Intellectual News* 10, no. 1 (2002): 28–44.

Petrucci, Franca. "Cognati, Imperia." In *Dizionario Biografico degli Italiani*, vol. 26 (1982). http://www.treccani.it/enciclopedia/imperia-cognati_(Dizionario-Biografico)/.

Quantaince, Courtney. *Textual Masculinity and the Exchange of Women in Renaissance Venice*. Toronto: University of Toronto Press, 2015.

Reato, Danilo. *Le maschere veneziane*. Venice: Arsenale, 1988.

Reiss, Sheryl E., and David Wilkins, eds. *Beyond Isabella: Secular Women Patrons in Renaissance Italy*. Kirkville, MO: Truman State University Press, 2001.

Rogers, Mary. "Fashioning Identities for the Renaissance Courtesan." In *Fashioning Identities in Renaissance Art*, edited by Mary Rogers, 91–103. Aldershot, UK: Ashgate, 2000.

Ruggiero, Guido. "Who's Afraid of Giuliana Napolitana? Pleasure, Fear, and Imagining the Arts of the Renaissance Courtesan." In *The Courtesan's Arts: Cross-Cultural Perspectives*, edited by Martha Feldman and Bonnie Gordon, 280–94. Oxford and New York: Oxford University Press, 2006.

Santore, Cathy. "Julia Lombardo, 'Somtuoaa Meretrize': A Portrait by Property." *Renaissance Quarterly* 41, no. 1 (1988): 44–83.

Scarabello, Giovanni. "Per una storia della prostituzione a Venezia (XIII–XVIII secc.)." *Studi Veneziani* 17 (2004): 15–101.

Schmitter, Monika. "The Quadro da Portego in Sixteenth-Century Venetian Art." *Renaissance Quarterly* 64, no. 3 (2011): 693–751.

Slim, H. Colin. "A Motet for Macchiavelli's Mistress and a Chanson for a Courtesan." In *Essays Presented to Myron P. Gilmore*, edited by Sergio Bertelli and Gloria Ramakus, volume 2, 457–72. Florence: La Nuova Italia Editrice, 1978.

Stollhans, Cynthia. "The Pious Act of an Impious Woman: The Courtesan Fiammetta as Art Patron in Renaissance Rome." In *Patronage, Gender and the Arts in Early Modern Italy: Essays in Honor of Carolyn Valone*, edited by Katherine A. McIver and Cynthia Stollhans, 231–47. New York: Italica Press, 2015.

Storey, Tessa. *Carnal Commerce in Counter-Reformation Rome*. Cambridge and New York: Cambridge University Press, 2008.

Thornton, Peter. *The Italian Renaissance Interior, 1400–1600*. New York: Harry N. Abrams, 1991.

Ugolini, Paola. *The Court and Its Critics: Anti-Court Sentiments in Early Modern Italy*. Toronto: University of Toronto Press, 2020.

Verini, Giovanni Battista. *Il vanto della cortigiana Ferrarese* (Venice, 1532). In *Attraverso il Cinquecento*, edited by Arturo Graf, 355–61. Turin: Ermanno Loescher, 1888.

CHAPTER 4

Fractured Politics, Seamless Art: Family Patronage in Bologna at the Turn of the Cinquecento

Saida Bondini

At the turn of the Cinquecento, Bologna was marked by important political and institutional changes that involved a plurality of actors—foreign and local, papal and patrician—and which uniquely reshaped the social structure of the city, its cultural fabric and patronage system.[1]

Officially under the Papal States, Bologna had long been dominated by the Bentivoglio family, who had remained at the head of the civic government for most of the fifteenth century.[2] The political primacy and extraordinary fortune of the family allowed it to oversee artistic endeavors of exceptional relevance, attracting first the attention of contemporary chroniclers and eventually modern scholars.[3] In 1506, the dominion of the Bentivoglio ended: Pope Julius II (1503–1513) formally reconquered Bologna, imposing an institutional overhaul that created a fracture in the political equilibrium of the city.[4]

This rupture has long been regarded as a watershed moment in Bolognese art. Modern scholarship has emphasized the leading role of the "princely" patronage of the Bentivoglio and the rulers' demise came to be associated with the end of a prolific artistic season, which involved a shift in style and

1 For an overview of the political, institutional, and artistic context in Bologna between the fifteenth and sixteenth centuries, see recently Rubin Blanshei, *A Companion to Medieval and Renaissance Bologna*.

2 In 1447, the *capitoli* promulgated by Pope Nicholas V established a mixed formed government involving a subdivision of power between the civic authority (the Senate) and the papal legate, which remained in force for the second half of the fifteenth century. Between 1446 and 1463, the Bolognese senate was headed by Sante Bentivoglio (1424–1463) and between 1463 and 1506, by Giovanni II Bentivoglio (1443–1508). On this topic, see the many studies by De Benedictis cited in this chapter's bibliography; Colliva, "Bologna dal XIV al XVIII"; Terpstra, "Republics by Contract"'; Rubin Blanshei, *Politics and Justice*; Duranti, *Diplomazia e autogoverno a Bologna*; and Idem., "*Libertas*, Oligarchy, Papacy."

3 On the extensive bibliography on the Bentivoglio family and their artistic patronage, see notably, Ady, *The Bentivoglio*; Basile, ed., *Bentivolorum Magnificentia*; Emiliani, *La stagione dei Bentivoglio*; Sorbelli, *I Bentivoglio*; and the more recent studies by Clarke and Drogin cited in this chapter's bibliography.

4 See the above-mentioned studies by De Benedictis; Robertson, *Tyranny under the Mantle*.

 | DOI:10.1163/9789004513938_006

patronage choices.[5] This historiographical paradigm has widely predisposed the understanding of artistic production in Bologna, enforcing a periodization that was modeled after political events.[6]

In the unstable political climate of sixteenth-century Bologna, an element of continuity can be found in the patronage of the other, often overlooked, protagonists of the city's social and cultural scene. Patrician families, wealthy merchants, cultivated notaries and university lecturers, among others, all contributed to fostering a broader sense of civic identity and artistic continuity throughout the Bentivoglio government and well after its demise in 1506.[7] An examination of the patronage of these illustrious figures, who formed the Bolognese urban elite, brings an alternative and more nuanced reading to light.

The patronage of the Bolognese urban elite was underscored by the need to assert its status, which underwent a transition concomitant with the administrative renovation of the city. During the late fifteenth century, the civic elite had to find its place around the hegemonic presence of the Bentivoglio, and did so by looking for official legitimation in knightly titles, financial power and, when possible, political offices.[8] In the years following the end of the Bentivoglio dominance, the institutional and legislative refashioning ordered by Julius II modified the participation of the urban elite in the civic government, giving power to a selected group of forty senators, who ruled the city jointly with the papal legate and gradually distinguished themselves as a separate caste.[9] Before and after this moment of transition, artistic patronage offered the Bolognese elite a tangible means by which it could legitimize

5 Fortunati Pietrantonio, ed., *Pittura bolognese*; Basile, ed., *Bentivolorum Magnificentia*; among others, and most recently Rossoni, *Raffaello e l'arte a Bologna*.

6 In line with the idea that stylistic variances can be read as indicators of "new social dynamics," see Previtali, *La periodizzazione*.

7 The artistic patronage of the Bolognese urban elite has been partly explored by Cavalca, "Dentro e Fuori il Palazzo"; Robertson, *Tyranny under the Mantle*; and the timely studies on individual figures, including, Bettini, *Palazzo Ghisilardi*, and Idem., *Il palazzo dei diamanti a Bologna*.

8 In the Quattrocento, the highest strata of Bolognese society encompassed a heterogeneity of offices, titles, and backgrounds, which only started to be framed within formal regulations in the second half of the century, notably following the promulgation of the 1454 civic statues. A restricted group of families found place in the *Sedici riformatori dello stato di libertà* (the highest committee of the local government), whose members constituted a privileged inner circle in Bolognese society. On this topic, see particularly Gardi, "Making of an Oligarchy"; Castelnuovo, *Être noble*; Donati, *L'idea di nobiltà*; Duranti, *Diplomazia e autogoverno*.

9 On the composition of the new papal government and social changes in this entail, see Duranti, "*Libertas*, Oligarchy, Papacy"; Reinhardt, *Macht und Ohnmacht*; Robertson, *Tyranny under the Mantle*.

its position, claiming and manifesting affiliation to a privileged group, while shaping its collective identity. However, patronage also served for this stratum as a defense mechanism, which allowed it to protect, renegotiate and reassert its standing in a moment of political upheavals. By fostering artistic endurance, the urban elite managed to navigate the turmoil that redefined the city at the turn of the Cinquecento, safeguarding the privileged position so hard-earned in the decades prior. The shift from "signorial" to senatorial administration imposed a transformation of the Bolognese patronage system; it did not, however, determine, or at least not immediately, a change in artistic trends.

The Augustinian church of Santa Maria della Misericordia provides an illuminating example of this articulated system of relationships that underlay the patronage of the Bolognese elite. Located just outside the medieval walls of the city, the Misericordia is today a secondary, seldom visited church, but throughout the late fifteenth century, it emerged as one of the main patronage *foci* of the local elite. This case study offers the opportunity to question the immediate connection between patronage choices and political events that have often served as arbitrary partitions in the scholarship of Renaissance Bologna.

1 Santa Maria della Misericordia: Innovations in Chapel Design and Decoration

In 1473, the abandoned church and adjacent monastery of Santa Maria della Misericordia were acquired by the Hermits of Saint Augustine of the Lombard province, who were already established in Bologna in the basilica of San Giacomo Maggiore (founded in 1267).[10] The Augustinians promptly oversaw the reconstruction and redecoration of their new suburban site. The refashioning started in the mid-1470s with the enlargement of the pre-existing church

10 The first mention of the complex of Santa Maria della Misericordia dates to 1236, when the monastery hosted a group of Ursuline nuns, see Archivio di Stato di Bologna (henceforth ASBo), Demaniale, *Santi Leonardo e Orsola*, 2/3244, n. 1 (in Gamberini, "Il complesso," 143). In 1432, the Misericordia was ceded to the Olivetan congregation of San Michele in Bosco. The monks left the monastery in 1454, which was eventually occupied by the Augustinians between 1473 and its suppression in 1796. The documents regarding the passages of property of the complex are in ASBo, Demaniale, *San Biagio e Santa Maria della Misericordia*, 1/7076 and *Libro di Memorie* (1558) by the prior Vincenzo da Bergamo, ASBo, Demaniale, *Miscellanea delle corporazioni religiose soppresse*, busta 4. On the history and refashioning of the Misericordia, see Supino, *L'arte nelle chiese*, 421–432; Raule, *La chiesa*; Gottarelli, *La chiesa*; Delbianco, "Le chiese di S. Martino"; Poli, *La chiesa*; Gamberini, "Il complesso."

and the construction of lateral chapels along its north aisle. The work continued intermittently between the 1490s and 1550s, expanding to the elevation of the façade, the extension of the frontal portico, and the addition of new chapels to the southern side of the church. Encouraged by papal indulgences, several of the wealthiest and most illustrious families of the city supported the enhancement and refashioning of the Misericordia through financial donations and *ius patronatus* purchasing of the chapels (fig. 4.1). Most donors already owned a chapel in a different church or basilica in the city, including San Giacomo Maggiore, but seized the opportunity offered by the *ex novo* reconstruction of the Misericordia to acquire and fashion, afresh, a new family space.

Among the noteworthy patrons of the Misericordia were Bartolomeo Felicini (d. 1504) and his wife Dorotea Ringhieri (d. 1525). The couple descended from affluent families of bankers and silk merchants and were known in Bologna for their wealth and illustrious family ties, which included the Bentivoglio.[11] In the 1490s, the Felicini-Ringhieri obtained the patronage rights of a chapel, probably the first to be built in the south aisle of the church. The construction began in the early 1490s and was followed by a second refashioning in the 1510s after structural damage occurred to the space.[12] The Felicini-Ringhieri chapel stands out in the Misericordia for its size, prominent location (adjacent to the high altar), and architectural features. In contrast to the standardized *cappelle* previously added to the opposite aisle of the church, the new Felicini-Ringhieri chapel (fig. 4.2) comprised a larger square space with adjoining *scarsella* articulated by a succession of Corinthian pilasters and covered by an umbrella dome. The formal sobriety, balanced architectural elements and decoration of the chapel drew upon local models and Florentine antecedents—from Michelozzo to Giuliano da Sangallo—combining them with features of unprecedented novelty in Bologna.

The resounding tone of innovation in the Felicini-Ringhieri chapel was further enhanced by the commission of a sumptuous altarpiece. The work was

---

11 For Bartolomeo Felicini and his family, see Dolfi, *Cronologia*, 315–319; Ghirardacci, *Historia di Bologna*, 232–237, 331, 595. For the Ringhieri, see Dolfi, *Cronologia*, 647; Dalla Tuata, *Istoria di Bologna*, 315. For the respective family trees, see Carrati, *Genealogie*, ms. B 699, vol. 2, plate 87 and ms. B 698, vol. 2, plate 98. Bartolomeo and Dorotea's firstborn, Giovanni Felicini Junior (1486–1528), married Giovanni II Bentivoglio's daughter Semiramide (called Isotta; d. 1560), see the account in Ghirardacci, *Historia di Bologna*, 331. Giovanni II Bentivoglio also acted as godfather of Giovanni Felicini Junior in 1486, see Archivio Generale Arcivescovile di Bologna, *Registro dei battesimi della cattedrale*, libro III, f. 114v.

12 The reconstruction of the chapel was undertaken around 1517 and probably involved the addition of the *scarsella* and cupola. On the dating of the chapel, its construction and refashioning, see Bondini, "Linguaggi architettonici."

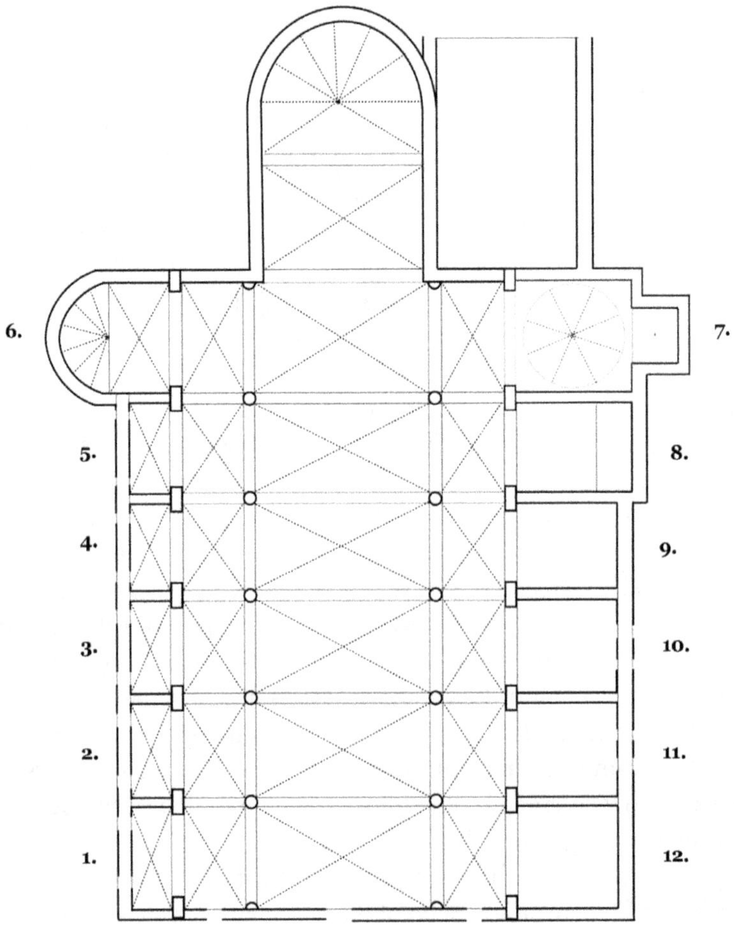

1. Chapel of the Virgin Mary (Casio family)
2. Chapel of St. Monica (Parati, later Grassi family)
3. Chapel of St. Sebastian (Malvezzi, later Amorini family)
4. Chapel of the Crucifixion (or Saint Gerome) (Gandolfi family)
5. Chapel of St. Nicholas of Tolentino (Fantuzzi, later Zamboli family)
6. Chapel of St. Augustine (Manzoli-Sacrati family)
7. Chapel of St. John the Baptist (Felicini-Ringhieri family)
8. Chapel of the Pentecost (Pepoli-Marescaldi family)
9. Chapel of the Annunciation (Volta-Ghislieri family)
10. Chapel of St. Catherine (Malavolta family)
11. Chapel of the Conception (Gozzadini later Zambeccari family)
12. Chapel of St. Anthony and St. Lucy (De' Turchi, later Malisardi family)

FIGURE 4.1 Ground plan of the Church of Santa Maria della Misericordia, Bologna
PHOTO © THE AUTHOR

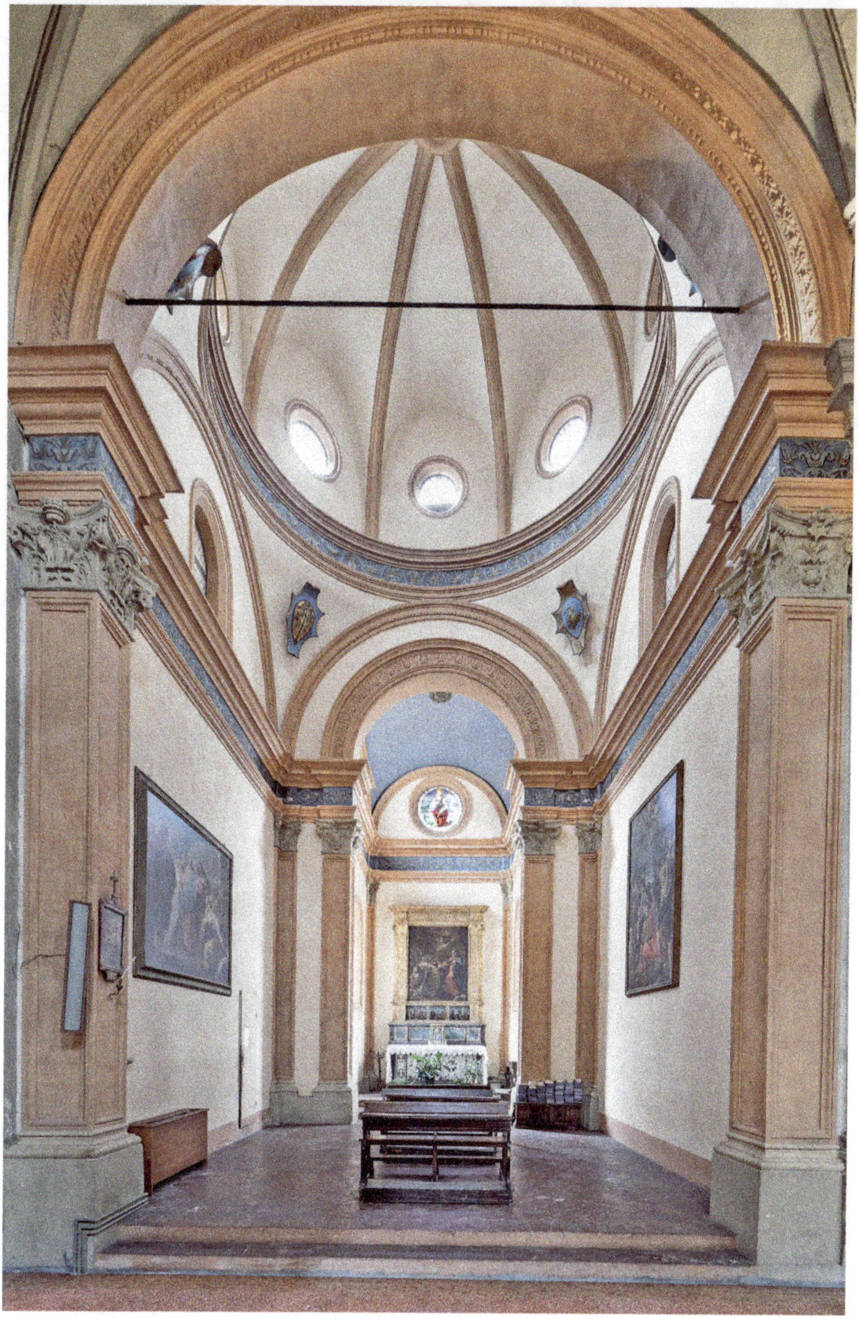

FIGURE 4.2 Felicini-Ringhieri chapel, 1490–1517, Church of Santa Maria della Misericordia, Bologna, frontal view
PHOTO © THE AUTHOR

painted around 1490 by Francesco Raibolini (known as Francia; ca. 1447–1517), who also designed the glass window for the chapel. Today disassembled, the original altarpiece included a central panel, a *cimasa* and a tripartite predella, which together formed an imposing structure of four meters (fig. 4.3).[13] The Felicini-Ringhieri altarpiece enjoyed favorable reception among contemporary and later sources; Vasari recalled it as the "first work" ever painted by Francia, noting that it "gave such satisfaction in Bologna" to inspire the commission of similar paintings by other patrons.[14] Indeed, the altarpiece produced for Bartolomeo Felicini embodied a certain "modern taste" with respect to local tradition, which would soon become popular in Bologna.[15] Following the Felicini-Ringhieri, Francia started to receive commissions for the altarpieces of the most illustrious families of Bologna, including the other donors of the Misericordia.

Around 1490, a new altarpiece by Francia was installed in the chapel directly opposite the Felicini-Ringhieri *cappella* in the north aisle of the church. The commission of both chapel and altarpiece was arranged in 1482 in the testament of Bartolomeo Manzoli (d. 1482), a wealthy member of the city's government magistracy (the *Anziani*) and cousin of Bartolomeo Felicini.[16] The construction of the chapel was concluded by the early 1480s, while the painting was only executed around 1490 for Bartolomeo's widow, the Ferrarese noblewoman Francesca Sacrati (d. 1508).[17] When implementing the wishes of her deceased husband, Francesca opted for an altarpiece that reflected the latest artistic trends proliferating in the city and that could confer a "modern look" to the chapel built in the previous years by Bartolomeo Manzoli. The original altarpiece by Francia was composed of a central panel depicting

13 On the Felicini altarpiece, see Negro and Roio, *Francesco Francia*, 134–138, cat. 8a–e; Bentini, [et al.] eds., *Pinacoteca*, vol. 1, 356–360, cat. 156a–b; Cavalca, *La pala d'altare*, 347–348, cat. 37.

14 "La prima tavola che egli [Francia] facesse fu una tavola non molto grande a messer Bartolomeo Felsini che la pose nella Misericordia [...] la qual opera, da lui fatta l'anno 1490, piacque talmente in Bologna che messer Giovanni Bentivogli, desideroso di onorar l'opere di questo nuovo pittore la cappella sua in S. Iacopo, gli fece fare in una tavola una Nostra Donna in aria e due figure per lato con due angeli da basso che suonano," Vasari, *Le vite*, vol. 3, 583–584.

15 For a stylistic analysis of the Felicini-Ringhieri altarpiece, see Cavalca, *La pala d'altare*, 193–199.

16 The testament of Bartolomeo Manzoli is in ASBo, *Famiglia Bentivoglio-Manzoli*, 1, busta 6, n. 34, (partly published by Delbianco, "Le chiese," 256, n. 18; Cavalca, *La pala d'altare*, 387). Bartolomeo's aunt, Dorotea, married Bartolomeo Felicini's father, Giovanni Felicini Senior, see Carrati, *Genealogie*, ms. 699, plate 87 and ms. 700, plate 4.

17 Da Bergamo, *Libro di Memorie*, f. 7.

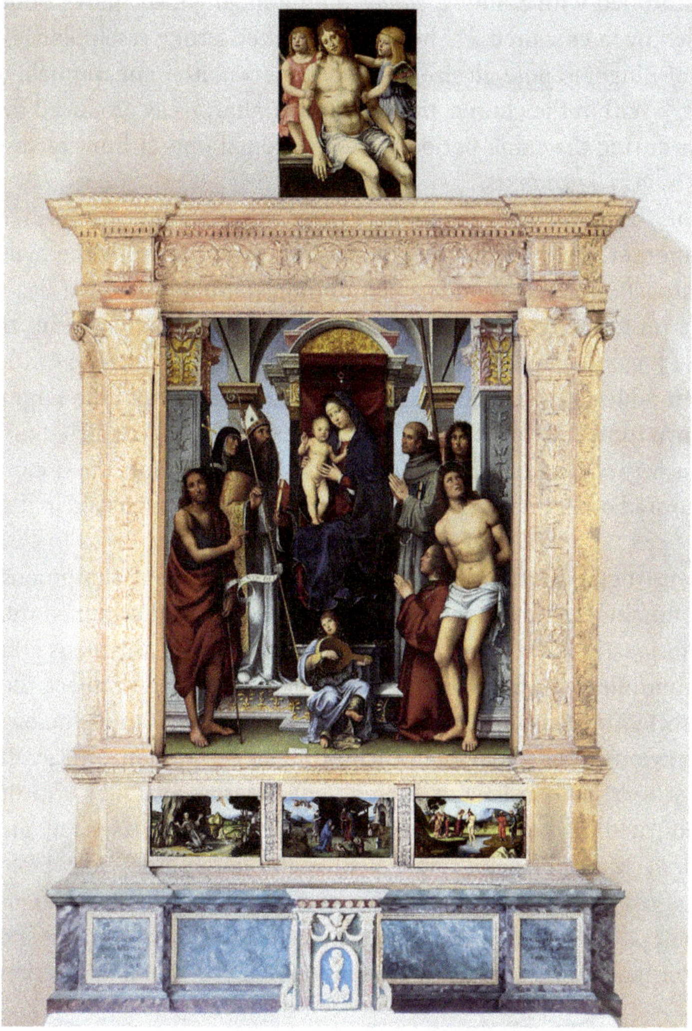

FIGURE 4.3 Francesco Raibolini (known as Francia, ca. 1447–1517), *Virgin and Child Enthroned with Saint John the Baptist, Saint Augustine, Saint Monica, Saint Proculus, Saint Francis, Saint Sebastian, the Donor and An Angel* [main panel], ca. 1490, oil on panel, 186.5 × 159 cm, Pinacoteca Nazionale di Bologna, Bologna; *Imago Pietatis* [cimasa], 1490, oil on wood, 83 × 63 cm, Pinacoteca Nazionale di Bologna, Bologna; *Stigmatization of Saint Francis* [predella left panel], 1490, oil on wood, 29.4 × 55.5 cm, Alana Collection, Newark (Delaware); *Nativity of Christ* [predella central panel], 1490, oil on wood, 32 × 55 cm, Kelvingrove Art Gallery and Museum, Glasgow; *Baptism of Christ* [predella right panel], 1490, oil on wood, 32.5 × 55.5 cm, Museu Calouste Gulbenkian, Lisbon
RECONSTRUCTION © THE AUTHOR

a Madonna enthroned with Saints, a *cimasa* and a large gilded frame, both lost but recorded by later sources.[18] The work presented strong resemblances with the Felicini-Ringhieri *pala*, in size, format, subject matter and, probably, carved framing.[19] Within the church, the two similar altarpieces produced by the same artist during the same period were positioned one in front of the other, working as visual *pendants*.

The effect of the decorative ensemble at the Misericordia was further enhanced by another work painted by Francia some years later for the high altar of the church. Between 1498 and 1499, Anton Galeazzo Bentivoglio (1472–1525), apostolic protonotary and second born of the city's ruler, Giovanni II Bentivoglio (1443–1508), commissioned Francesco Francia and Lorenzo Costa (1460–1535) to produce a large altarpiece intended as an *ex-voto* to the Virgin for his safe return from the Holy Land.[20] The altarpiece (fig. 4.4) depicted the scene of the *Nativity of Christ* and included among the holy group, the donor, Anton Galeazzo, and other members of the Bentivoglio family portrayed in the guise of saints.

The new Bentivoglio *pala* constituted the largest and more sumptuous altarpiece commissioned from Francia at the Misericordia and occupied the most prestigious location in the church, simultaneously acting as a pious gesture and a celebration of the family ruler.[21] In implementing their project, the Bentivoglio resorted to that same painter—Francia—and the same typology of altarpiece previously chosen by the Felicini-Ringhieri and Manzoli-Sacrati families. This search for consistency thereby engendered a subtle form of direct emulation within the church: originally aligned in the transept, the Felicini-Ringhieri, Manzoli-Sacrati and Bentivoglio altarpieces inevitably induced a visual comparison of the magnificence of the works and, by extension, that of their patrons. Within the same space, the Misericordia *pale* made evident the interplay between collective affiliation and individual distinction

18 Malvasia, *Pitture*, 216–218; see also Cavalca, *La pala d'altare*, 348.

19 Negro and Roio, *Francesco Francia*, 138–140, cat. 9; Bentini [et al.], eds., *Pinacoteca*, vol. 1, 360–362, cat. 157; and Cavalca, *La pala d'altare*, 348–349, cat. 38, who suggested a resemblance between the lost Manzoli frame and the woodcarving of the Felicini-Ringhieri altarpiece.

20 On the Bentivoglio altarpiece, see Negro and Roio, *Francesco Francia*, 144–146, cat. 14; Bentini [et al.], eds., *Pinacoteca*, vol. 1, 364–365, cat. 159; Cavalca, *La pala d'altare*, 218–224, 358–359, cat. 54. For its commission and the travel of Anton Galeazzo Bentivoglio to Jerusalem (also mentioned in the inscription at the base of the altarpiece's frame), see Lamo, *Graticola*, 64–65; Dalla Tuata, *Istoria di Bologna*, 399; Alberti, *Historie di Bologna*, 124–125; Vasari, *Le Vite*, vol. 3, 584; Ghirardacci, *Historia di Bologna*, 294–295.

21 Cavalca, *La pala d'altare*, 358.

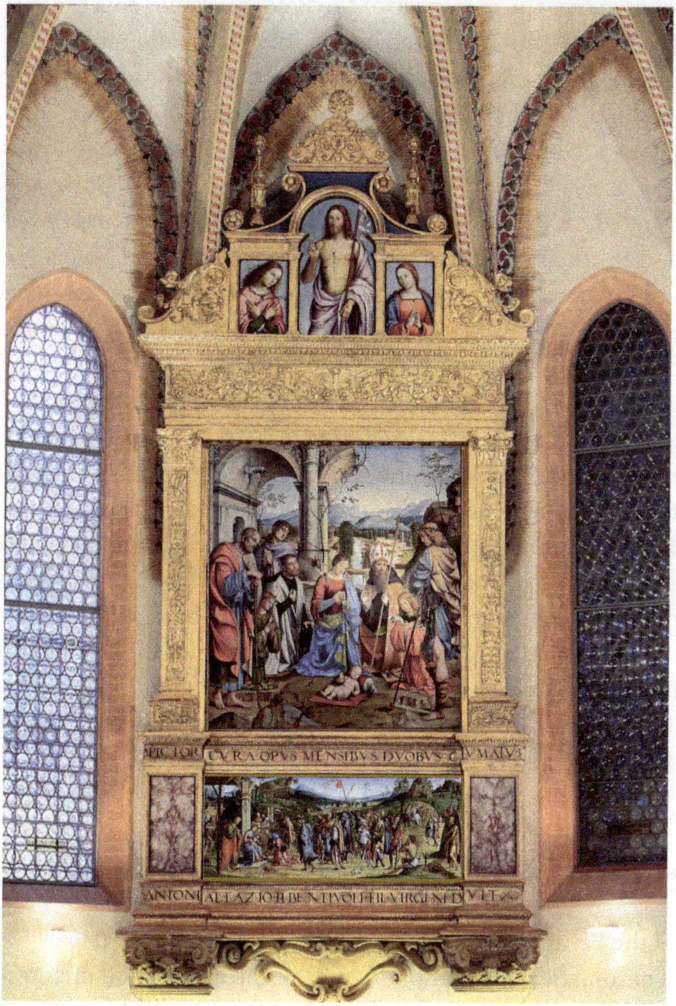

FIGURE 4.4 Francesco Raibolini (known as Francia, ca. 1447–1517), *Adoration of the Child with Saint Joseph, Saint Francis, Saint Augustine, the Donors* [central panel], 1498–99, oil on panel, 209.3 × 190 cm, Pinacoteca Nazionale di Bologna, Bologna; Lorenzo Costa, *The Risen Christ between Saint Gabriel the Archangel and the Virgin Annunciate* [cimasa], 1498–1499, oil on wood, respectively 105 × 55 cm, 56 × 35 cm, 56 × 35 cm, high altar, Church of Santa Maria della Misericordia, Bologna; Lorenzo Costa, *Adoration of the Magi* [predella], 1499, oil on panel, 75 × 181.3 cm, Pinacoteca di Brera, Milan. *Reconstruction*
PHOTO © THE AUTHOR

that involved in those years the patronage of the Bolognese elite on a broader scale. These interventions were motivated by the wish of the donors, such as the Felicini-Ringhieri, to display innovative artistic solutions, which could showcase their cultural and social ambitions; at the same time, these commissions adhered to a common language that signaled that their patrons belonged to an exclusive social group. Comparable altarpieces by Costa and Francia were exhibited on the high altars of prestigious churches and basilicas of the city and in the new chapels of the most distinguished Bolognese families, including the *cappella* of the Bentivoglio at San Giacomo Maggiore (1493–1494), the Paltroni in San Martino Maggiore (1506), the chapel of the merchant Francesco Ghedini in San Giovanni in Monte (1497) and that of the wealthy senator Mino De' Rossi at San Petronio (1492), among others.[22] These works testify to a shared taste that from the 1490s gradually became popular in Bologna and which found in the civic elite one of its main promoters. This wider phenomenon found a quasi-systematic response in the Misericordia, whose reconstruction gave the urban elite a platform on which their patronage could directly interact and, in a sense, collaborate with one another. It is by no means a coincidence that in the church the exception to this pattern can be traced in the commission of one of the few non-aristocratic Misericordia patrons, the poet and merchant, Girolamo Pandolfi (known as Casio; 1467–1533), who turned to a foreign painter, the Milanese Giovanni Antonio Boltraffio (1467–1516), for his altarpiece (1500).[23]

2 The Misericordia following 1506

In 1506, the fall of the Bentivoglio and the establishment of the new papal government did not automatically determine a shift in the artistic and architectural trends in the city, nor in the decoration of the Misericordia. Many of the choices that characterized the urban elite at the Misericordia persisted in the commissions of the patrons gravitating around the renewed papal administration, including some of its highest-ranking members.

Giovanni Gozzadini (1477–1517) was one of such figure. Of crucial importance in the reformed Bolognese society, he was lecturer in Law at the *Studium*,

22 On these examples, see the entries in Cavalca, *La pala d'altare*.

23 The chapel was allocated to Girolamo's brother, Francesco Casio, and his wife Laura at the end of the fifteenth century, see Cavalca, *La pala d'altare*, 224–225, 362–363, cat. 58. On the Casio altarpiece (today at the Musée du Louvre) and its patron, see Berselli, "Un committente"; Ballarin, [et al.], eds., *Leonardo a Milano*; Luzio and Renier, *La coltura*, 196 ff.

apostolic protonotary and datary, and archdeacon of the city. Having started his career in the Roman Curia, Gozzadini returned to Bologna as one of Julius II's most trusted men.[24] On 11 November 1506, he led the triumphal parade organized to acclaim the papal "reconquest" of the city, preceding the Pope and throwing celebrative gold and silver coins to the crowds.[25] Gozzadini's return to Bologna was marked by ambitious artistic commissions, including the refashioning of the church of San Bartolomeo in Porta Ravegnana, the transformation of the related priory house into a splendid palace, and the construction of a new sepulchral chapel. As his burial site Gozzadini chose, and probably not by chance, the Misericordia. Between 1512 and 1516, Gozzadini renounced the patronage rights of the chapel previously owned by his father in the church and invested a substantial amount of money (2,100 Bolognese *lire*) to construct and decorate a new, sumptuous space that could suit and reflect his social aspirations and political rank.[26] Notably, the chosen forms for the Gozzadini's novel chapel were those previously introduced by the Felicini-Ringhieri. The Gozzadini chapel (fig. 4.5) faithfully replicated the architectural scheme of the first *cappella* built in the 1490s by Bartolomeo Felicini and Dorotea Ringhieri. The overall architectural resemblance was presumably encouraged by the Misericordia friars, who likely wished to maintain formal consistency within the southern aisle of their church. Yet, the correspondences between the two chapels extended to very specific solutions, including the glass window of the central lunette and the project for the altarpiece, which both involved, once again, Francesco Francia. Francia provided the cartoon for the polychrome window featuring the chapel's patron (the Virgin) and painted the predella of the altarpiece with a highly unusual and sophisticated iconography

24 On Giovanni Gozzadini, see Dalla Tuata, *Istoria di Bologna*, 440, 637; Dolfi, *Cronologia*, 384; Ciuccarelli, "Giovanni Gozzadini."

25 "Poi il pontefice era portato sopra una sedia di velluto cremese [...] avanti a lui andava Giovanni Gozzadini datario del papa, con un altro, spargendo del popolo danari d'argento et d'oro, la qual moneta da una parte haveva queste lettere: BONONIA PER JULIUM A TYRANNO LIBERATA, et dall'altra: JULIUS II PONT. MAX.: si gettarono in tutto tre mila ducati fra oro et moneta," Ghirardacci, *Historia di Bologna*, 355; see also Alberti, *Historie di Bologna*, 210–211.

26 "Reverendissimus dominus D. Iohannes Gozadinus prothonotarius et tunc Regis gubernator, filius domini Bernardini de Gozadinis, ab anno 1512 in diem x Iulii 1516, vice capelle quam alias acceptatam per dictum dominum Bernardinum [...] ipse renuntiavit, construi fecit capellam Conceptionis beate Virginis in nostra ecclesia pulcherrimam et adornatam tabula seu anchona. In que omnia expendit libras 2100 bononinorum," Da Bergamo, *Libro di Memorie*, f. 23.

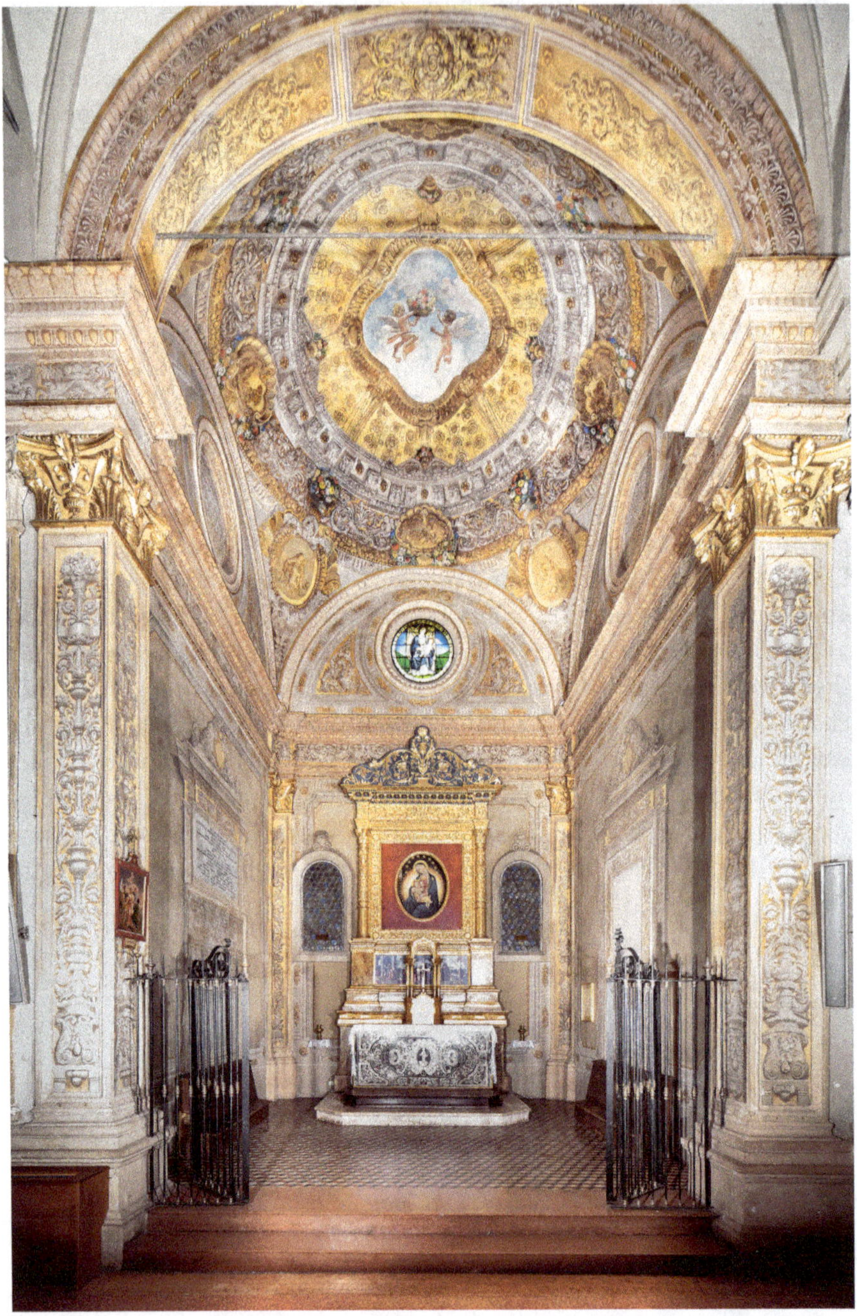

FIGURE 4.5 Gozzadini chapel, 1512–1516, Church of Santa Maria della Misericordia, Bologna, frontal view
PHOTO © THE AUTHOR

(1514–1516?).[27] The new altarpiece was meant to comprise a detached fresco with a *Nursing Madonna* (1397) by Lippo di Dalmasio (ca. 1352–d. before 1421) framed by a carved woodwork attributed to Andrea Marchesi (known as Formigine; ca. 1485–1559).[28] The new predella referenced some of the solutions employed earlier in the Misericordia altarpieces, especially in the representations of the Nativities of the Bentivoglio's main panel and Felicini's predella. The panel, like the rest of the Gozzadini altarpiece and chapel, presented elements of iconographical and formal novelty, but also adapted to pre-existing schemes—stylistically and formally, Gozzadini's choices set in line with those promoted by the former Misericordia donors, including the Bentivoglio. Notwithstanding his many years in Rome, Gozzadini did not try to counter, for taste or ideological reasons, with the artistic trend that distinguished the Bolognese elite of the previous period, on the contrary, he embraced it.

The construction of the funerary chapel of the distinguished apostolic datary at the Misericordia attracted the attention of prospective patrons and further enhanced the prestige of the site in Bologna. Six years after Gozzadini's death (1517), Giovanni Battista Malavolta (d. 1533), a juriconsult and doctor in law at the University, entrusted in his last will (dated 26 March 1523) the Augustinian friars of the Misericordia with the construction of a new chapel in their church. Malavolta had already acquired a funerary chapel in the Augustinian basilica of San Giacomo Maggiore, where his effigy and sepulchral monument (ca. 1533) are extant. In 1523, Malavolta decided to build an additional family chapel in the increasingly popular church of the Misericordia, for which he left specific instructions: his testament established that within six years after the passage of his inheritance from his widow to the Augustinians, the latter party had to construct a chapel located between the *cappella* of the Gozzadini and that of the Felicini (fig. 4.1). Most significantly, the document specified that the chapel could not be inferior ("non minoris") in any way—value, price and splendor—to that of the Gozzadini, with regard to both its paintings and to

27 The predella merges the representation of the Nativity of Christ with the apocryphal scene of Saint Augustine in a state of doubt between the blood of Christ and the milk of the Virgin. The painting is currently dated to 1508, but is most likely ascribable to the 1510s when the Gozzadini chapel was constructed. In 1880, the predella was substituted by a copy and moved to the Pinacoteca Nazionale, see Negro and Roio, *Francesco Francia*, 187; Bentini [et al.], eds. *Pinacoteca*, vol. 1, 375–376, cat. 165.

28 The provenance of the detached fresco is unknown, but the sources suggest a previous location in the apse of the Misericordia, see Malvasia, *Felsina Pittrice*, 293. Malvasia also notes that the fresco was then retouched by Bagnacavallo. For the Gozzadini glass window, see Medica, "Francesco Francia," 55–56.

other ornaments ("tam in picturis quam in aliis ornamentis").[29] The testamentary provision is extremely interesting in this respect, as it openly expresses the patron's intentions and his deliberate and conspicuously comparative approach: a faithful resemblance of the Malavolta chapel with the commissions of the previous Misericordia patrons is not only implied by visual evidence, nor imposed by the Order, but explicitly requested, on paper, by the donor himself.

Many years passed before the provisions set out in Malavolta's 1523 will were fulfilled and his chapel built. Construction in the church could only begin in the 1550s, after the death of his wife and the allocation of his inheritance to the Misericordia friars.[30] In the years that separated the building of the Gozzadini chapel from the commission and later completion of the Malavolta *cappella*, cultural climate in Bologna had changed. The second and third decades of the Cinquecento saw an increasing interest by artists, and demand by patrons, of the artistic novelties of the Papal Court. The "Roman taste", that gradually spread following the political reformation of Bologna, found its main protagonists in artists like Innocenzo Francucci (known as da Imola; ca. 1490–1545), Biagio Pupini (fl. 1511–1551), and Girolamo Marchesi (known as Cotignola; ca. 1480–1550), who could provide patrons with local, yet faithful, interpretations of the latest Roman, and especially Raphaelesque works.[31]

The ongoing change of actors in Bolognese art also progressively involved the decoration of the Misericordia. Following the death of Francesco Francia in 1517, the church donors looked to the painter Bartolomeo Ramenghi (known as Bagnacavallo Senior; 1484–1542) for the realization of their new altarpieces.[32] The artist was entrusted with the commission of at least two paintings for the Misericordia: one for the chapel dedicated to Saint Nicholas of Tolentino, likely under the patronage of the Zamboli family, the other for the *cappella* of Saint

29 "Item dominus testator reliquit [...] fieri facere eius impensis in ipsa ecclesia Sancte Marie de Misericordia unam pulcram et honorabilem cappellam non minoris pretii, valoris et estimationis et pulchritudinis quam sit illa de Gozadinis sita in dicta ecclesia tam in picturis quam in aliis ornamentis [...] et quod ea debeat construi infra capellam illorum de Felicinis et capellam illorum de Gozadinis," ASBo, Demaniale, *San Giacomo*, 28/1634, n. 65, ff. 3v–4r.

30 The construction of the Malavolta chapel is fully documented by an extant expense book, which allows us to date the building works between 1552/1554 and 1557, ASBo, Demaniale, *San Biagio e Santa Maria della Misericordia*, 1/7076, n. 76 (in Malaguzzi Valeri, *L'architettura a Bologna*, 89–90).

31 On this topic, see Bernardini, *Antefatti bolognesi*; Perini Folesani, *Carmi di Raffaello*.

32 Bernardini, *Il Bagnacavallo*; Ugolini, "Ramenghi, Bartolomeo."

Monica, recently acquired by the Parati.[33] In spite of the variation in authorship, the new interventions did not distance themselves entirely from the previous decoration of the church, as the case of the Parati altarpiece confirms. In 1520, Francesco di Filippo Parati (d. 1540), a doctor in law and member of the new senatorial government formed by Julius II, accepted the patronage rights of the Misericordia chapel, which he soon after endowed with "an altarpiece featuring portraits of himself, his wife and his son."[34] The original features of the disassembled altarpiece can be inferred from a drawing, currently at the Uffizi (fig. 4.6).[35] The sheet illustrates the project for a large *pala* comprising a main panel with the *Coronation of the Virgin* and a *cimasa* with a *Pietà*, framed by architectural woodwork, and accompanied by measures in Bolognese feet.[36] Remarkably, the ensemble shows close similarities with the *pale* conceived for the Misericordia in the previous years. Notably, the rectangular central panel, the crowning *Imago Pietatis* and the gilded frame repeat those of the Felicini-Ringhieri (fig. 4.3), Bentivoglio (fig. 4.4), and probably Manzoli-Sacrati altarpieces. The similarity is particularly striking upon comparison with the surviving frames of the Bentivoglio and Felicini-Ringhieri altarpieces and its *cimasa*, which features an almost identical representation to the Uffizi drawing. Such correlations seem to imply Bagnacavallo's close study of the existing decoration of the church and especially of the altarpieces previously conceived by Francia. Three decades after Francia's interventions, the Uffizi

33 The Zamboli chapel was built between 1478 and 1480 by Bartolomeo Fantuzzi and changed patronage in the sixteenth century, when new donations by Elisabetta Zamboli (1506) and her niece Barbara (1531) are recorded, see Da Bergamo, *Libro di Memorie*, f. 21. The main panel was identified with a painting currently in Pinacoteca Nazionale, see Bentini [et al.], eds., *Pinacoteca*, vol. 2, 46–47, cat. 31; Bernardini, *Il Bagnacavallo*, 110–111, cat. 32; Lucco, "Innocenzo da Imola," 190–191 attributed the painting to Girolamo da Treviso Junior. The altarpiece is described by Cavazzoni, *Pitture*; Malvasia, *Pitture*, 218.

34 "Die 20 Iulii 1520 [...] acceptavit in nostra ecclesia capellam Sancte Monice quam mox satis pulcra anchona seu tabula decoravit [...]; adornavit insfrascriptam capellam *anchona in qua est ipsius, uxoris sue, ac filii sui imago* et argenteo calice in quo est eius insigne et patena," (italics mine), see Da Bergamo, *Libro di Memorie*, f. 26. This new document helps to redate the painting previously ascribed to the 1530s.

35 The extant main panel depicting *The Coronation of the Virgin with Saint Monica, Saint Francis and three donors* today hangs on the north wall of the Manzoli chapel at the Misericordia.

36 Faietti, ed., *Il Cinquecento a Bologna*, 122, cat. 24. The relationship between the drawing and the Parati altarpiece was first suggested by Bernardini in Fortunati Pietrantonio, ed., *Pittura bolognese*, vol. 1, 124–125, also Bernardini, *Il Bagnacavallo*, 106–108, cat. 30; Cavalca, *La pala d'altare*, 61–62. The identification and attribution to Bagnacavallo is refused by Lucco, "I due Girolami," 172, n. 22, who, however, correctly dates the altarpiece to the 1520s.

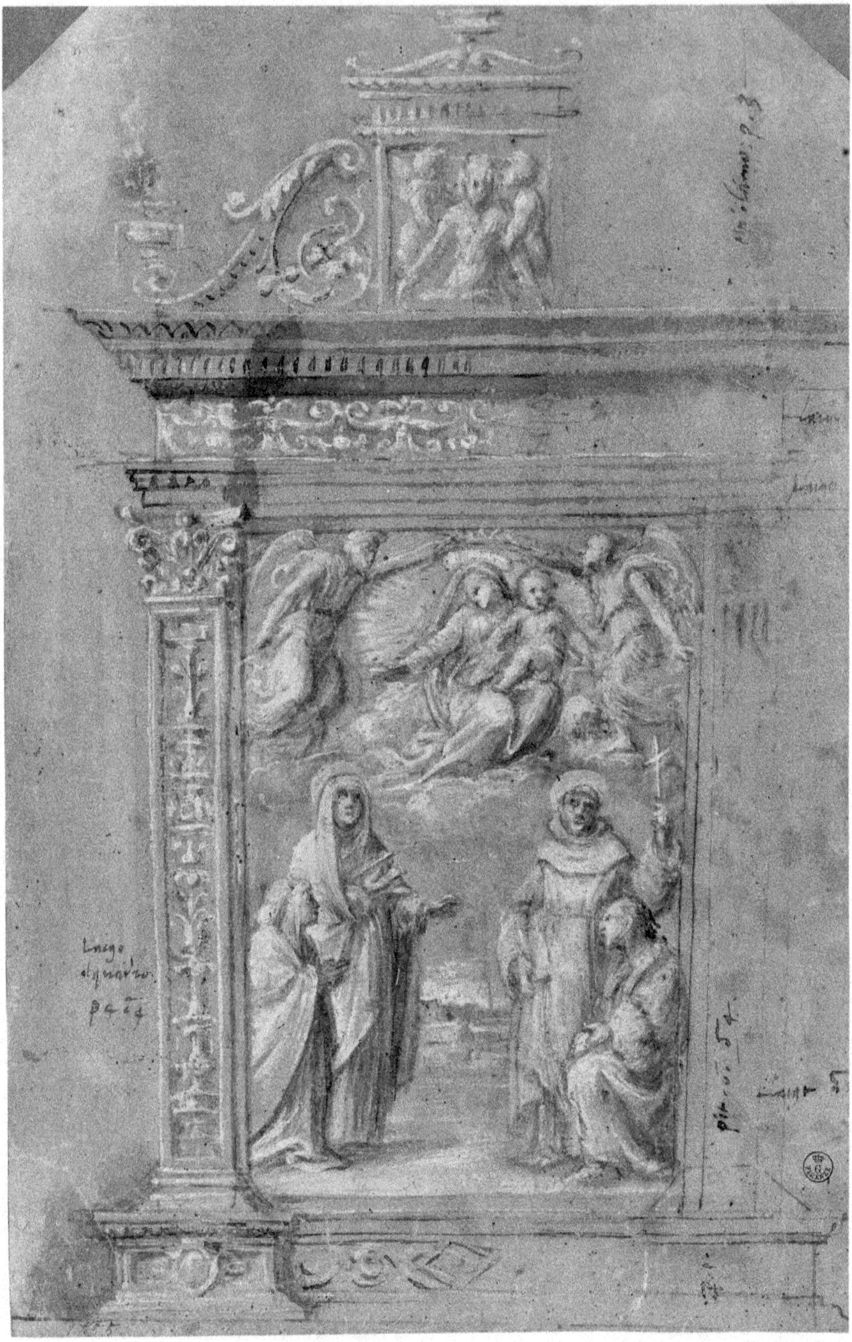

FIGURE 4.6 Bartolomeo Ramenghi (known as Bagnacavallo Senior, 1484–1542), *Design for an altarpiece*, early 1520s, ink and gouache on brown paper, 370 × 240 mm
GABINETTO DEI DISEGNI E DELLE STAMPE DELLE GALLERIE DEGLI UFFIZI, FLORENCE

drawing suggests a persisting willingness of patrons, and artists, to maintain a certain consistency in forms within the Misericordia.

3 The Misericordia and the Bolognese Urban Elite: A Collective Work

In less than thirty years, the interventions of the Bolognese urban elite had transformed the abandoned peripheral church of the Misericordia into a lively artistic center. The refashioning of the church attracted patrons of the highest caliber: from the ruling family of the Bentivoglio and the apostolic protonotary Giovanni Gozzadini to the cultivated senator Francesco Parati. The church's donors constituted a representative sample of Bolognese highest society and its variety. Its dynamics followed and mimicked the artistic fashions and patronage relationships that involved Bologna on a broader scale. The interventions promoted in the church reveal the establishment of a consistent artistic and architectural language with which the Bolognese urban elite came to identify and that found their spokesmen in artists like Francia. These examples testify to a collective form of patronage, which was often stimulated, albeit not determined, by a distinguished presence—be it the Felicini, Bentivoglio or Gozzadini.

In the Misericordia church, patrons combined to create a final collective and cohesive work. Artistic consistency was not enforced by the religious Order, but intentionally pursued by donors, as the documents confirm. This joint effort was certainly not lacking in individual ambition, which clearly manifested in personal artistic choices of particular splendor as in the prominent display of the arms and portraits of the patrons. From the 1470s, their *insigna* started to be affixed to the capitals, nave and portico of the Misericordia, while their likenesses populated almost every altarpiece completed after 1490, including the Felicini-Ringhieri, Bentivoglio, Casio, Parati and Zamboli and the lost painting of De' Turchi family, which featured "the image of Saint Stephen protomartyr and at his sides the patron [Giuseppe] and his father Stefano de' Turchi."[37]

The collective language and patronage of the Bolognese elite survived the important transitions that followed 1506. In the city, as in the Misericordia church, the political shift was not marked immediately by an artistic fracture, but, rather, was hidden by resilient continuity.

---

37 "[…] ducati centum auri in una pulchra anchona in qua picta sint imago sancti Stephani prothomartiris et ab eius lateribus imagines ipsius, ac domini Shephani de' Turchi patris sui," Da Bergamo, *Libro di Memorie*, f. 38.

In the following years, Bologna was gradually transformed by the construction of new senatorial palaces, prestigious chapels and *pale*, such as the *cappella* designed by Baldassarre Peruzzi (1481–1536) for the nobleman Ludovico Ghisilardi (d. 1531) in 1530.[38] The Misericordia remained a lasting reminder of the transitional moment that characterized the city at the turn of the Cinquecento, in which the reformed political milieu of the city coexisted and merged almost seamlessly with the artistic inheritance of the preceding era. Until its suppression in 1796, the church, its chapels and altarpieces displayed, one next to the other, the traces of the old "signorial" regime and the glories of papal domination—visual testimony of Bologna's unique history and art.

Bibliography

Ady, Cecilia. *The Bentivoglio of Bologna. A Study in Despotism.* London: Oxford University Press, 1937.

Alberti, Leandro. *Historie di Bologna. 1479–1543 [ante 1543]*, edited by Armando Antonelli and Maria Rosaria Musti. Bologna: Costa, 2006.

Ballarin, Alessandro, [et al.] eds. *Leonardo a Milano. Problemi di leonardismo milanese tra Quattrocento e Cinquecento. Giovanni Antonio Boltraffio prima della pala Casio.* Verona: Edizioni dell'Aurora, 2010.

Basile, Bruno, ed. *Bentivolorum Magnificentia. Principe e Cultura a Bologna nel Rinascimento.* Rome: Bulzoni, 1984.

Benati, Daniele, and Giacomo Calogero, eds. *Arte e Umanesimo a Bologna (1460–1530): Materiali e nuove prospettive.* Bologna: Bononia University Press, 2020.

Bentini, Jadranka, [et al.] eds. *Pinacoteca Nazionale di Bologna: Catalogo generale.* 1. *Dal Duecento a Francesco Francia.* Venice: Marsilio, 2004.

Bentini, Jadranka, [et al.] eds. *Pinacoteca Nazionale di Bologna: Catalogo generale.* 2. *Da Raffaello ai Carracci.* Venice: Marsilio, 2006.

Bernardini, Carla. *Il Bagnacavallo Senior. Bartolomeo Ramenghi, pittore (1484?–1542?).* Rimini: Luisè, 1990.

Bernardini, Carla. "Antefatti Bolognese: Una traccia." In *L'Estasi di Santa Cecilia di Raffaello da Urbino nella Pinacoteca Nazionale di Bologna*, edited by Carla Bernardini, Andrea Emiliani and Gabriella Zarri, 2–19. Bologna: Nuova Alfa, 1983.

Berselli, Elisabetta. "Un committente e un pittore alle soglie del Cinquecento: Girolamo Casio e Giovanni Antonio Boltraffio." *Schede Umanistiche* 2 (1997): 123–143.

38 Bettini, *Baldassarre Peruzzi.*

Bettini, Sergio. *Baldassare Peruzzi e la Cappella Ghisilardi*. Parma: Diabasis, 2003.

Bettini, Sergio. *Palazzo Ghisilardi. Il sogno rinascimentale di un notaio bolognese*. Ferrara: Edisai, 2004.

Bettini, Sergio. *Il palazzo dei diamanti a Bologna. La committenza artistica di Nicolò Sanuti nell'età dei Bentivoglio*. Parma: Diabasis, 2017.

Bondini, Saida. "Linguaggi architettonici e dinamiche di committenza: La cappella Felicini-Ringhieri nella chiesa di Santa Maria della Misericordia." In *Arte e Umanesimo a Bologna (1460–1530): Materiali e nuove prospettive*, edited by Daniele Benati and Giacomo Calogero, 233–260. Bologna: Bononia University Press, 2020.

Carrati, Baldassarre Antonio Maria. *Genealogie delle famiglie bolognesi, 18th c.*, Biblioteca Comunale dell'Archiginnasio di Bologna, mss. B 699–735.

Castelnuovo, Guido. *Être noble dans la cité: Les noblesses italiennes en quête d'identité (XIII*e*–XV*e *siècle)*. Paris: Garnier, 2014.

Cavalca, Cecilia. *La pala d'altare a Bologna nel Rinascimento. Opere, artisti e città 1450–1500*. Milan: Silvana, 2013.

Cavalca, Cecilia. "Dentro e Fuori il Palazzo. Ricchezza Privata e Magnificenza pubblica a Bologna: Alcuni esempi attorno e oltre ai Bentivoglio." In *The Taste of Virtuosi: Collezionismo e mecenatismo in Italia 1400–1900*, edited by Andrea Leonardi, 17–34. Florence: Edifir, 2018.

Cavazzoni, Francesco. *Pitture et sculture et altre cose notabili che sono in Bologna e dove si trovano* [1603], edited by Marinella Pigozzi. Bologna: CLUEB, 1999.

Ciuccarelli, Cecilia. "Giovanni Gozzadini." In *Dizionario Biografico degli Italiani*, vol. 58. Rome: Istituto della Enciclopedia italiana, (2002).

Clarke, Georgia. "Magnificence and the City: Giovanni II Bentivoglio and Architecture in Fifteenth-Century Bologna." *Renaissance Studies* 13 (1999): 397–411.

Clarke, Georgia. "Giovanni II Bentivoglio and the Uses of Chivalry Towards the Creation of a 'Republican Court' in Fifteenth-Century Bologna." In *Artistic Exchange and Cultural Translation in the Italian Renaissance City*, edited by. Stephen J. Campbell and Stephen J. Milner, 162–186. Cambridge: Cambridge University Press, 2004.

Colliva, Paolo. "Bologna dal XIV al XVIII secolo: governo misto o signoria senatoria?" In *Storia dell'Emilia Romagna*, edited by Aldo Berselli, 12–34. Bologna: Bononia University Press, 1976–1977.

Da Bergamo, Vincenzo. *Libro di Memorie*, 1558, Archivio di Stato di Bologna, Demaniale, *Miscellanea delle corporazioni religiose soppresse*, busta 4.

Dalla Tuata, Fileno. *Istoria di Bologna* [*ante* 1521], edited by Bruno Fortunato. Bologna: Costa, 2005.

De Benedictis, Angela. "Quale *corte* per quale *signoria*?" In *Bentivolorum Magnificentia. Principe e cultura a Bologna nel Rinascimento*, edited by Bruno Basile, 13–33. Rome: Bulzoni, 1984.

De Benedictis, Angela. "'… sendo la parte de' Bentivoglio confirmata et unita': per una storia del costituirsi dei rapporti di potere in una realtà della prima età moderna." In *"Familia" del principe e famiglia aristocratica*, vol. 2, 437–469. Rome: Bulzoni, 1988.

De Benedictis, Angela. "Il governo misto." In *Storia di Bologna 3. Bologna nell'età moderna*, vol. 1, 201–269. Bologna: Bononia University Press, 2008.

De Benedictis, Angela. "Popular Government, Government of the *Ottimati*, and the Languages of Politics: Concord and Discord (1377–1559)." In *A Companion to Medieval and Renaissance Bologna*, edited by Sarah Rubin Blanshei, 289–309. Leiden and Boston: Brill, 2018.

Delbianco, Maria. "Le chiese di S. Martino Maggiore e di S. Maria della Misericordia." *Strenna storica bolognese* 45 (1995): 245–257.

Dolfi, Pompeo Scipione. *Cronologia delle famiglie nobili di Bologna*. Bologna: Ferroni, 1670.

Donati, Claudio. *L'idea di nobiltà in Italia* (*secoli XIV–XVIII*). Rome and Bari: Laterza, 1995.

Drogin, David J. "Bologna's Bentivoglio Family and Its Artists: Overview of a Quattrocento Court in the Making." In *Artists at Court. Image Making and Identity 1300–1550*, edited by Stephen J. Campbell, 72–90. Boston: Isabella Stewart Gardner Museum, 2004.

Drogin, David J. "Art, Patronage and Civic Identity in Renaissance Bologna." In *The Court Cities of Northern Italy*, edited by Charles M. Rosenberg, 244–324. Cambridge: Cambridge University Press, 2010.

Drogin, David J. "The Fifteenth-Century Bentivoglio: Art Patronage, Rulership, and Emulation." In *Bologna. Cultural Crossroads from the Medieval to the Baroque: Recent Anglo-American Scholarship*, edited by Gian Mario Anselmi, Angela de Benedictis, Nicholas Terpstra, 85–96. Bologna: Bononia University Press, 2013.

Drogin, David J. "Art and Patronage in Bologna's 'Long' Quattrocento." In *A Companion to Medieval and Renaissance Bologna*, edited by Sarah Rubin Blanshei, 559–600. Leiden and Boston: Brill, 2018.

Duranti, Tommaso. *Diplomazia e autogoverno a Bologna nel Quattrocento* (*1392–1466*). Bologna: CLUEB, 2009.

Duranti, Tommaso. "*Libertas*, Oligarchy, Papacy: Government in the Quattrocento." In *A Companion to Medieval and Renaissance Bologna*, edited by Sarah Rubin Blanshei, 260–288. Leiden and Boston: Brill, 2018.

Emiliani, Andrea. *La stagione dei Bentivoglio nella Bologna rinascimentale*. Bologna: Minerva, 2006.

Faietti, Marzia, ed. *Il Cinquecento a Bologna. Disegni dal Louvre e dipinti a confronto*. Milan: Electa, 2002.

Fanti, Mario. "Chi fu il committente del 'San Rocco' del Parmigianino in San Petronio?" *Strenna storica bolognese* 66 (2016): 171–181.

Fortunati Pietrantonio, Vera, ed. *Pittura bolognese del '500*. Bologna: Grafis, 1986, 2 vols.

Gamberini, Elisa. "Il complesso di Santa Maria della Misericordia di Bologna attraverso i suoi documenti." *I quaderni del M.A.E.S.* 10 (2007): 141–161.

Gardi, Andrea. "Making of an Oligarchy: The Ruling Classes of Bologna." In *A Companion to Medieval and Renaissance Bologna*, edited by Sarah Rubin Blanshei, 310–334. Leiden and Boston: Brill, 2018.

Ghirardacci, Cherubino. *Historia di Bologna* [*ante* 1598], edited by Albano Sorbelli. Città di Castello: Lapi, 1915–1932.

Gottarelli, Elena. *La chiesa di Santa Maria della Misericordia attraverso i secoli*. Bologna: Tamari, 1981.

Lamo, Pietro. *Graticola di Bologna: gli edifici e le opere d'arte della città nel 1560* [1560], edited by Marinella Pigozzi. Bologna: CLUEB, 1996.

Lucco, Mauro. "Innocenzo da Imola." *Arte a Bologna* 3 (1993): 185–191.

Lucco, Mauro. "I due Girolami." In *Studi di storia dell'arte in onore di Jürgen Winkelmann*, edited by Sylvie Béguin [et al.], 165–183. Naples: Paparo 1999.

Luzio, Alessandro, and Rodolfo Renier. *La coltura e le relazioni letterarie di Isabella d'Este Gonzaga*. Milan: Bonnard, 2005.

Malaguzzi Valeri, Francesco. *L'architettura a Bologna nel Rinascimento*. Rocco S. Casciano: Cappelli, 1899.

Malvasia, Carlo Cesare. *Pitture, scolture ed architetture delle chiese, luoghi pubblici, palazzi, e case della città di Bologna, e suoi subborghi* [*1686*], edited by Andrea Emiliani. Bologna: Nuova Alfa, 1969.

Malvasia, Carlo Cesare. *Felsina Pittrice. Lives of the Bolognese Painters* [*1678*]. Vol. 1, *Early Bolognese Painting*, edited by Elizabeth Cropper and Lorenzo Pericolo. Turnhout: Harvey Miller, 2012.

Manca, Joseph. *Cosmè Tura. The Art and Life of a Painter in Estense Ferrara*. Oxford: Oxford University Press, 2000.

Medica, Massimo. "Francesco Francia e la produzione vetraria a Bologna." In *Il genio di Francesco Francia. Un orafo pittore nella Bologna del Rinascimento*, edited by Elena Rossoni and Mario Scalini, 53–57. Venice: Marsilio, 2018.

Negro, Emilio, and Nicosetta Roio. *Francesco Francia e la sua scuola*. Modena: Artioli, 1998.

Perini Folesani, Giovanna. "Carmi inediti di Raffaello e sull'arte della prima metà del Cinquecento a Roma e Ferrara e il mondo dei *Coryciana*." *Römisches Jahrbuch der Bibliotheca Hertziana* 32 (1997–1998): 367–407.

Poli, Marco. *La chiesa di Santa Maria della Misericordia*. Bologna: Inchiostri Associati, 1997.

Previtali, Giovanni. "La periodizzazione della storia dell'arte italiana." In *Storia dell'arte italiana*, I. *Materiali e problemi, 1. Questioni e metodi*. Turin: Einaudi, 1979, 5–95.

Raule, Angelo. *La chiesa di Santa Maria della Misericordia in Bologna.* Bologna: Nanni, 1961.

Reinhardt, Nicole. *Macht und Ohnmacht der Verflechtung. Rom und Bologna unter Paul V.* Tübingen: Bibliotheca Academica, 2000.

Robertson, Ian. *Tyranny under the Mantle of St. Peter: Pope Paul II and Bologna.* Turnhout: Brepols, 2002.

Rossoni, Elena. "Raffaello e l'arte a Bologna dopo la cacciata dei Bentivoglio tra Giulio II e Leone X." *Strenna storica Bolognese* 70 (2020): 347–368.

Rubin Blanshei, Sarah. *Politics and Justice in Late Medieval Bologna.* Leiden and Boston: Brill, 2010.

Rubin Blanshei, Sarah, ed. *A Companion to Medieval and Renaissance Bologna.* Leiden and Boston: Brill, 2018.

Sorbelli, Albano. *I Bentivoglio signori di Bologna.* Bologna: Cappelli, 1969.

Sricchia Santoro, Fiorella. "Ricerche intorno all'Antifonario di Leone X della Biblioteca Vaticana." *Prospettiva* 96–96 (1999): 155–168.

Stemp, Richard. "Cosimo Tura and the Sacrati Chapels in Ferrara." *Musei Ferraresi* 17 (1990–1991): 61–69.

Supino, Igino Benvenuto. *L'arte nelle chiese di Bologna: secoli XV–XVI.* Bologna: Zanichelli, 1932–1938.

Terpstra, Nicholas. "'Republics by Contract.' Civil Society in the Papal State." In *Sociability and its Discontents. Civil Society, Social Capital, and Their Alternatives in Late Medieval and Early Modern Europe*, edited by Nicholas Eckstein, Nicholas Terpstra, 293–311. Turnhout: Brepols, 2009.

Ugolini, Andrea. "Ramenghi, Bartolomeo, detto Bagnacavallo Sr." In *Dizionario Biografico degli Italiani*, vol. 86. Rome: Istituto della Enciclopedia italiana, 2016.

Vasari, Giorgio. *Le vite de' più eccellenti pittori, scultori e architettori: nelle redazioni del 1550 e 1568* [1550, 1568], edited by Paola Barocchi and Rosanna Bettarini. Florence: Sansoni, 1966–1987.

CHAPTER 5

"Our Insatiable Desire for All Things Antique": Isabella d'Este as Patron and Collector

Stephen K. Scher

Raised in the sophisticated Este court of Ferrara, the center of a rich humanist culture in the arts, literature and philosophy, Isabella (1474–1539), who was born on the 18th of May 1474, grew to become one of the most fascinating and accomplished persons in the Italian Renaissance.[1] Because of the fortunate survival of much of her voluminous correspondence (16,000 copies of outgoing letters; 28,000 incoming), and the availability of contemporary opinions and descriptions we possess a deep understanding of her character and personality, essential to a study of her collecting and patronage of the arts. We know of her considerable achievements, often under difficult circumstances, as regent of Mantua during the frequent absences of her husband, Francesco II Gonzaga (1466–1519), and as a clever and practiced diplomat, but she was also a poet, accomplished musician, singer, and innovative patron of musicians and composers of secular music,[2] a friend and patron to many of the most distinguished artists, writers, humanists, and political and ecclesiastical dignitaries of the High Renaissance, as well as a devoted mother of eight children, of whom six survived. She was also a well-known arbiter of fashion and a designer not only in Italy, but in many of the European courts.

As well as being highly intelligent, talented, creative, and innovative, a loyal friend, pious and chaste, among other virtues, she was also vain, domineering, and, most importantly, as a collector, determinedly acquisitive, ruthless, and even unscrupulous.

1 "… *lo insociabile desiderio nostro de cose antique.*" Clifford Brown. *Per Dare Qualche Splendore*, 237–238, letter 38c to Nicolò Frisio, Mantua: January 2, 1507. The standard biography of Isabella d'Este is Cartwright. *Isabella d'Este*; other valuable studies include Marek. *The Bed and the Throne*; Fletcher, "Isabella d'Este," 51–64; Alsop, *Rare Art Traditions*, esp. 430–446; San Juan, "The Court Lady's Dilemma," 67–78; *Isabella d'Este: "La prima donna del mondo"*; Jardine, *Worldly Goods*; Welch. *Shopping in the Renaissance*.

2 Fenlon, "The Gonzaga and Music," 87–94; Thornton. *Scholar in His Study*, 122–123; Gallico, "Appunti sulla Musica," 202–207; Shephard, "Constructing Isabella d'Este's Musical Decorum," 684–706.

 | DOI:10.1163/9789004513938_007

1 Representations of Isabella d'Este

We cannot be certain of Isabella's appearance despite the few portraits that exist among the many that were produced and have disappeared.[3] Nor can we rely upon contemporary, flattering descriptions, or the opinions of later biographers. She was very demanding of her portraitists, rejecting a representation by Andrea Mantegna (1431–1506) because she considered it not to be a good likeness. She was thrilled by the widely distributed medal fashioned by Giancristoforo Romano (1456–1512), her own example of which, mounted in gold and jewel-encrusted with her name in diamonds, she placed in her *studiolo* next to a spectacular ancient cameo double portrait, thus associating herself with the ancient world (fig. 5.1).[4]

When Leonardo da Vinci (1452–1519) visited Mantua in 1499, he made a drawing of the marchesa that she approved, but she could never persuade him to do a painted version.[5] Francesco Bonsignori's (1460–1519) preparatory sketch (National Gallery, London) for his altarpiece of the Beata Osanna Andreassi (1449–1505) (Palazzo Ducale, Mantua) is perhaps a more realistic portrayal of the marchesa.[6] One of the most familiar of her portraits was painted by Titian (1490–1576) between 1534 and 1536 and is now in Vienna (Kunsthistorisches Museum).[7] The portrait was not done from life, when Isabella was around 60 years old, but copied from an earlier painting executed in 1511 possibly by Francesco Francia (1450–1517). In a letter to Francia dated November 25th, 1511, Isabella remarks: "And since, through your art, you have made us much more beautiful than nature did, we thank you as much as is possible."[8] She expresses a similar sentiment in a letter of May 29th, 1536 to Benedetto Agnello: "Our portrait by the hand of Titian pleases us so much that we doubt if we were ever

3 *Isabella d'Este: "La prima donna del mondo,"* 86–118; Beverly Brown, "Portraiture at the Courts of Italy," 45–47.

4 *Splendours*, eds. Chambers and Martineau, 55, 168, cat. no. 118; *Isabella d'Este: "La prima donna del mondo,"* 301–304, cat. nos. 96, 97; Syson, "Reading Faces," 281–294; Scher and Ng, *Scher Collection*, 56, cat. no. 31 (entry by Alessandra Di Croce).

5 *Splendours*, eds. Chambers and Martineau, 50; Ames-Lewis. *Isabella & Leonardo*. See also Viatte, *Leonard da Vinci/Isabelle d'Este*.

6 Pouncey, "A Drawing by Bonsignori," 99–101; *Splendours*, eds. Chambers and Martineau, 178–179, cat. nos. 139, 140.

7 *Isabella d'Este: "La prima donna del mondo,"* 111–113; Hickson, "'To see ourselves'," 305–306.

8 Luzio. *La galleria dei Gonzaga*, 212: "Havemo recevuto il ritratto che ni haveti mandato ... avedoni vui cum l'arte vostra facta assai più bella che non ni ha facto natura, ringratiamovine quanto più potemo." Archivio Gonzaga, Archivio di Stato, Mantova, 2996 libro 29 cc.72r–v; ed. and trans. by Shemek. *Selected Letters*, 352, letter 475.

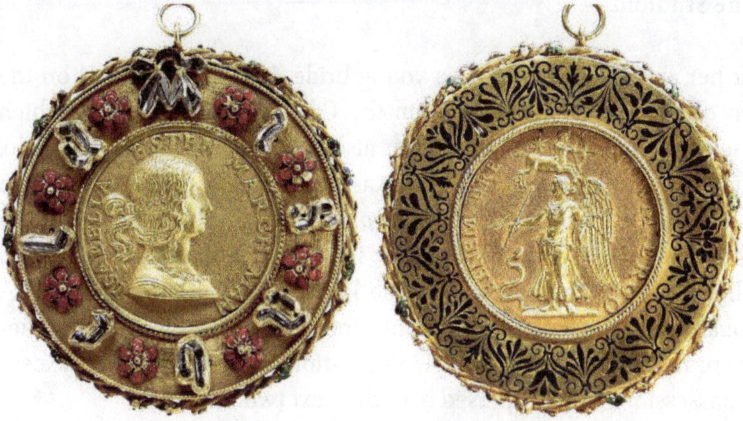

FIGURE 5.1 Giancristoforo Romano (ca. 1465–1512), *Medal of Isabella d'Este*. Gold, cast, with an enameled and jeweled frame, 69 mm
KUNSTHISTORISCHES MUSEUM, VIENNA, MÜNZKABINETT. INV. NO. 6.8.33BIS

as beautiful as this, even at the age at which he has represented us."[9] This was actually the second of two portraits by Titian, the first, now lost, but known from a copy by Rubens (1577–1640; Kunsthistorisches Museum, Vienna), having been rejected because it portrayed her in too realistic a fashion, showing her age and weight.[10]

There is, finally, the terra cotta bust in the Kimbell Art Museum, Fort Worth, tentatively identified as Isabella and attributed to Giancristoforo Romano and which has always disturbed me as a purported representation of the marchesa. If compared with the busts of Isabella's husband, Francesco, and of her sister, Beatrice (1475–1497), both by Giancristoforo Romano, that are indisputably portraits, this impersonally idealized beauty is not convincing.

9 *Isabella d'Este: "La prima donna del mondo,"* 114, cat. no. 51: The original of the full text is quoted here: "Il ritratto nostro di man di Tiziano ne piace di sorte che dubitiamo di non esser stata in quell'etade ch'egli rappresenta di quella beltà che in sé contiene. Havemo ben pensato di far qualche dimostracione con esso Tiziano per la fatica usata in esso, ma habbiamo deliberato di voler prima il ritratto de Zanninelli, il che gli farete intendere sollecitando che lo restituisca, accio che homai sia renduto a quei gentilhomini che con desiderio l'aspettano et ben hanno ragione." (Archivio Gonzaga busta 2936, libro 311. C.141).

10 Ibid., 114–117, cat, no. 52.

2 The Studiolo

Soon after her arrival in Mantua as a young bride, Isabella embarked on the decoration of her private apartments in the Castello di San Giorgio, which included not only her living quarters, but also, in the Torretta di San Nicolò, two additional chambers designed to serve as a private office or *studiolo*, and a new style of room below it that she called a *grotta*. In 1522, three years after the death of her husband, she moved to a new *studiolo* and *grotta* on the ground floor of the section of the Palazzo Ducale known as the Corte Vecchia.[11] A posthumous 1542 inventory of the contents and the specific placement of her collections provides us with invaluable information, since, with but few exceptions, her possessions were dispersed over the next two centuries.[12]

In the Renaissance, the *studiolo* was an important part of a nobleman's dwelling, a place where he could find the solitude required for privacy, quiet study, and the reception of special friends. There were certainly such locations belonging to women, but strictly circumscribed for female activities. Isabella would have known of the *studioli* in Ferrara of her uncles, Leonello (1407–1450) and Borso d'Este (1413–1471), and those of Federico da Montefeltro (1422–1482) in Urbino and Gubbio, the latter now at the Metropolitan Museum of Art, New York, and she would certainly have drawn inspiration from her mother's *studioli*.[13] Isabella, however, had an inventive, independent mind and a very strong will, and she transformed her *studiolo* and *grotta* into something much more extensive and unique, in effect, appropriating and even expanding the functions of an environment usually reserved for men. It was a place where she could not only read, compose her correspondence, host musical entertainments, and receive her closest friends, but also display her growing collection of art and precious objects. It became, finally, a kind of celebrated mini-museum, a necessary destination for visiting dignitaries.[14]

---

11 The most complete introduction to Isabella's rooms in the ducal palace in Mantua can be found in Clifford Brown. *Isabella d'Este in the Ducal Palace*; see also, *Isabella d'Este: "La prima donna del mondo,"* 145–184; Anderson, "*What was Ferrarese about Isabella d'Este's* Camerino," 337–352.

12 Clifford Brown, *Per dare qualche splendore*. For the 1542 inventory see especially 319–362.

13 Thornton, *Scholar in His Study*, 91–92.

14 Clifford Brown, *Per Dare Qualche Splendore*, 25; Syson and Thornton. *Objects of Virtue*, 83. As was done so effectively by Molly Bourne, it is important and fascinating to compare the activities of Isabella and her husband, Francesco II, in decorating their respective environments, the former in the Ducal Palace, the latter in his new city palace of San Sebastiano (1506–1512). Francesco chose to present in frescoes and separate paintings Gonzaga family emblems, and celebrations of his roles as ruler and *condottiere*, the most significant of which were the extraordinary canvases of the *Triumphs of Caesar*

Some idea of her forceful personality even at age seventeen is evident in letters she sent to the painter in charge of preparing the first set of rooms:

Letter of October 2, 1491, Ferrara:

To Giovanni Luca Liombeni (d. ca. 1495):[15]

> Having realized that you are as long in finishing a picture as you are in your person, [apparently he was tall] we hereby notify you at this time you will have to change your nature. Because if you have not finished the studiolo by the time we return, we will have to imprison you in the bridge dungeon, and that will be no joke.[16]

In a follow-up letter a month later she wrote:

> In response to your letter, we say that we are pleased you are disposed to finish our studiolo soon so as not to end up in the bridge dungeon ... Do your best to make it beautiful and striking.... Nothing gauche: we would only make you redo it all at your own expense and then send you to the dungeon for the whole winter. You might enjoy spending a night there to get a taste of how well you like the room; then maybe you would be more responsive.[17]

While Isabella was agitated about the completion of the decoration of her *studiolo*, by 1492 she had embarked on a highly original concept, the commissioning of a succession of allegorical mythological paintings for its walls, the realization of this project occupying roughly thirty-four years.[18] Although the subjects of the seven paintings, all of which are now in the Louvre, are interrelated, they do not seem to be the result of an overall plan, each canvas

---

(1485–1488, Royal Collection, Hampton Court Palace, England), whereas, as we shall describe below, Isabella embarked on a complex and sophisticated series of allegories expounding moralizing themes of virtue and learning as an environment in which to display her collecting activities. Bourne, "Renaissance Husbands and Wives," 93–123.

15 Little is known about Liombeni, whose adopted son was Lorenzo Leonbruno (Leombruno; 1477–1537), who also worked for Isabella d'Este and her husband, Francesco II Gonzaga on some of the frescoes in their respective rooms in the ducal palace.

16 Shemek, *Selected Letters*, 46, letter 48.

17 Ibid., 46, letter 49.

18 The standard study of the paintings in the studiolo of Isabella d'Este is Campbell. *Cabinet of Eros*. See also Verheyen. *Paintings in the Studiolo*; Gilbert, "*What Did the Renaissance Patron Buy?*" 392–450, especially 416–426.

inspired by its predecessor and generally linked by several manifestations of two roughly interrelated common themes: the victory of Virtue over the Vices associated with a thinly-veiled celebration of the marchesa herself. Although Isabella consulted with writers and humanists such as Paride da Ceresara (1496–1532), Pietro Bembo (1470–1547), Pietro Aretino (1492–1556), and Mario Equicola (ca. 1470–1525), she was always closely involved in dictating the complicated details.

The attempts by Isabella to engage various artists to contribute paintings to her *studiolo* provide us with a fascinating narrative. Over the course of her long life she befriended or at least was in direct contact with an impressive array of many of the most distinguished artists of the late fifteenth and sixteenth centuries, earning her the sobriquet "a Tenth Muse."[19]

Although the marchesa had brought with her from Ferrara several artists to execute her first two *studiolo* paintings, she chose, instead, the long-established Mantuan court artist, Andrea Mantegna (1431–1506), who produced first the *Parnassus*,[20] completed in 1497, followed by *Pallas Expelling the Vices from the Garden of Virtue* painted between 1499 and 1502 (fig. 5.2).[21] In both cases, the development of their subjects involved elaborate allegories, the first celebrating the support of the arts in Mantua under the protection of Mars and Venus, who possibly refer to Isabella and her husband. The second offers a fascinating and complex collection of strange creatures in a dense and powerful composition in which, once again, the central figure, Pallas, would seem to be an allegorical representation of Isabella, who expels from the Garden of Virtue a congregation of unseemly creatures, the whole being as much literary as pictorial.

In April 1497, Isabella considered approaching Pietro Perugino (1446/50–1523) in Florence but did not actively contact him until September 1502.[22] This commission is a striking example of how obsessively involved she was in

19 Campbell, *Cabinet of Eros*, 337, note 24, explains the origins and subsequent appearances of the phrase describing Isabella as "*una decima musa*." The full text is reproduced from a letter of Battista Guarino (ca. 1434–1503) dated March 31st, 1493. The phrase is used again by Mario Equicola in 1505 and Julius Caesar Scaliger (1484–1558) in 1512.

20 Cody, "Mantegna and the Orators," 51–77.

21 Schottenstein, "*Pallas Expelling Vices*."

22 Shemek, *Selected Letters*, 198, letter 282, September 15, 1502; Campbell, *Cabinet of Eros*, 169–90, especially 172–173 and 350–351 for a full translation of the letter and the original Italian text, and Appendix Two by Clifford M. Brown (Digest of the Correspondence Concerning the Paintings Commissioned for the *Studiolo* in the Castello (1496–1515), 285–298). Campbell gives a detailed history of Isabella's complicated and at times turbulent relationship with Perugino related to engaging the artist to contribute paintings to the studiolo, including the listing of a long series of relevant letters.

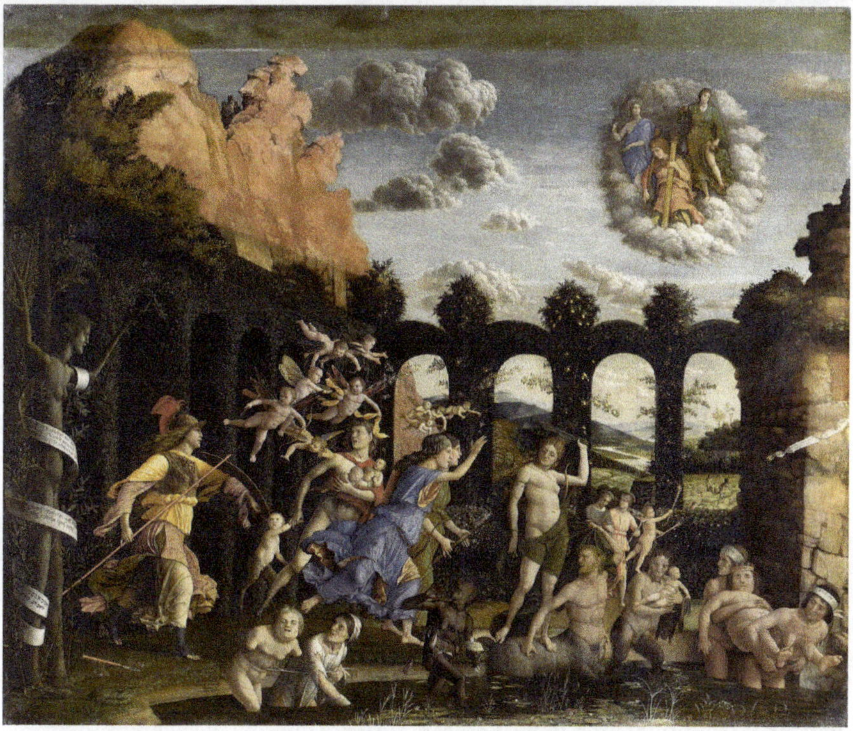

FIGURE 5.2 Andrea Mantegna (1431–1506), *Pallas Drives the Vices from the Garden of Virtue*, 1499–1502. Tempera on canvas, 160 × 192 cm (63 × 77 in.)
MUSÉE DU LOUVRE, PARIS, DÉPARTEMENT DES PEINTURES, INV. NO. 371

the project, sending some seventy letters related to the painting to a variety of recipients, including the artist. In a letter to Perugino dated January 12th, 1504 she encloses pieces of thread showing the desired heights of the figures in the painting, the latter partly because each city had its own standards of measurement.[23] In the most famous of the relevant letters, this one addressed to Francesco Malatesta[24] and dated January 19, 1503, she includes an impossibly long and characteristically detailed description of exactly how she wished the painting to appear, enclosing sketches.[25] She was even concerned about the direction of the light in each painting so that it would correspond with the lighting in the *studiolo*. After much angry badgering, Perugino finally completed

23 Shemek, *Selected Letters*, 244, letter 328.

24 Francesco Malatesta was the Gonzaga agent in Florence; his life dates are not available, but correspondence exists dated 1502, 1503, and 1528.

25 Campbell, *Cabinet of Eros*, 172–173, 291, note 42, 350–351 for the original Italian text.

the work in 1505. Entitled *A Battle Between Chastity and Lasciviousness*, it is a flawed work affected by the strained relationship between artist and patron.

In November 1496 Isabella had indirectly approached Giovanni Bellini (1430–1516) with a request to contribute a painting to the *studiolo*, but the idea languished until 1501 and eventually came to naught, since Bellini would not subject himself to the restrictive demands of such an overbearing patron.[26] In March 1501, she then attempted to interest Leonardo da Vinci with a similar request and had equally discouraging results.[27]

The fourth painting was commissioned from Lorenzo Costa (1460–1535), who was to replace Mantegna as Mantuan court artist after the latter's death in 1506. The subject of this painting, *The Coronation of the Poet*, or *Allegory of Isabella d'Este's Coronation* was produced between 1505 and 1506. As a representative of heavenly and virtuous love in contrast to earthly and carnal, Isabella is the central figure being crowned with myrtle by Anteros and Venus. At the same time, it is a celebration of her patronage of the arts and letters.

Costa was also the author of the fifth painting, *The Reign of Comus*, completed between 1506 and 1511. In this painting, as complex in its imagery and meaning as those that preceded it, Comus, the god of revelry and celebration, particularly of marriage, is only one among many other important divinities: the two Venuses and Cupids, Bacchus and Ariadne, Mercury, Janus, and others. Beyond a triumphal arch Janus and Mercury are chasing away Envy and three other figures, while the crowded landscape seems filled with melody as a reference to Isabella's love of music and skill as a performer.

After a gap of twenty years, Isabella commissioned the final two paintings for the *studiolo* from Antonio Allegri, called Correggio (1489–1534): *The Allegory of Virtue* (fig. 5.3) and *The Allegory of Vice*, now dated sometime between 1528 and 1529 and bearing titles given to them in the seventeenth century.[28] The two paintings are a testimony to Isabella's original instructions when she first thought of commissioning paintings for her *studiolo*, that only the finest artists in Italy should be approached. In this case, not only was the choice of Correggio more or less consistent with this command, but the results seem to exemplify her remarkable ability to perceive and accept the latest developments in painting, for in contrast to the first group of five paintings, which, by this later date would have been considered old-fashioned, these two are decidedly contemporary.

---

26 Ibid., 284, 286, cat. no. 1; 289, cat. no. 29bis.

27 Shemek, *Selected Letters*, 158–159, letter 229, n. 60; Campbell, *Cabinet of Eros*, 285, 288, cat. no. 13.

28 Verheyen, *Paintings in the Studiolo*, chapter v, 55–61; Campbell, *Cabinet of Eros*, 222–249.

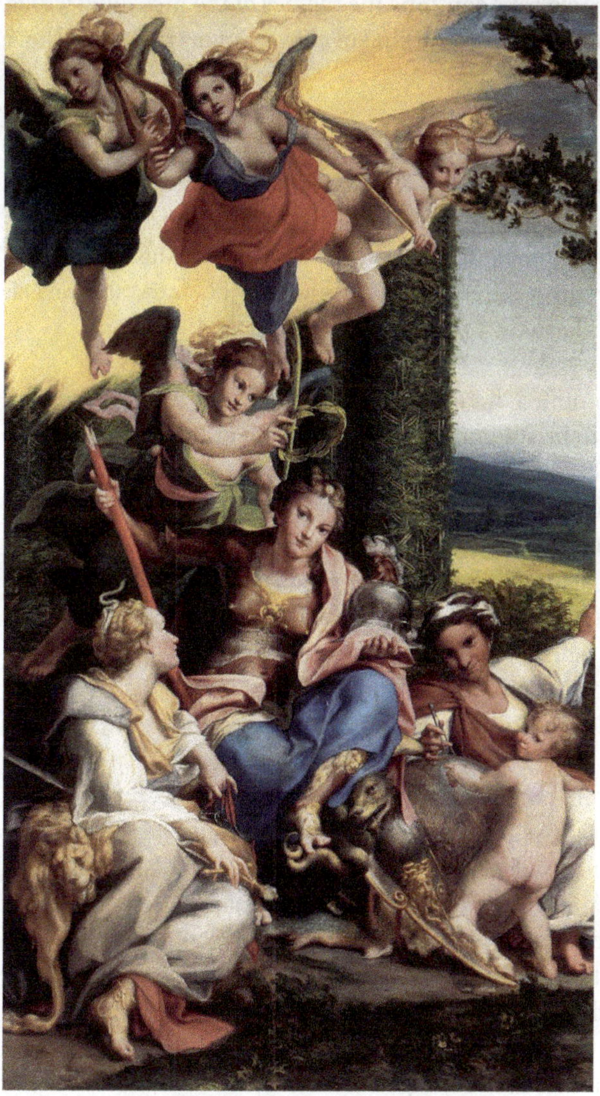

FIGURE 5.3 Antonio Allegri da Correggio (1489–1534), *Allegory of Virtue*, 1531. Oil on canvas, 149 × 88 cm (58.6 × 34.6 in.)
MUSÉE DU LOUVRE, PARIS, DÉPARTEMENT DES ARTS GRAPHIQUES, INV. NO. 5926

If Mantegna's *Pallas Expelling the Vices from the Garden of Virtue* shows the goddess in the midst of performing her ultimately successful task, Correggio's painting shows her in triumph. The pendant work, the so-called Allegory of Vice, is more ambiguous. The central figure being tortured and flayed has been equated with Laocoön, Marsyas, and Silenus and represents the punishment of earthly passions. The two thus continue the themes of the preceding works, providing an environment to inspire the kind of conversations that would have taken place in Isabella's precious *studiolo*.

3 Collecting Antiquities

It was Isabella's early intention upon becoming established in Mantua to begin collecting antiquities.[29] In a letter, dated November 13[?] 1497, she reveals much about how she will usually proceed in this endeavor.

> We heard that Dominico di Piero the Venetian jeweler has died and left many antiquities to be sold under the supervision of the jeweler Giovan Andrea da Fiore. Since we have an enormous desire to see them so we can buy some of them, we wrote to the aforesaid Giovan Andrea asking him to go to the appropriate people and have the antiques sent here. We will pay for those that are beautiful. But because we suspect that when our most illustrious lord father, [Ercole I d'Este (1431–1505)] who delights in these things, arrives, he will take the best ones, we would be very pleased if you would see in every possible way that they are sent before His Excellency arrives. You could do nothing for which we would be more grateful.[30]

Her concern here about possible competition, even from her father, and the obsessive desire to possess works from antiquity would never diminish throughout her life, and would, more than a few times, lead her to commit less than honorable actions. Regarding her available finances, it is important to realize that Isabella did not have access to large sums, since, as was common for women in her position as a consort, she had her own limited budget that was not only dedicated to maintaining her considerable personal household, but to contributing to her husband's financial needs when necessary.[31] With some frequency, she found herself having to pawn her jewelry to meet both her own and his demands. This situation made it difficult for her to compete with more wealthy collectors, who were almost exclusively male. Her sister, Beatrice, who did not collect, had married the wealthy duke of Milan, Ludovico Sforza,

---

29 C[lifford]. Brown, "'Lo Insociabile Desiderio'," 324–353; Paolucci. *I Gonzaga e l'Antico*; Clifford Brown, *Per dare qualche splendore*, 13–20.

30 Ibid., 127, a.; Shemek, *Selected Letters*, 116–117, letter 157.

31 Cartwright, *Isabella d'Este*, I, 226–227; San Juan, "The Court Lady's Dilemma," 71; Shemek 2017, 194–195, letter 276, Mantua, May 18, 1502.

il Moro (1452–1508), prompting Isabella, in a moment of jealousy, to exclaim: "Would to God that we who spend so willingly should have so much!"[32]

The 1542 inventory, compiled by the notary Odoardo Stivini,[33] of what was contained in the *studiolo* and *grotta* lists around 1,620 items, including:[34]

- 1240 coins and medals in gold, silver, and bronze, both ancient and contemporary
- 46 engraved gems, 29 cameos, and 3 statuettes in pietre dure
- 72 vases, flasks, and cups in pietre dure, agate, jasper, and chalcedony
- 48 bronze statuettes, at least twelve of them by contemporary artists such as Antico, and 17 in marble
- 13 portrait busts
- 3 reliefs

Yet the inventory does not represent the entire collection, since there are other possessions mentioned in the correspondence and located throughout the marchesa's apartment. This would have been the sum of roughly forty years of determined collecting, not including other areas of activity of this enthusiastic shopper, namely jewelry, books (especially the products of the great Venetian publisher Aldus Manutius (1449–1515)), fashionable clothing, musical instruments, essential oils for the perfumes that Isabella herself formulated. And all this on a habitually restrained budget.[35]

From 1490 to 1497 Isabella was purchasing antique intaglios and engraved semi-precious stones from Venetian craftsmen, but by the latter date she was already looking further afield, telling her agents in the following year that "we now want other things than cameos; rather we are now interested in owning some figurines and heads in bronze and marble."[36] After 1498 Isabella established relations with several contacts, particularly in Venice and Rome, both of which cities were major sources for the antiquities that were attracting large numbers of collectors. In fact, Rome was being stripped of so much of its

---

32 *Splendours*, eds. Chambers and Martineau, 51–52.

33 No life dates available.

34 C[lifford] Brown, *Lo Insociabile Desiderio*, 325, 345, n.6.; *Isabella d'Este: "La prima donna del mondo,"* 263–288, cat. no. 95 (Daniela Ferrari), transcribes the entire inventory; Ferrari, "L'inventario dell Gioie," 20–43.

35 Welch, *Shopping in the Renaissance*; see especially chapter nine, *Shopping with Isabella d'Este*, 246–273. Welch provides a detailed and extensive picture of Isabella's finances, methods of acquisition, financial status, range of purchases, and her motivations for such purchases.

36 C[lifford] Brown, *Lo Insociabile Desiderio*, 331, 349, n. 52, 350, n. 54; Brown, *Per dare qualche splendore*, 128–129, file d. Isabella d'Este to Giovanni Andrea Fiore, Mantua, April 4, 1498: "Ve respondemo che nui desideramo anchora molto più de havere qualche figuretta et teste de bronzo et marmore …"

ancient material that strict controls were instituted by successive popes, causing Isabella to resort to various subterfuges to obtain the objects she desired.

As her knowledge of ancient works developed, Isabella also frequently relied upon the advice of artists regarding the quality and authenticity of works in which she might have an interest, especially Giancristoforo Romano, Pier Jacopo Alari-Bonacolsi called Antico (1460–1528), Andrea Mantegna, and occasionally Leonardo da Vinci. Eventually she, herself, was sometimes approached for opinions about the quality and authenticity of works of art.

The complicated story of the two Sleeping Cupids, one attributed to the Greek 4th century BCE sculptor Praxiteles, the other allegedly by Michelangelo (1475–1564), is one of the more revealing insights into Isabella's collecting methods.[37] One of her closest and most enduring friendships was with her sister-in-law, Elisabetta Gonzaga (1471–1526), the consort of Guildobaldo da Montefeltro (1472–1508), duke of Urbino, whose extensive collection contained two supposedly ancient marble sculptures, a Venus and a Sleeping Cupid that had been given to him by Cesare Borgia (1475–1507). Despite their supposed friendship, on the 21st of June 1502, the notorious Borgia had treacherously entered and taken possession of Urbino, while Guidobaldo and his wife were absent. Hearing this news, on June 30th Isabella immediately sent the following letter to her brother in Rome, Cardinal Ippolito d'Este (1509–1572):

> Most Reverend Father in God, my dear and honored Brother
>
> The Lord Duke of Urbino, my brother-in-law, had in his house a small Venus of antique marble, and also a Cupid, which were given to him some time ago by His Excellency the Duke of Romagna [Cesare Borgia]. I feel certain that these things must have fallen into the said Duke's hands … And since I am very anxious to collect antiques for the decoration of my studio, I desire exceedingly to possess these statues, which does not seem impossible, since I hear that His Excellency [Cesare Borgia] has little taste for antiquities … I am quite willing…. that you should mention my name and say that I have asked for them very urgently …[38]

37 Norton, "The Lost *Sleeping Cupid*," 251–257; *Isabella d'Este: "La prima donna del mondo,"* 310–316, "Isabellas Schlafende Eroten des Michelangelo und Praxiteles"; Weil-Garris Brandt, "Sogni di un *Cupido dormante*," 313–323; Clifford Brown, *Per dare qualche splendore*, 111–112, file 6 a, b.; 120–121; 156–159, file 22, file a–g, 23, file a–u; 177–180, file 28 a–c; 325; 338, 345, 352–356; Campbell *Cabinet of Eros*, 91–107.

38 Brown, *Per dare qualche splendore*, 157, file 22, b. Isabella d'Este to Cardinal Ippolito d'Este, Mantua, June 30, 1502.

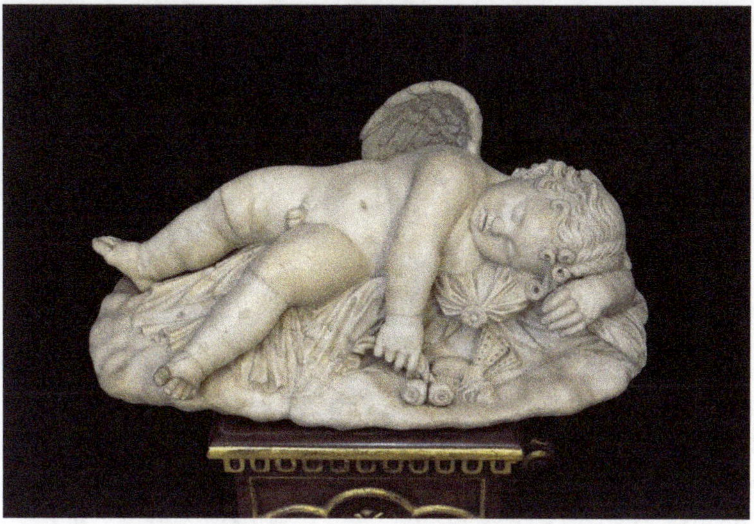

FIGURE 5.4 Roman, Imperial Period. *Sleeping Cupid*. 2nd century CE White marble, length, 69 cm, Florence, Galleria degli Uffizi, inv. no. 1914, n. 392 (usually referred to as the prototype for Michaelangelo's lost *Sleeping Cupid*)

Cesare was, in fact, quite amenable to the marchesa's request, and on July 22, the marbles were safely installed in her *grotta*. This, however, was not the end of the story. At the close of 1503, when Guidobaldo had been restored as ruler of Urbino, he requested Isabella to return his Cupid, which she refused to do, maintaining that he had given Borgia permission for her to possess the sculptures.[39] When it came to the desire for a work of art, Isabella's loyalty was clearly on the side of art rather than family.

This Cupid (fig. 5.4) had originally been reported to Isabella in 1496 by an agent in Rome without any mention that it was by Michelangelo but was not purchased because it was considered to be modern.[40] It is not clear if Isabella was aware that the Cupid was by Michelangelo, whose reputation as an exceptional young talent was beginning to make his work desirable to own, but she admitted that as a modern work it had no equal.[41] Certainly, in her correspondence of 1502 she only refers to the sculptures that she covets in Urbino as "antiquities." Nonetheless, it has always been assumed that she eventually

39 Ibid., 177–189, file 28, a–c, December 8, 1503–January 22, 1504.

40 Ibid., 111–112, file 6, a–b, June 27–July 26, 1496.

41 Ibid., 158, file 22, d., Isabella d'Este to Francesco II Gonzaga, Mantua, July 22, 1502: "il Cupido, per cosa moderno, non ha paro."

knew the piece was not only modern, but by the great Florentine sculptor. In the inventory of 1542, it is described as by Michelangelo and thus has always been associated with a Sleeping Cupid he carved in 1496, supposedly treated to look as if it were ancient and sold to a dealer, who then sold it to Cardinal Raffaele Riario (1461–1521). When the cardinal discovered that the sculpture was "modern," he returned it whereupon it then passed through several hands, finally arriving in Urbino.

Of equal importance was a genuinely ancient Sleeping Cupid, attributed to Praxiteles (395 BCE–330 BCE), that was in a collection in Rome and that was originally offered in 1496 to Isabella's husband, Francesco. Negotiations for the piece continued with Isabella until finally, in 1506, she obtained the statue, which she placed next to the alleged Michelangelo for comparison.[42] Eventually, both Sleeping Cupids were acquired in the 1630's by Charles I (1600–1649) of England as part of his purchase of the Mantuan collections, and disappeared when his collections were sold after his execution in 1649.[43]

In reference to the title of this volume, the youthful Michelangelo is "modern" because he is not ancient, although as a young sculptor he is partly developing his skills by inventing works in an ancient style.

The widespread and passionate interest in Greek and Roman art and the fierce competition to own originals also led to the production of small bronzes that reproduced the subjects of famous statues or portrayed mythological subjects. Pier Jacopo Alari-Bonacolsi, called Antico, was a leading Mantuan artist in this genre whose first patron was Gianfrancesco Gonzaga (1446–1496), for whom he produced a series of small bronzes and portrait medals. By at least 1497 he was in contact with Isabella, but on March 27, 1500, turned down a request from her for sculpture to decorate the door of her *camerino*.[44] He would, however, become increasingly active on her behalf as an artist, adviser, and restorer of ancient sculpture. Beginning in 1510, but most actively around 1519, he cast a series of bronze statuettes for Isabella, eight of which still survive in various collections (fig. 5.5).[45]

Isabella's *studiolo* and *grotta* were, collectively, a tribute to antiquity where the paintings delivered their message of the triumph of good over evil not

42 *Isabella d'Este: "La prima donna del mondo,"* 310–314, cat. No. 101; Clifford Brown, *Per dare qualche splendore*, 120, file 23, a–u, October 22, 1502–May 18, 1506.

43 Norton, "The Lost Sleeping Cupid," 252–254.

44 Ferrari, "L'Antico nelle fonti d'archivio," 309, doc. 35.

45 Allison, "The Bronzes of Antico," 37–309; Leithe-Jasper, "Isabella d'Este und Antico," 317–362; Allison, "Antico e Isabella d'Este," 128–153; *Antico: The Golden Age of Renaissance Bronzes*. Johnson, "In the Hand of the Beholder," 183–197.

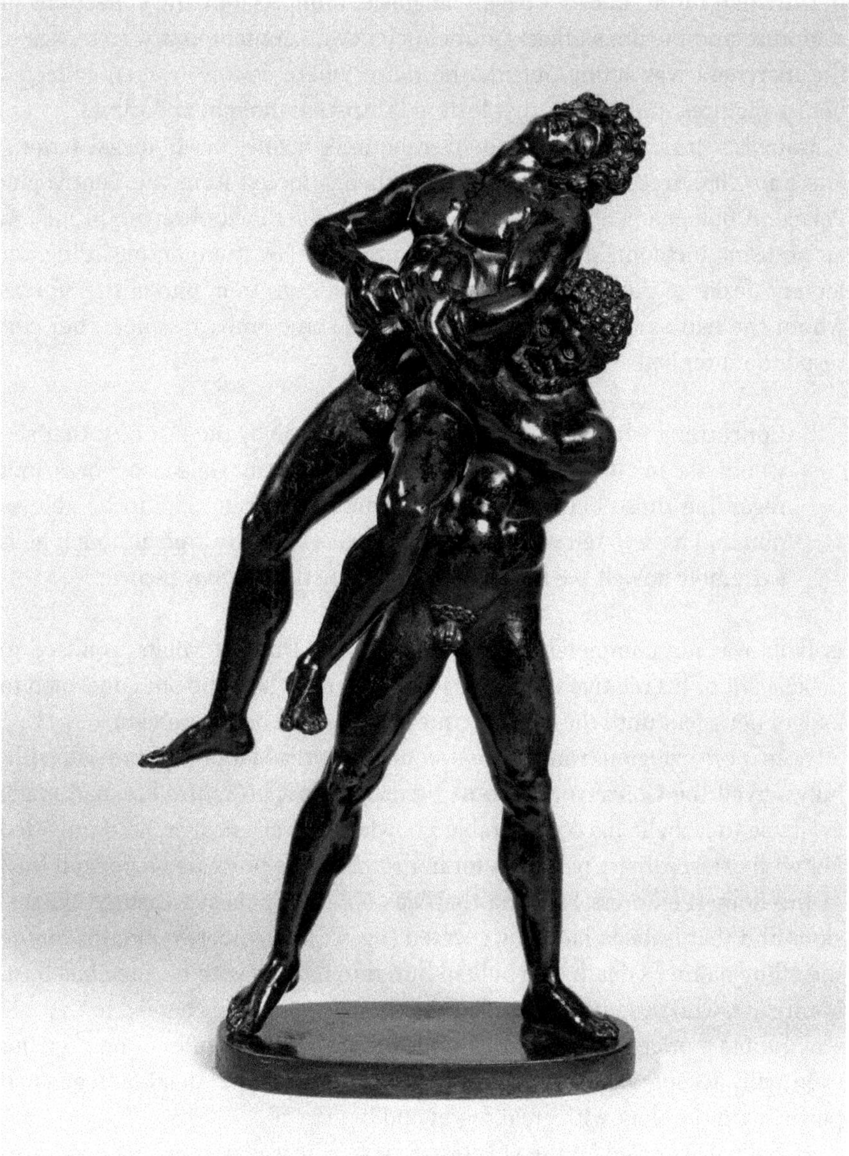

FIGURE 5.5 Pier Jacopo Alari-Bonacolsi, called Antico (1460–1528), *Hercules and Antaeus*, ca. 1500. Bronze with inlaid silver eyes, cast, H. 39.1 cm (15.3 in.) with base, 40.7 cm. (16 in.)
VICTORIA AND ALBERT MUSEUM, LONDON, INV. NO. A. 37–1956

in Christian terms, but in a pagan language, reinforced by the collections of sculpture and precious objects, both ancient and contemporary. Here, again, the marchesa was acting outside the norm where courtly women collected books, pictures, and objects that fostered Christian thought and values.

Isabella's "insatiable desire" could sometimes involve her in illegal actions. She knowingly received stolen alabaster heads looted from the Bentivoglio Palace in Bologna.[46] She was also a shameless deathbed observer. In 1515, in an amusing incident, she wrote to a Gonzaga in-law in Milan regarding her fervent desire to purchase some important antiques from one of the Sforzas whom she had assumed had passed away. In some embarrassment, her correspondent replied:

> Concerning what your Excellency wrote to me by the last post that she would like me to do, following the death of Signor Galeazzo Sforza, and regarding those belongings of his which you would like to be able to obtain, I have to tell you Signor Galeazzo is still alive, and although he is extremely unwell, we have not lost all hope that he may recover.[47]

Isabella was not completely reassured when the Duke of Milan promised to make a gift of his relative's antiques whenever he should die but continued to badger her agent until the works in question were in her possession.

Even more egregious was her treatment of Andrea Mantegna, who had faithfully served the Gonzaga as a court painter almost his entire life, had made available to Isabella his considerable knowledge of classical art, and provided her with extraordinary paintings for her *studiolo*. He possessed a portrait bust of the Roman empress Faustina that was one of his most treasured possessions and that Isabella had long coveted (fig. 5.6). In 1506, two months before the ailing painter's death, she bullied him into parting with his precious bust. Mantegna, who desperately needed the money, reluctantly agreed to the sale and quoted a price of 100 ducats. Isabella replied with an offer of only 25, but eventually accepted the artist's price. It was reported to her that Mantegna had parted with the work with great regret and in tears.[48]

Isabella d'Este died on the 13 February 1539. She was still making purchases in 1538 and had drawn up her Last Will and Testament in 1535 wherein she

46 Clifford Brown, *Per dare qualche splendore*, 236–238, file 38, docs. a–d, The Bentivoglio antiquities, November 2, 1506–September 30, 1507.

47 Ibid., 268, file 54, d. Giovanni Gonzaga to Isabella d'Este, Milan, April 4, 1515.

48 *Isabella d'Este: "La prima donna del mondo,"* 308–309, cat. no. 100; Clifford Brown, *Per dare qualche splendore*, 231–235, file 36, docs. a–I, July 13–August 7, 1506.

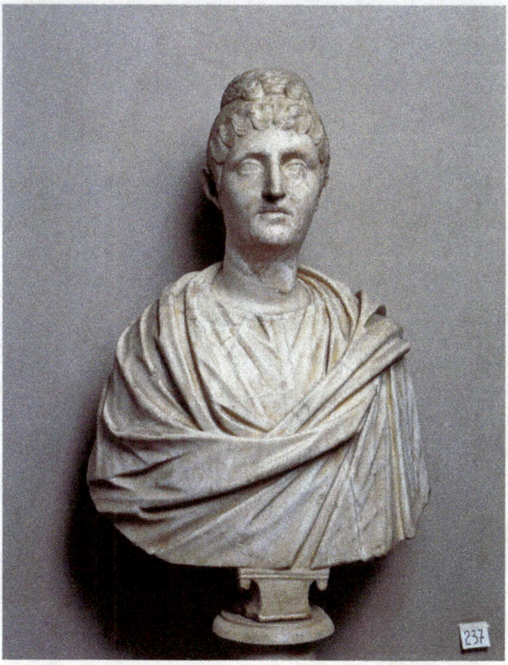

FIGURE 5.6
Roman, Imperial Period. *Faustina the Elder* (ca. 100–140 CE). White marble, overall height, 68 cm (26.8 in.); height of head, 25 cm (9.8 in.). ca. 140 CE Palazzo Ducale, Mantua, inv. no. 6749

bequeathed to her heirs almost all of what she had gathered over a period of some forty-one years. The *studiolo* and *grotta* remained intact at least to the end of the sixteenth century, but in the seventeenth century much had been moved to other locations in the ducal palace and related ducal properties. In addition, the financial problems of successive impoverished dukes had led to the sale of large segments of the collection, especially the famous sale in 1627–1628 of the Gonzaga collection to Charles I of England, and the acquisition by Cardinal Richelieu (1585–1642) of five of the *studiolo* paintings from Charles I Gonzaga of Nevers, 8th duke of Mantua (1580–1627–1637) during the Sack of Mantua in 1630 in the War of the Mantuan Succession (1628–31), who in turn gave them to Louis XIV (1638–1715), their eventual disposition after the French Revolution being the Louvre.

Except for a very few objects that can be identified such as the cameo vase in Braunschweig (fig. 5.7),[49] several ancient reliefs—the *Dancing Satyrs*[50] and

49 *Splendours*, eds. Chambers and Martineau, 168–169, cat. no. 119; *Isabella d'Este: "La prima donna del mondo,"* 306–307, cat. no. 99.

50 Ibid., 166–167, cat. no. 116.

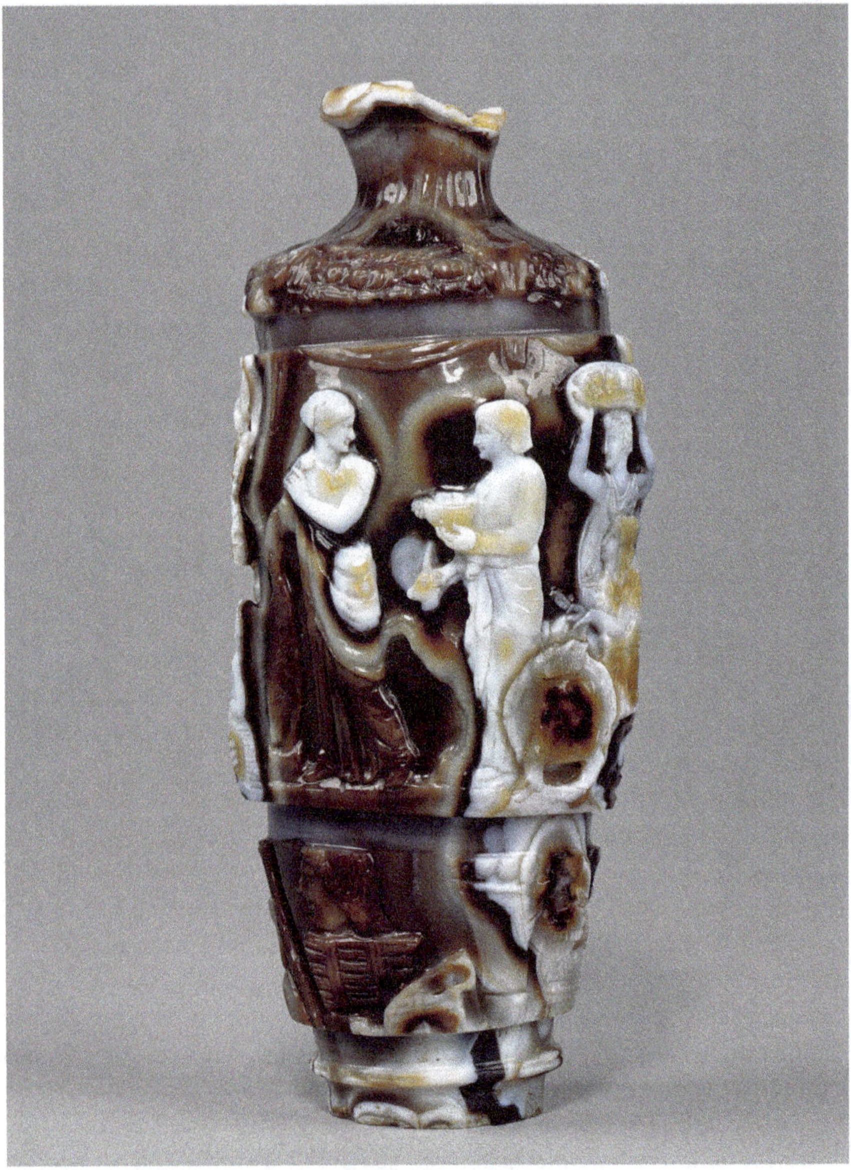

FIGURE 5.7 Roman, Imperial Period, *Lekythos*, ca. 198 CE Five-layered Sardonyx, H. 15.3 cm (6 in.)
HERZOG ANTON ULRICH-MUSEUM, BRAUNSCHWEIG

the *Return of Proserpina*[51]—and Mantegna's bust of Faustina,[52] all still in place in the *studiolo* and *grotta*, and the statuettes by Antico, Isabella's extensive collection is lost.[53]

Isabella's unquestionable fame rests not only on her intelligence, her many talents, and her wide range of accomplishments, especially as a patron and collector, but that, as a pioneer, they were achieved by a woman playing many roles beyond those expected of her gender. It is thus not difficult to understand why Isabella's cousin, the *preux chevalier* and poet, Niccolò da Correggio (1450–1508), dubbed her "LA PRIMA DONNA DEL MONDO."[54]

Bibliography

Allison, Ann Hersey. "The Bronzes of Pier Jacopo Alari–Bonacolsi, called Antico." *Jahrbuch der Kunsthistorischen Sammlungen in Wien* 53/54 (1993/1994): 37–310.

Allison, Ann Hersey. "Antico e Isabella d'Este." In *Isabella d'Este: La primadonna del Rinascimento*, edited by Daniele Bini, 128–153. Modena: Il Bulino edizioni d'arte: 2001.

Alsop Joseph. *The Rare Art Traditions: The History of Art Collecting and Its Linked Phenomena*. Bollingen Series XXXV. 27. Cambridge: Harper and Row, 1982.

Ames-Lewis, Francis. *Isabella and Leonardo*. New Haven: Yale University Press: 2012.

Antico: The Golden Age of Renaissance Bronzes (exh. cat., National Gallery of Art, The Frick Collection), edited by Eleanora Luciano, Denise Allen, Claudia Kryza-Gersch. London: Paul Holberton Publishing, 2011.

Bini, Daniele, ed. *Isabella d'Este: La primadonna del Rinascimento*, Modena: Il Bulino, edizioni d'arte, 2001.

Bourne, Molly. "Renaissance Husbands and Wives as Patrons of Art: The *Camerini* of Isabella d'Este and Francesco II Gonzaga." In *Beyond Isabella: Secular Women Patrons of Art In Renaissance Italy*. Sixteenth Century Essays and Studies, vol. 54. edited by Sheryl Reiss, David G. Wilkins, 93–123. Kirksville, Missouri: Truman State University Press, 2001.

Brown, Beverly Louise. "Portraiture at the Courts of Italy." In *The Renaissance Portrait from Donatello to Bellini* (exh. cat.), edited by Keith Christiansen and Stefan

51 Ibid., 167–168, cat. no. 117.

52 Ibid., 170, cat. no. 122; Ferino-Pagden 1994, 308–309, cat. no. 100.

53 See above, note 37.

54 Cartwright, *Isabella d'Este*, vol I, 83 and n. 2; An interesting perspective on Isabella's role in the political life of Mantua and in her relationship with her husband, Francesco Gonzaga, can be found in Cockram, "Epistolary Masks," 20–37.

Weppelmann 26–47. New Haven and London: The Metropolitan Museum of Art and Yale University Press, 2011.

Brown, Clifford M. "'Lo Insociabile Desiderio Nostro de Cose Antique': New Documents on Isabella d'Este's Collection of Antiquities." In *Cultural Aspects of the Italian Renaissance: Essays in Honour of Paul Oskar Kristeller*, edited by Cecil Clough, 324–353. Manchester: Manchester University Press, 1976.

Brown, Clifford M. *Isabella d'Este in the Ducal Palace in Mantua: An Overview of Her Rooms in the Castello di San Giorgio and the Corte Vecchio*. Rome: Bulzoni Editore, 2005.

Brown, Clifford M., with Anna Maria Lorenzoni. "The Grotta of Isabella d'Este." *Gazette des Beaux-Arts* 89 (1977): 155–171; 91 (1978): 72–82.

Brown, Clifford M., with Anna Maria Lorenzoni and Sally Hickson. *'Per dare qualche splendore a la gloriosa cità di Mantua': Documents for the Antiquarian Collection of Isabella d'Este*. Biblioteca del Cinquecento 106. Rome: Bulzoni Editore, 2002.

Brown, David Allen. "Leonardo and the Ladies with the Ermine and the Book." *Artibus et Historiae* 11, no. 22 (1990): 47–61.

Campbell, Stephen J. *The Cabinet of Eros: Renaissance Mythological Painting and the Studiolo of Isabella d'Este*. New Haven: Yale University Press, 2006.

Campbell, Stephen J., and Evelyn Welch, eds. *Artists at Court: Image-Making and Identity 1300–1550* (2002 symposium papers). Fenway Court, vol. 31. Boston: Isabella Stewart Gardner Museum, 2004.

Cartwright, Julia Maria. *Isabella d'Este, Marchioness of Mantua, 1474–1539: A Study of the Renaissance*. 2 vols. New York: E.P. Dutton, 1903.

Cockram, Sarah. "Epistolary Masks: Self-Presentation and Dissimulation in the Letters of Isabella d'Este." *Italian Studies* 64, no. 1, Spring, 2009, 20–37.

Cody, Steven J. "Mantegna and the Orators: The Invention of the 'Mars and Venus' for Isabella d'Este Gonzaga." *Artibus et Historiae* 75 (2017): 51–77.

Fenlon, Iain. "The Gonzaga and Music." In *Splendours of the Gonzaga*, (exh. cat.), edited by David Chambers and Jane Martineau, 87–94. London: Victoria and Albert Museum, 1981.

Ferrari, Daniela. "L'Antico nelle fonti d'archivio." In *Bonacolsi l'Antico: Uno scultore nella Mantova di Andrea Mantegna e di Isabella d'Este*, edited by Filippo Trevisani and Davide Gaspirotto, 300–328, (exh. cat., Museo di Palazzo Ducale, Mantua). Milan: Electa, 2008.

Gallico, Claudio. "Appunti sulla Musica all'Epoca di Isabella d'Este." In *Isabella d'Este: La primadonna del Rinacsimento*, edited by. Daniele Bini, 202–207. Modena: Il Bulino edizioni d'arte, 2001.

Gilbert, Creighton E. "What did the Renaissance Patron Buy?" *Renaissance Quarterly* 51 (1998): 392–450.

Giovinezza di Michelangelo (exh. cat., Palazzo Vecchio, Florence), edited by Kathleen Weil-Garris Brandt, Christina Acidini Luchinat, James David Draper, Nicolas Penny. Florence: Articifio Skira, 1999.

Hickson, Sally. "'To See Ourselves as Others See Us': Giovanni Frances Zaninello of Ferrara and the Portrait of Isabella d'Este by Francesco Francia." *Renaissance Studies* 23, no. 3 (2009): 288–310.

Isabella d'Este: "La prima donna del mondo"; Fürstin und Mäzenatin der Renaissance (exh. cat.), edited by Sylvia Ferino-Pagden. Vienna: Kunsthistorisches Museum, 1994.

Jardine, Lisa. *Worldly Goods: A New History of the Renaissance*. New York: Nan A. Talese, Bantam Doubleday Dell Publishing Group, Inc., 1996.

Johnson, Geraldine A. "In the Hand of the Beholder: Isabella d'Este and the Sensual Allure of Sculpture," In *Sense and the Senses in Early Modern Art and Cultural Practice*, edited by Alice E. Sanger and Siv Tove Kulbrandstad Walker, 183–197. New York: Taylor and Francis, 2016.

Luzio, Alessandro. *La galleria dei Gonzaga vendata all'Inghilterra nel 1627–1628: Documenti degli archivi di Mantova e Londra raccolti ed illustrati*. Milan: L. F. Cogliati, 1913, facsimile reprint: Rome: Bardi 1974.

Marek, George. *The Bed and the Throne: The Life of Isabella d'Este*. New York: Harper and Row, 1976.

Norton, Paul F. "The Lost *Sleeping Cupid* of Michelangelo," *The Art Bulletin* 39 (1957): 251–257.

Ozzola, Leandro. "Isabella d'Este e Tiziano." *Bolletino d'Arte* 10 (1930–1931): 491–494.

Paolucci, Antonio. *I Gonzaga e l'Antico: Percorso di Palazzo Ducale a Mantova*. Rome: Fratelli Palombi, 1988.

Pouncey, Philip. "A Drawing by Francesco Bonsignori." *The British Museum Quarterly* 16, no. 4 (January 1952): 99–101.

The Renaissance Portrait from Donatello to Bellini (exh. cat.), edited by Keith Christiansen and Stefan Weppelmann. New York: The Metropolitan Museum of Art and New Haven: Yale University Press, 2011.

San Juan, Rose Marie. "The Court Lady's Dilemma: Isabella d'Este and Art Collecting in the Renaissance." *Oxford Art Journal* 14, no. 1 (1991): 67–78.

Scher, Stephen K., and Aimee Ng. *The Scher Collection of Commemorative Medals*. New York: The Frick Collection in association with D. Giles Limited, New York and Lewes (UK), 2019.

Schottenstein, Tal. "*Pallas Expelling Vices from the Garden of Virtues* by Andrea Mantegna: Towards a New Approach." Master's thesis, The Hebrew University of Jerusalem, Faculty of Humanities: Department of History of Art, 2018.

Shemek, Deanna, ed. and trans. *Isabella d'Este: Selected Letters*. Arizona Center for Medieval and Renaissance Studies, Tempe, Arizona. Toronto: Iter Press, 2017.

Shephard, Tim. "Constructing Isabella's Musical Decorum in the Visual Sphere." *Renaissance Studies* 25, no. 5 (2011): 684–706.

Splendours of the Gonzaga, (exh. cat.), edited by David Chambers and Jane Martineau. London: Victoria and Albert Museum, 1981.

Syson, Luke. "Consorts, Mistresses and Exemplary Women: The Female Medallic Portrait in Fifteenth-century Italy." In *The Sculpted Object 1400–1700*, edited by Stuart Currie and Peta Motture, 43–58 plus illustrations. Brookfield, Vermont: Ashgate, 1997.

Syson, Luke. "Reading Faces: Gian Cristoforo Romano's Medal of Isabella d'Este." In *La Corte de Mantova nell'età di Andrea Mantegna: 1450–1550*, edited by Cesare Mozzarelli, Robert Oresko, Leandro Venturi, 281–294 plus illustrations. Rome: Bulzoni Editore, 1997.

Syson, Luke, and Dora Thornton. *Objects of Virtue: Art in Renaissance Italy*. Los Angeles: J. Paul Getty Museum, ca. 2001.

Thornton, Dora. *The Scholar in His Study: Ownership and Experience in Renaissance Italy*. New Haven: Yale University Press, 1997.

Verheyen, Egon. *The Paintings in the Studiolo of Isabella d'Este at Mantua*. New York: New York University Press, 1971.

Weiss, Roberto. *The Renaissance Discovery of Classical Antiquity*. Oxford: Basil Blackwell, 1969.

Welch, Evelyn. *Shopping in the Renaissance: Consumer Cultures in Italy 1400–1600*. New Haven: Yale University Press, 2005.

CHAPTER 6

Cleaning Out the Workshop: How Preparatory Drawings Became Collector's Treasure in Renaissance and Baroque Italy

John Marciari

In traditional histories of the Italian Renaissance, Giorgio Vasari (1511–1574) is often described not only as the first art historian of the period but also the first major collector of Italian drawings. We know now that neither of those descriptions is strictly true. With regard to the collecting of drawings, for example, the work of Evelyn Karet, Peter Windows, and others have made us familiar with figures such as Felice Feliciano (1433–1479), that quintessential Renaissance man of Verona, a humanist, antiquarian, poet, and collector, whose will of 1466 discussed his drawings collection, and whose collector's mark (even if often effaced) allows us to identify sheets that were in his collection, among them works by Stefano da Verona (1379–1451). Other early collectors include Antonio Badile the Younger (1424–1507/12), who before his death had managed to assemble the group of drawings that were long part of the now-dismembered Badile Album.[1] They and others all predated Vasari, who was only born in 1511.

Vasari still stands as a pivotal figure, however, in a distinct kind of drawing collecting, and his scholarly, historical interests can be said to have led him there. Specifically, it seems that Vasari can be credited with a mode of consistently collecting not only the autonomous drawings, fancy portrait heads, and relatively finished compositional studies that were the mainstay of most collections up to (and beyond) Vasari's time, but also scrappy preparatory sketches, works that were generally not understood by their creators to have inherent pictorial values, but which were instead the functional working material of the studio (fig. 6.1).[2] The working drawing, a quick compositional idea or a study made to work out the pose of a figure, was inherently a different sort of object. Paintings, of course, were made to commission, or with the intention

1 On Feliciano, Badile, and other early collectors, see Karet, "The Tradition of Collecting," with references to earlier bibliography.

2 It bears noting that while this sheet might stand in for the kinds of drawings that Vasari collected, the question of whether the arrangement and mounting of the sheets was by (or for) Vasari, or for Niccolò Gaddi, is a question that needs to be considered further, as Andrew Morrogh has demonstrated; see Morrogh, "Vasari's Libro."

 | DOI:10.1163/9789004513938_008

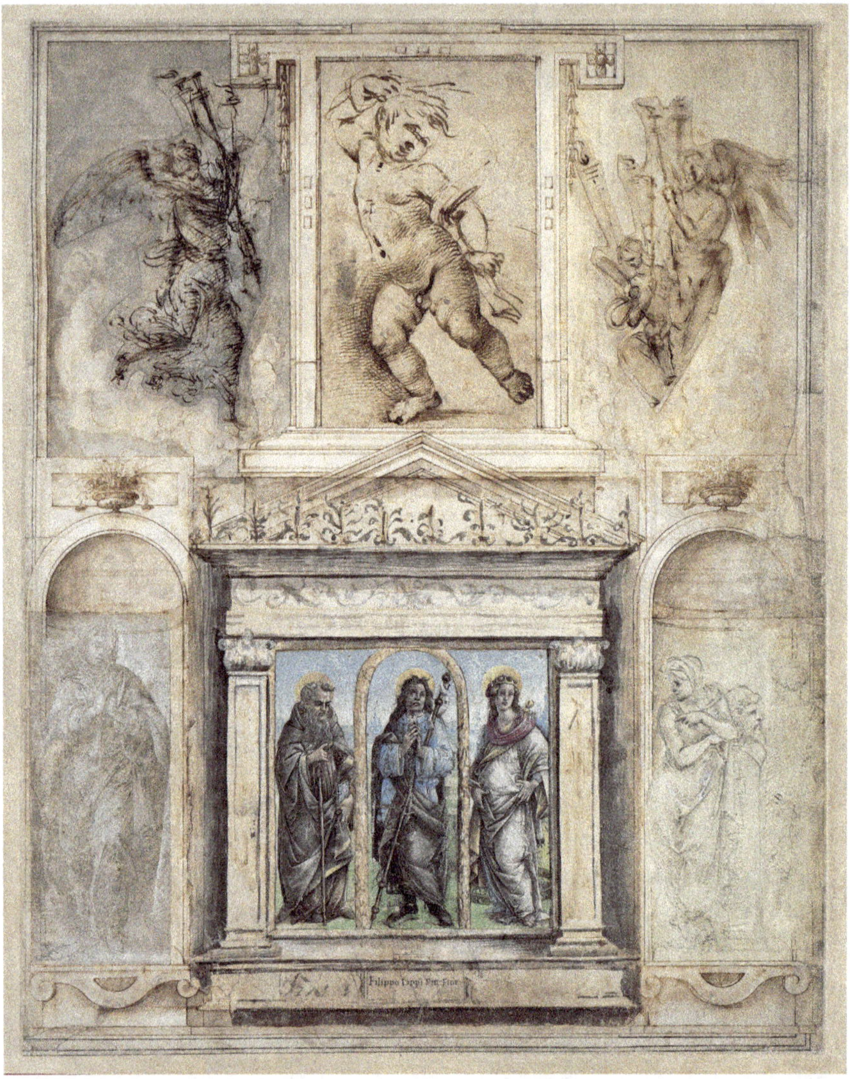

FIGURE 6.1 Filippino Lippi (1457–1504), Sandro Botticelli (1445–1510), and Raffaellino del Garbo (1466–1527), *Studies mounted on a page of Vasari's Libro de' Disegni*, after 1524. 56.7 × 45.7 cm (22 15/16 × 18 in.)
NATIONAL GALLERY OF ART, WASHINGTON, DC, INV. 1991.190.1

that they be sold and shown. Worked-up compositional drawings, moreover, might be required by contracts or else just shown to the patron of a work as part of conventional habit. These drawings were thus made with the intention or expectation that they would be seen and shown, and they became, rather naturally, collectable. The distinctions between a compositional *modello* and an autonomous drawing—a drawing made as an end in itself—thus easily blur. The working sketch or figure drawing, however, was a different beast. For the most part, painters of the fifteenth and sixteenth centuries only reluctantly surrendered such materials to collectors, partly because they were elements of a studio's working material but also because most painters did not understand them as works demonstrating their full abilities. And while painters often maintained this view well into the seventeenth century, the attitude of collectors had changed, and working drawings both new and old increasingly found their way into collectors' hands. It is this process of cleaning out the workshop, of the ways both practical and theoretical by which preparatory drawings became collectors' material, that this chapter will address.[3]

1 Types of Drawings and the Desires of Collectors

It is an art historical commonplace that during the Italian Renaissance, the practice of sketching came to be valued as never before. The sketch, that is, was understood to be a marker of artistic genius, representing a moment in which an artist seized upon inspiration and, in a godlike act, brought a new creation into being. Elements of this belief can be found in the treatise on painting by Leon Battista Alberti (1404–1472), and it is a historical phenomenon with which Leonardo da Vinci (1452–1519) is particularly associated.[4]

And yet, even if theorists and artists began to think this way by the early fifteenth century, actual collecting practices seem to have lagged behind, for a good portion of those drawings that actually survive from the quattrocento are highly finished works that seem to have been made not for the artists' own purposes, but as items for patrons and collectors. These include not only highly finished portrait drawings but also refined compositional drawings on parchment, a costly material not used for casual sketching but for more formal works. A *Judith Handing the Head of Holofernes to Her Maid* (fig. 6.2) by Francesco Francia (ca. 1450–1517) is a typical example.[5] As mentioned above,

3 Long ago, Julius Held touched on some of these same questions in his "The Early Appreciation of Drawings." That essay remains an important survey of the various fates that drawings endured in the sixteenth and seventeenth centuries, and when, after writing and delivering this paper at the Frick conference, I went back to Held's article for another reason, I was surprised at how much overlap there was between his piece and my own. What I offer here might be considered an expansion and refinement of some of the same arguments.

4 The fundamental essay on this topic is Gombrich, "Leonardo's Method."

5 See Eitel-Porter and Marciari, *Italian Renaissance Drawings*, no. 15, for further discussion of the sheet including other versions produced by Francia and his workshop.

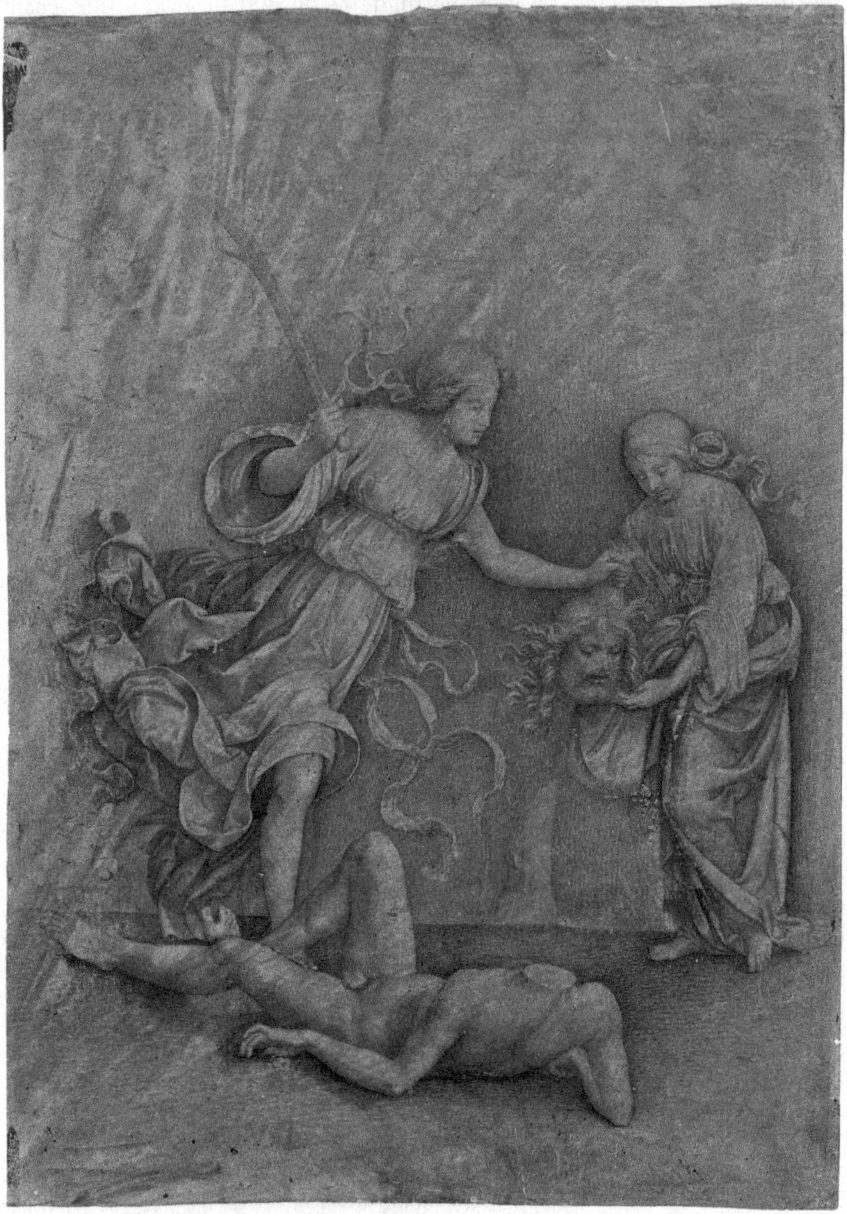

FIGURE 6.2 Francesco Francia, (1450–1517), *Judith Handing the Head of Holofernes to Her Maid*, ca. 1500–1508. Brown ink over traces of red chalk, with brown and green wash and white opaque watercolor, on parchment, 359 × 259 mm (14 1/8 × 10 3/8 in.)
MORGAN LIBRARY & MUSEUM, NEW YORK, INV. I, 94

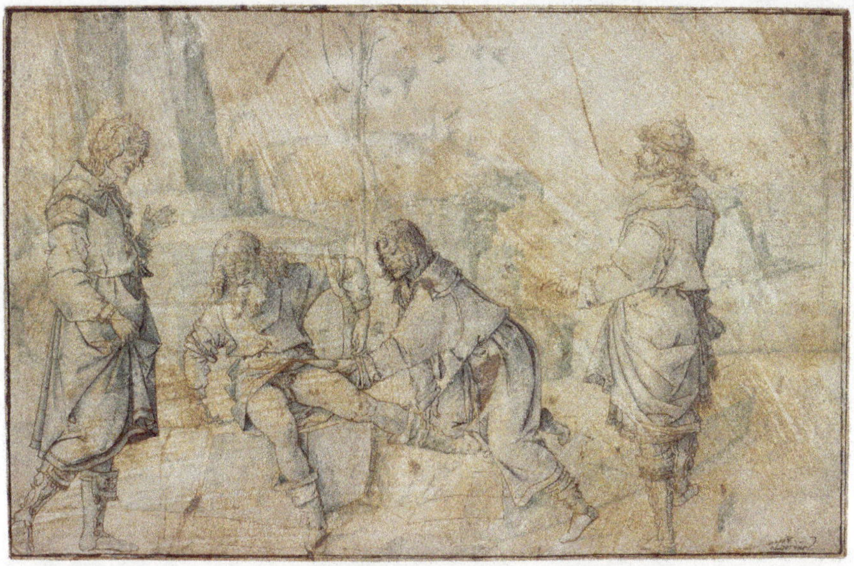

FIGURE 6.3 Bartolomeo Montagna (1450–1523), *Drunkenness of Noah*, ca. 1482–83. Pen and brown ink, blue and purple wash, over black chalk, on parchment, 228 × 357 mm (9 × 14 in.)
MORGAN LIBRARY & MUSEUM, NEW YORK, INV. I, 95

compositional drawings often fall into the same category, and the line between the modello and the autonomous drawing is not always clear. Bartolomeo Montagna's (1450–1523) *Drunkenness of Noah* (fig. 6.3), for example, is on parchment and makes use of the colored wash seen in the Francia and in other autonomous drawings; the yellow streaks, moreover, are the residue of a very old varnish applied to the drawing, presumably by a collector who treated it as akin to a painting and hung it on the wall. And yet, Montagna produced a *Drunkenness of Noah* in 1483 for the Scuola di San Marco in Venice, and there is some evidence that this is a drawing that he had to show to his patrons as part of the contractual approval process.[6] Similarly, some of the most impressive early drawings to survive—works such as the *Presentation of the Virgin* by Taddeo Gaddi (ca. 1300–1366), connected to his frescoes in the Baroncelli chapel at Santa Croce in Florence,[7] or the *Arrest and Martyrdom of San Miniato* by Cenni di Ser Francesco Cenni (active 1369–1415), probably related to lost

6 Verdigel, "Colore in Disegno," especially 152–53.

7 Musée du Louvre, Paris, inv. 1222.

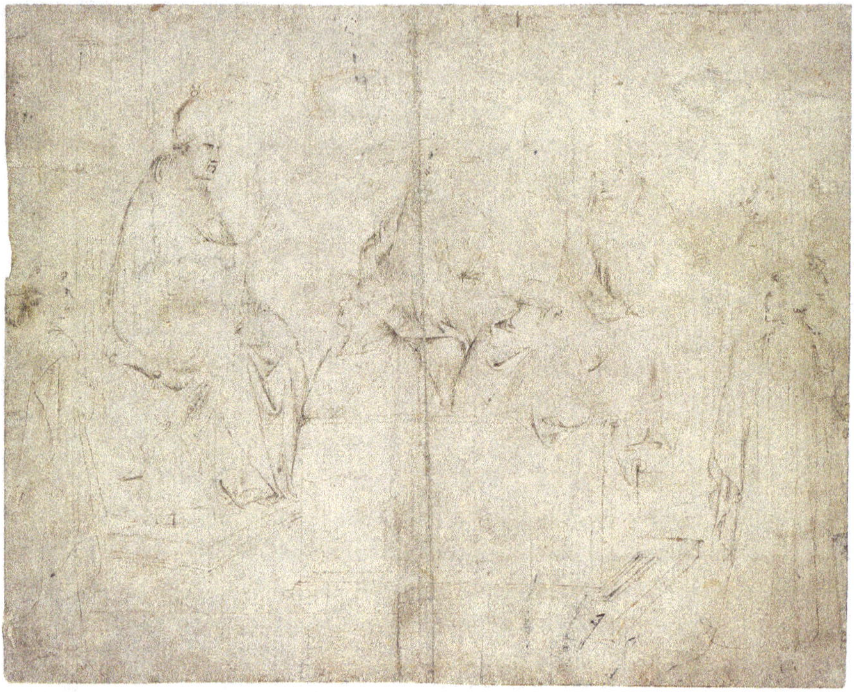

FIGURE 6.4 Spinello Aretino (1350–1410), *Miracles of Thomas Becket Read to Pope Alexander III*, ca. 1407–8. Pen and brown ink, 282 × 361 mm. (11 1/8 × 14 3/16 in.)
MORGAN LIBRARY & MUSEUM, NEW YORK, INV. I, 1A

frescoes done in the town of San Miniato west of Florence[8]—are connected to painting projects. Some believe these to be contract drawings, and others that they are *ricordi* of paintings, in which case they must also have been made for some special purpose. Either way, they are highly finished, but to a degree that went beyond anything normally required for the preparation of a painting; other considerations must have been at work.

The truly amazing survival from the early Renaissance, however, is not of a highly finished work, as rare as such things are, but rather, of a sheet like the *Miracles of Thomas Becket Read to Pope Alexander III* (fig. 6.4) by Spinello Aretino (1346–1410). This is a *sketch*: a working compositional drawing, a trial run modified in the final work, for his frescoes in the Palazzo Pubblico in Siena, done around 1408. As a marker of just how rare such a thing is, consider that

8 Morgan Library & Museum, New York, inv. I, 1; see Eitel-Porter and Marciari *Italian Renaissance Drawings*, cat. 4.

it has been identified as the earliest working sketch for an extant painting.[9] It seems striking that nothing predates the fifteenth century. And in this case, it was almost certainly an accidental survival. The paper was reused when Spinello's son Parri Spinelli (ca. 1387–1453) made an elaborate figure drawing on the other side of the sheet, the sort of drawing that would have had a continuing role in the working of the studio and was almost certainly the reason the sheet with Spinello's sketch was saved and made its way through time.

Other examples further illustrate the emphasis on finished, pictorial drawings in pre-Vasarian collecting. One case in point is the collector Gabriele Vendramin (1484–1552) in Venice. The notes made by Marcantonio Michiel (1484–1552) when he visited the collection, a will drawn up before Vendramin's death in 1552, and posthumous inventories from the 1560s allow us to reconstruct his holdings.[10] He, for example, owned the drawing book by Jacopo Bellini (ca. 1400–ca. 1470) now in the British Museum,[11] as well as the paired portrait drawings by Giovanni Bellini (ca. 1435–1516) and Vittore Belliniano (fl. 1507–1529) now at Chantilly.[12] What is much more surprising is that Vendramin had Roman works as well as Venetian, including a number of fancy compositional drawings from Raphael (1483–1520) and his workshop, among them the *Appearance of Sts. Peter and Paul to Attila and Pope Leo* and *Adoration of the Shepherds* in the Louvre.[13] There was obviously a trade in such drawings that went far beyond the artists' immediate circle.

Turning to Rome, we can cite the collection of Fulvio Orsini (1529–1600), which has been reconstructed by Michel Hochmann and others.[14] Orsini served as librarian and antiquarian to the Farnese cardinals, but he built a collection of his own as well. His drawings were—typically for the time—shown framed, mixed with paintings and conceptually akin to them, not kept in albums or portfolios as rare objects. Again, these were a combination of autonomous drawings, highly finished compositional models, and cartoons or cartoon fragments. They included a Michelangelo (1475–1564) *Fall of Phaeton*, perhaps the one that was later in the Farnese collection and is now in the Royal Collection at Windsor; Orsini was librarian to Alessandro Farnese (1520–1589), and his collection was later merged into the Farnese's own. He also owned a study by

9 See Weppelmann, "Spinello Aretino's *Canonization*," and more recently, Eitel–Porter and Marciari *Italian Renaissance Drawings*, cat. 5.

10 See Windows, "New Identifications"; and Idem., "Gabriele Vendramin's '*disegni divini*'."

11 British Museum, London, inv. 1855,0811.1-98.

12 Musée Condé, Chantilly, inv. DE118 and DE121.

13 Musée du Louvre, Paris, inv. 3873 and 3460.

14 See especially Hochmann, "Les dessins de Fulvio Orsini."

Giulio Clovio (1498–1578) after Michelangelo's *Crucifixion*.[15] Drawings taken to this level of refinement were inherently precious objects. Similarly, exceptions to the general rule of preferring pictorial compositional drawings might be made for treasures by someone like Raphael, especially in the decades after the painter's early death. Orsini also seems to have owned Raphael's study of Aeneas and Anchises for the Vatican fresco the *Fire in the Borgo*.[16]

Orsini's Roman contemporary Antonio Tronsarelli (d. 1601) formed an analogous collection in the latter half of the Cinquecento.[17] It was heavily weighted toward works by Tronsarelli's contemporaries and included compositional drawings such as the *Presentation of the Virgin* by Perino del Vaga (1501–1547) now in the Metropolitan Museum of Art, or the *Allegory of Peace* by Francesco Salviati (1510/11–1563) in the British Museum.[18] Highly finished drawings in the Michelangelesque mode, in which a figure drawing was carried to such a degree of refinement that it became an end in itself also began to appear in collections in this moment later in the sixteenth century: examples in Tronsarelli's holdings included Daniele da Volterra's (1509–1566) *Dido*. While many of Tronsarelli's drawings were framed and hung on the wall like those of Orsini, there were 150 more kept in an album. This album seems not, however, to have been organized according to any historical principles, for one page had drawings by Salviati, Raphael, Beccafumi, and Perino del Vaga on it, while another juxtaposed sheets by Perino, Raffaelle da Montelupo, Perugino, and Salviati. Most pages of the album had a single drawing on them, but these pages with multiple drawings indicate that Orsini was willing to acquire smaller sketches as well.

There is a body of evidence that clearly suggests that a distinction between the collectable, finished drawing and the working sketch persisted, and it was one maintained not only by the collectors, but also by the artists themselves. We can learn this, for example, from the surviving correspondence that documents the efforts of Niccolò Gaddi (1537–1591), one of the most ambitious drawings connoisseurs of the Cinquecento, to build a collection.[19] He followed Giorgio Vasari's lead in his collecting practices and acquired Vasari's *Libro de' Disegni* and expanded it, building an enormous collection of drawings.

15 Musée du Louvre, Paris, inv 843.

16 Albertina Museum, Vienna, inv. 4881.

17 See Lafranconi, "Antonio Tronsarelli."

18 Metropolitan Museum of Art, New York, inv. 63.75.1, and British Museum, London, inv. 1946,0713.52.

19 On Gaddi's collection, see Morrogh "Vasari's Libro," as well as Acidini Luchinat, "Niccolò Gaddi collezionista." For Gaddi's collection-related correspondence, see Bottari and Ticozzi, *Raccolta di lettere*, vol. 3.

To do so, he employed a network of agents in Rome, Venice, Bologna and elsewhere. Like Vasari, but like few collectors before the seventeenth century, Gaddi collected according to historical principles, and he was distinctly interested in working sketches, something that seems at times to have baffled the artists whom Gaddi or his agents approached.

In 1581, for example, Gaddi wrote to Francesco Bassano (1549–1592), requesting drawings by Francesco and his father, Jacopo (ca. 1510–1592). Bassano first apologized and then demurred:

> [I]f these drawings are not to your excellency's taste, you must excuse me, because we [the Bassano family] have never drawn very much, nor have we made a profession of drawing, but certainly we have employed every kind of study in order to produce works of art, which we have wanted to realize in the best possible way.[20]

What does this mean: *we employ every kind of study, but we have never drawn very much*? It could be suggested that this was a matter of a Venetian responding to the perceived differences between Venetian and Tuscan art. In likewise fashion, a few years earlier in 1574, the Bolognese dealer Ercole Basso had written to Gaddi from Venice, expressing frustration with the difficulty of finding drawings there: "I am sending your excellency four pieces," Basso wrote, "which don't satisfy me. Nonetheless, I am sending them because I went to such difficulty to find them, the case being that these painters paint without drawing."[21] But he had the drawings, and as Bassano said, "we have employed every kind of study." More than likely, this was less a matter of finding drawings, but of finding drawings like those they expected Gaddi would want.

In support of this idea, the letters that Giovanni Antonio Dosio (1533–1611) wrote to Gaddi provide interesting insights. The architect Dosio served as Gaddi's agent in Rome, and he wrote extensively about his search for drawings there in 1574.[22] He was unsuccessful in his attempt to find drawings by Sebastiano del Piombo (1485–1547), and because Federico Zuccaro (1539–1609) was off on his travels in the wake of the *Porta Virtutis* scandal, Dosio could not offer Gaddi any drawings by Federico or his brother Taddeo (1529–1566): the family workshop must have been closed up tight. The most telling line in his letter, however, relates to his attempt to get drawings by Girolamo Muziano

20 Bottari and Ticozzi *Raccolta di lettere*, vol. 3: 265–66.

21 Bottari and Ticozzi *Raccolta di lettere*, vol. 3: 272–94. On Basso, see also McCrory, "The Dukes and Their Dealers."

22 Bottari and Ticozzi *Raccolta di lettere*, vol. 3: 300–301.

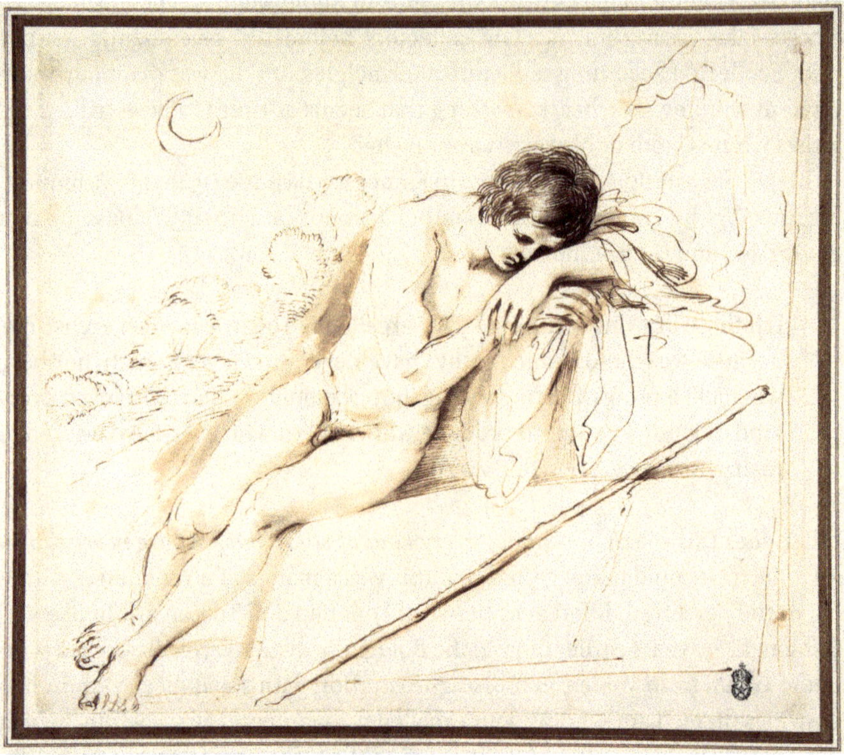

FIGURE 6.5 Guercino (1591–1666), *Endymion*, ca. 1630–35. Pen and brown ink and wash, 212 × 248 mm (8 3/8 × 9 ¾ in.)
THE METROPOLITAN MUSEUM OF ART NEW YORK, INV. 68.171

(1532–1592). Muziano was an avid and beautiful draftsman, who created highly finished landscapes in pen and ink as well as refined figure studies especially in red chalk. Yet, Dosio wrote, "Muziano gives us difficulty, not having things that satisfy, and wanting to send something good." It was inconceivable that Muziano did not have drawings in the workshop, for his figure studies and landscape drawings are among the most refined examples surviving from mid-Cinquecento Rome, but perhaps he did not have the sort of "good drawing" that he expected Gaddi to want. That is, I believe, he did not have any autonomous drawings, or elaborate compositional drawings, or at least was not willing to give them up.

Even seventy-five years later in 1650, in a letter to his patron Don Antonio Ruffo (1610/11–1678), Guercino (1591–1666) would explain that he could not send any drawings because his poor health necessitated that he paint directly to the canvas. Yet, at that time, Guercino was painting a full-length canvas of

Endymion for Ruffo, perhaps using a drawing now at the Metropolitan Museum of Art as his model (fig. 6.5).[23] Even if the drawing was more than a decade old by 1650, which to judge from its style seems not unlikely, the point is that Guercino was not going to surrender it to Ruffo. Guercino's reuse of an earlier sketch in fact tells part of the story, for the artist often returned to his earlier drawings and used an older study of a subject as the starting point for a new painting. For some artists, it might have been a case of misunderstanding what the collectors wanted, but for others like Guercino, it seems a matter of deliberate evasiveness.

2 Workshop Practice and the Preservation of Drawings

Alongside this pattern of exchange (and in some cases the reticence to do so), which reveals how both artists and collectors understood the ideas around collecting practices, a related phenomenon deserves consideration: the desire for an artist to have his workshop pass to his heirs largely intact, with all of the working drawings, especially as long as the artist had an heir who was himself a painter. In the case of Guercino, some of the painter's drawings made it out into the world during his lifetime, but he left the overwhelming majority to his two nephews, Benedetto (1633–1715) and Cesare Gennari (1637–1688), who were themselves painters. Benedetto, the elder, died without heirs, so the drawings then passed to Cesare's sons Filippo Antonio (1677–1751) and Gianfrancesco (1671–1727), and it was after their death, three generations after Guercino's own, that Gianfrancesco's son Carlo (1716–1790) began selling off the family drawings in earnest, with one large group passing through the hands of the Bolognese dealer Francesco Forni (fl. ca. 1740–50) to the Englishman John Bouverie (ca. 1722–1750),[24] and much of the rest being acquired by Richard Dalton (ca. 1715–1791) for the British Royal Collection, where more than 800 examples remain.[25]

Jacopo Tintoretto (1518/19–1594) offers an earlier but similar example of an artist preserving his workshop. With his death in 1594, his workshop passed wholly intact to his elder son Domenico (1560–1635), who continued operating

23 The drawing was first connected with the Ruffo letter and commission by Mahon, *Omaggio al Guercino*, 8; see also Griswold, "Guercino."

24 It was after Guercino's death that many of his drawings were laid onto the familiar and distinctive "Casa Gennari" mounts, though whether these were added by the Gennari, Francesco Forni (as seems most likely to the present author), or Bouverie remains an open question; see Marciari, *Guercino: Virtuoso Draftsman*, 22–24 for a recent summary.

25 See Mahon and Turner, *The Drawings of Guercino*.

the studio until his own death in 1635. It then passed to Sebastiano Casser (1596–after 1678), a German painter who was a member of the studio, and who became the heir to it when he married Domenico's sister Ottavia (1570–1646), notwithstanding the fact that Ottavia was already 69 years old at the time of the marriage, and that Casser was some 26 years her junior.[26] According to the terms of Domenico's will, Casser was to be given, among other things, a bust of Vitellius (the model for so many drawings in the Tintoretto studio), a statue and two torsos, all the drawings Casser had done as a student in Domenico's workshop, and 150 sketches of male figures and fifty of female figures, in addition to all the pigments, brushes and a porphyry stone still in the studio—in other words, the working material for the studio, including drawings. Domenico's younger brother Marco (1561–1637), however, was to get the sketches and paintings of Jacopo and the so-called *disegni buoni*.

This distinction between the "good drawings" by Jacopo and the working material of the studio is an important one. Famously, almost none of Jacopo's compositional drawings survive; more than likely, most of them passed to Marco and were somehow subsequently lost. Accidents happen. The figure drawings, however, remained in the workshop. Leopoldo de' Medici (1617–1675), to whom we will return, acquired about 150 of them late in his life, using his agents to buy them from Casser. We also know that in 1678, Antonio Saurer, an agent acting on behalf of Don Gasparo de Haro y Guzman, Marqués del Carpio (1629–1687), visited the aged Casser, who sold him further remnants of the studio including the compositional drawings by Domenico Tintoretto now in the British Museum.[27] Indeed, the extant drawings by Jacopo and his workshop seem mainly to have been sold off in two large groups: the Medici set now in the Uffizi, and a second set—all figure drawings—that bears the inscription *Giacomo Tintoretto* or *G Tintoretto*, added by an unknown collector. It is not clear how or when this group left the workshop, but its relatively high quality (with many sheets by Jacopo himself) suggests that these were not the dregs left when Saurer visited the workshop in 1678. Whatever its original source, most—possibly all—of this latter group made its way together down to the collection of Joshua Reynolds (1723–1792), after which the group was broken

26 On Casser, see Mazzucco, *Jacomo Tintoretto*, 651, 761–762, 909, 924, 925, as well as Zarrillo, "The Neurosis of Visual Legacy."

27 On Saurer's visit to Casser, see Checa Cremades, "El Marqués del Carpio." The large group of ex-Carpio drawings in the British Museum, though now clearly recognizable as by Domenico, were long believed to be the work of Jacopo and were presumably passed off by Casser as the master's work.

up. These sheets are now scattered in collections in England, the United States, Rotterdam, Vienna, Berlin, and elsewhere.[28]

Niccolò Gaddi's attempt to buy drawings by the Bassano discussed above finds its rejoinder some 80 years later in 1654, when Leopoldo de' Medici's agent Paolo del Sera (1617–1672) tracked down Giovanni Domenico Biava (fl. ca. 1620–50), who was the heir and executor of Gerolamo Bassano (1566–1621). He was able to send a group of drawings to Florence, although he noted that at least one of these was *solo per discorso pittoresco*, yet another sign that the workshop was yielding not elaborately finished studies but rather working sketches.[29]

Above all, the fact that working drawings generally stayed together in a workshop, as long as there was an heir to inherit them, and especially if there was an heir who was an artist, cannot be over-emphasized. Explicit documentation of this is found in the will of Peter Paul Rubens (1577–1640), who explained that his drawings—both those he made, and those by other artists—were not to be sold until his youngest child was eighteen, and then only if none of his sons had become a painter, and if none of his daughters had married one.[30]

The issue of inheritance becomes more complicated when there was no heir, or when the heir was not an artist. Federico Barocci (ca. 1533–1612), for example, gave some of his drawings to his primary assistants, Ventura Mazzi (1560–1638) and Antonio Viviani (1560–1620), but the overwhelming mass of them passed to his nephew, Ambrogio (fl. ca. 1650), who was not an artist. Ambrogio would eventually sell more than 800 sheets to Leopoldo de' Medici's agents Giovanni Battista Staccoli in 1658 and Domenico Maria Corsi in 1673 (again explaining why such a large group of drawings came to the Uffizi).[31] Some of Mazzi's drawings wound up in the collection of Pierre Crozat (1665–1740) and probably include those in the Louvre,[32] but the most amazing footnote in this history of dispersal concerns the drawings that Barocci gave to Viviani (fig. 6.6). These remained in the house of Viviani's family in Urbino

28 On the groups of drawings extracted from Tintoretto's workshop en bloc, see also Marciari, "*Drawing in Tintoretto's Venice.*"

29 Garofalo and Faietti, "Il fondo antico dei Bassano."

30 Belkin, "The Classification of Rubens's Drawings." Furthermore, the drawings were grouped in the studio not by artist (as a collector or historian might have them), but rather, by iconography, further indication that they were working materials.

31 Regarding the drawings that Ambrogio stubbornly kept together until they were sold to Leopoldo, see Baldinucci, *Notizie*, 6: 71–75, 82–87.

32 For Mazzi's drawings see Sangiorgi, ed., *Committenze milanesi*, 66–68.

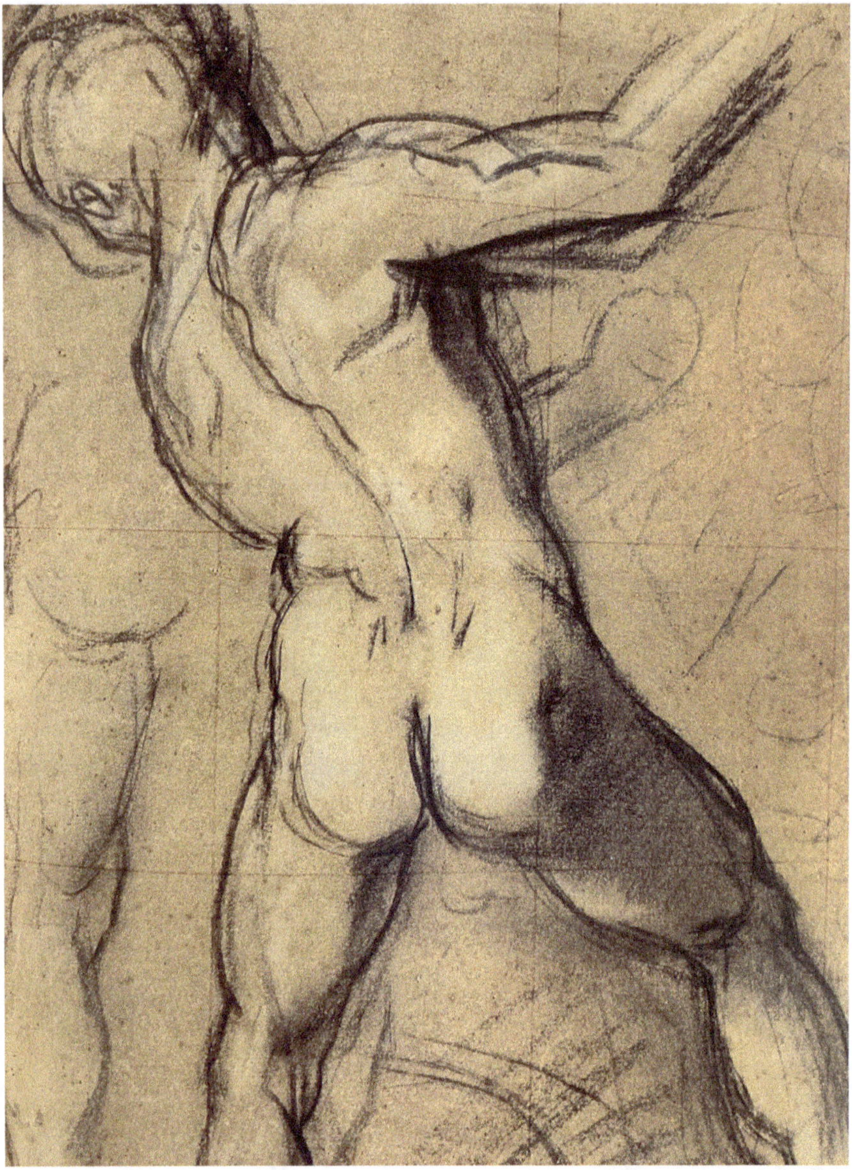

FIGURE 6.6 Federico Barocci, (1535–1612), *Study of a Male Nude* for the *Martyrdom of St. Vitalis*, 1583. Charcoal and white chalk, squared in red chalk, on brown paper, 340 × 250 mm (13.3 × 98.4 in.)
GALLERIA NAZIONALE DELLE MARCHE, URBINO, INV. 1990 DIS 39

through the 1920s; astonishingly, August Schmarsow found some still hanging on the wall when he went to Urbino 300 years after Barocci's death.[33]

Further evidence falls in line with this pattern. Giovanni Battista Armenini (1530–1609) notes that Perino del Vaga's daughter sold her father's drawings to "a Mantuan Merchant," and we learn from other sources that this occurred around 1555, about a decade after Perino's death, and that the Mantuan merchant was the antiquary Jacopo Strada (1515–1588).[34] Strada was a voracious collector and seems to have realized how to work the system of buying from an artist's heirs when there was no later painter in the family. He also bought some drawings by Giulio Romano (1499–1526) from the artist's son, a purchase that probably included the best sheets not only by Giulio, but also by his master Raphael.[35] According to Vasari, Raphael died without heirs and had left drawings to his assistants Giovan Francesco Penni (ca. 1496–after 1528) and Giulio. After Strada left Mantua and moved to Vienna in 1556, he remained an active buyer, and his famous portrait by Titian was painted in 1568 during a trip to Venice in which Strada tried unsuccessfully to acquire the previously mentioned Vendramin collection for Duke Albrecht of Bavaria.[36] And yet, even Strada cannot have bought everything that Giulio left behind in Mantua, for Rubens also managed to acquire a notable group of Giulio's drawings during his years in the city long afterwards.[37]

While general patterns become clear, there are exceptions in almost every case of the retention or dispersal of workshop drawings. Despite Guercino's notable stinginess, for example, and the desire of his immediate heirs Benedetto and Cesare Gennari to keep the drawings together, many of Guercino's drawings nonetheless left the Casa Gennari before the eighteenth century. Christina of Sweden (1626–1689) was able to acquire some, possibly during her visit to

33 See Schmarsow, *Federigo Baroccis Zeichnungen*, as well as Bernini Pezzini, "Diesgni baroccheschi." I am grateful to Ian Verstegen for sharing the story of the Barocci drawings with me. The drawings are all now in the Galleria Nazionale delle Marche, for which see Arcangeli, *Federico Barocci*.

34 Popham, "On Works by Perino del Vaga," 59. Another case that might be cited is that of Parmigianino, for which see Popham, "The Baiardo Inventory." Popham suggests that Parmigianino's heirs (not artists themselves) may have exchanged the master's stock of drawings for the money owed to his patron Francesco Baiardo (1486–1561), who had provided surety on a contract left unsatisfied at the artist's early death.

35 Jansen, *Jacopo Strada*, 630–33.

36 Anderson, "A Further Inventory." The portrait is in the Kunsthistorisches Museum, Vienna, inv. GG81.

37 Wood, "Rubens's Collection of Drawings"; see also Jaffe, "Rubens and Giulio Romano," 325.

the artist near the end of his life.[38] Other Guercino drawings that were subsequently in the English collections of Peter Lely (1618–1680) and of the Dukes of Devonshire were perhaps sold to them by Benedetto Gennari after he moved to England in 1674. Still others were acquired by Carlo Cesare Malvasia (1616–1693), probably from the Gennari family in Bologna.

Annibale Carracci (1560–1609) provides a similar example: the enormous collection of drawings in the Royal Collection at Windsor represents the remnants of his studio, and we have an unbroken line of provenance: Annibale left these to Domenichino (1581–1641), who in turn left them to his assistant Francesco Raspantino (fl. 1637–1664). They were bought from Raspantino by Carlo Maratti (1625–1713), who sold them to the Albani Pope Clement XI (1649–1721); they were then acquired from the Albani collection for the British Royal Library. Not surprisingly for a group of drawings that were the remnants of the workshop, this group includes sheets not only by Annibale himself, but also by his assistants in Rome; there remain even today among the so-called "Annibale" drawings at Windsor sheets probably by Domenichino, Francesco Albani (1578–1660), Giovanni Lanfranco (1582–1647), and others. One can imagine the studies for a given project being gathered together at the end of work, regardless of which artist had made them, and passing down through history together. And yet, if the workshop remnants went to Domenichino, there are hundreds of other Carracci drawings that had already left the studio. During Annibale's lifetime, a group of drawings was somehow acquired by the Bonfiglioli family of Bologna; it is tempting to think that these were drawings from Annibale's early years, left behind when the artist moved to Rome. These were later acquired by Joseph Smith (1682–1770) and were sold by him to the Royal Collection, but having been integrated with the ex-Albani drawings, there seems no way to be sure which came from which source. Malvasia also managed to acquire a large group of Carracci drawings; one also wonders whether these were somehow extracted from the Bonfiglioli holdings in Bologna. In Rome, however, Francesco Angeloni (1559–1652), a friend of the artist, was also said to have had 600 drawings. These were surely studied by Angeloni's nephew and heir, Giovanni Pietro Bellori (1613–1696), who was meant to inherit them, but after Angeloni's death, they were dispersed, with a large group going to France with Nicolas Mignard (1606–1668) and eventually finding their way into the collections of Crozat, Pierre-Jean Mariette (1694–1774), and ultimately the Louvre.[39]

---

38 van Tuyll, *Guercino*, 20, notes that despite a common presumption, the Guercino drawings in the Teylers Museum, containing many rough sketches and fragments, are unlikely to have been the drawings that Guercino bestowed upon the Queen during the visit, even if many of the Teylers Italian drawings ultimately descend from her collection.

39 Wittkower, *Drawings of the Carracci*, 18–22.

3 Collectors and Historians

With the mention of Bellori and Malvasia we come to a key moment in the history of drawing collecting, one in which the historian-collectors (those interested in all kinds of drawings) take over. There were relatively few of these in the sixteenth century, with Vasari and Gaddi serving as notable examples. Yet, by the seventeenth century, a distinct and different pattern emerges, with scholars both collecting for themselves and overseeing the princely and ducal collections. The case seems to be more than one of very rich aristocrats simply buying up everything that was available; instead, there was a paradigm shift of sorts, in which any drawing—sketches as well as more finished drawings and works by minor artists in addition to the great masters—had newly understood value. Two key figures here are Cardinal Leopoldo de' Medici and his advisor Filippo Baldinucci (1625–1696). Leopoldo acquired the collection of Niccolò Gaddi (and the core of Vasari's *Libro de' Disegni* as part of it), and he and Baldinucci set out to continue what Vasari and Gaddi had begun. They employed a network of agents across Italy, among them the above-mentioned agents buying remnants of Tintoretto's workshop from Sebastiano Casser, and of Barocci's workshop from Ambrogio Barroci. In a letter to one of his correspondents, Bernardo della Penna (fl. ca. 1670), Leopoldo explained that he would "always take the drawings of the great masters, already having a good collection," but he was also interested in the others, those not of the best class or from an earlier age, for he had few examples. His collecting practices were a novelty, one he had to explain to his agents.[40]

In addition to Baldinucci in Florence, Leopoldo's agents included Malvasia and Bonaventura Bisi (1601–1659) in Bologna, and Marco Boschini (1602–1681) in Venice, among many others, and one can imagine how his own collection would have been perceived and emulated by those who became historians and collectors themselves.[41] Leopoldo's drawings became the core of the Uffizi collection today, the greatest single resource for Italian drawings. Baldinucci himself formed a collection of some 1200 drawings, arranged chronologically in four volumes, although ironically, these eventually passed not into the Uffizi, but rather, into the Louvre, which acquired the albums in Florence in 1806 after they had descended through the Pandolfini family.[42] Long before that time, of course, the Louvre collections had acquired a similar flavor of the historical collection, thanks in no small part to the influence of later historian-collectors like Mariette.

40 Baldinucci, *Notizie*, 6:93.

41 On Bisi, see Stone, "Il frate con l'orecchino d'oro."

42 See Bacou and Bean, *Disegni fiorentini*; see also Tordella, "Documents inédits."

The pattern of artists trying to hold on to their working drawings did not shift significantly and would continue into the eighteenth century—one thinks of the Tiepolo family organizing their drawings in albums prior to their move to Spain[43]—but by that time, there were few collectors who hesitated to buy drawings of any sort as soon as they were available. There would always be (and there will always be) collectors who preferred the big pictorial sheets, especially compositional *modelli*, that were prized by the earliest collectors, but so long as the scholarly approach to drawing collecting prevailed, the workshop remnants were eagerly purchased, and the working drawing had become valuable collectors' treasure.

Bibliography

Acidini Luchinat, Cristina. "Niccolò Gaddi collezionista e dilettante del Cinquecento." *Paragone Arte* 31, nos. 359/361 (1980): 141–75.

Anderson, Jaynie. "A Further Inventory of Gabriel Vendramin's Collection." *The Burlington Magazine* 121 (1979): 639–48.

Arcangeli, Luciano. *Federico Barocci: I disegni della Galleria Nazionale delle Marche.* Rome: Miligraf, 2012.

Bacou, Roseline, and Jacob Bean. *Disegni fiorentini del Museo del Louvre dalla collezione di Filippo Baldinucci* (exh. cat.). Rome: Gabinetto Nazionale delle Stampe, 1959.

Baldinucci, Filippo. *Notizie dei professori del disegno da Cimabue in qua.* Florence: Studio per edizioni scelte, 1975.

Belkin, Kristin Lohse. "The Classification of Rubens's Drawings Collection." *Wallraf–Richartz–Jahrbuch* 55 (1994): 105–114.

Bernini Pezzini, Grazia. "Disegni baroccheschi nella collezione Viviani di Urbino." In *Studi in onore di Giulio Carlo Argan*, edited by Silvana Macchioni, 227–233. Florence: La Nuova Italia, 1984.

Bottari, Giovanni Gaetano, and Stefano Ticozzi. *Raccolta di lettere sulla pittura, scultura ed architettura scritta da' più celebri personaggi dei secoli XV, XVI e XVII.* Milan: G. Silvestri, 1822; (reprint Hildesheim and New York: G. Olms, 1976).

Checa Cremades, Fernando. "El Marqués del Carpio (1629–1687) y la pintura veneciana del Renacimiento. Negociaciones de Antonio Saurer." *Anales de Historia del Arte* 14 (2004): 193–212.

Eitel–Porter, Rhoda, and John Marciari. *Italian Renaissance Drawings at the Morgan Library & Museum.* New York: Morgan Library & Museum, 2019.

43 See Knox, *Catalogue of Tiepolo Drawings*, 3–9.

Garofalo, Cristiana, and Marzia Faietti. "Il fondo antico dei Bassano agli Uffizi: Fisionomia, consistenza. Percezione storica di Jacopo disegnatore." In *Jacopo Bassano: I figli, la scuola, l'eredità*, edited by G. Ericani, C. Caramanna, and F. Millozzi, *Atti del Convegno Internazionale di Studio (Bassano del Grappa, Museo Civico; Padova, Università degli Studi, Archivio Antico del Bò, 30 marzo–2 aprile 2011). In Bollettino del Museo Civico Musei Biblioteca Archivio di Bassano* n.s. 30–34 (2009–2013), 2: 548–69.

Gombrich, Ernst. "Leonardo's Method for Working out Compositions." In *Norm and Form: Studies in the Art of the Renaissance*. London, 1971, 1: 58–63.

Griswold, William. "Guercino." *The Metropolitan Museum of Art Bulletin* n. s. 48, no. 4 (Spring 1991): 40–41.

Held, Julius. "The Early Appreciation of Drawings." *Studies in Western Art: Acts of the Twentieth International Congress of the History of Art* (Princeton, 1963), vol. 3, 72–95.

Hochmann, Michel. "Les dessins et les peintures de Fulvio Orsini et la collection Farnèse." *Mélanges de l'Ecole française de Rome. Italie et Méditerranée* 105 (1993): 49–91.

Jaffe, Michael. "Rubens and Giulio Romano at Mantua." *Art Bulletin* 40 (1958): 325–29.

Jansen, Dirk Jacob. *Jacopo Strada and Cultural Patronage at The Imperial Court*. Leiden: Brill, 2019.

Karet, Evelyn. "The Tradition of Collecting Drawings in Northern Renaissance Italy before Vasari." In *A Demand for Drawings: Five Centuries of Collectors and Collecting Drawings*, edited by John Marciari, 15–29. New York: Morgan Library & Museum, 2018.

Knox, George. *Catalogue of the Tiepolo Drawings in the Victoria and Albert Museum*. London: Her Majesty's Stationery Office, 1960.

Lafranconi, Matteo. "Antonio Tronsarelli: A Roman Collector of the Late Sixteenth Century." *The Burlington Magazine* 140 (1998): 537–50.

Mahon, Denis. *Omaggio al Guercino* (exh. cat.). Cento: Pinacoteca Comunale, 1967.

Mahon, Denis, and Nicholas Turner. *The Drawings of Guercino in the Collection of Her Majesty the Queen at Windsor Castle*. Cambridge: Cambridge UP, 1989.

Marciari, John. *Guercino: Virtuoso Draftsman* (exh. cat.). New York: Morgan Library & Museum, 2019.

Marciari, John. "*Drawing in Tintoretto's Venice*: Marginal Notes to an Exhibition." *Artibus et Historiae* 81 (2020): 237–52.

Mazzucco, Melania G. *Jacomo Tintoretto ed i suoi figli: Storia di una famiglia veneziana*. Second edition. Milan: Rizzoli, 2009.

McCrory, Martha. "The Dukes and Their Dealers: The Formation of the Medici Grand-ducal Collections of the Sixteenth Century." In *The Art Market in Italy*, edited by Marcello Fantoni, Louisa C. Matthew, and Sara F. Matthews-Grieco, 355–66. Modena: Panini, 2003.

Morrogh, Andrew. "Vasari's Libro and the Drawings Collection of Niccolò Gaddi: The Frames." In *A Demand for Drawings: Five Centuries of Collectors and Collecting Drawings*, edited by John Marciari, 31–43. New York: Morgan Library & Museum, 2018.

Popham, A.E. "On Some Works by Perino del Vaga," *The Burlington Magazine* 86 (1945), 59–66.

Popham, A.E. "The Baiardo Inventory." In *Studies in Renaissance and Baroque Art Presented to Anthony Blunt on his 60th Birthday*, edited by Jeanne Courtauld et al., 26–29. London and New York: Phaidon, 1967.

Sangiorgi, Fert, ed. *Committenze milanesi a Federico Barocci e alla sua scuola*. Urbino: Accademia Raffaello, 1982.

Schmarsow, August. *Federigo Baroccis Zeichnungen, 2: Die Zeichnungen in den übrigen Sammlungen Italiens*. Leipzig: Teubner, 1910.

Stone, David M. "Il frate con l'orecchino d'oro: Bonaventura Bisi, pittore e mercante d'arte, e un nuovo ritratto del Guercino." In *Nuovi Studi sul Guercino: da Cento a Roma, da Piacenza a Bologna*, edited by Daniele Benati and David Stone, 57–70. Piacenza: Stampa TEP, 2020.

Tordella, Piera Giovanna. "Documents inédits sur l'entrée au Musée du Louvre de la collection de dessins de Filippo Baldinucci." *La Revue du Louvre* 5/6 (1996): 78–87.

Tuyll, Carel van. *Guercino 1591–1666: Drawings from Dutch Collections*. 's-Gravenhage: Schwarz/SDU, 1991.

Verdigel, Genevieve. "Colore in Disegno: A Reappraisal of the Use of Color in Fifteenth-century Draftsmanship in the Veneto." *Master Drawings* 58 (2020): 148–68.

Weppelmann, Stefan. "Spinello Aretino's *Canonization of Thomas Becket* and Trecento Drawing Practice." *Master Drawings* 41 (2003): 3–13.

Windows, Peter. "New Identifications in the Drawings Collection of Gabriele Vendramin." *Master Drawings* 50 (2012): 33–48.

Windows, Peter. "Gabriele Vendramin's '*disegni divini*': The Anatomy of an Early Collection of Drawings." *Journal of the History of Collections* 26 (2014): 1–19.

Wittkower, Rudolf. *The Drawings of the Carracci in the Collection of Her Majesty the Queen at Windsor Castle*. London: Phaidon, 1952.

Wood, Jeremy. "Rubens's Collection of Drawings: His Attributions and Inscriptions." *Wallraf-Richartz Jahrbuch* 55 (1994), 333–51.

Zarrillo, Taryn Marie. "The Neurosis of Visual Legacy: Seicento Venetian Painters Confront Their Past." In *The Enduring Legacy of Venetian Renaissance Art*, edited by Andaleeb Badiee Banta, 11–24. London and New York: Routledge, Taylor & Francis Group, 2016.

CHAPTER 7

Modern Michelangelos? Copies, Fakes, and New Economies of Taste in the Early Seicento

Hannah Joy Friedman

1 Introduction: Copies Everywhere

In his preface to the reader of *Il Microcosmo della Pittura* (1657), the physician and art theorist Francesco Scannelli (1616–1663) presents his credentials as an expert in matters of art, not only by announcing his firsthand knowledge of the beautiful works that he discusses, but also by emphasizing his ability to distinguish these from the numerous copies that often supplant them and tarnish the names of the great masters:

> I know (and it is true) that in various public places there are pictures of rare beauty, and also in private homes there are very excellent and valuable works; and to most of these I can testify as an eyewitness [*testificare di vista*], as in the homes of great Princes of Italy, and Lords of great worth; and I am equally aware of that which experience itself then discloses, whereas quite often the copies of paintings unduly pass for originals, being served by obscurity; which pictures of modest character mostly bear upon the panel the name of a good master so as to pass frankly for their work; and the copies, gaining credibility through time and diligence, and through the original having on occasion faded, or been carried off to some faraway place, [the copies] obtain the foremost place; and through the studios being filled with works by certain Masters whose activities never went beyond the boundaries of their own regions, thus [do] their works, and similarly their names, as though ill-born, succumb and die.[1]

As this passage of the *Microcosmo* attests, copies abounded in Italian art collections by the mid-seventeenth century. The potential for these copies to make tacit and spurious claims as to their authorship is a source of indignation for

1 Scannelli, *Il Microcosmo della Pittura*, preface, unnumbered, translated by the author, with warm thanks to Alessandra di Croce for her help.

 | DOI:10.1163/9789004513938_009

Scannelli, whose straightforward equation of quality with the elite autograph gives an impression of continuity with museum and collecting practice today. On the one hand, Scannelli gives an example of the seventeenth century's sensitivity to autograph status and anxieties over forgeries and derivations after select painters' works. On the other hand, the very predominance of copies, whether evident imitations or forgeries, also suggests that such pictures remained interesting and desirable for collectors regardless of whether they were seen as inferior to "originals." In Scannelli's text, the discernment of quality inherent in the distinction between originals and copies is tied specifically to the performance of taste. The preface to the *Microcosmo* follows a pattern of practicing art criticism as an ennobling activity that links the connoisseur or *intendente* with noble collectors through a shared exercise of taste. Scannelli praises the *Microcosmo*'s dedicatee, the Duke of Modena Francesco I D'Este (1610–1658), for "discerning ... with extraordinary taste the true beauties and most recondite perfections" in the work of the artists whom Scannelli prizes most highly.[2] The Duke's discernment and "extraordinary taste" thus become shared traits uniting Scannelli to his noble patron. The adroit (if commonplace) maneuver by which Scannelli creates this ennobling bond illustrates how art could generate social capital through a display of taste.[3]

2 Replication and the Value of Objects, Past and Present

The preface to the *Microcosmo* also raises the question of where copies fit into the economy of taste that evolved between the sixteenth and seventeenth centuries. Scannelli's remarks as to the ubiquity of copies after the Cinquecento masters he discusses in the *Microcosmo*, such as Titian (Tiziano Vecellio, 1490–1576), Raphael (Raffaello Santi, 1483–1520), and Correggio (Antonio Allegri da Correggio, 1489–1534), are borne out by documentary studies of the art market in the seventeenth century.[4] In (and well beyond) early modern Italy, imitation, repetition, and derivation were the norm of artistic production, and having only one clear master version of a successful composition was the exception, as numerous scholars have demonstrated.[5] For instance, Patrizia

2 Ibid.

3 See for instance Bourdieu, *La Distinction*; Honig, *Painting and the Market*; Ho, "Invitation to Compare"; Gage "'Some Stirring or Changing of Place'"; Ago, *Gusto for Things*.

4 See Cavazzini, *Painting as Business*; Spear and Sohm, *Painting for Profit*; both with extensive further bibliography.

5 Key studies include Gombrich, *Art and Illusion*; Cropper, "Tuscan History"; Muller, "Measures of Authenticity"; Feigenbaum, "Drawing and Collaboration"; Melion, "Hendrick Goltzius";

Cavazzini's analysis of the Roman market for copies in the early Seicento unpacks the synergy between the art market and the processes of apprenticeship and training, both of which generated large amounts of pictures that were at once byproducts of a learning process of copying and salable versions of successful pictures, often retouched or finished by an established artist.[6] Art history's current nomenclatures might label such pictures as anything from "copy" to "circle of [artist]," "after [artist]," "workshop of [artist]," or as a more or less tenuous attribution to "[artist]?" As Maria Loh indicates in a compelling study of the topic, in artistic theory and practice at the beginning of the seventeenth century, repetition and originality were closely intertwined, and existed in dynamic synergy rather than in conflict with one another.[7] Loh is one of many art historians who have investigated the multifaceted attitudes towards copies in the early modern period. Nevertheless, the abundance of scholarship on this topic often seems divorced from the treatment of objects in today's museum and collecting practices. In a 1990 study of drawing in the Carracci academy, Gail Feigenbaum pointed out a discrepancy between the historical circumstances of art's production and the contemporary handling of most of the art thus produced. Rightly noting that the yes/no formulation of attribution debates was ill-adapted to the historical material under investigation, she observed that "after connoisseurs had plucked the best original Carracci drawings out of the boxes, the residue was regarded—intellectually—as dross, of no interest or value whatsoever."[8] On the one hand, the overlapping subjects of imitation, originality, copying, and connoisseurship have been (as just noted) the focus of a lively and still-expanding scholarly discussion in the decades following Feigenbaum's essay. On the other hand, the gradual rehabilitation of copies and fakes from the status of uninteresting dross coexists with the persistence of a deeply ingrained autograph-versus-knockoff dichotomy when it comes to assigning value to works of art in practice. This tendency is visible, for instance, in the physical treatment of copies in terms of display and

---

Feigenbaum, "Practice in the Carracci Academy"; Bury, "On some engravings by Giorgio Ghisi"; Mena Marqués, "Titian, Rubens, and Spain"; Bury, *The Print in Italy*; Spear, "Di Sua Mano"; Wallace, "Michelangelo and Venusti"; Cavazzini, "Claude's Apprenticeship"; Loh, "New and Improved"; Pon, *Raphael, Dürer, and Raimondi*; Cropper, *The Domenichino Affair*; Neer, "Poussin and Imitation"; Loh, *Titian Remade*; Balis, "Rubens and His Studio"; Cavazzini, *Painting as Business*; Sparti, "Copie dipinte"; Tummers, *The Eye of the Connoisseur*; Cavazzini, "Il mercato delle copie"; Mazzarelli, *La Copia*; Tummers and Jonckheere, *Art Market and Connoisseurship*; Robertson, "Late Annibale"; Calvillo, "Authoritative Copies"; Hansen, *Michelangelo's Mirror*.

6 Cavazzini, "Il mercato delle copie."

7 Loh, "New and Improved."

8 Feigenbaum, "Drawing and Collaboration," 146.

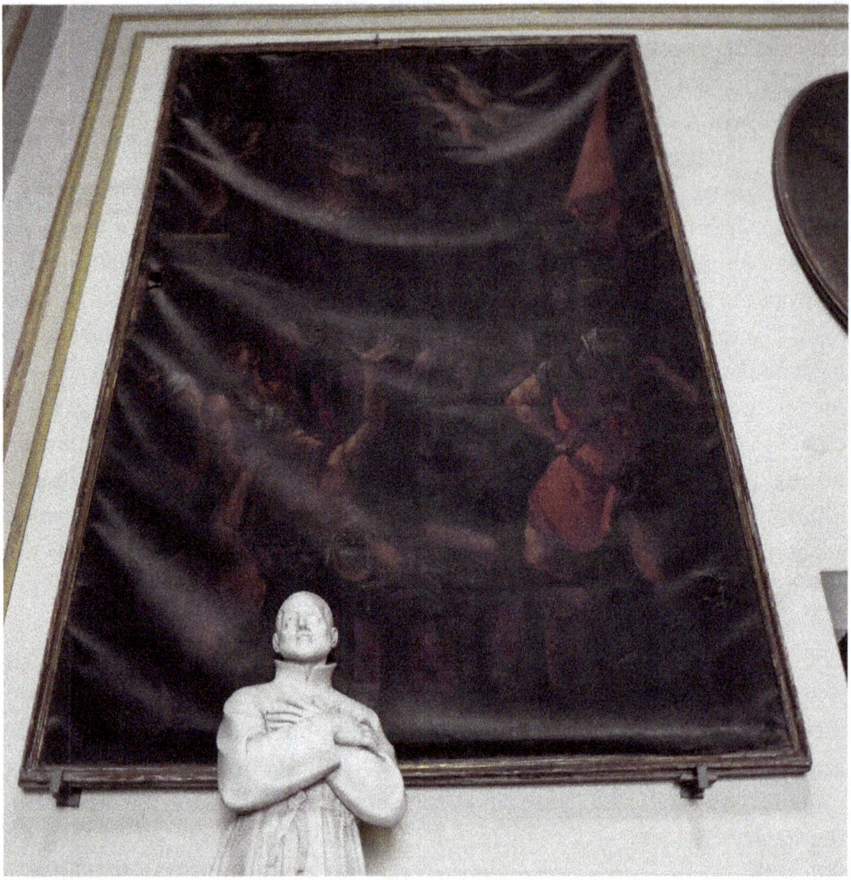

FIGURE 7.1 Anonymous, after Titian (1490–1576), *Martyrdom of Saint Lawrence*, probably 1570–1650. Chiesa di San Paolo Maggiore, Naples
PHOTO: AUTHOR

conservation, as may be seen, for example, in an anonymous copy of Titian's *Martyrdom of Saint Lawrence* that has received rather less care than would be expected were there any sort of Titian attribution attached to it (fig. 7.1). This composition is one that was frequently repeated by Titian and his workshop, and also replicated in print by Cornelis Cort (1533–1578).[9]

Given the robust scholarship on imitations of this composition and the high profile of many of its iterations, nowadays one might expect the inherent multiplicity of this image to make the idea of the original master version

9 On replication in Titian's workshop practice, see Cole, "Titian and Originality"; Joannides, "Titian's Repetitions"; Loh, *Titian Remade*; M. Mancini, "Tiziano e il controllo."

irrelevant. Yet today, the presence or absence of a named artist still plays a key role in determining the care and attention paid to a given object, as the ruinous state of the anonymous copy illustrates. The same cult of the master and the autograph manifests itself in several ways: in the strong propensity of museum labels to upgrade pictures from workshop products or copies to autograph works; in the over-attribution of pictures to a small roster of big names despite all evidence as to the impressive number and diversity of artists working in a given time and place;[10] and of course, most conspicuously, in the monetary value that attaches to works of art.

A well-documented incident from the recent past casts a wry light on the place of copies in contemporary art historical practice. In 2006, a gentleman who had inherited an anonymous picture after Caravaggio's (Michelangelo Merisi da Caravaggio, 1571–1610) *Cardsharps* decided to sell his painting at auction through Sotheby's; the picture in question belongs to the endless stream of early modern replicas of Caravaggio's works, particularly his early genre subjects.[11] The gentleman's anonymous painting fetched the respectable price of £42,000, reflecting its high quality within the larger body of copies after Caravaggio. The painting's new owner happened to be the Seicento scholar Sir Denis Mahon, who promptly declared the picture to be by Caravaggio himself, and found support for this claim among other scholars who take what has been called an "expansionist" view of Caravaggio attributions.[12] In consequence, the painting's value swung abruptly from £42,000 to over £10,000,000, and later became the object of a landmark court case against the auction house. When it comes to the actual value assigned to objects, arguments as to the intellectual, historical, and artistic value of copies are—literally and figuratively—academic, hopelessly outmatched by the enduring myth and mystique of the autograph.

For our purposes, the significance of this anecdote is not the unflattering view it presents of connoisseurship, but rather the way it delineates both a discrepancy and a shared set of concerns between audiences now and in the early modern period. Seicento artists and viewers definitely drew distinctions of value based on who had made a picture and whether it was regarded as a prototype or a derivation, but practices of connoisseurship in the long Renaissance tended to deal with gradations of value rather than yes or no

10 Cavazzini, *Painting as Business*, 13–41.

11 Spear, *Caravaggio's "Cardsharps,"* is a meticulous study of the Sotheby's incident, the ensuing trial, its outcomes, its implications, and its art historical background.

12 Ibid., 2.

answers, even to questions of attribution.[13] The same artists whose names can now mark a multi-million-dollar difference between "by" and "after" nearly all produced multiples of successful works, either by their own hands, or by well-supervised workshop assistants.[14] Scholarly investigations of derivative images have understandably gravitated toward the most prestigious end of the spectrum, focusing on tour-de-force copies or performances of style that are themselves autograph works by major artists, such as Peter Paul Rubens' (1577–1640) famous copies after Titian, or Hendrick Goltzius's (1558–1617) masterful reformulations of other artists' graphic *maniere*.[15] Yet these ambitious and inventive derivations may still have much in common with pictures in the lesser ranks of early Seicento copying, such as the ill-loved replica of Titian's *Martyrdom of Saint Lawrence* mentioned above.

Let us pursue the idea that "routine" copies and forgeries, like the more ambitious bravura copies of major artists, might have held a high degree of interest for their early modern viewers and makers. Loh's excellent study of Baroque repetition affirms a clear distinction—one that scholars already enact in practice—between ambitious copies and utilitarian ones: "Repetition cannot be compared ... to forgery, which is a form of imitation that does not seek identification; the forger does not want the viewer to see the deception, whereas the artist of repetition does."[16] While the distinction is important, it is perhaps also worth considering a more porous boundary between these categories. What exactly does the sagging and dust-covered anonymous *Martyrdom of Saint Lawrence* hold in common with a copy by Rubens, Cort, or Titian himself? To what extent would Seicento artists and audiences have separated the intent to deceive from the intent to impress?

3 A New Economy of Taste

What was even considered a copy in early modern Italy? Works that one might generically term "derivative" (which, as noted, included the overwhelming majority of the Seicento's painting and graphic arts) existed not only across a broad spectrum of price and quality, but also responded to a wide range of

13 Spear, "Di Sua Mano."

14 Caravaggio himself is probably an exception; for different perspectives on his studio methods and production setup, see for instance Christiansen, "Caravaggio and 'L'esempio'"; Maccherini, "Caravaggio nel carteggio"; Papi, *Ribera a Roma*, 13–14; Cardinali and De Ruggieri, "Da copia evidente"; Gregori, "Come dipingeva il Caravaggio."

15 For example, Mena Marqués, "Titian, Rubens, and Spain"; Melion, "Hendrick Goltzius."

16 Loh, "New and Improved," 478.

motivations, expectations, and ideas about artistic practice.[17] On the one hand, there was a keen awareness of fakes in the art world of the early Seicento. The pejorative undertone of the English term *fake* is in this context at once appropriate and misleading: deliberately misrepresenting a picture's authorship could be an act of shameful fraud or of honorable achievement, depending entirely on the terms in which artist and audience received the deception. The first systematic treatise on connoisseurship, the *Considerations on Painting* by the Sienese physician and *intendente* Giulio Mancini (1559–1630), contains an explicit *caveat emptor* passage warning Roman buyers of Cinquecento pictures about how forgers could create an appearance of age by painting over a cheap image on an old support, or burning damp straw and holding a picture in the smoke.[18] On the other hand, the practice of replicating works by a range of acknowledged masters was the very substance of making art, and the craft of drawing in particular was acquired through a long discipline of copying.[19] Given the importance of using drawings to learn drawing, works on paper by and after certain exemplary artists acquired a wide range of functions and layers of value: a drawing by a major artist could be private, public, frivolous, utilitarian, a collector's item, a crucial studio tool, a source for eminently marketable prints, a palimpsest of hands and source images, or several of the above all at once. Both drawn and printed copies after prestigious Cinquecento artists—particularly Michelangelo Buonarroti (1475–1564)—could take on multiple levels of authority and authorship, with a value as collectibles that often outstripped their pedagogical or studio use.[20] For instance, a page from the seventeenth-century printmaker Luca Ciamberlano's (1580–1641) drawing book, the *Scuola perfetta per imparare a disegnare*, was probably based on one of the numerous drawn copies of an anatomical study of legs by Michelangelo (fig. 7.2). The drawing book overall is anchored in studies of features and body parts by Agostino Carracci (1557–1602), who also excelled at copying and adapting the work of other artists. For the numerous drawings that emulated and propagated this type of study, it is impossible to make any meaningful distinction between forgery (with a ready market for Michelangelo drawings and a fat profit margin for any that could pass muster as autograph), routine

17 See for instance Vincenzo Giustiniani's delineation of numerous forms and levels of copying in his "Discourse on Painting;" Giustiniani, *Discorsi sulle Arti*, 41–43.

18 G. Mancini, *Considerazioni sulla Pittura*, 1:134. On Mancini, see especially Gage, "'Some Stirring'"; De Renzi and Sparti, "Giulio Mancini."

19 Children of Mercury; Cavazzini, *Painting as Business*, 49–80; Sparti, "Copie dipinte"; Lukehart, *Accademia Seminars*.

20 See for instance Bambach, "'Il Divin' Disegnatore," 21–30, with further bibliography. See also Marciari's chapter in this volume.

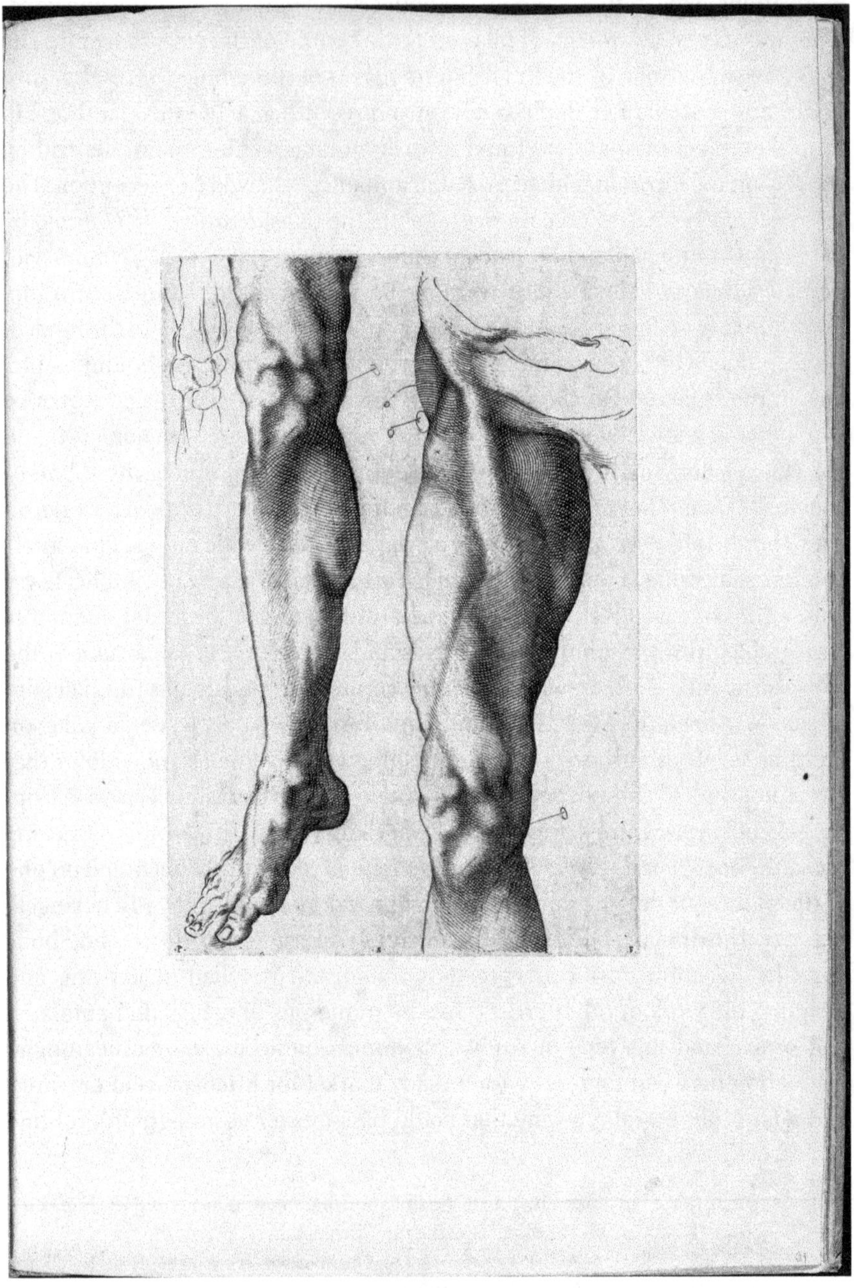

FIGURE 7.2 Luca Ciamberlano (1580–1641), after Agostino Carracci (1557–1602), *Studies of legs*, from the *Scuola perfetta per imparare a disegnare*, circa 1610–1620. Etching and engraving, 16 × 10.5 cm (6.3 × 4.1 in.). National Gallery of Art, Washington, DC, Gift of Arthur and Charlotte Vershbow
COURTESY NATIONAL GALLERY OF ART, WASHINGTON

practice (an effort to emulate a difficult model as an essential part of training), and ambitious performance. To return to Loh's terms, there is no discernable distinction here between replication that seeks recognition and replication that avoids it.[21]

A sufficiently well-executed drawing after this type of Michelangelesque study had the potential to function as a fake, but with painting especially, most copies after Cinquecento artists tended to be seen as serviceable, unproblematic stand-ins for master compositions, or as translucent incorporations of a high-profile work into a younger artist's oeuvre and reputation.[22] One sees this, for instance, in two paintings by Michele Tosini (1503–1577) in the Galleria Colonna in Rome, which are based on two extremely well-known works by Michelangelo: the statue of *Dawn* from the New Sacristy of San Lorenzo in Florence, and the much-replicated *Venus and Cupid* (fig. 7.3).[23] No early modern viewer (or present-day Italian museum visitor) would have failed to recognize these as derivations from Michelangelesque prototypes—there is no mystery to the fact that these are after and not by Michelangelo himself. That being said, discerning viewers might have engaged in a lively game of connoisseurship to determine whose copies they are, and how good.[24] The level of attention that early Seicento writers lavished on fine *sfumature* of quality and type between different varieties of copies is eloquent evidence of the interest that the evaluation of copies held for early modern *intendenti*.[25] Across the wide spectrum reaching from the anonymous *Martyrdom of Saint Lawrence* discussed earlier to Tosini's refined interpretations of Michelangelo in the Galleria Colonna, copies of many kinds shared the capacity to stage a game of performative evaluation. Inherent in their status as copies, of any quality whatsoever, was a reinforced and specific invitation to discuss their quality and their attribution, an activity that tapped into the economy of taste in which art collections translated into social capital.

This performative practice of evaluation is amplified and enlivened by the modern-day hang of the Galleria Colonna pictures, which invites a comparison between them, and closely reflects historical practice. By the seventeenth century, owners of paintings took an increasingly active interest in staging this kind of comparison in order to draw out discussion of the merits and themes

21 Loh, "New and Improved," 478.

22 See especially Cavazzini, "Il mercato delle copie"; Loh, *Titian Remade*.

23 Negro, *Venere e Amore*.

24 An early seventeenth-century instance of connoisseurship as a social game is in Bizoni, *Diario di viaggio*, 29.

25 G. Mancini, *Considerazioni sulla Pittura*, 1:135–38; Giustiniani, *Discorsi sulle Arti*, 41–43; Spear, "Di Sua Mano."

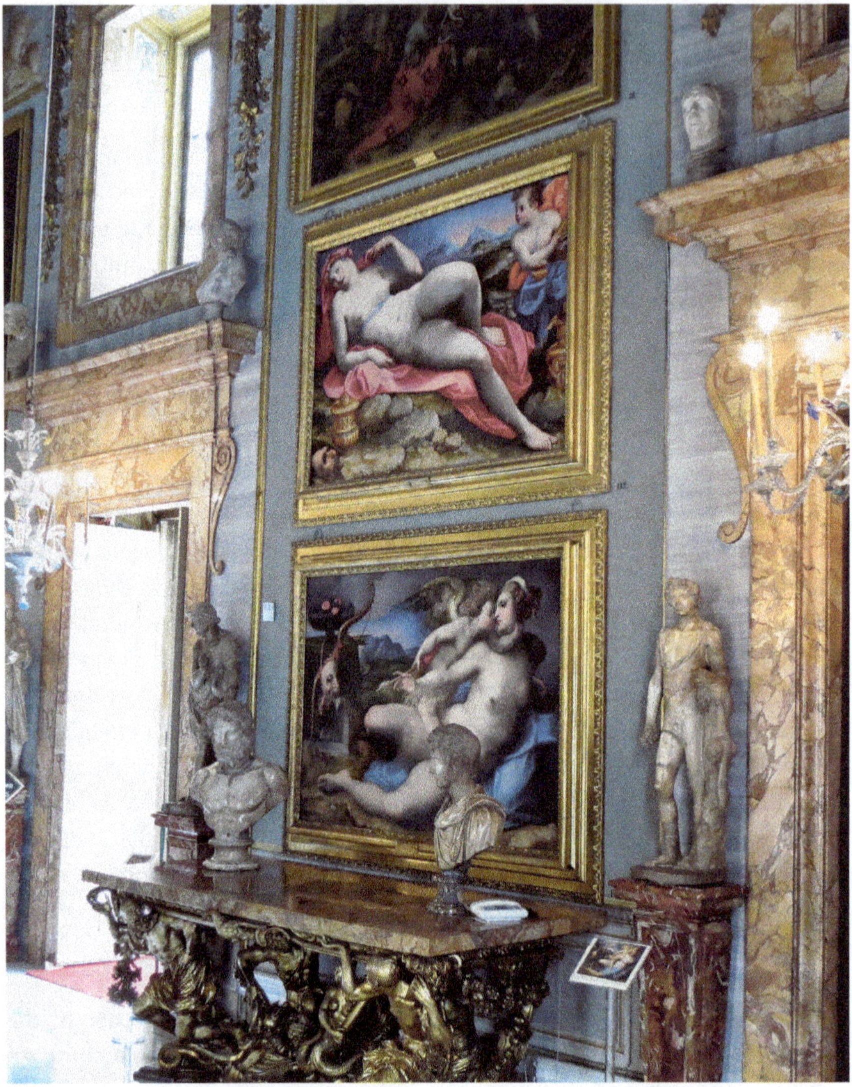

FIGURE 7.3 Interior, Galleria Colonna, Rome, with view of *Dawn* and *Venus and Amor* by Michele Tosini (1503–1577)
PHOTO: AUTHOR

of their pictures through eloquent juxtapositions.[26] In a sense, this particular comparison would be less interesting if both of these works had been painted by Michelangelo himself and not Tosini. The contemporary hang of the pictures gives an example of how owning two such works could cue a discussion

26 Feigenbaum and Freddolini, *Display of Art*; Ho, "Invitation to Compare."

of the *paragone* or rivalry between sculpture and painting, with the top image representing (and translating across media) one of Michelangelo's sculptures, while the bottom image, after a cartoon, refers to his work as a draftsman and painter. The core function of the painting/sculpture *paragone* as a parlor game goes back at least to Baldassare Castiglione's (1478–1529) *Book of the Courtier* (1528).[27] The forms and challenges of the two sorts of copying (after two- and three-dimensional works of art, respectively) thus become an important component in generating interest in the Colonna paintings. In unpacking and comparing what went into the process of producing the two Tosini pictures, viewers would perform what Mancini termed the "recognition of painting." Such performances, and the displays of taste that they occasioned, were closely bound to the whole point of owning and viewing art. Taste was the fluctuating currency of an economy in which spoken discernment and connoisseurship functioned as a playful yet high-stakes social competition.[28] For instance, as noted by Elizabeth Cropper and Charles Dempsey, the novel practices of collecting and display of the Marquis Vincenzo Giustiniani (1564–1637) are intimately tied to his understanding of *taste*, or *gusto*, a notion that was evolving between Cinquecento and Seicento.[29] While the general principle of showcasing one's refinement through an art collection is nothing new, what shifts in the Seicento is the loosening of that refinement's definition: taste no longer necessarily means the most rare and expensive of everything, but shifts instead towards the notion of personal inclination as a noble prerogative.[30]

4 Copies, Connoisseurship, and Competition

Where do copies—and more particularly, the unloved subset of fakes—come into this economy of taste? What is at stake for patrons and for artists in creating something that tries to pass itself off as something older and more prestigious? One striking example of the generative overlap between fraudulent fake and ambitious copy is Michelangelo's *Bacchus*, which an important contemporary text frames as a bravura forgery of antique statuary (fig. 7.4).[31] The *paragone* between ancient and modern that animates the *Bacchus* allows for a spectrum of interpretation from general competition with the ancients to the

27 Castiglione, *Book of the Courtier*, 96–102.

28 See for instance Fumaroli, "Rome 1630"; De Benedictis, Roani, and Mancini, *Riflessioni*; Ho, "Invitation to Compare"; Ago, *Gusto for Things*.

29 Cropper and Dempsey, *Nicolas Poussin*, 64–105; D'Angelo, "Il gusto in Italia e Spagna."

30 Cropper and Dempsey, *Nicolas Poussin*, 88–105.

31 Lieberman, "Regarding Michelangelo's 'Bacchus.'"

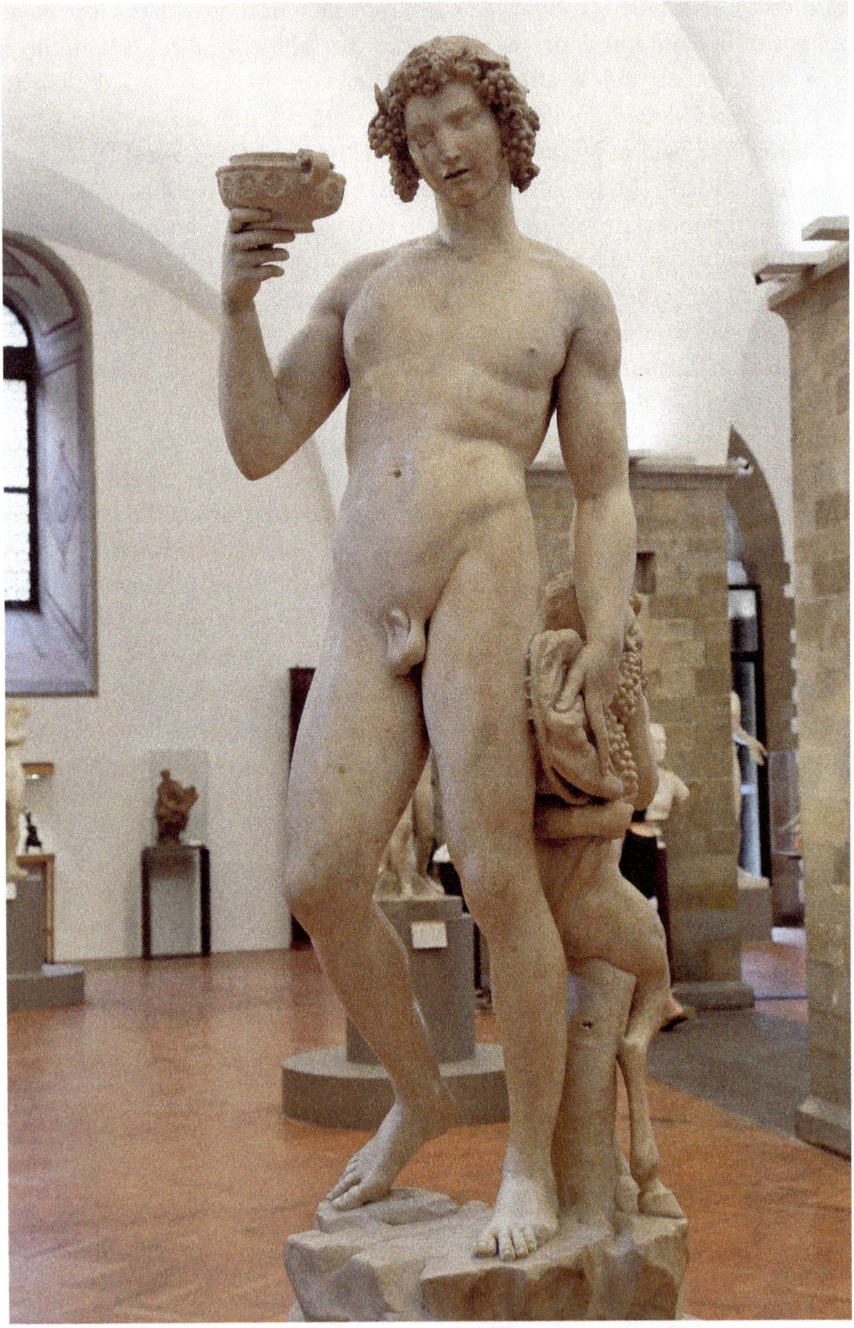

FIGURE 7.4 Michelangelo Buonarroti (1475–1564), *Bacchus*. Marble, h. 203 cm (80 in.). Museo Nazionale del Bargello, Florence
PHOTO BY ATTILIO

more specific intention of deceiving the viewer as to the work's origins.[32] A later commentary on Michelangelo's Bacchus interprets the statue group as an attempt to pass as a genuine antiquity, demonstrating how interpretations of the degree and nature of deceitfulness in a work of art could change over time or for rhetorical effect. In his 1548 treatise *On Antique Painting*, the Portuguese artist Francisco de Holanda (1517–1584) writes about this work of sculpture in his discussion of how ancient statues show movement:

> Now in Rome a marble god Bacchus with a young satyr carrying a basket of grapes on his back was shown to me as an antique and marvelous work. It appeared to me to be the work of an able artist, and yet not an antique one, even if in the color of the marble and in all its perfections it was; and when some Romans asked what I thought, I said that it was very fine and done by an able artist, but I declared that it was not antique, and this because its arms and hands were raised halfway, which was outside the limits and rigor of antiquity, for they were neither very low nor raised very high, and likewise that the movement and placement of the legs of the Bacchus were weak and lacking the stability and firm implantation of the antique, even though the perfections and the invention and the proportions and the satyr with the basket looked antique. Then they were amazed by my words and told me in response that it was a work that Michelangelo had done days earlier in order to deceive the Romans and the pope with that antique object; and Michelangelo learned that his work had not deceived me.[33]

Here we have another inversion of the ancient contest between the painters Zeuxis and Parrhasius (Pliny, *Natural History*, 35:65–66).[34] Unlike Zeuxis, who is taken in by Parrhasius's deceptive painted curtain, Holanda sees through the trick, and thus bests Michelangelo in the artistic contest. The phrase "Michelangelo learned that his work had not deceived me," when even the pope and the other Roman *intendenti* were presumably taken in, shows how connoisseurship—or what Mancini would later refer to as the "recognition of painting"—functioned as an arena for social and professional one-upmanship. This performative competition was not only among artists (Michelangelo competing with antiquity, Holanda competing with Michelangelo) but also

---

32 See also Extermann, "Copie e falsificazioni"; Luciano, Allen, and Kryza-Gersch (ed.), *Antico*.

33 Holanda, *On Antique Painting*, 110–11.

34 Pliny, *Natural History*, 9:309–11; see also Blake McHam, *Pliny and Artistic Culture*, 264–303.

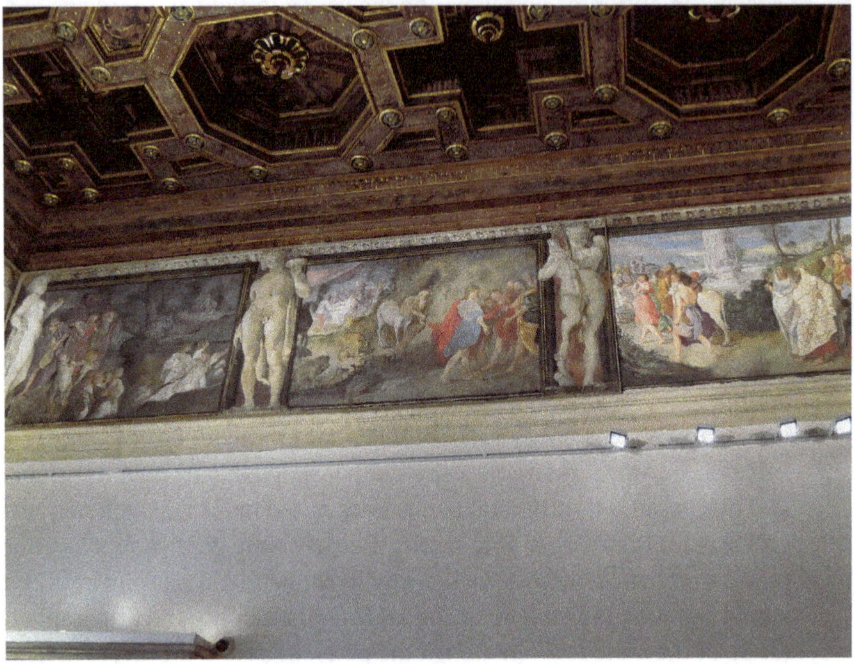

FIGURE 7.5 Annibale (1560–1609), Agostino (1557–1602), and Ludovico Carracci. (1555–1619), Detail: Jason Frieze, 1584. Fresco. Palazzo Fava, Bologna
PHOTO: AUTHOR

between artists and patrons (Michelangelo tricking the pope, Holanda seeing through the deception to the amazement of the people who show him the statue).

We can see the continued relevance of this ambitious brand of competitive forgery near the end of the sixteenth century: one of the major early fresco cycles by the Carracci in Bologna, the 1584 *Story of Jason* frieze in Palazzo Fava, depicts scenes from ancient poetry in up-to-the-minute manipulations of style and trompe l'oeil effects. The Carracci's updated contest between ancient and modern also proudly courts a *paragone*-driven comparison with Michelangelo, whose *Bacchus* has been turned from sculpture into dazzlingly illusionistic paint, and whose fake antiquity the Carracci are both honoring and outdoing in the fresco cycle as a whole (fig. 7.5).[35] If the Carracci were directly aligning their mastery of deceptive effects with Michelangelo's bravura forgeries of the antique, their commentators were just as aware as Holanda of the artistic and social stakes of the game. Carlo Cesare Malvasia's (1616–1693) biography of the

35 Boschloo, *Annibale Carracci*; Robertson, "I Carracci"; Campbell, "The Carracci"; Perini, "Il fregio."

Carracci contains a highly entertaining series of anecdotes about how Annibale (1560–1609) and Agostino (1557–1602) would deceive the powerful patrons who gave themselves airs for their knowledge of art. Malvasia first recounts many amusing incidents in which the Carracci, like Zeuxis, tricked several animals, as well as studio assistants, innkeepers, cooks, valets, and other hapless laypersons, with trompe l'oeil pranks.[36] Malvasia then introduces the forgery-based tricks of the Carracci, with an overt comparison to the pranks' Plinian antecedents: "Therefore the following jokes, which did not deceive mindless beasts, but men of the finest judgment, should also be mentioned."[37] Malvasia begins with "[an] instance where the lack of discernment of a great personage was exposed and chastened."[38] In these episodes, both envious fellow artists and learned, socially prominent patrons are taken in by "Titians" on which the paint is still wet, and by drawings that send would-be connoisseurs into ecstasies about Correggio and Parmigianino, and which of course turn out to have been freshly made by the Carracci. In fact, one could argue that they are still taking in connoisseurs to this day, given how many of the Carracci's drawings have shared attributions with Correggio and Parmigianino over the years.

Furthermore, Malvasia underscores the very methods of fraud about which Mancini warns potential buyers of paintings: the fake Titians are painted over cheap old pictures, and the fake Parmigianino drawings are on old paper smudged and darkened with a mix of black ink, soot, and soapy water.[39] In all of these stories, the sting of the joke is the moment when the Carracci puncture the antiquarians' and monsignors' inflated pretensions of taste and expertise. As in Holanda's pride at seeing through a trick that even (as we are led to presume) took in the pope, the stakes of forgery are social rather than financial. We find here an echo of another Plinian anecdote, that of Alexander the Great in the studio of his painter Apelles (*Natural History* 35: 85–86). In an endeavor to impress with his understanding, the great king overreaches and winds up sounding foolish, so much so that the boys who grind the colors are laughing, as Apelles gently points out.[40] The episode was gleefully depicted in print by Salvator Rosa, to whom the story's emphasis on the artist's social and intellectual cachet evidently appealed (fig. 7.6). In the wide arena of artistic practice in the background of Malvasia's anecdotes, the forging of pictures by great Cinquecento masters opened an opportunity for "great personages" to appear to disadvantage next to artists. Fakes, in other words, could provide access to a level of social ascendancy that money alone could not necessarily buy.

36 Malvasia, *Life of the Carracci* 270–90.

37 Ibid., 278.

38 Ibid., 278–79.

39 Ibid., 279–81.

40 Pliny, *Natural History*, 9:325; Blake McHam, 225–26.

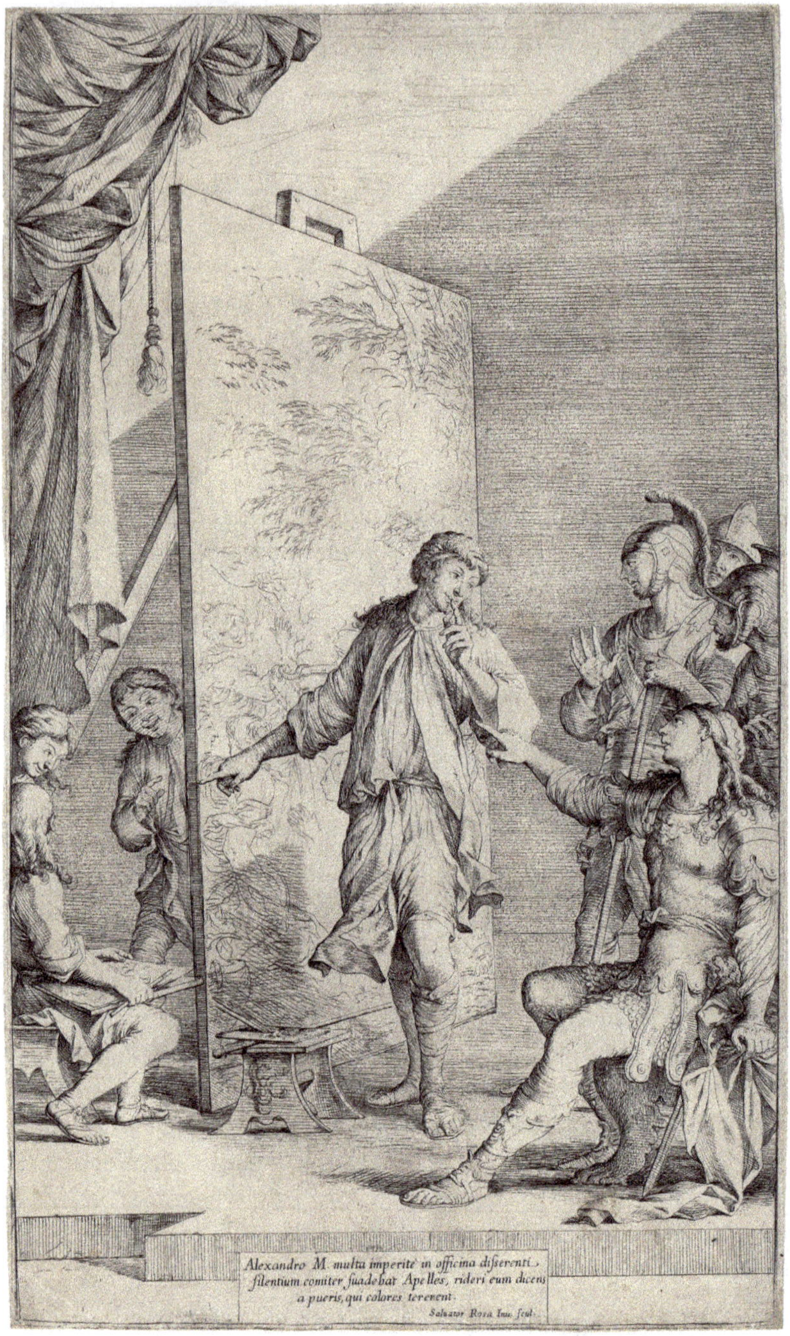

FIGURE 7.6 Salvator Rosa, (1615–1673), *Alexander in the Studio of Apelles*, c.1662. Etching and drypoint, 45.5 × 27.5 cm (17 15/16 × 10 13/16 in.). National Gallery of Art, Washington, DC, Alisa Mellon Bruce Fund
COURTESY NATIONAL GALLERY OF ART, WASHINGTON

5 Conclusion: Honorable Fraud

So much, then, for what artists stood to gain through copying and forgery: a chance to compete with each other, with their most revered predecessors and colleagues, and with their social superiors. But what did patrons stand to gain from copies? There are ample hints that the owners of copies enjoyed the game of connoisseurship even if they didn't always win at it. One of Malvasia's sources for his Carracci stories is a forgery episode recounted by Giulio Mancini, the papal physician and pioneering theorist of connoisseurship mentioned earlier.[41] Mancini's stance on copies and copying is far from one-sided. On the one hand, his warnings against fraudulent copies might be taken to include, in one direction, the very raw comparison he draws (in a letter to his brother) between a picture being copied and a woman being raped.[42] On the other hand, he himself actively sought to commission and purchase copies, and his discussion of them in the *Considerations on Painting* is geared more towards the recognition of their quality than towards their dismissal or devaluation.[43] His warnings about fake Cinquecento pictures being painted on old supports are followed immediately by an anecdote about Annibale Carracci using exactly these techniques to take an arrogant patron down a notch with a fake Sebastiano del Piombo.[44] The episode illustrates Mancini's claim that forgery specifically is often done more for honor ("per zelo d'honore") than for profit.

Mancini concludes both the anecdote and his warnings about forgeries with a ringing vindication of Annibale's fraudulent copy that explicitly equates deception with ambition: "And by such eminent men [as Annibale] I too should like to be deceived, and of such manner of copies as these I believe it to be true which the Grand Duke of Tuscany said, that in these are two arts, one of the author and the other of the copyist who simulates him, and truly they are gems among paintings."[45] Like Holanda's, Mancini's practice of connoisseurship is a calculated performance of taste. Mancini's appreciation of Annibale's fraud is an opportunity to show discernment ("I know that what I'm looking at is a copy"), taste ("I can tell that the copy is better"), and flagrant name-dropping ("and the Grand Duke of Tuscany agrees with me").

Even partial anecdotal evidence such as this suggests that copies, and specifically forgeries, enabled a form of evaluative discussion that was an exclusive

41 G. Mancini, *Considerazioni sulla Pittura*, x–xii.

42 Maccherini, "Caravaggio nel carteggio," 80.

43 Differing perspectives on the issue emerge, for instance, in Maccherini, "Caravaggio nel carteggio"; De Benedictis, Roani, and Mancini, *Riflessioni*, 17; Sparti, "Novità su Giulio Mancini."

44 G. Mancini, *Considerazioni sulla Pittura*, 1:135.

45 Ibid., 1:135. Translated by the author.

property of pictures that tried to pass for something else. In the performative social space of the Roman picture gallery, the game of seeing through a fake was one that the owners of copies could draw guests into, taking on the role of Apelles/Annibale and inviting their visitors to embarrass or distinguish themselves. Two brief concluding proposals remain: first, that the ocean of attribution problems in Caravaggist painting is one symptom of the desirability of copies specifically in an open market where collectors were showing their taste in what they bought more than they were showing their wealth.[46] Secondly, that copies specifically were being acquired not just for their esthetic merits, but for their ability to act as conversation pieces and as litmus tests for the perspicacity of their viewers. If this is so, the enormous prevalence of themes of trickery and deception in Caravaggist painting takes on a further humorous layer of significance: centuries later, the artists' jokes are still on us.

Acknowledgements

I am grateful to the Center for Advanced Study in the Visual Arts at the National Gallery of Art, Washington, DC for generous research funding in the form of a Paul Mellon Predoctoral Fellowship. I also wish to thank Alessandra di Croce, Frances Gage, Patrizia Cavazzini, Yoko Hara, Felipe Pereda, Stephen Campbell, Elizabeth Schwartz, and Alex Neroth van Vogelpoel for their help, kindness, and friendship.

Bibliography

Ago, Renata. *Gusto for Things. A History of Objects in Seventeenth-Century Rome.* Translated by Bradford Bouley, Corey Tazzara, and Paula Findlen. Chicago: University of Chicago Press, 2013.

Balis, Arnout. "Rubens and His Studio: Defining the Problem." In *Rubens, a Genius at Work* (exh. cat.), edited by Michel Draguet, 30–51. Brussels: Royal Fine Arts Museum, 2007.

Bambach, Carmen C. "'Il Divin' Disegnatore." In *Michelangelo: Divine Draftsman and Designer*, edited by Elisa Urbanelli, Marcie M. Muscat, and Margaret Aspinwall, 15–30. Exh. cat. New York: Metropolitan Museum of Art, 2018.

Bizoni, Bernardo. *Diario di viaggio di Vincenzo Giustiniani.* Edited by Barbara Agosti. Porretta Terme: I Quaderni del Battello Ebbro, 1995.

46 Cavazzini, *Painting as Business*, 119–51.

Blake McHam, Sarah. *Pliny and the Artistic Culture of the Italian Renaissance: The Legacy of the* Natural History. New Haven: Yale University Press, 2013.

Boschloo, Anton W. A. *Annibale Carracci in Bologna: Visible Reality in Art After the Council of Trent.* 2 vols. The Hague: Government Publishing Office, 1974.

Bourdieu, Pierre. *La Distinction. Critique sociale du jugement.* Paris: Editions de Minuit, 1979.

Bury, Michael. "On Some Engravings by Giorgio Ghisi Commonly Called 'Reproductive'" *Print Quarterly* 10 (1993): 4–19.

Bury, Michael. *The Print in Italy: 1550–1620.* Exh. cat. London: The British Museum, 2001.

Calvillo, Elena. "Authoritative Copies and Divine Originals: Lucretian Metaphor, Painting on Stone, and the Problem of Originality in Michelangelo's Rome." *Renaissance Quarterly* 66, no. 2 (2013): 453–508.

Campbell, Stephen J. "The Carracci, Visual Narrative, and Heroic Poetry after Ariosto: the 'Story of Jason' in Palazzo Fava." *Word & Image* 18, no. 2 (2002): 210–30.

Cardinali, Marco, and Maria Beatrice De Ruggieri. "Da copia evidente a replica presunta. Le traccie materiali nei doppi di Caravaggio." In *La Copia: Connoisseurship, storia del gusto e della conservazione: Giornate di studio del 17–18 maggio 2007, Museo Nazionale Romano, Palazzo Massimo alle Terme*, edited by Carla Mazzarelli, 99–126. San Casciano Val di Pesa: Libro Co. Italia, 2010.

Castiglione, Baldassare. *The Book of the Courtier* [1528]. Translated by George Bull. New York: Penguin Books, 1976.

Cavazzini, Patrizia. "Claude's Apprenticeship in Rome: The Market for Copies and the Invention of the *Liber Veritatis*." *Konsthistorisk Tidskrift* 73, no. 3 (2004): 133–46.

Cavazzini, Patrizia. *Painting as Business in Early Seventeenth-Century Rome.* University Park: Penn State University Press, 2008.

Cavazzini, Patrizia. "Il mercato delle copie nella Roma di primo Seicento." In *La Copia: Connoisseurship, storia del gusto e della conservazione: Giornate di studio del 17–18 maggio 2007, Museo Nazionale Romano, Palazzo Massimo alle Terme*, edited by Carla Mazzarelli, 257–70. San Casciano Val di Pesa: Libro Co. Italia, 2010.

Children of Mercury: The Education of Artists in the Sixteenth and Seventeenth Centuries. Exh. cat. Providence: Bell Gallery, List Art Center, Brown University, 1984.

Christiansen, Keith. "Caravaggio and 'L'esempio davanti del naturale.'" *Art Bulletin* 68, no. 3 (1986): 421–45.

Cole, Bruce. "Titian and the Idea of Originality in the Renaissance." In *The Craft of Art: Originality and Industry in the Italian Renaissance*, edited by Andrew Ladis and Carolyn Wood, 86–112. Athens: University of Georgia Press, 1995.

Cropper, Elizabeth. "Tuscan History and Emilian Style." In Henry A. Millon, et al., *Emilian Painting of the 16th and 17th Centuries: A Symposium*, 49–62. Bologna: Nuova Alfa Editoriale, 1987.

Cropper, Elizabeth. *The Domenichino Affair: Novelty, Imitation, and Theft in Seventeenth-Century Rome.* New Haven: Yale University Press, 2005.

Cropper, Elizabeth, and Charles Dempsey. *Nicolas Poussin: Friendship and the Love of Painting*. Princeton: Princeton University Press, 1996.

D'Angelo, Paolo. "Il gusto in Italia e Spagna dal Quattrocento al Settecento." In *Il Gusto: Storia di una Idea Estetica*, edited by Luigi Russo, 11–34. Palermo: Aesthetica Edizioni, 2000.

De Benedictis, Cristina, Roberta Roani, and Giulio Mancini. *Riflessioni Sulle "Regole Per Comprare Collocare E Conservare Le Pitture" Di Giulio Mancini*. Florence: Edifir, 2005.

De Renzi, Silvia, and Donatella Livia Sparti. "Giulio Mancini." In Treccani, *Dizionario Biografico degli Italiani*. http://www.treccani.it/enciclopedia/giulio-mancini_%28Dizionario-Biografico%29/.

Extermann, Grégoire. "Copie e falsificazioni: L'industria dell'antico nella bottega di Guglielmo della Porta." In *La Copia: Connoisseurship, storia del gusto e della conservazione: Giornate di studio del 17–18 maggio 2007, Museo Nazionale Romano, Palazzo Massimo alle Terme*, edited by Carla Mazzarelli, 225–57. San Casciano Val di Pesa: Libro Co. Italia, 2010.

Feigenbaum, Gail. "Drawing and Collaboration in the Carracci Academy." In *IL 60: Essays Honoring Irving Lavin on his Sixtieth Birthday*, edited by Marilyn Aronberg Lavin, 145–66. New York: Italica Press, 1990.

Feigenbaum, Gail. "Practice in the Carracci Academy." *Studies in the History of Art* 22 (1993): 58–76.

Feigenbaum, Gail, and Francesco Freddolini, eds. *Display of Art in the Roman Palace 1550–1750*. Los Angeles: Getty Research Institute, 2014.

Fumaroli, Marc. "Rome 1630: Entrée en scène du spectateur." In *Roma 1630: Il trionfo del pennello* (exh. cat.), edited by Olivier Bonfait, 53–82. Florence: Villa Medici, 1994.

Gage, Frances. "'Some Stirring or Changing of Place:' Vision, Judgement and Mobility in Pictures of Galleries." *Intellectual History Review* 20, no. 1 (2010): 123–45.

Gage, Frances. *Painting as Medicine in Early Modern Rome: Giulio Mancini and the Efficacy of Art*. University Park: Penn State University Press, 2016.

Giustiniani, Vincenzo. *Discorsi sulle Arti e sui Mestieri*, edited by Anna Banti. Florence: Sansoni, 1981.

Gombrich, Ernst. *Art and Illusion: A Study in the Psychology of Pictorial Representation*. Princeton: Princeton University Press, 1969.

Gregori, Mina. "Come dipingeva il Caravaggio." In *Sir Denis Mahon e l'arte italiana del XVII secolo: Da Guercino a Caravaggio*, edited by Anna Coliva and Mina Gregori, 63–66. Rome: "L'Erma" di Bretschneider, 2014.

Hansen, Morten Steen. *Michelangelo's Mirror: Perino del Vaga, Daniele da Volterra, Pellegrino Tibaldi*. University Park: Penn State University Press, 2013.

Ho, Angela. "Invitation to Compare: Frans van Mieris's 'Cloth Shop' in the Context of Early Modern Art Collecting." *Renaissance Studies* 23, no. 5 (2009): 694–717.

Holanda, Francisco. *On Antique Painting*. Translated by Alice Sedgwick Wohl. University Park: Penn State University Press, 2013.

Honig, Elizabeth. *Painting and the Market in Early Modern Antwerp*. New Haven: Yale University Press, 1998.

Joannides, Paul. "Titian's Repetitions." In *Titian: Materiality, Likeness, "Istoria"*, edited by Joanna Woods-Marsden, 37–51. Turnhout: Brepols, 2007.

Lieberman, Ralph. "Regarding Michelangelo's 'Bacchus.'" *Artibus et Historiae* 22, no. 43 (2001): 65–74.

Loh, Maria. "New and Improved: Repetition as Originality in Italian Baroque Practice and Theory." *Art Bulletin* 86, no. 3 (2004): 477–504.

Loh, Maria. *Titian Remade: Repetition and the Transformation of Early Modern Italian Art*. Los Angeles: Getty Research Institute, 2007.

Luciano, Eleonora, Denise Allen, and Claudia Kryza-Gersch, eds. *Antico: The Golden Age of Renaissance Bronzes*. Exh. cat. Washington, DC: National Gallery of Art, 2011.

Lukehart, Peter M., ed. *The Accademia Seminars: The Accademia di San Luca in Rome, c. 1590–1635*. Washington, DC: Center for Advanced Study in the Visual Arts, 2009.

Maccherini, Michele. "Caravaggio nel carteggio familiare di Giulio Mancini." *Prospettiva* 86 (1997): 71–92.

Malvasia, Carlo Cesare. *Malvasia's* Life of the Carracci. *Commentary and Translation* [1678]. Edited and translated by Anne Summerscale. University Park: Penn State University Press, 2000.

Mancini, Giulio. *Considerazioni sulla Pittura*. 2 vols. [1617–1621; unpublished]. Edited by Adriana Marucchi. Rome: Accademia dei Lincei, 1956.

Mancini, Matteo. "Tiziano e il controllo dell'immagine riprodotta." *Venezia Cinquecento* 36, no. 2 (2008): 121–58.

Mazzarelli, Carla, ed. *La Copia: Connoisseurship, storia del gusto e della conservazione: Giornate di studio del 17–18 maggio 2007, Museo Nazionale Romano, Palazzo Massimo alle Terme*. San Casciano Val di Pesa: Libro Co. Italia, 2010.

Melion, Walter. "Hendrick Goltzius's Project of Reproductive Engraving." *Art History* 13, no. 4 (1990): 458–487.

Mena Marqués, Manuela B. "Titian, Rubens, and Spain." In *Titian and Rubens: Power, Politics, and Style* (exh. cat.), edited by Hilliard T. Goldfarb, 69–94. Boston: Isabella Stewart Gardner Museum, 1998.

Muller, Jeffrey M. "Measures of Authenticity: The Detection of Copies in the Early Literature on Connoisseurship." *Studies in the History of Art* 20 (1989): 141–49.

Neer, Richard. "Poussin and the Ethics of Imitation." *Memoirs of the American Academy in Rome* 51/52 (2006–2007): 297–344.

Negro, Angela. *Venere e Amore di Michele di Ridolfo del Ghirlandaio: Il mito di una Venere di Michelangelo tra copie, repliche, e pudiche vestizioni*. Rome: Campisano, 2001.

Papi, Gianni. *Ribera a Roma*. Cremona: Soncino, 2007.

Perini, Giovanna. "Il fregio con le storie di Giasone dipinto dai Carracci a Palazzo Fava, Bologna." In *Mediterranean Myths from Classical Antiquity to the Eighteenth Century. Mediteranski miti od antike do 18. Stoletja*, edited by Metoda Kokole, Barbara Murovec, Marjeta Šašel Kos, et al., 189–211. Ljubljana: Založba ZRC, 2006.

Pliny the Elder. *Natural History*. Edited and translated by Harris Rackham. Cambridge, Mass.: Harvard University Press, 1961.

Pon, Lisa. *Raphael, Dürer, and Marcantonio Raimondi: Copying and the Italian Renaissance Print*. New Haven: Yale University Press, 2004.

Robertson, Clare. "I Carracci e l'invenzione: Osservazioni sull'origine dei cicli affrescati di Palazzo Fava." *Atti e Memorie* 32 (1993): 271–314.

Robertson, Clare. "Late Annibale and His Workshop: Invention, Imitation and Patronage." *Mitteilungen des Kunsthistorisches Institut in Florenz* 54, no. 2 (2012): 267–94.

Scannelli, Francesco. *Il Microcosmo della Pittura, overo trattato diviso in due libri*. Cesena: Neri, 1657.

Sparti, Donatella Livia. "Copie dipinte nell'educazione artistica seicentesca in Italia." In *Les Académies dans L'Europe Humaniste: Idéaux et Pratiques*, edited by Marc Deramaix, Perrine Galand-Hallyn, Ginette Vagenheim, and Jean Vignes, 391–423. Geneva: Librairie Droz, 2008.

Sparti, Donatella Livia. "Novità su Giulio Mancini: Medicina, arte e presunta 'Connoisseurship.'" *Mitteilungen des Kunsthistorischen Institutes in Florenz* 52, no. 1 (2008): 53–72.

Spear, Richard. "Di Sua Mano." *Memoirs of the American Academy in Rome* (2002): 79–98.

Spear, Richard. *Caravaggio's "Cardsharps" on Trial: Thwaytes v. Sotheby's*. London: The Burlington Press, 2020.

Spear, Richard, and Philip Sohm, eds. *Painting for Profit: The Economic Lives of Seventeenth-Century Italian Painters*. New Haven: Yale University Press, 2010.

Tummers, Anna. *The Eye of the Connoisseur: Authenticating Paintings by Rembrandt and His Contemporaries*. Amsterdam: Amsterdam University Press, 2011.

Tummers, Anna, and Koenraad Jonckheere, eds. *Art Market and Connoisseurship: A Closer Look at Paintings by Rembrandt, Rubens, and Their Contemporaries*. Amsterdam: Amsterdam University Press, 2008.

Wallace, William E. "Michelangelo and Marcello Venusti: A Case of Multiple Authorship." In *Reactions to the Master: Michelangelo's Effect on Art and Artists in the Sixteenth Century*, edited by Francis Ames-Lewis, 137–56. Burlington, Vermont: Ashgate, 2003.

CHAPTER 8

Trading Caravaggio: Giovan Angelo Altemps, Prospero Orsi, and the Roman Art Market of Caravaggesque Painting

Fausto Nicolai

Towards the end of sixteenth century, buying a painting in Rome had become very easy and it was no longer necessary for the sellers to be painters, or the buyers to be established collectors.[1] "Un po' tutti per Roma vendevan quadri" (almost everyone was selling paintings in Rome), as the art expert Marquis Vincenzo Giustiniani (1564–1637) pointed out; and recent studies have reinforced his observation, noting that almost everyone in Rome was buying paintings with procurement and accessibility methods comparable to the modern art market.[2] The broadening of picture assets held in all strata of Roman society is a recognized historical phenomenon whose direct consequences are reflected in the generalized enjoyment of these artifacts regardless of the quality and function of the object itself (devotional, portraits, etc.). The growing demand for paintings no longer only involved the wealthy elite, including aristocracy, clergy and the business/mercantilist class, but extended to a myriad of workers such as butchers, fishmongers, cobblers and others, whose houses and shops were frequently decorated with paintings, sometimes in surprising numbers and often of unexpectedly high quality. Alongside the widespread possession of paintings is another, concomitant and parallel phenomenon of the birth of a method of collecting activity based on the systematic research of a specific author or a "type" of subject. If in the past centuries the iconography or subject had represented the main reason for the commission of a painting, and if in the past the painting itself was made only on commission, by the sixteenth century the trend had changed: a precise style or genre became desirable, and painters created their works independently from the directives of a customer but rather than for a large audience of potential buyers. In other words, a widespread increase in demand corresponded to a proportionate supply according

1 For a general overview about the development of painting trade in seventeenth-century Rome see: Cavazzini, *Painting as a Business*; Idem, "Middle-class patronage"; Idem, "Marketing strategies"; Nicolai, *Mecenati a confronto*.

2 Giustiniani, *Discorso sulle arti*, 45.

 | DOI:10.1163/9789004513938_010

to the accepted rules of market. To cope with the increased demand, painters modified their working methods by integrating works made on commission with the serial production of paintings for direct sales. It is not difficult to recognize in this new course of collecting and workshop methodology the contribution of Caravaggio (Michelangelo Merisi; 1571–1610) and Caravaggism, which, in fact, paved the way for the search for a very specific style and compositions that were to become popular. It is no coincidence, in fact, that an entire generation of painters belonging chronologically and culturally to the latest phase of Mannerism "converted" to the revolutionary Caravaggesque style, certainly more for economic opportunity than for artistic infatuation. Many were lured by the prospect of the deal and chose to emulate Caravaggio's style and his compositions in order to sell their own form of the Caravaggesque novelty. Caravaggio attracted and seduced collectors of early seventeenth-century Rome and even more so, for obvious reasons, his imitators did the same once the master disappeared from the city leaving an apparently unbridgeable void. In this context Giovan Angelo Altemps (1587–1620), a noble scholar and collector, did not escape the wave of Caravaggesque fashion.

1 Giovan Angelo Altemps

Giovan Angelo Altemps was just born when his father Roberto, accused of repeated adultery, was unexpectedly and tragically sentenced to death at the will of an intransigent Pope Sixtus V (1521–1590).[3] Obviously, this decision reflected the Pope's unease with the rich and increasingly powerful father of Roberto, Cardinal Marco Sittico Altemps (1533–1595). It was not uncommon in the Rome of those years that high prelates conceived children, much less frequent however was their legal recognition of their offspring which Marco Sittico had decided to grant to Roberto.

We do not know how much the premature and violent death of his father may have affected Giovan Angelo's childhood but certainly the environment in which he grew up was influenced by his grandfather, who commissioned the beautiful family palace in Rome near the Piazza Navona and created the rich library called the Altempsiana.[4]

From the papers of the Altemps family's archive, it appears that Giovan Angelo grew up under the tutelage of his mother Cornelia Orsini (1566–1643)

3 Merola, "Altemps," 134.
4 Scoppola, *Palazzo Altemps.*

until he was twenty years old, when he took over the reins of the family.[5] In fact, in the family records one can see that from 1607 through 1620 the whole patrimony is managed by Duke Giovan Angelo as owner and holder.[6] Although little information relating to the cultural background of the young Giovan Angelo survives, both direct and indirect testimonies offer insight into a personality dedicated to study with a passion for mathematics and astronomy.[7] After his marriage in 1605 to Maria Cesi (1583–1609), his brother-in-law Federico Cesi (1585–1630), founder in 1603 of the famous Accademia dei Lincei, played a key role in Giovan Angelo's scientific training.[8] In the context of the academy Giovan Angelo was able to develop his scientific interests which culminated in a rather close friendship with the greatest scientist of the time, Galileo Galilei (1564–1642).[9] Some correspondence attests to their relationship and attests to how much Giovan Angelo admired Galilean discoveries and inventions starting with the telescope. Alongside astronomy and mathematics, Giovan Angelo also cultivated a personal literary vein, publishing two comedies and a biography of Pope Sant' Aniceto (92–168).[10] Comedy was a very popular literary genre at the beginning of the seventeenth century and Giovan Angelo organized theatrical performances with sets and music in his palace in Rome.[11] Giovan Angelo was also a fine bibliophile, a passion inherited from his paternal grandfather that led him to considerably expand the already rich family library. With the 1611 purchase of the book collections of Filippo Colonna (1578–1639), which included the library earlier assembled by Cardinal Cervini (1501–1555), Giovan Angelo made the Altempsiana one of the most important and celebrated private libraries in seventeenth-century Rome.[12]

2 Prospero Orsi and the Formation of the Altemps Collection

In light of this excursus, Giovan Angelo's high intellectual profile is undeniable and establishes a foundation for an analysis of his collecting taste and artistic choices. In this context a fundamental role was played by Prospero Orsi

5 Nicolai, *Mecenati a confronto* 62.
6 Ibid.
7 Serrai, *La biblioteca Altempsiana*, 25–26.
8 Ibid., 27.
9 Serrai, *La biblioteca Altempsiana*, 26.
10 Merola, "Altemps," 134.
11 Nicolai, *Mecenati a confronto*, 178.
12 Serrai, *La biblioteca Altempsiana*, 24–27.

(1560–1633), who procured numerous paintings for the duke, in particular of the Caravaggesque style.[13] The study of the formation of the Altemps painting collection and the relationship Giovan Angelo had with Orsi illuminates much about the dynamics of the art market in the early seventeenth- century Rome, particularly the developments of Caravaggism as a collecting and trading phenomenon, after Merisi's death.

Unlike his grandfather Cardinal Marco Sittico, who in life collected few paintings, Giovan Angelo had a particular interest in painting, especially with regard to the current contemporary styles.[14] Various archival sources make possible a reconstruction of the painting collection Giovan Angelo created in just over a decade, from 1608 to 1620 the date of his untimely death: 1) the accounting records of the Altemps family archive; 2) an inventory of all the assets owned by Giovan Angelo dating back to 1618–19, which is today preserved in Chicago at the Newberry Library; 3) the inventory of assets drawn up after Giovan Angelo's death in 1620, preserved among the papers of a notary in the Archivio di Stato di Roma.

The 1618–19 inventory includes the description of all the belongings held by Giovan Angelo at that time, from dishes, to silverware, to books, to paintings, and was drawn up by an anonymous author, while the duke was still alive. The document lists more than 300 paintings of various subjects plus 153 *Portraits of Illustrious Men*, for a total of over 450 pieces estimated to be worth 13,013 Roman scudi.[15] Unlike the 1620 posthumous inventory in which the paintings have only a few attributions, the Chicago manuscript records the names of the creators of about half of the works. Most of them are by contemporary painters belonging to both the Caravaggesque and the Carracci schools. In particular, eight canvases directly assigned to Caravaggio stand out: "un putto che sona il liuto" (A young lute player), "Un pastore che sona il flauto" (A shepherd who plays a flute), "Retratto del Caravaggia [sic] che li morde una lucertola" (A portrait of Caravaggio in which he is bitten by a lizard), "Un quadro de' frutti dove è la carafa" (A painting with fruits and a carafe), and furthermore, "tre Teste di Vecchio" (three Heads of elder men).[16]

13 Luigi Spezzaferro was the first to discuss this topic in a fundamental essay: Spezzaferro, "Caravaggio accettato." I personally contributed with additional data and reflections (Nicolai, *Mecenati a confronto*, 59–85).

14 Spezzaferro, "Caravaggio accettato," 37–43; Nicolai, *Mecenati a confronto*, 59–63.

15 The list reports 266 records with some of them including more than a painting for a total of more than 300 works. Nicolai, *Mecenati a confronto*, 62. More recently Vannugli has published the complete inventory: Vannugli "L' iconografia del cardinale Marco Sittico Altemps," 141–146.

16 Spezzaferro, "Caravaggio accettato," 41–42; Nicolai, *Mecenati a confronto*, 59–63.

The inventory also lists other paintings with a clear Caravaggesque style: "David che ammazza Golia" (David killing Goliath), "un Xpo [Cristo] in Emmaus con doi discepoli e un oste" (Christ at Emmaus with two disciples and one innkeeper) both assigned to an unspecified "Bartolomeo" and a "San Tomaso che mette il deto nella costa di Xpo [Cristo]" (Saint 'Thomas who puts his finger in Christ's ribs) without attribution.[17] Finally, works attributed to Carlo Saraceni (1579–1620), Antiveduto Gramatica (1571–1626), Antonio Pomarancio (1560–1620) and Ottavio Leoni (1578–1630) complete the group of painters from the Caravaggesque school. The Carraccesque school is also well represented with works assigned to Annibale (1560–1609), Ludovico (1555–1619) and Agostino (1557–1602) Carracci and Guido Reni (1575–1642).[18] The inventory also records names of older painters of the first and second half of the sixteenth century, such as Raphael (1483–1520), Sebastiano del Piombo (1485–1547), Francesco Francia (1459–1517), Scipione Pulzone and others, although the attributions remain rather difficult to confirm because they are more distant in time.[19] For that reason, and with the aim of updating and providing new insights, this chapter focuses only on the works assigned to Caravaggio and "Caravaggesque" painters that are mentioned in the Altemps papers and belonged to Giovan Angelo, all of which he bought from Prospero Orsi between 1611 and 1613.

The 1618–19 inventory illustrates the quantitative and qualitative consistency of Giovan Angelo's collection in the final phase of its formation. To understand how the collection was formed over time, however, it is necessary to refer to other documents such as the expense records in the Altemps Archive dated from the end of the sixteenth century onwards.

The accounting records of the Altemps archive document almost daily purchases and commissions made by Giovan Angelo between 1607 and 1620, and they provide crucial information about the names of the artists or sellers, prices and attributions assigned to the paintings at the time of each transaction. A representative case study is an analysis of the records relating to purchases made through Prospero Orsi which begin in 1611. More precisely, Prospero Orsi appears for the first time in the Altemps accounts in August 1611 when he received a payment of 20 scudi for having sold to Giovan Angelo four paintings depicting doctors of the church for which the artist is not specified.[20] Noteworthy is that from the very beginning Orsi appears essentially as a "dealer" of paintings. A few months later, in October 1611, Orsi's

17 Spezzaferro, "Caravaggio accettato," 43; Nicolai, *Mecenati a confronto*, 68–69.

18 Ibid.

19 Spezzaferro, "Caravaggio accettato," 39; Nicolai, *Mecenati a confronto*, 64–66.

20 Spezzaferro, "Caravaggio accettato," 37; Nicolai, *Mecenati a confronto*, 211.

name again appears in the archive this time as a painter who, together with Tarquinio Ligustri (1564–before 1621), received the first down payment for the fresco decoration of the new library of Palazzo Altemps.[21] The two artists had most likely already collaborated a few years earlier in the decoration of the Gallery of Palazzo Massimo alle Colonne (1602).[22] It is not unlikely, therefore, that it was Ligustri, already at work in the old part of the Altemps library since the summer of 1611, who introduced Orsi to Giovan Angelo Altemps. The relations between duke Altemps and Orsi thus developed along the double track of patronage and brokering the sales of paintings. Soon after the initiation of work in the new Altemps library, the transactions between Orsi and Giovan Angelo followed at a fast pace and continued beyond the completion of the decoration. It would seem, therefore, that the commission for the decoration of the library had consolidated the trust between the two. In fact, on the same day that Orsi received the deposit for the painted decoration of the new library, he also sold four paintings to the Duke of Altemps for 80 scudi: "Un bagno di Calisto del Caracciolo" (Calisto at her bath by Caracciolo), "Un contadino del Caravaggio e una tavola di frutti" (A peasant by Caravaggio and a table of fruits), "un Orfeo di Bassano" (an Orpheus by Bassano).[23] The first painting is cited in the 1618–1619 inventory as "un quadro di Calisto del Caracciolo" with an estimated value of 100 roman *scudi*, and again in the 1620 Giovan Angelo Altemps' posthumous inventory with a more precise description that includes the dimensions: "Un quadro di Calisto con Diana a paisagio di palmi 5 del Caracciolo" (a painting with Callisto and Diana in a landscape 5 roman *palmi* long by Caracciolo).[24] According to the seventeenth-century sources, the name Caraciolo or Caracciolo was used to indicate Annibale Carracci and in fact the subject of Altemps' painting seems to be related to the production of the Bolognese master.[25] The painting *Diana and Callisto* attributed to

21 Nicolai, *Mecenati a confronto*, 45–46.

22 L. Sickel, "Un affresco inedito." 93–98.

23 Nicolai, *Mecenati a confronto*, 63.

24 Ibid., 64. A Roman *palmo* corresponds to about 20–22cm or 8–8.5 inches.

25 The author of the Altemps inventory refers several paintings to "Caracciolo" or "Carracci" to signify as by either Annibale, Agostino and Ludovico Carracci and not by the Neapolitan Caravaggesque painter Giovan Battista Caracciolo (1578–1635). It was quite common in the 17th century to encounter the mangling of the name Carracci into Caracciolo, as we see in the correspondence of the well-known connoisseur Giulio Mancini with his brother Difebo. Mancini frequently referred to Annibale Carracci as Caracciolo or Carracciolo, likely reporting a common way to name the Bolognese master. See: Maccherini, "Caravaggio nel carteggio famliare di Giulio Mancini" 71–92.

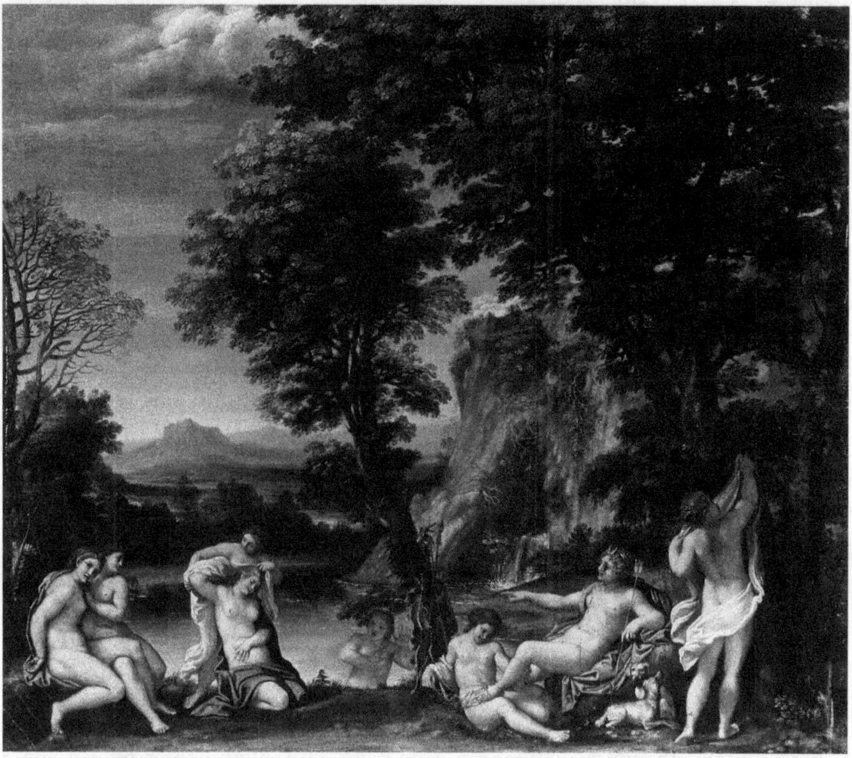

FIGURE 8.1 Annibale (1560–1609) or Agostino (1557–1602) Carracci, *Diana and Callisto in a Landscape*, ca. 1599
DUKE OF SUTHERLAND COLLECTION, MERTOUN – ST. BOSWELL'S, SCOTLAND

Annibale or his brother Agostino was acquired by the Duke of Sutherland in 1798 (fig. 8.1).[26] An argument that the Sutherland *Callisto* can be identified with the Altemps painting lies with the same dimensions and the fact that this work has not been present in the Roman collection since the end of the seventeenth century.[27] We know that the Sutherland painting was brought to Paris by the

26 Bellori in his biography of Annibale Carracci mentions "la favola di Callisto al bagno con Diana" (the tale of Callisto taking a bath with Diana) as *pendant* of a *Toilette of Venus* both in the collection of the French abbot de la Noue after being brought to Paris from Italy by the painter Jacques Stella in the 1634 (Bellori, *Le vite*, 86–87). Clovis Whitfield convincingly attributes the painting to Agostino Carracci rather than Annibale. See: Whitfield, "Agostino risarcito."

27 The painting does not appear in the 1691 inventory of goods that belonged to Pietro Altemps (1607–1691), Giovan Angelo's heir. As I will report later, there are no sales of paintings recorded in the Altemps papers between 1620 and 1691. More likely the painting could have been moved/donated to some other member of the family before 1634 and then potentially sold by the new owner. AA, Inventory of the goods that belonged to Duke

painter Jacques Stella (1596–1657) in 1634 and then passed to the Orléans collection where it remained until 1798 before being purchased by the current owner.[28] It is possible, therefore, that the painting belonged to Giovan Angelo Altemps and had left Rome shortly after the Duke's death in 1620, although confirmation is still lacking.

The painting described as "Orpheus" and attributed to Bassano (likely Jacopo Bassano), (1510–1592) is also mentioned in the 1620 posthumous inventory of Giovan Angelo Altemps with more details: "quadro grande di palmi 7 in circa d'un paisagio con la favola di Orfeo" (a large painting of about seven roman palmi of a landscape with the tale of Orpheus).[29] There are different versions of this subject attributed to both Francesco (1549–1592) and Leandro (1557–1622) Bassano, but with different dimensions. The only one with dimensions compatible with the Altemps version (about 140 cm, or seven palmi) was recently offered at a Sotheby's auction after being located in a private collection in Chicago.[30] The comparable dimensions alone do not, however, allow for an assured identification.

Two paintings attributed to Caravaggio complete the purchase Orsi arranged. In the two Altemps inventories of 1618–19 and 1620 they are reported respectively with these descriptions: "quadro d'un pastor che sona un flauto del Caravaggio" (a painting with a shepherd playing a flute by Caravaggio) e un "un quadro di diversi frutti del medesimo" (a painting with many fruits by the same), which subsequently become "una testa d'un villano che sona un cifalo ad olio alto palmi 3 et largo palmi 2" (a head of a peasant playing a flute 3 palmi high and 2 palmi wide) and "una tavola con molti frutti sopra con una caraffa di vino di palmi 4" (a table with many fruits on top and a carafe of wine measuring 4 palmi).[31] The generic description of the still life with fruit does correspond with known works by Caravaggio, but it is nevertheless impossible to trace the current location of the Altemps picture. By contrast, no painting of a flute player by Caravaggio appears in any ancient or modern collection records. In a recent essay Laura Teza proposed that the Altemps painting could be related to a "portrait of a farmer / peasant" mentioned in one of the most important sources for the biography of Caravaggio, the manuscript of Giulio

Pietro Altemps, 1691. Significantly, no purchases of paintings with a similar subject appear in the Altemps family records after 1620.

28 D. Posner, *Annibale Carracci. A Study on the Reform of Italian Painting around 1590*, New York-London 1971, 50, (118–119).

29 Nicolai, *Mecenati a confronto*, 64.

30 Sotheby's, *Master paintings*, lot. 122.

31 Nicolai, *Mecenati a confronto*, 64.

Mancini's *Considerations on Painting* (ca. 1616–20).[32] It is not known whether it could be the same painting or at least the same composition, certainly the omission of the flute in Mancini's quotation seems to further call this possibility into question. An Altemps family's inventory dated 1747 records "un quadro con un giovane che sona il ciufalo di bona mano" (a young man playing a flute by a good hand) that can most likely be identified with the painting sold by Prospero Orsi in 1611, recognized for its good quality, but no longer attributed to Caravaggio.[33] Traces of the painting are lost after that date.

On September 1st 1612 Giovan Angelo bought some other paintings from Prospero Orsi: "quattro quadri e cioè doi del Caravaggio et un San Carlo et un altro" (four paintings namely two by Caravaggio, a *San Carlo* and another one) for a total cost of 155 scudi,[34] By cross-checking the data we can establish with certainty that the two paintings "by Caravaggio" indicated here correspond to the "putto che sona un liuto del Caravaggio" (a boy playing a lute by Caravaggio) and "un quadro del retratto del Carravaggia [sic] che li morde una lucertola del Caravaggio" (a painting with the portrait of Caravaggio bitten by a lizard by Caravaggio), respectively at numbers 85 and 124 of the 1618–19 inventory and valued at 100 and 60 scudi.[35] The two paintings are also mentioned in the 1620 posthumous inventory without attribution but with more details and measurements: "un giovane che sona il liuto con una caraffa di fiori di palmi 6 longo" (a young man playing the lute with a jug of flowers 6 palmi long) valued 60 scudi and "un ritratto di Caraccio [sic] dove li morsica una licerta di palmi 3 e ½" (portrait of Caravaggio where he is bitten by a lizard 3 ½ palmi long) estimated at 18 scudi.[36] These are two famous compositions by Merisi and the fact that Prospero Orsi sold them to the Duke of Altemps makes the story even more interesting. Luigi Spezzaferro considered these works to be copies or at best replicas made by good painters, perhaps under Orsi's direct guidance.[37] In other words, they could be good pieces for the nascent Roman art market, especially at a time after Merisi's death when the demand for his works became the main commercial trend.

As the examples above make clear, there are significant differences in the evaluations between the 1618–19 inventory now in Chicago and the one drawn up shortly after Giovan Angelo's death in 1620. The author of the Chicago inventory is unknown, while the posthumous document was written by the

32 Teza, "Considerazioni sul Mondafrutto."

33 Nicolai *Mecenati a confronto*, 238.

34 Ibid., 66, 239.

35 Ibid., 66.

36 Ibid.

37 Spezzaferro, "Caravaggio accettato," 39.

painters Antonio Pomarancio (1560–1620) and Baldassare Aloisi (1578–1638), the latter directly involved in the reproduction of works by Caravaggio and therefore expert in judging paintings of that style.[38] The difference in the estimates can also be explained by the fact that the inventory of 1618–1619 was drawn up when Giovan Angelo was still alive and he himself could have influenced the prices upwards. The estimation of only 18 scudi assigned by the two authors to the *Boy Bitten by the Lizard* leaves little doubt that it is in fact a copy of the already famous Caravaggesque composition and was judged as such in the 1620 inventory. There are at least four known versions of the Boy bitten by a green lizard, two believed to be autograph (National Gallery London; and Longhi Collection, Florence) and two recognized copies.[39] The dimensions of the Altemps painting do not correspond to any of the versions known today and, therefore, it cannot be connected to any of those identified so far.

A different discussion concerns the *Lute Player* and the possibility of a new hypothesis regarding the version that belonged to Giovan Angelo Altemps. To date, there are three examples of this famous composition that are considered authentic works by Caravaggio: one ex-Wildenstein collection, one currently in the Hermitage Museum (Saint Petersburg, Russia—fig. 8.2) that belonged to Vincenzo Giustiniani (1638), and another which was bought in Italy by the third Duke of Beaufort in 1726 and remained at Badminton House (England) for almost three centuries (fig. 8.3).[40] The Wildenstein version shows some musical instruments on the table in front of the young player, while a carafe with water and flowers is featured in both the ex-Giustiniani and ex-Badminton compositions. The latter was for a long time considered a copy of the Hermitage version but more recently, thanks to a providential cleaning, it has been accepted as original by most scholars.[41] In fact, today this version is almost universally recognized as the one that belonged to Cardinal Francesco Maria del Monte (1549–1627) painted by Caravaggio around 1596.[42] The work is described in detail by Giovanni Baglione (1566–1643), a reliable biographer of Caravaggio. In particular, Baglione recalls the intense vividness of the still life on the table, emphasizing the "flashes of light" and the reflection of the room

38 Nicolai, *Mecenati a confronto*, 62.

39 Marini, *Caravaggio "Pictor prestantissimus,"* 45–58; Zuccari, "Le due versioni" 64–73; Berra, *Il Ragazzo morso*.

40 Christiansen, *A Caravaggio rediscovered*; Marini, *Caravaggio "Pictor prestantissimus,"* 381–383; Gregori, "Il suonatore di liuto," 129–131.

41 Mina Gregori recognizes the ex-Badminton version as the prototype for the ex-Giustiniani and now Hermitage painting (Gregori, "Il suonatore di liuto," 130).

42 Ibid. Even before cleaning, the ex-Badminton painting was identified with Del Monte's picture by Clovis Whitfield ("Der Lautenspieler," 242–244); see also Strinati, "Il suonatore," 115–127.

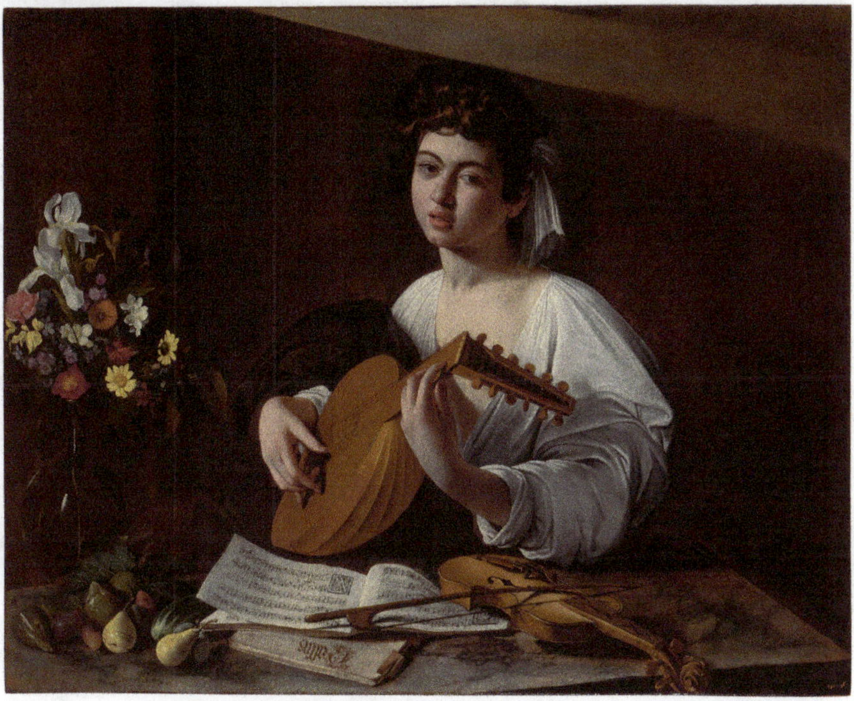

FIGURE 8.2 Caravaggio (Michelangelo Merisi; 1571–1610), *Lute Player*, c.1596 Oil on canvas 94 × 119 cm (37 × 47 in). The State Hermitage Museum, Saint Petersburg, Inv. no. GE-45
PHOTOGRAPH © THE STATE HERMITAGE MUSEUM. PHOTO BY PAVEL DEMIDOV

on the carafe and the drops of dew on the flowers.[43] Indeed, these details seem to exactly match the ex-Badminton version more than the others. The presence of a carafe of flowers was also explicitly mentioned in the 1620 inventory record of the version that belonged to Giovan Angelo Altemps: "un giovane che sona il liuto con una caraffa di fiori di palmi 6 longo" (a young man playing the lute with a jug of flowers long 6 palmi).[44] Despite this correspondence, when I first studied the Altemps collection I came to the conclusion that the painting belonging to Giovan Angelo must have been lost and not identifiable with either the ex-Badminton version or the undisputed version at the Hermitage.[45] The recent discovery by Riccardo Gandolfi of a "new" biography of Caravaggio written by Gaspare Celio presumably around 1614 could

43 Baglione, *Vite*, 136.
44 Nicolai, *Mecenati a confronto*, 67.
45 Ibid.

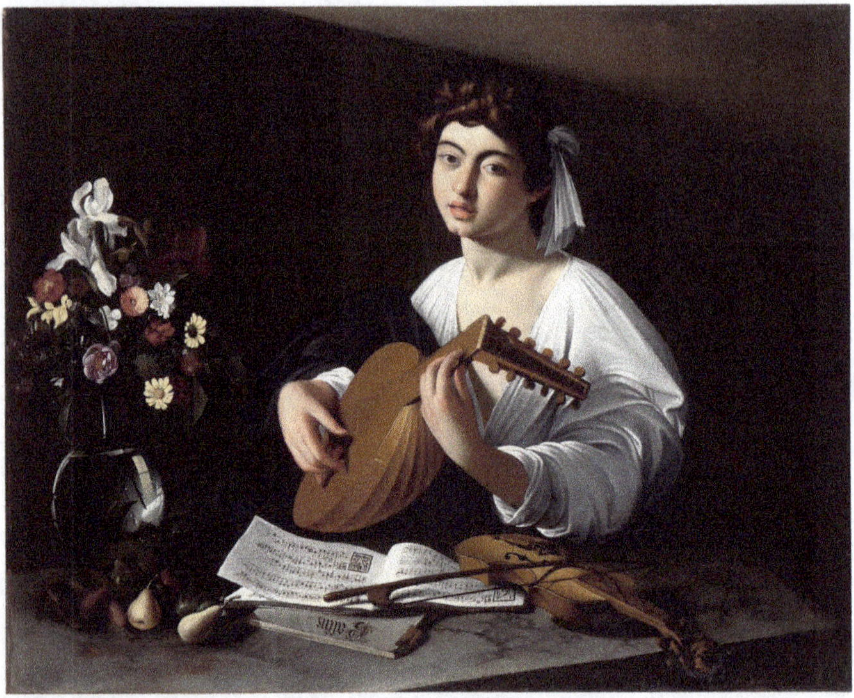

FIGURE 8.3 Caravaggio (Michelangelo Merisi; 1571–1610), *Lute Player*. ca. 1596. Oil on canvas 96 × 121 cm (38 × 48 in.)
EX-BADMINTON HOUSE GLOUCESTERSHIRE

open up a new possible scenario.[46] Celio recalls that Caravaggio painted a *Lute Player* in Prospero Orsi's house.[47] Is this perhaps the painting that Orsi sold to the Duke of Altemps just after Caravaggio's death? The hypothesis is intriguing but requires further investigation. All Altemps documents favor a solid attribution of the *Lute Player* to Caravaggio. If the identification of the Del Monte version with that of Badminton House is valid, then one should wonder what happened to the ex-Orsi and presumably ex-Altemps version. Gandolfi suggests that the ex-Orsi painting, datable to 1597, could be identified with the Hermitage version (formerly Giustiniani) without indicating a possible passage through the Altemps collection.[48] Clovis Whitfield, on the other hand,

46 Gandolfi, "La biografia di Caravaggio." 136–151.

47 "Poi fattosi amico Prosperino Orsi, delle Grottesche, si pose in casa di esso Prospero a fare alcuna cosa dal naturale, dove fece un putto che sonava il leuto ..." (Gandolfi, "La biografia di Caravaggio," 137).

48 Ibid., 141.

more explicitly argues that the Hermitage painting is precisely the one sold by Orsi to the Duke of Altemps and by his heirs to the Marquis Vincenzo Giustiniani.[49] Corroborating this hypothesis is the fact that the painting is mentioned in the posthumous inventory of the possessions of Vincenzo Giustiniani dated 1638 and not before. Since the *Lute Player* is apparently no longer present in the Altemps inventories subsequent to 1620, one might think that at some point between that date and 1638 the painting passed to Giustiniani.

When Giovan Angelo prematurely passed away in 1620 at the age of 33, the Altemps family faced a difficult financial situation. With the principal heir Pietro (1607–1691), son of Giovan Angelo, still a minor, the economic administration was managed for about four years by his mother Cornelia Orsini and Fausto Latini.[50] At this juncture, it could be assumed that important pieces from the collection may have been sold to raise cash, among them the *Lute Player*. The hypothesis sounds captivating, although various circumstances may affect its reliability.

In his testament Giovan Angelo Altemps established the *fidecommesso* on all his hereditary assets, including paintings.[51] This legal condition prohibited the heirs from selling or dispersing the collection, which thus had to remain intact. After careful research among the entries of the Altemps family's accounting records between 1620 and 1640, I was able to ascertain that in reality, just after the death of Giovan Angelo, the administrators of the inheritance sold some important assets, failing to respect the *fidecommesso*. In particular, in 1621 a pearl necklace valued at 3000 scudi was sold to Olimpia Aldobrandini and in 1622 part of the collection of ancient statues sold to Cardinal Ludovisi for 946 scudi.[52] However, no sales relating to paintings and no direct contact with Vincenzo Giustiniani or other members of that family emerged. Moreover, another point in Giovan Angelo's testament leads us to believe that the passage of the *Lute Player* from the Altemps to the Giustiniani is rather unlikely. Giovan Angelo "entrusted" his son and principal heir Pietro (1607–1691), still a minor, to the "protection" of the reigning pope Paul V (1550–1621) and the cardinal-nephew Scipione Borghese (1577–1633).[53] That Scipione Borghese was obsessed with possessing works by Caravaggio is well known. He even went so far as to have the Cavaliere d'Arpino (Giuseppe Cesari, 1568–1640)

49 Whitfield, "Novità e conferme," accessed March 2020.

50 Archivio di Stato di Roma (ASR), Notai Auditor Camerae (AC), VOL. 2951, October 5th 1620, ff. 354–359. The testament was openend on October 5th but it has been drawn up in March 11th 1620.

51 See note 50.

52 AA, Libro delle Entrate et Uscite 1620–1622, May 12 1621, 1 February 1622.

53 ASR, Notai AC, vol. 2951, f. 358. See also: Nicolai, *Mecenati a confronto*, 164.

unjustly imprisoned for the sole purpose of taking possession of his collection of paintings, including authentic ones by Merisi.[54] It is difficult to think that a personality like that, once involved in the Altemps legacy and certainly aware of the "Caravaggios" contained therein, would not have taken advantage. Given the conditions, a sale to Scipione Borghese would have been rather simple and "smoother" than to Giustiniani.

The prohibition of selling hereditary assets, and the fact that, no sales of paintings are reported in the Altemps papers between 1620 and 1638, seem to reasonably exclude a potential passage of the work to Giustiniani. Perhaps, then the *Lute Player* remained in the Altemps collection longer than previously thought and far from the prying eyes of Cardinal Borghese and others. An interesting clue comes from the legacy of Pietro Altemps. As I reported in 2009, there is no *Lute Player* in the list of paintings that belonged to him that were kept in the Altemps palace in Rome. However, the inventory of the paintings conserved in the Gallese family castle at the death of Pietro Altemps in 1691 records a picture as "un giovane in camiscia [sic!] che sona e canta" (a young man wearing a shirt who plays and sings).[55] The lute and the table with the still life are not mentioned, but the detail of the shirt worn by the young man and the fact that he sings and plays is intriguing. In fact, in addition to wearing an eye-catching white shirt, the Caravaggesque lute player, particularly in the Badminton version, also plays and actually sings. Considering that the author of the inventory must have been a local notary from Gallese village or possibly his assistant, it is little wonder that he simply reported what he saw—a young man in a shirt in the act of playing and singing—rather than noting every detail of the composition to mention the musical instrument. Even the fact that the painting is in Gallese and not in Rome can be explained by the particular preference of Pietro Altemps for the family castle where he resided for long periods, and which he restored and adorned with frescoes and many paintings from the collection of his father Giovan Angelo.[56] This painting must have belonged to Giovan Angelo's collection since there is no trace of a purchase

54 Cirinei, "Conflitti artistici" 255–305.

55 AA, Inventarium bonorum hereditariorum cla: me: Ducis Petri et respectivè fideic.rorum Cla: Me: Card.lis et Ducis Joannij Angeli in Civitate Gallesiis sub die Julij 16 anno 1691 (Inventory of the goods belonged to Pietro Altemps located in the Gallese Castle in 1691), f. 11. See also Bellori, *Le Vite*, 218, who emphasizes the "camicia" as a salient element of the composition.

56 For the restoration and decoration of the Gallese castle see: Nicolai, *Mecenati a confronto*, 55–59. There are 165 paintings listed in 1691 inventory of the goods kept in the Gallese castle. See note 55.

of it or works with a comparable subject in the Pietro account records from 1622 to 1691. In the subsequent inventory of Altemps family assets dated 1713 there is no longer any trace of the painting and from this moment and on no painting even slightly recognizable as a *Lute Player* is mentioned.

If, therefore, the current data tend to exclude any correspondence between the Altemps *Lute Player* and the one owned by Vincenzo Giustiniani now at the Hermitage, there might yet be the possibility, albeit theoretical, of a relationship with the ex-Badminton version. The dimensions of the Altemps version are compatible with those of the ex-Badminton picture, an important though certainly not conclusive point for identification.

In conclusion, the fact that Orsi potentially owned a *Lute Player* by Caravaggio could lead one to think that copies may have been made by Orsi himself or perhaps by another skilled copyist. Orsi may have taken advantage of both the possession of the painting and the death of Caravaggio to freely place copies of the painting on the market, passing them off as originals, using his credit as a long-time friend of Merisi. If the same applies to the version of the Lute Player Orsi sold to Altemps in 1611, then the Altemps painting would have to be a different version from the ex-Badminton picture and still unlocated.

Giovan Angelo Altemps bought other paintings from Prospero Orsi with an attribution to Caravaggio in 1613. Two of these paintings, a still life and an old man's head, were already attributed to Caravaggio at the time of purchase and then were recorded the same way in the inventory of 1619: "un quadro di frutti e fiori dipinti del Caravaggio" (a painting with fruits and flowers by Caravaggio) and "un quadretto d'una testa d'un vecchio del Caravaggio" (a painting with an Old Man's head by Caravaggio), valued, respectively at 60 and 20 scudi.[57] To these must be added other "tre teste di vecchio del Caravaggio" (three elderly men's heads by Caravaggio) listed in the 1618–19 inventory that were purchased by Orsi without attribution in 1613.[58] Unfortunately, the current location of these paintings mentioned for the last time in a late 1837 Altemps inventory is unknown.[59] Basically, all the paintings ascribed to Caravaggio that were purchased by the Duke of Altemps belong to the Lombard master's early period and they are in all cases genre paintings. In particular, the unusual presence of elderly men's heads may be significant, in light of the young Caravaggio's work in the workshop of Lorenzo Siciliano at the time of his earliest stay in

57 Nicolai, *Mecenati a confronto*, 65, 238.

58 Ibid.

59 Ibid., 238.

Rome, works that may have remained in the possession of Orsi.[60] It seems that Orsi implemented a precise commercial strategy to guarantee the authenticity of the paintings he was selling. This was based on his proven friendship with Caravaggio, on the notoriety of the compositions, and on the fact that no one, starting from the "inventor" of those subjects, could argue the presumption of authenticity of the works.

Giovan Angelo's passion for the Caravaggesque style is also demonstrated through the purchases of works by followers of Merisi. In the 1618–19 inventory "un quadro di Nostro Signore che appare alli doi discepoli di Bartolomeo" (a painting of Our Lord appearing to the two disciples by Bartolomeo) and "un David che ha in mano la testa di Golia di Bartolomeo Ottimo Scolare del Caravaggio del naturale" (a David holding the head of Goliath by Bartolomeo Excellent scholar of Caravaggio in full figure).[61] In the 1620 inventory details on the dimensions and subjects are added: "un Cristo in Emmaus con doi discepoli a un oste di *palmi* 10 longo" (a Christ at Emmaus with two disciples and an innkeeper 10 palmi long) and "un quadro grande di David che ammazza Golia di *palmi* 10 alto" (a large painting with of David killing Goliath 10 palmi high).[62] It is not clear to whom the indication "Bartolomeo Ottimo Scolare di Caravaggio" refers. Cautiously Spezzaferro believed that was Bartolomeo Manfredi while Gianni Papi more recently proposed the name of Bartolomeo Cavarozzi.[63] Revisiting my previous opinion closer to Spezzaferro's hypothesis, I now consider Papi's proposed identification more convincing. Supporting this conclusion is the fact that two paintings, a *Supper at Emmaus* today at the J. Paul Getty Museum (fig. 8.4) and a *David with the Head of Goliath* (location unknown) are both attributable to Cavarozzi and almost certainly are formerly from the Altemps collection.[64] The *Supper at Emmaus* now at the Getty is about 30 cm narrower than the Altemps painting, but a possible reduction of the canvas in the course of subsequent re-framing cannot be excluded.[65] The date of this painting, based on its style, to the early second decade of the seventeenth century would also correspond to the citation in the 1618–19 Altemps inventory.[66]

60 Curti, "Sugli esordi di Caravaggio." 65–75.

61 Nicolai, *Mecenati a confronto*, 65, 238.

62 Ibid.

63 Spezzaferro, "Caravaggio accettato," 41; Papi, *Bartolomeo Cavarozzi*, 24.

64 Papi, *Bartolomeo Cavarozzi*, 24–25.

65 Papi rightly points out that the length of the painting reported in the Altemps inventory could include the frame and that would explain the difference in size comparing to the painting now in the Getty Museum. See: Papi, *Bartolomeo Cavarozzi*, 24 and note 81.

66 For the date of the painting see: Papi, *Bartolomeo Cavarozzi*, 25.

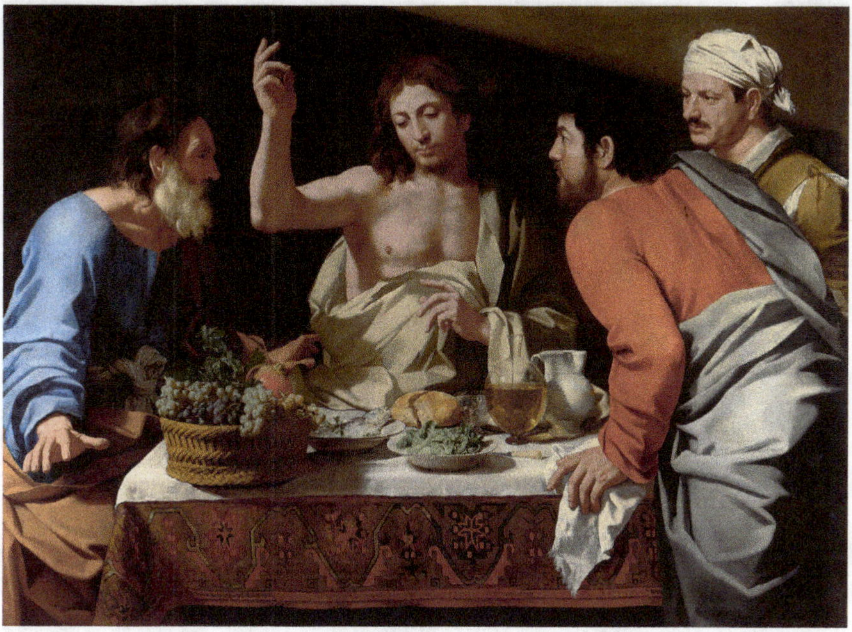

FIGURE 8.4 Bartolomeo Cavarozzi, (Italian, 1587–1625), *The Supper at Emmaus*, ca. 1612–1615. Oil on canvas; 139.7 × 194.9 cm (55 × 76 ¾ in.)
J. PAUL GETTY MUSEUM, LOS ANGELES, 72.PA.11

One of Caravaggio's followers Giovan Angelo Altemps must have been particularly fond of was Carlo Saraceni, as is attested by the six paintings attributed to him recorded in the inventory of 1618–1619. Among these the most important ones for their size and value are "un quadro grande con la Madonna e Santa Elisabetta e Nostro Signore con un angiolo" (a large Saint Elizabeth and Our Lord with an angel) and "una Giuditta" (a Judith).[67] These are two of Saraceni's most felicitous compositions which are known in different autograph versions, copies and workshop derivations.[68] In addition to the "small" version at the Academy Arts in Honolulu (Hawaii), another larger version (94×130 cm, 37"×51.2") has recently come to be considered as the likely prototype (fig. 8.5), for numerous derivations and copies scattered in various private collections and museums.[69] Yuri Primarosa, who published the painting, has also proposed that this prototype can be identified with the work owned by Giovan Angelo Altemps, on the basis of both the subject and the measurements

67 Nicolai, *Mecenati a confronto*, 66, 239.
68 Primarosa, "L'originale ritrovato." 174–180.
69 Primarosa, "Nuova luce su Carlo Saraceni," 73–74.

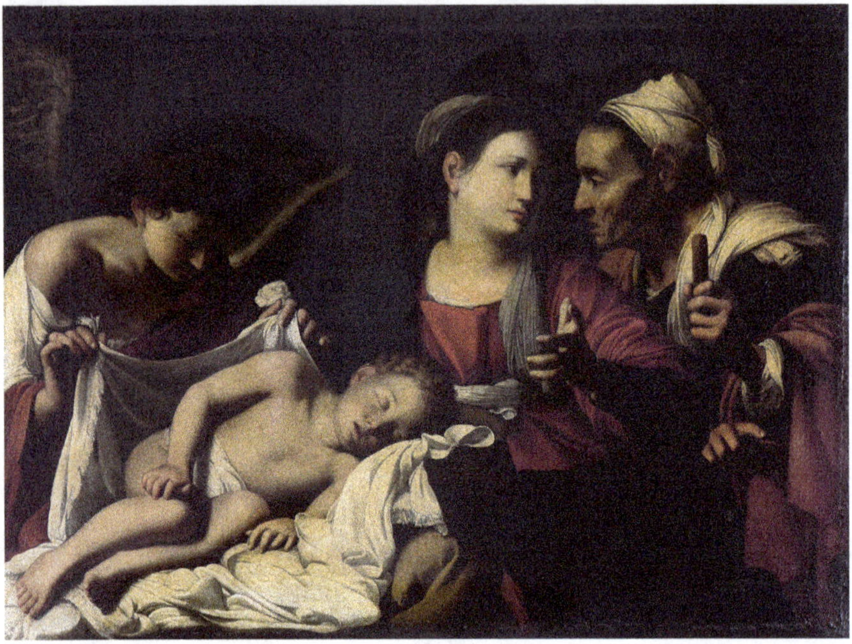

FIGURE 8.5 Carlo Saraceni (1579–1620), *Saint Anne, Elizabeth and the Christ Child with an Angel*, ca. 1608–1610
PRIVATE COLLECTION

("large" = large). Confirming this proposal is a further quotation from the inventory of the assets of the Altemps family of 1713, in which the work is described as: "quadro di sei e quattro [palmi] con effigie della Madonna Ss.ma, Sant'Elisabetta, il Bambino Giesù [sic] che dorme dentro un panno bianco et un angeletto [sic] che alza detto panno" (a picture of six and four [palmi] with the effigy of the Holy Madonna, Saint Elizabeth, the Child Jesus who sleeps inside a white cloth and a little angel who lifts that cloth).[70] The description leaves no doubt about the exact correspondence of the Altemps painting with the picture recently published by Primarosa whose dimensions are also 4×6 palmi, or approximately 90 × 130 cm. The work is dated on a stylistic basis to 1608–10, which would not exclude a direct commission by Giovan Angelo Altemps, although no documentary evidence has yet confirmed such a direct association with Altemps.[71]

70 AA, Inventory of the goods belonged to Giuseppe Maria Altemps, 1713.

71 For the date of the painting see: Primarosa, "Nuova luce su Carlo Saraceni," 73–74. In Giovan Angelo's expense records there are no direct payments to Carlo Saraceni to confirm a commission for the work, however, it cannot be ruled out that the payment may

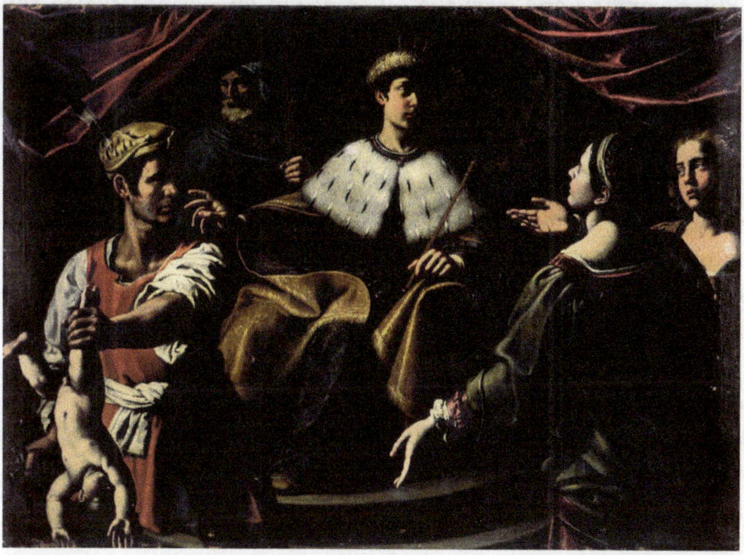

FIGURE 8.6 Antiveduto Gramatica (1571–1626), *The Judgment of Solomon*, ca. 1612–1614
KOELLIKER COLLECTION, MILAN

Giovan Angelo personally knew Saraceni, due to the works that the artist had carried out in the palace in Montecavallo (Quirinale Hill) that were completed in 1618. It should therefore come as no surprise that a large number of works by the Venetian painter was recorded in the Duke's collection some of which may have been made on commission.[72] With regard to the *Judith*, among the various authentic and workshop replicas of this famous composition by Saraceni, the example in the Koelliker collection could be the one that belonged to Giovan Angelo Altemps due to its similar size.[73]

Also in the Koelliker collection is another fine example of Caravaggesque painting that belonged to Giovan Angelo Altemps, *The Judgment of Solomon* attributed to Antiveduto Gramatica.[74] (fig. 8.6) The descriptions of the painting recorded in the Altemps inventories of 1618–19 and 1620 correspond exactly

have been made through intermediaries who were then reimbursed but without specifying the nature of the outlay. For example, very often in the Altemps accounting papers are reported to the "maestro di casa" or "our agent" for generic "wardrobe expenses," which could also include paintings or other furnishings.

72 Nicolai, *Mecenati a confronto*, 54.

73 Nicolai, *Mecenati a confronto*, 66.

74 Ibid.

to the Koelliker painting and even the difference in dimensions, which can be explained by a reduction in the length of the canvas over time, does not affect this identification.[75] Also, in this case, the dating of the work itself on the basis of style to 1615 fits perfectly with the timing of the citations in the Altemps inventories.

Giovan Angelo Altemps quickly formed a collection of undoubted value and, as we have seen, he certainly gravitated towards the more "modern" and innovative painting styles popular in the early seventeenth century Rome. Prospero Orsi contributed in a decisive way to the formation of Giovan Angelo's collection and most likely shaped the owner's taste. Doubts that remain about the authenticity of the various works attributed to Caravaggio that were sold by Orsi notwithstanding, what is certain is the innovative force with which the Caravaggesque style permeated collectors' choices and the Roman artistic market in the first decades of the seventeenth century and of which the Altemps collection offers a formidable example.

Acknowledgements

I would like to express my gratitude to the people who assisted me in preparing this essay: Inge Reist for inviting me to participate in this publication and for all her efforts in refining my text; Donna Lucrezia Hardouin and Donna Altea Altemps for their kind hospitality in Gallese during my research in the Altemps Archive; Yuri Primarosa and Clovis Whitfield, Gabriele Reina (Koelliker Collection), Fabio Marcelli and Gianni Papi for their essential assistance with images and advice, my wife Athena who was fundamental for the English translation of the present paper.

Bibliography

Archival Sources

Archivio Altemps (Gallese, Italy), reported as AA.
Archivio di Stato di Roma (ASR), Rome, Italy.

Published Sources

Baglione, Giovanni. *Vite de'pittori, scultori et architetti dal tempo di Gregorio XIII nel 1572, al tempo di Urbano Ottavo nel 1642*. Rome: Andrea Fei, 1642.

75 *Orazio Borgianni*, 140–141.

Bellori, Giovanni Pietro. *Le vite de' pittori, scultori et architetti moderni*. Rome: Mascardi, 1672.

Berra, Giacomo. *Il "Ragazzo morso da un ramarro" del Caravaggio: L'enigma di un morso improvviso*. Florence: Libro Co., 2016.

Cavazzini, Patrizia. *Painting as a Business in the Early Seventeenth-Century Rome*. University Park: Penn State University Press, 2008.

Cavazzini, Patrizia. "Middle-class Patronage, Collecting, and the Art Market." In *A Companion to Early Modern Rome, 1492–1692*, edited by P. M. Jones, Barbara Wisch, and S. Ditchfield, 412–426. Leiden and Boston: Brill, 2019.

Cavazzini, Patrizia. "Marketing Strategies and the Creation of Taste in Seventeenth-century Rome." In *The Art Market in Rome in the Eighteenth-century Rome*, edited by P. Cohen, 65–85. Leiden and Boston: Brill, 2018.

Christiansen, Keith. *A Caravaggio Rediscovered: The Lute Player*. New York: The Metropolitan Museum of Art, 1990.

Cirenei, A. "Conflitti artistici, rivalità cardinalizie e patronage a Roma fra Cinque e Seicento: il caso del processo criminale contro il Cavalier d'Arpino." In *La nobiltà romana in età moderna: Profili istituzionali e pratiche sociali*, edited by Maria Antonietta Visceglia, 255–305. Rome: Carocci, 2001.

Curti, Francesca. "Sugli esordi di Caravaggio a Roma: La bottega di Lorenzo Carli e il suo inventario." In *Caravaggio a Roma, Una vita dal vero*, (exh. cat., Archivio di Stato di Roma), edited by Michele Di Sivo and Orietta Verdi, 65–76. Rome: De Luca Editori d'Arte, 2011.

Gandolfi, Ricardo. "La biografia di Michelangelo da Caravaggio nelle *Vite* di Gaspare Celio." in *Storia dell'Arte* 151–152 (2020): 136–151.

Giustiniani, Vincenzo. *Discorsi sulle arti e sui mestieri*, edited by Anna Banti. Florence: Sansoni, 1981.

Gregori, Mina. "Il suonatore di liuto 'ex-Badminton.'" In *Monteverdi e Caravaggio* (exh. cat.), edited by F. Cacciatori and V. Villa, 129–131. Cremona: Museo del Violino, 2017.

Maccherini, Michele. "Caravaggio nella corrispondenza familiare di Giulio Mancini." *Prospettiva* 87 (1997): 71–92.

Marini, Maurizio. *Caravaggio "Pictor praestantissimus"*.... Rome: Newton & Compton, 2005.

Merola, Antonio. "Altemps, Giovanni Angelo." In *Dizionario Biografico degli Italiani*, vol. 2. Rome: Istituto della enciclopedia italiana, 1960.

Nicolai, Fausto. *Mecenati a confronto. Committenza, collezionismo e mercato dell'arte nella Roma del primo Seicento. Le famiglie Massimo, Altemps, Naro e Colonna*. Rome: Campisano, 2009.

Orazio Borgianni. Un genio inquieto nella Roma di Caravaggio, (exh. cat., Palazzo Barberini, Rome), edited by Gianni Papi. Milan: Skira, 2020.

Palazzo Altemps: Indagini per il restauro della fabbrica Riario, Soderini, Altemps, edited by Francesco Scoppola. Rome: De Luca, 1987.

Papi, Gianni. *Bartolomeo Cavarozzi*, Cremona: Soncino, 2016.

Posner, Donald. *Annibale Carracci. A Study on the Reform of Italian Painting around 1590*. New York and London: Phaidon, 1971.

Primarosa, Yuri. "Nuova luce su Carlo Saraceni. La Madonna del Pilar di Santa Maria in Monserrato e altri inediti." *Storia dell'Arte* 146/147 (2017): 69–76.

Primarosa, Yuri. "L'originale ritrovato. Carlo Saraceni e 'l'Angelo che veglia il Bambino Gesù con la Vergine e Sant'Anna,' tra repliche autografe, derivazioni e copie." In *Originali, repliche, copie*, edited by Pietro Di Loreto, 174–180. Rome: Ugo Bozzi, 2018.

Serrai, Alfredo. *La biblioteca Altempsiana. Ovvero. Le raccolte librarie di Marco Sittico III e del nipote Giovan Angelo Altemps*. Roma: Bulzoni, 2008.

Sickel, Lothar. "Un affresco inedito di Tarquinio Ligustri: la 'prospettiva' nel Palazzo Massimo alle Colonne." *Bollettino d'Arte* 120 (2003): 93–98.

Sotheby's, *Master paintings*, (auction catalogue). October 14, 2020, New York, lot.122.

Spezzaferro, Luigi. "Caravaggio accettato. Dal rifiuto al mercato." In *Caravaggio nel IV centenario della Cappella Contarelli*, edited by Caterina Volpi, 23–50. Rome: CAM, 2002.

Strinati, Claudio. "Il suonattore di liuto di Caravaggio." In *Monteverdi e Caravaggio* (exh. cat.), edited by F. Cacciatori and V. Vila, 115–127. Cremona: Museo del Violino, 2017.

Teza, Laura. "Considerazioni sul Mondafrutto, sul Bacchino malato e su 'ritratto di un villano.'" In *Il giovane Caravaggio "sine ira et studio,"* edited by Alessandro Zuccari, 56–63. Rome: De Luca, 2018.

Vannugli, Antonio. "L'iconografia del cardinale Marco Sittico Altemps: Da ignoto lombardo a Cati, da De Magistris a Leoni, da Pulzone a Bays, con l'inventario Altemps del 1618–1619." *Studi di Storia dell'Arte* 31 (2020): 119–146.

Whitfield, Clovis. "Der Lautenspieler." In Caravaggio: *Originale und Kopien im Spiegel der Forschung* (exh. cat., Museum Kunst Palast, Düsseldorf), edited by Jürgen Harten and Jean-Hubert Martin, 242–244. Stuttgart: Hatje Cantz, 2006.

Whitfield, Clovis. "Agostino risarcito." *About Art Online*, July 2017. https://www.aboutartonline.com/agostino-risarcito-la-vera-grandezza-del-maggiore-dei-fratelli-carracci-un-saggio-c-whitfield-1-parte-with-english-text/. Accessed July 2020.

Whitfield, Clovis. "Novità e conferme dalla 'Vita di Caravaggio' di Gaspare Celio." *About Art Online*, https://www.aboutartonline.com/novita-e-conferme-dalla-vita-di-caravaggio-di-gaspare-celio-clovis-whitfield-text-with-italian-translation/. Accessed March 2020.

Zuccari, Alessandro. "Le due versioni del *Ragazzo morso dal ramarro* attribuite a Caravaggio." In *Il giovane Caravaggio "sine ira et studio,"* edited by Alessandro Zuccari, 64–73. Rome: De Luca, 2018.

CHAPTER 9

From the Art Market to St. Peter's: The Cases of Nicolas Poussin and Valentin de Boulogne

Patrizia Cavazzini

Between 1628 and 1629 Nicolas Poussin (1594–1665) and Valentin de Boulogne (1591–1632), two French artists who lived in Rome most of their lives, painted two of the smaller altarpieces in the basilica of St Peter's, respectively the *Martyrdom of St. Erasmus* and the *Martyrdom of the Saints Processus and Martinianus*.[1] The task, one of the most prestigious in the city, signaled their success, in particular as they had both obtained it through the intervention of the powerful cardinal Francesco Barberini (1597–1679), nephew of Pope Urban VIII (1568–1644). The famous erudite Cassiano dal Pozzo (1588–1657) possibly suggested Nicolas Poussin's name for the altarpiece, but his intervention might have been superfluous, as Poussin had just completed the *Death of Germanicus* for the cardinal.[2] Valentin had also already received a commission from Francesco Barberini for a lost *Decollation of St John the Baptist*.[3] Like Poussin, Valentin was close to Cassiano dal Pozzo, whom he portrayed and who paid for his medical expenses when the painter became ill and died in 1632.[4] Both painters had also already worked for Ascanio Filomarino (1583–1666), who was part of the Barberini's circle and became cardinal in 1641.[5]

Thus, at first sight, both Poussin's and Valentin's careers were conforming to the patterns of patronage that are well-known for Rome, relying on commissions from the most influential characters in the Roman art world.[6] It has become increasingly clear though that in the city, from the beginning of the seventeenth century, patronage was not the only way for a painter to make a living.[7] Working only for patrons was an ideal to which artists aspired,

1 Rice, *Altars and Altarpieces* 225–238; *Poussin et dieu*, 164–166.
2 Bellori, *Le vite*, 428.
3 Lavin, *Barberini Documents*, 42.
4 Mazzetti di Pietralata, "Joachim von Sandrart."
5 Lorizzo, *La collezione del Cardinale Filomarino*, 34, 117.
6 While the bibliography is too vast to be cited here, the seminal work remains Haskell, *Patrons and Painters*.
7 Costello, "The Twelve Pictures," is the earliest and fundamental study; Cavazzini, "Marketing Strategies," with further bibliography.

 | DOI:10.1163/9789004513938_011

but difficult to achieve in practice. Few painters were so busy with commissions that they could avoid the world of trade, and in many cases, it was that world that brought them to the patrons' attention. This is what happened to Caravaggio (Michelangelo Merisi; 1571–1610) who became cardinal Francesco Maria del Monte's (1549–1627) protégé after the cardinal bought his early pictures in the shop of the painter Lorenzo Carli.[8]

1 Paths to the Profession: Workshops and Palaces

At least from Michelangelo's (1475–1564) time, and increasingly towards the end of the Cinquecento, many painters in Rome struggled to affirm the nobility of their profession. In particular they wanted to distinguish themselves from the myriad artisans with little training who could freely establish themselves as painters in the city. A rare case in Europe, the painters' guild in Rome did not require any formal training, did not limit the number of its members, and did not hinder foreigners. As a consequence, many cheap pictures were produced in Rome in the late sixteenth century, "so awkward that they move to laughter not to devotion."[9] The founding of the academy of St Luke in 1593 tried to make clearer the distinction between two different kinds of painters: the academicians who practiced a liberal art and the "bottegari," or painter-merchants, who were considered artisans.[10] The latter were members of the "compagnia," heir to the medieval corporation, a minor branch of the academy unhappily coexisting with the main body. "Bottegari" were allowed to own shops where they kept stocks of paintings for sale, while academicians were not, and therefore they worked at home.[11] "Bottegari" relied on quantity and not on quality, turning out mostly single figures or heads, portraits, landscapes, still-lifes and many copies, in any case works that were not considered to require great powers of invention. Academicians had to be more skilled, and able to conceive a composition on their own without relying on somebody else's drawing. In practice it was not always clear who belonged to which branch of the institution and according to which criteria; a painter could move from one branch to the other, as happened to Antiveduto Gramatica (1571–1626), who started

8 Curti, "Sugli esordi di Caravaggio," 74–75.

9 Archivio dell'Accademia di San Luca, Statuti 1607, ff. 21–21v.

10 Missirini, *Memorie per servire*, 71; Rossi, "La compagnia di San Luca," 367–394; Cavazzini, "Pittori eletti e bottegari"; Salvagni, *Da Universitas ad Accademia*, II, in particular 239–253 for the most recent interpretation of the early history of the institution, which became more structured and efficient only in the 1620's.

11 For an example, Sickel, "Anthonis Santvoort," 39–62; see also notes 12, 18, 19 *infra*.

out by painting "sibyl's heads" and portraits but became head of the painters' academy towards the end of his life.[12] Moreover many painters in Rome in the early Seicento practiced the profession without being a member of either the academy or a compagnia.

Ideally the academicians, as members of a noble profession, were not supposed to be tainted by commercial transactions. They could only work for pleasure, not for gain, and could only bestow their works, receiving a gift in return, not a payment. Their canvases could not be priced merely according to the labor necessary to complete them, a criterion deemed appropriate only for artisanal objects. The success of a composition and the fame of its author were more relevant in determining the final price, rarely settled in advance with private patrons.[13] These principles, impossible to carry out in practice, colored many transactions between painters and patrons, and caused contemporary sources, in particular biographers, to minimize the role of the art-market.

Even though a "bottegaro" could make a good living, establishing oneself as a painter in Rome was extremely competitive. Youngsters found that the better artists from the late Cinquecento were no longer willing to train apprentices with any degree of continuity.[14] Many established painters hired collaborators by the day, a system under which training, food and lodging were not contemplated. Almost no famous artist offered notarial contracts of employment to novices, who therefore had no guarantee of steady employment and could be easily dismissed at a moment's notice. On the contrary, "bottegari" underwrote such contracts with apprentices, commonly used in all manual professions, but considered inappropriate for a liberal artist. These masters took their task seriously, at least on paper, offering to "teach the art of painting with every diligence and solicitude" for a number of years, and to provide a youth with food and lodgings.[15] In exchange, they acquired full rights to the apprentice's labor, which was usually applied both to the workshop and domestic services. Thus, a youth could devote only a limited number of hours to learning the profession, and usually nothing of what he produced belonged to him until his contribution to the revenues of the workshop became significant.

Many painters, especially those who went to Rome relatively young, found themselves working not for the more established artists, but for the vast underworld of anonymous personalities who ran shops. A list of shops

12 Sperindei, "Due pittori e 'bottegari' marchigiani."

13 Cavazzini, "'Patto fermo' o cortesia." For a different approach, Spear and Sohm, *Painting for Profit*.

14 Cavazzini, "Riflessioni sull'apprendistato."

15 For one of many examples of this kind of contract, ASR, 30 Notai, uff. 9, 13 febbraio 1593, f. 259, as cited by Sickel. "Gli esordi di Caravaggio," 38.

compiled around 1625 tallies over 140 "botteghe" belonging to painters and painter-guilders in Rome.[16] It is well-documented that Giovanni Baglione (1566–1643), Antiveduto Gramatica and many others, were apprenticed in such places. Indeed, this is the main reason why so little is known about the training and early careers of many painters who arrived in Rome with scant instruction in the profession, such as Jusepe de Ribera (1591–1652): deemed demeaning, such beginnings were hardly ever advertised.[17] From Baglione's and Gramatica's examples, it is evident that contacts between master and pupil lasted decades, and continued even when the latter started to work independently.[18] Antiveduto worked for ten years with the "bottegaro" Giovan Domenico Angelini (born ca. 1560), on an intermittent basis, and kept collaborating with him even after having set up his own shop.[19]

Painters, young and old, could also make a living by formally enrolling in a nobleman's or a cardinal's household. These positions were honorific, meaning that they required no specific service, and assured lodgings, a space to work, food, a small monthly stipend, and other benefits which could include the maintenance of a servant and a horse.[20] Canvases would be commissioned and paid for separately, in addition to the stipend, and a painter was free to work for other patrons or for the market. Living in the palace was not necessarily a requirement, and all these subsidies were bestowed even if the painter was ill or unable to work for any reason. The Cavalier d'Arpino (1568–1640), from his youth and throughout his life, was always in somebody's service and the benefits he received from cardinal Pietro Aldobrandini (1571–1621) were substantial, the equivalent of 200–250 scudi a year, even when he was working in the Sala di Campidoglio in the Conservators palace.[21] Gerrit van Honthorst (1592–1656), David de Haen (1585–1622), Nicolas Régnier (1591–1667) and Joachim Sandart (1606–1688) all were in the service of Vincenzo Giustiniani (1564–1637) in subsequent years, but perhaps not too many of these valuable positions existed, certainly fewer than those mentioned by biographers.[22]

Second-rate artists could become "familiari" as well: Pope Urban VIII had the painter-gilder Simone Lagi in his roll, and cardinal Francesco Barberini the little-known Giovan Domenico Marziani, called Maltese, who had frescoed

16 Biblioteca Apostolica Vaticana (BAV), Barberini Latini, 4835.

17 Porzio and D'Alessandro, "Ribera between Rome and Naples."

18 Cavietti and Curti, "La bottega di Morelli," 434–435.

19 Bertolotti, "Gian Domenico Angelini," 70–78; Sickel, "The 'Madonna dei Cappuccini'."

20 Cavazzini, "Painters vs. Architects"; Byatt, "Aspetti giuridici," 616–617.

21 Cavazzini, "Painters vs architects," 30.

22 Capitelli, "Dutch Caravaggists in Rome," 13–23.

some angels in the church of Santa Bibiana.[23] In Marziani's case, he was enrolled as a "gentleman extraordinaire," like the librarian Luca Holstenio (1596–1661), who had a much better salary, 15 scudi a month versus Marziani's 3.60.[24] Because Marziani was in the cardinal's service, he was even considered for the altarpiece in St Peter's—the one that was then painted by Valentin—obviously a commission which would have been another huge advantage of his position. Lodgings, with fewer or no other benefits, could be offered to painters by any sort of patron, of any social class, and in general patrons of lower social standing offered fewer benefits and less freedom to work for other artists' customers.

2 Valentin's Early Career and Arrival in Rome

The case of Valentin de Boulogne is emblematic, as he made his way in Rome from rather unpretentious beginnings. He had arrived in the city by 1609, when he was eighteen, presumably having briefly trained in France with his father, a glass-painter. In that year a "Valentino apprentice," of unknown nationality, lived with the Florentine painter Pietro Veri (d. 1611) at Sant'Andrea delle Fratte.[25] Veri, who worked also as an architect, occupied a middle ground between painter and decorator; responsible for the modest *Saint Francis* altarpiece in the Scarlatti chapel in San Giovanni dei Fiorentini, he was at that time painting coffered ceilings and decorative friezes in Palazzo Firenze.[26] Veri, whose household records are missing for 1610, became ill in 1611, dying in August the same year. His apprentice Valentino seems to have moved to the workshop of an even more obscure painter, Polidoro Mariottini also from Florence—indeed it was common for youths to move between workshops, especially if their owners shared a common geographical origin.[27] The "Valentino apprentice" in Veri's household in 1609 almost certainly is the "Valentino French painter" living with Mariottini in 1611: the combination of the two records suggests that this is indeed Valentin de Boulogne.[28] Mariottini associated with sculptors, in particular with Stefano Maderno (1576–1636) and Nicolas Cordier (1567–1612) from Lorraine, therefore it might well be in this

23 Rice, *The Altars and Altarpieces*, 233, 236; Nessi, *Andrea Camassei*, 51, 55, note 14.

24 BAV, Archivio Barberini, Computisteria, Giustificazioni vol. 45, f. 357 [unpublished].

25 Lemoine, "Bowing to No One," 3; Vodret, *Ghiongrat*, 488.

26 Sickel, "Pietro Veri"; *Roma di Sisto V*, 547–548; Daniele, "Pietro Veri a Montegiordano," 127–131.

27 Pampalone, "Pittori fiorentini a Roma," 421. For Mariottini, Fausto Nicolai, *Mecenati a confronto*, 48, 221, 223.

28 Vodret, *Ghiongrat*, 488.

workshop that Valentin met the sculptor David Delariche (d. 1626), also from Lorraine, his roommate from 1620 until the latter's assassination in 1626.[29]

Valentin is then mentioned in May 1614, when he reconciled, after a skirmish or verbal confrontation, with another insignificant painter, a Frenchman called Nicolas Noel.[30] Noel was another "bottegaro" who did sign notarial contracts with apprentices, promising to teach, house and feed them.[31] It is not possible to establish if Valentin ever worked for him; however it is intriguing that the only traces of Valentin that can be found in Rome for more than a decade are all in this underworld of minor painters. It is obvious that he looked at canvases by Bartolomeo Manfredi (1582–1622), Cecco del Caravaggio (fl. ca. 1610–1620) and Jusepe de Ribera, but it is not known what his relationship with them might have been, possibly only an informal and casual one. Until 1620 there is no further trace of Valentin, and until he painted the *Last Supper* (Rome, Galleria Nazionale d'Arte Antica) for the gallery of Palazzo Mattei, around 1625, there is no proof that he worked on commission or interacted with patrons.[32] In 1624 a small *Head of a Soldier*, now lost, was listed in the death inventory of monsignor Costanzo Patrizi; in 1627 a *Denial of St Peter's* (Florence, Longhi Foundation), perhaps painted as early as 1615, was in the collection of the lawyer Giovan Battista Mellini (d. 1627).[33] There is no evidence that these works were commissioned, and even the first painting by Valentin owned by Francesco Barberini, a *David* now in a private collection in California, was bought on the market and not commissioned. Paid for in June 1627, it was almost immediately followed by a commission from the cardinal.[34] (fig. 9.1).

Even after Valentin became sought after by Francesco Barberini and his circle of intellectual friends, he did not stop working for dealers. Leaving behind the world of painter-merchants where he had been trained, he met with one of the more skilled players in the Roman art-market, the Genoese Giovanni Stefano Roccatagliata (1596–1652), an attaché to the antechamber of Urban VIII, a prestigious if poorly paid role that put him in contact with the

29 Vodret, *Ghiongat*, 488, 519. For Delariche Pierguidi, "Ermafrodito," 86–87; Cavazzini, "Success and Failure."

30 Ibid., 20.

31 ASR, 30 Notai, uff. 19, 17 Novembre 1616, f. 707, for a contract of apprenticeship between Nicolas di Claudio Natalis, "pictor in urbe" and a Flemish apprentice.

32 Lemoine, *Valentin de Boulogne. Beyond Caravaggio*, 231.

33 Nicolai, "'Le molte pitture moderne buone'."

34 Lavin, *Barberini Documents*, 42; see also BAV, Archivio Barberini, Contabilità, Giustificazioni di Francesco Barberini, vol. 44, f. 197, ristretto delle spese del mese di giugno: "A Valentino franzese pittore per un David compro per ordine del signor Filomarino scudi 15."

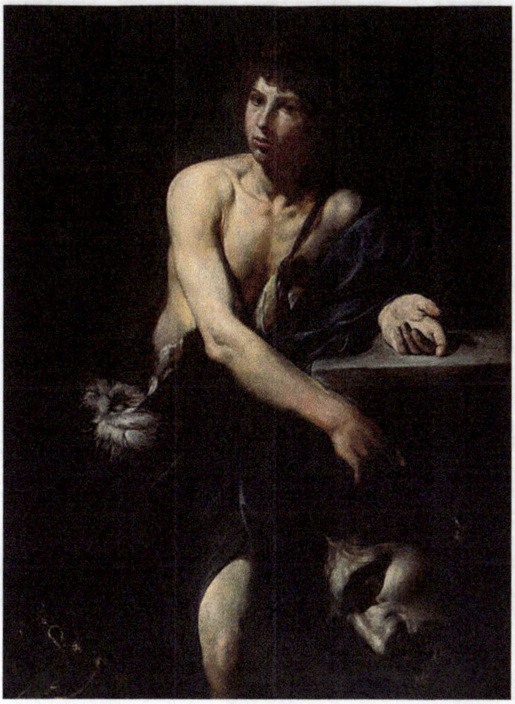

FIGURE 9.1
Valentin de Boulogne (1591–1632), *David*, 1626–27. Oil on canvas, cm 136 × 103 (53.5 × 40.6 in.)
PRIVATE COLLECTION, CALIFORNIA

pope and his visitors.[35] Roccatagliata supplemented his income by trading in pictures, in particular he promoted new talents, both Italians and foreigners, recently arrived in Rome, buying paintings on the cheap and selling them years later for multiples of their cost. Because of his position at the papal court, he knew many of its members, including the chamberlain Angelo Giori (1586–1662) who in 1629 bought from him the *St John the Baptist* and the *St Jerome* by Valentin now in Camerino.[36] Giori had also used Roccatagliata as a middleman when he commissioned a *Rebecca at the Well* from Valentin (Rome, private collection).[37] For Roccatagliata, Valentin had also painted at least one of the two versions of the *Judgment of Solomon* (Paris, Musée du Louvre; Rome, Galleria Nazionale d'Arte Antica, fig. 9.2) sold by the dealer to Fabrizio Valguarnera (d. 1631), a Sicilian nobleman who bought paintings in order to launder stolen diamonds.[38] In the same year Valentin painted for Valguarnera

35 Costello, "The Twelve pictures"; Cavazzini, "Nicolas Poussin, Cassiano dal Pozzo"; Pierguidi, *Note sui dipinti.*

36 *Valentin de Boulogne. Beyond Caravaggio*, 208–209, cat. no. 45/46 (Christiansen) for "St. John the Baptist/St Jerome."

37 Lemoine, "Chronology," 232.

38 Costello, "The Twelve pictures"; *Valentin de Boulogne. Beyond Caravaggio*, 169–170, cat no. 33 (Christiansen) for "The Judgement of Solomon."

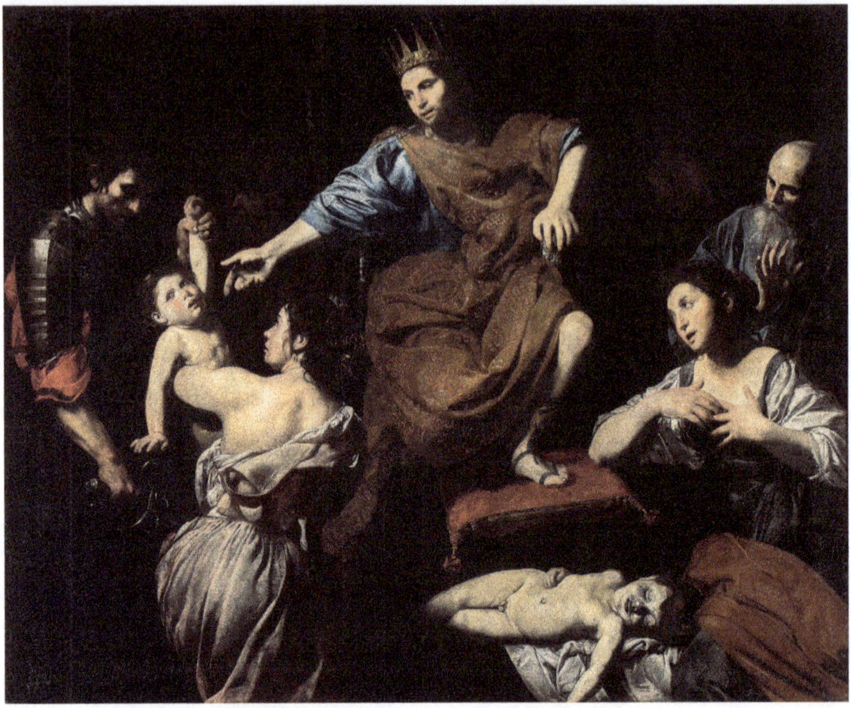

FIGURE 9.2 Valentin de Boulogne (1591–1632), *The Judgement of Salomon*, ca. 1629. Oil on canvas, 174 × 213 cm (68.5 × 83.8 in.). Galleria Nazionale di Arte Antica, Rome (C) GALLERIE NAZIONALI DI ARTE ANTICA, ROMA (MIC)—BIBLIOTHECA HERTZIANA, ISTITUTO MAX PLANCK PER LA STORIA DELL'ARTE/ENRICO FONTOLAN

a large *Musical Company with Fortune Teller* (Liechtenstein, The Princely collection), presumably also destined to the art market, as Valguarnera too was an art-dealer, not a collector.[39]

Presumably Valentin was one of the many painters who went to Rome from the last quarter of the Cinquecento "all of a sudden," or "without a fixed abode," as sources say, without any idea of where he would end up or how to make a living.[40] Neither upon his arrival, nor later did he enter a nobleman's or a cardinal's service, or that of a less exalted protector.[41]

---

39 *Valentin de Boulogne. Beyond Caravaggio*, 223–227, cat. no. 50 (Christiansen) for "A Musical Company with a Fortune Teller."

40 Lukehart, "Appendix"; Bellori, *Le vite*, 213.

41 Valentin was never in Francesco Barberini' s service; in Lemoine, "Chronology," 235 the evidence is misinterpreted.

3 Poussin's Early Career in Rome

Like Valentin, Poussin was never enrolled in any noble family, or in any other household. His desperate letter of 1630 to Cassiano dal Pozzo, in which he stated that an illness left him without means of survival, is a sure sign that he had to fend for himself, as no painter in a household would find himself in such a dire condition.[42] When he arrived in Rome in 1624, at the age of 30, Poussin meant to establish himself in the Barberini circle through the intervention of the poet Giovan Battista Marino (1569–1625) and the banker Marcello Sacchetti, (1586–1629) a strategy that failed because Marino and cardinal Francesco Barberini left Rome. Poussin did not quickly find employment with the cardinal, contrary to what is generally assumed: Francesco bought his *Sack and Destruction of the Temple of Jerusalem* in February 1626 from a third party, not from the painter, who did not receive any remuneration at all from this transaction.[43] It took two more years of toil before he saw any compensation from the Barberini, until the beginning of 1628, when he was paid the modest amount of 60 scudi for the *Death of Germanicus* (Minneapolis Institute of Arts).[44]

Cassiano Dal Pozzo was certainly an important patron for Poussin, and in his letter of 1630 mentioned above the painter remarked on the many favors already received from him. However, his role during Poussin's early years in Rome must have been limited, because of his travels abroad with Francesco Barberini in 1625 and 1626. By 1689, at the death of Cassiano's brother Carlo Antonio, (1606–1689) the dal Pozzo collection included many paintings by Poussin, and many of his early ones, but not all of them were commissions.[45] Some, such as the *Rebecca at the Well* and its pendant *Christ and the Woman of Samaria*, possibly painted in 1627, were clearly meant for the family, as they are focused on a well, "pozzo" in Italian.[46] Others originally belonged not to Cassiano, but to the art-dealer Roccatagliata, a close friend of his.[47] Perhaps Roccatagliata bought what Poussin painted on spec, or perhaps he commissioned specific themes of the painter, always with the intention of trading them as soon as it became profitable to do so. Though he was in contact with the Barberini and the dal Pozzo, he was not a supportive patron who shared

42 For the dating of this episode, Rice, "Poussin's Elephant"; Abbing, "Poussin's Elephant Revisited," with an unlikely interpretation of the text of the letter; Mahon, *Nicolas Poussin*. 44.

43 Cavazzini, "Nicolas Poussin"; Mahon, *Nicolas Poussin*, 62–72.

44 Lavin, *Barberini Documents*, 28.

45 Standring, "Some pictures"; Standring, "Come fare l'inventario."

46 Standring, "Some Pictures," 622–624; Mahon, *Nicolas Poussin*, 31, 118.

47 Fumagalli, "Poussin et les collectionneurs," 52–53.

cultural interests with Poussin, but a shrewd dealer who favored erotic images easy to sell on the art-market.[48]

At various dates Roccatagliata owned at least nine early paintings by Poussin, and many copies after his works. Three of the originals he owned in the early 1630's ended up in the dal Pozzo collection, after 1637 at the earliest, years after they were painted. These were the *Venus and Adonis* (Kimbell Art Museum, Fort Worth), the *Amor Vincit Omnia* (Cleveland Museum of Art); the *Ark of Noah* (Tatton Park; or perhaps a similar picture), and a lost *Reclining Venus with Satyrs and Putti.*[49] Roccatagliata bequeathed two more—the *Agony in the Garden* on copper (on deposit at the Metropolitan Museum), and the *Cephalus and Aurora* (Hovingham Hall)—to Cassiano's brother Carlo Antonio in 1652, together with a *Holy Family* (Detroit Institute of Arts), a later picture painted in Paris between 1641 and 1642.[50] The dealer also owned the *King Midas at the Source of the River Pactolus*, (Musée Fesch Ajaccio,);[51] the *King Midas and Bacchus* (Alte Pinakothek, Munich)[52] (fig. 9.3) and a small *Mercury and Venus* unidentified thus far, all autograph.[53]

This long list of pictures owned by Roccatagliata clarifies his support of Poussin during the first six or seven years the painter spent in Rome: possibly his role was even more significant. If he sold paintings by Valentin to Angelo Giori, Roccatagliata could also have sold him two early canvases by Poussin, the *Death of Narcissus* (Musée du Louvre) and the *Death of Adonis* (Musée

48 Cavazzini, "Nicolas Poussin"; Standring, "Poussin's erotica"; Costello, "The Twelve Pictures."

49 The *Venus*, which must have been similar to the *Sleeping Venus* in Dresden, was described in 1636 as "un altro [quadro] di tela di quattro palmi dello stesso [Nicolas Poussin] figuratovi una Venere giacente con figure di satiri et de amori," in Cavazzini, "Nicolas Poussin," 810, 812 (see the whole article for the complicated transaction). Sparti, "The dal Pozzo Collection," 563, where the 1695 inventory, at number 88, lists the *Venus and Satyrs* as "altro di 4 palmi con satiri del Pusino." The same painting, described as "un quadro in tela di palmi quattro per traverso con figura di una donna nuda che dorme con amorini e altre figure" was sold in 1730 from the da Pozzo collection, Standring, "Some Pictures," 612.

50 Fagiolo dall'Arco, *Jean Lemaire*, 29, 273, for Roccatagliata's death inventory, in particular "un'orazione all'horto in rame con cornice nera"; Standring: "A Lost Poussin"; Mahon, *Nicolas Poussin*, 27–28, note 44. *Poussin et dieu*, 168 dismisses the idea that the *Agony in the Garden* belonged to Roccatagliata, *ivi*, 206, for the *Holy Family*.

51 Rosenberg, *Le cardinal Fesch*, 28.

52 The *Midas and Bacchus* in Munich was bought by Prince Max Emmanuel in 1698 for 900 florins, see Krempel, "Max Emmanuel als Gemäldesammler," vol. 1, 223; the dal Pozzo still had two versions in 1741, but possibly they never owned the original, Standring, "Come fare l'inventario," 208, note 53.

53 Standring, "Three new inventories," 616–617; Standring, "A Lost Poussin"; Standring, "Some Pictures." The *Mercury and Venus* might have been a smaller copy of the composition now divided between the Louvre and the Dulwich gallery, Rosenberg, *Nicolas Poussin*, 57.

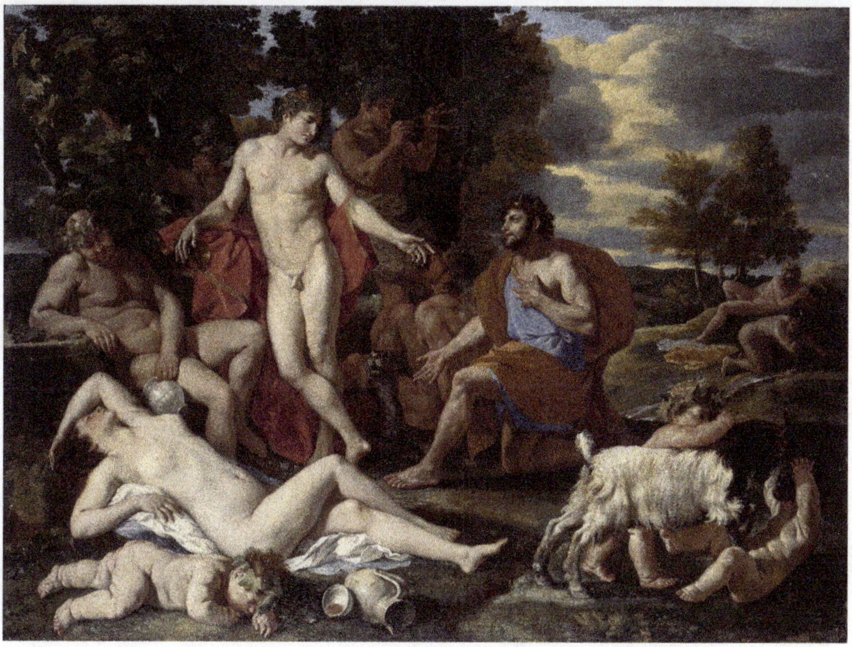

FIGURE 9.3 Nicolas Poussin (1594–1665), *King Midas and Bacchus*, ca. 1624. Oil on panel, 98.5 × 135 cm (38.7 × 53.15 in.). Alte Pinakothek, Bayerische Staatsgemäldesammlungen, Munich

de Caen), that almost certainly were in his collection.[54] As many other merchants did, Roccatagliata, when in possession of a good autograph, often had it replicated, by the same painter or by others; it is clear for example that he had the *King Midas* in Munich copied more than once.[55] By the early 1630s Roccatagliata owned copies after various early canvases by Poussin, such as the *Mars and Venus* in the Museum of Fine Arts in Boston, which were in the dal Pozzo collection by 1689 (fig. 9.4).[56] It cannot be taken for granted that the autographs were commissions from Cassiano or from his brother: they might have bought them from their friend the dealer. Poussin painted two versions on copper, a support he almost never used, of the *Agony in the Garden*, around 1627–28: one belonged to Roccatagliata, and entered the dal Pozzo collection at his death in 1652, and one listed in Taddeo Barberini's death inventory in

54 Corradini, "La collezione del cardinale Angelo Giori"; Rosenberg, *Nicolas Poussin*, 76–83.
55 Cavazzini, "Nicolas Poussin," 812; Rosenberg, *Le cardinal Fesch*, 30.
56 Mahon, *Nicolas Poussin*, 32–33.

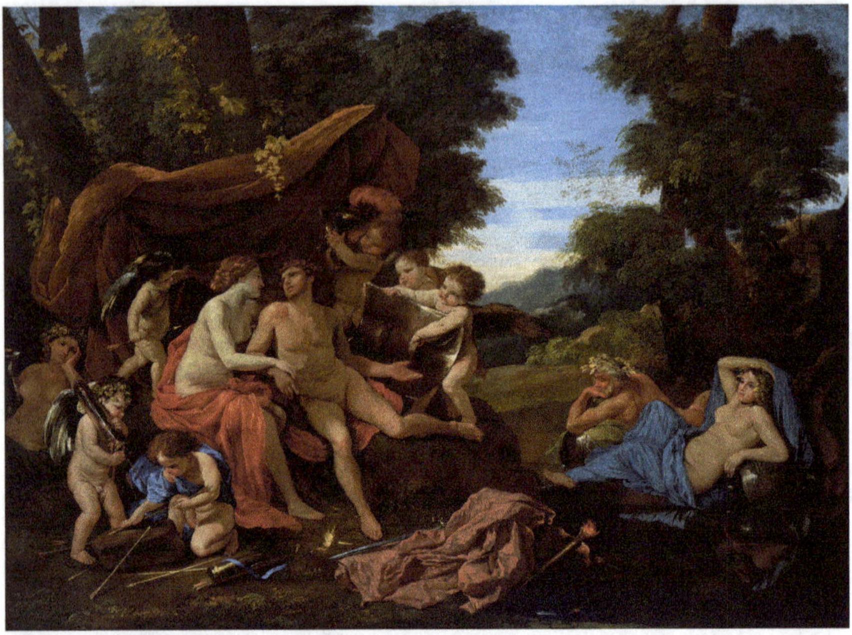

FIGURE 9.4 Nicolas Poussin (1594–1665), *Mars and Venus*, ca. 1630. Oil on canvas, 154.9 × 213.7 cm (61 × 84 1/8 in.). Museum of Fine Arts, Boston, Augustus Hemenway Fund and Arthur William Wheelwright Fund, 40.89

1648 (previously on deposit at the J. Paul Getty Museum) (figs. 9.5 and 9.6).[57] Roccatagliata himself, and not Cassiano dal Pozzo as is generally assumed, might have suggested to Poussin to paint a variant of his picture. Both compositions were then duplicated, the one belonging to Roccatagliata on copper and the other on canvas, an indication that he might have been behind this proliferation of similar images.[58]

Other paintings by Poussin before 1631 were also produced outside the traditional mechanism of patronage. He was forced to sell many canvases for "vile prices," including two battle pictures sold for seven scudi, presumably the ones now in Russia.[59] Other early canvases by Poussin belonged to fellow artists, such as Agostino Tassi (1578–1644) and Gian Lorenzo Bernini (1598–1680),

57 *Poussin et dieux*, 167, Lavin, *Barberini Documents*, 210, n. 470. The copy on canvas that belonged to Sir Anthony Blunt is most likely autograph, see Standring, "*Another version*."

58 Brigstocke, "Variantes."

59 Bellori, *Le vite*, 425–426; Rosenberg, *Nicolas Poussin*, 134–137.

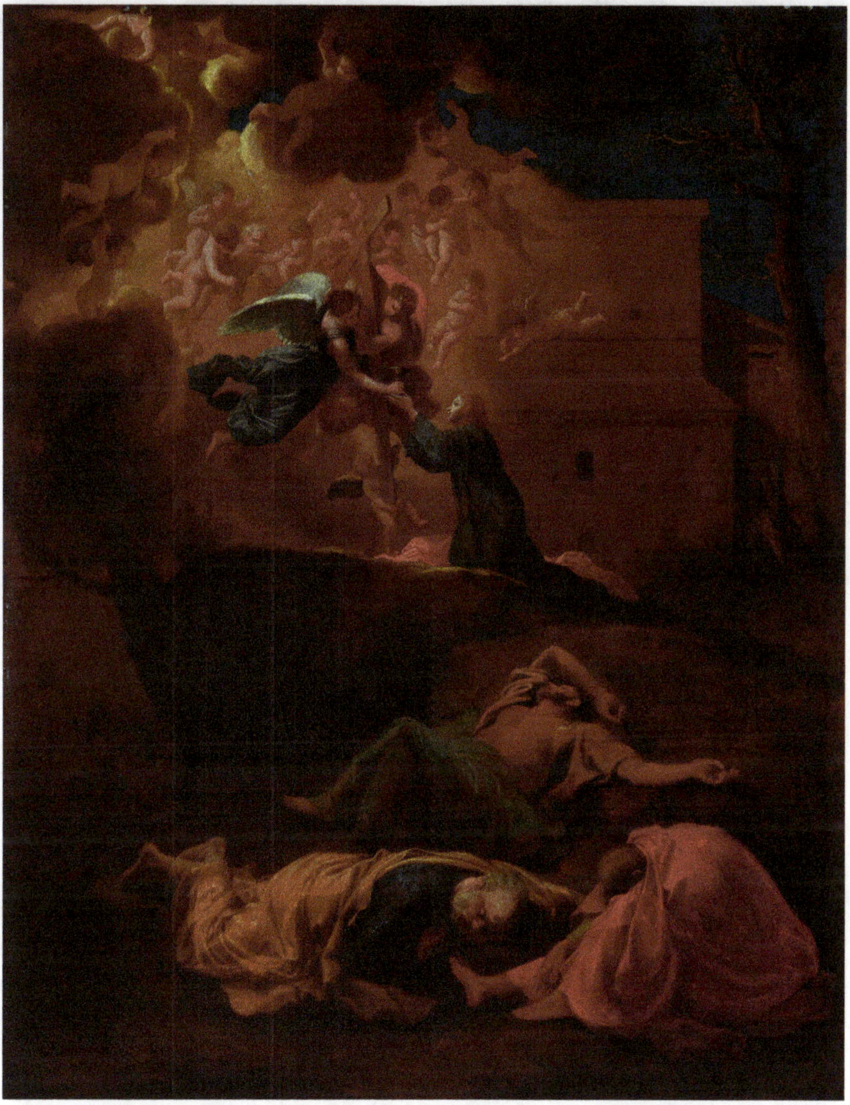

FIGURE 9.5 Nicolas Poussin (1594–1665), *The Agony in the Garden*, ca. 1627/28. Oil on copper, 65.6 × 48.1 cm (24 × 18.9 in.)
PRIVATE COLLECTION

who both sold those works they owned.[60] The sculptor and art-dealer Matteo Bonuccelli (fl. 1630–1654?), the husband of Bernini's famous lover Costanza bought the *Plague at Ashdod* (Musée du Louvre, Paris) and the *King Midas* in

60 Cavazzini, "Quadri per vendere."

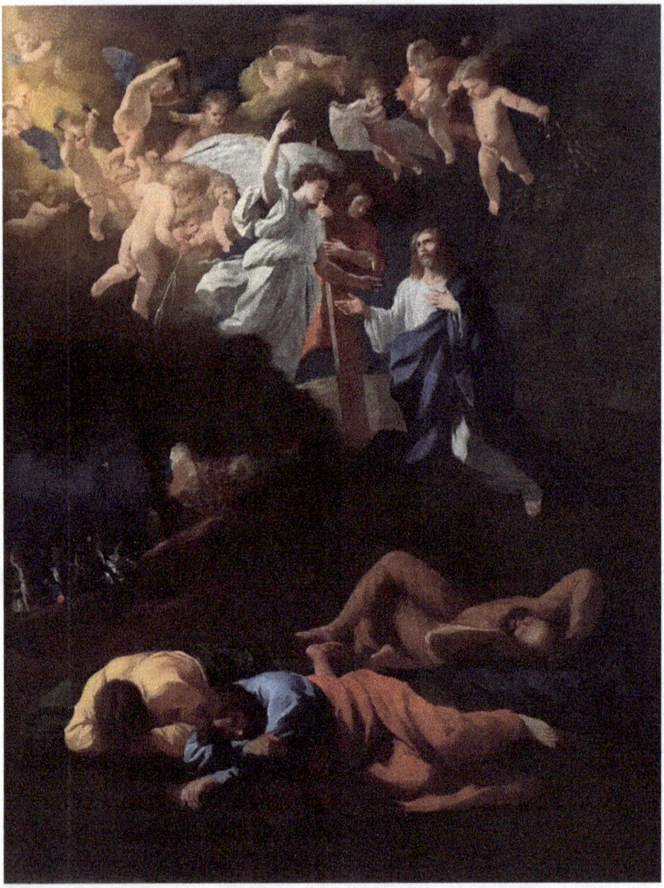

FIGURE 9.6 Nicolas Poussin (1594–1665), *The Agony in the Garden*, ca. 1627/28. Oil on copper, cm 60 × 47 cm (23.6 × 18.5) PRIVATE COLLECTION © PHOTO COURTESY OF THE J. PAUL GETTY MUSEUM

Ajaccio in 1631, at the sale following the death in prison of Fabrizio Valguarnera. It is remarkable that no major collector was interested in purchasing them.[61] Bonuccelli also owned the *Parnassus* (Museo del Prado; 1631), the two early *Bacchanals of Putti* (Galleria Nazionale d'Arte Antica, Rome), and possibly the *Nymph Astride a Goat* (Hermitage, St. Petersberg).[62] It is not known how he came into their possession.

61 McPhee, *Bernini's Beloved*, 71, 99–100; Rosenberg *Nicolas Poussin*, 98.

62 McPhee, *Bernini's Beloved*, 91–92, 96–97, 99–100, 106–107. See also Rosenberg, *Nicolas Poussin*, 206, for the *Parnassus*, with the wrong identification of the sculptor.

4 Conclusion

Thus, even though Poussin had painted an altarpiece for St Peter's, it took a while before he severed his connections with the world of trade. For many years in Rome, both Poussin and Valentin, to a large extent, worked outside the main channels of patronage: Valentin, who was young and inexperienced when he arrived, learned the profession in humble workshops, while Poussin was able to make a living through the support of a skillful talent scout. They came to the attention of Francesco Barberini through the art-market and only later did the cardinal commission works by them, presumably paying them much more than merchants. As shown, we should be open-minded when examining provenances: not all large and multifigured compositions in Rome were painted on commission.

Bibliography

Archival Sources

Archivio dell'Accademia di San Luca, Statuti 1607, ff. 21–21v.

Archivio di Stato di Roma (ASR), 30 Notai Capitolini, uff. 9, 13 febbraio 1593, f. 259. Cited in Lothar. Sickel, "Gli esordi di Caravaggio a Roma," *Römisches Jahrbuch der Biblioteca Hertziana* 39 (2009/2010): 225–265, 238, note 148.

Archivio di Stato di Roma (ASR), 30 Notai Capitolini, uff. 19, 17 novembre 1616, f. 707.

Biblioteca Apostolica Vaticana (BAV), Barberini Latini, 4835.

BAV, Archivio Barberini, Computisteria, Giustificazioni di Francesco Barberini, vol. 44, f. 197.

BAV, Archivio Barberini, Contabilità, Giustificazioni di Francesco Barberini, vol. 44, f. 197, ristretto delle spese del mese di giugno.

BAV, Archivio Barberini, Computisteria, Giustificazioni di Francesco Barberini, vol. 45, f. 357.

Published Sources

Abbing, M. Roscam. "Poussin's Elephant Revisited." *Source. Notes in the History of Art* 3972 (2020): 109–119.

Bellori, Giovanni Pietro. *Le vite de' pittori, scultori, e architetti moderni* (Rome, 1672), edited by Evelina Borea. Turin: Giulio Einaudi, 1976.

Bertolotti, Antonino. "Gian Domenico Angelini pittore perugino e i suoi scolari." *Giornale di erudizione artistica* 5 (1876): 65–87.

Brigstocke, Hugh. "Variantes, copies et imitation: Quelques reflexions sur le méthodes de travail de Poussin." In *Nicolas Poussin (1594–1665). Actes du colloque organisé au*

Musée du Louvre, edited by Alain Mérot, 203–228. Paris: La documentation française, 1996.

Byatt, Lucinda. "Aspetti giuridici e finanziari di una 'familia' cardinalizia del XVI secolo: Un progetto di ricerca." In *Familia del principe e famiglia aristocratica*, edited by Cesare Mozzarelli, vol. 2, 611–630. Rome: Bulzoni Editore, 1988.

Capitelli, Giovanna. "Dutch Caravaggists in Rome." In *Caravaggio and the Painters of the North* (exh. cat.), edited by Gert Jan van der Sman, 32–41. Madrid: Museo Thyssen-Bornemisza, 2016.

Cavazzini, Patrizia. "'Patto fermo' o cortesia negli accordi tra pittori e committenti a Roma nel Seicento." *Ricerche di storia dell'arte* 101 (2010): 5–20.

Cavazzini, Patrizia. "Pittori eletti e bottegari nei primi anni dell'Accademia e Compagnia di San Luca." *Rivista d'arte: Periodico internazionale di storia dell'arte medievale e moderna* 1 (2011): 79–96.

Cavazzini, Patrizia. "Nicolas Poussin, Cassiano dal Pozzo and the Roman Art Market in the 1620s." *The Burlington Magazine* 155 (2013): 808–14.

Cavazzini, Patrizia. "Marketing Strategies and the Creation of Taste in Seventeenth-century Rome." In *The Art Market in Rome in the Eighteenth Century*, edited by Paolo Coen, 68–85. Leiden: Brill, 2019.

Cavazzini, Patrizia. "Quadri per vendere o per nobilitare: Le raccolte dei pittori a Roma nella prima metà del Seicento e la collezione di Onorio Longhi." In *Le collezioni degli artisti in Italia*, edited by Francesca Parrilla and Matteo Borchia, 31–42. Rome: Artemide, 2019.

Cavazzini, Patrizia. "Riflessioni sull'apprendistato dei pittori a Roma." *Studiolo* 17 (2020–2021): 142–153.

Cavazzini, Patrizia. "Success and Failure in a Violent City. Bartolomeo Manfredi, Nicolas Tournier, Valentin de Boulogne." In *Valentin de Boulogne. Beyond Caravaggio*, (exh. cat., The Metropolitan Museum of Art and Musée du Louvre), edited by Keith Christiansen and Annick Lemoine, 17–28. New Haven and London: Yale University Press, 2016.

Cavazzini, Patrizia. "Painters vs. Architects at the Papal Court." In *The Court Artist in Seventeenth Century Italy*, edited by Elena Fumagalli, Raffaella Morselli, 21–47. Rome: Viella, 2014.

Cavietti, Marco, and Francesca Curti. "La bottega di Francesco Morelli pittore: Giovanni Baglione, Vittorio Tavagni, Tommaso Salini tra formazione, parentele, committenze e rivalità all'arrivo di Caravaggio a Roma." In *"L'essercitio mio è di pittore." Caravaggio e l'ambiente artistico romano*, edited by Francesca Curti, Michele di Sivo, Orietta Verdi, 373–454. *Roma Moderna e contemporanea* 19. Rome: Università Roma Tre-CROMA, 2012.

Corradini, Sandro. "La collezione del cardinale Angelo Giori." *Antologia di Belle Arti* 1 (1977): 83–94.

Costello, Jane. "The Twelve Pictures Ordered by Velasquez and the Trial by Valguarnera." *Journal of the Warburg and Courtauld Institute* 13 (1950): 237–284.

Curti, Francesca. "Sugli esordi di Caravaggio a Roma: La bottega di Lorenzo Carli e il suo inventario." In *Caravaggio a Roma, Una vita dal vero*, (exh. cat., Archivio di Stato di Roma), edited by Michele Di Sivo and Orietta Verdi, 65–76. Rome: De Luca Editori d'Arte, 2011.

Daniele, Giulia. "Pietro Veri a Montegiordano: Un inedito 'ricordo di pitture' per Virginio Orsini." In *Gli Orsini e i Savelli nella Roma dei papi, arte e mecenatismo di antichi casati dal feudo alle corti europee*, edited by Cecilia Mazzetti di Pietralata e Adriano Amendola, 127–131. Cinisello Balsamo: Silvana editoriale, 2017.

Fagiolo dall'Arco, Maurizio. *Jean Lemaire pittore antiquario*. Rome: Ugo Bozzi, 1996.

Fumagalli, Elena. "Poussin et les collectionneurs romains au XVII siècle." In *Nicolas Poussin 1594–1665*, (exh. cat., Galeries Nationales du Grand Palais), edited by Pierre Rosenberg and Louis-Antoin Prat, 48–57. Paris: Réunion des Musées Nationaux, 1994.

Haskell, Francis. *Patrons and Painters in Seventeenth-century Italy: A Study in the Relations between Italian art and Society in the Age of the Baroque*, London: Chatto and Windus, 1963.

Krempel, Ulla. "Max Emmanuel als Gemäldesammler." In *Kurfürst Max Emanuel, Bayern und Europa um 1700*, edited by H. Glaser, vol. 1, 221–225. Munich: Hirmer, 1976.

Lavin, Marilyn Aronberg. *Seventeenth-century Barberini Documents and Inventories of Art*. New York: New York University Press, 1975.

Lemoine, Annick. "Bowing to No One. Valentin's Ambitions." In *Valentin de Boulogne. Beyond Caravaggio* (exh. cat., The Metropolitan Museum of Art and Musée du Louvre), edited by Keith Christiansen and Annick Lemoine, 1–28. New Haven and London: Yale University Press, 2016.

Lemoine, Annick. "Chronology of the Life and Work of Valentin de Boulogne." In *Valentin de Boulogne. Beyond Caravaggio* (exh. cat., The Metropolitan Museum of Art and Musée du Louvre), edited by Keith Christiansen and Annick Lemoine, 229–235. New Haven and London: Yale University Press, 2016.

Lorizzo, Loredana. *La collezione del Cardinale Ascanio Filomarino; Pittura, scultura e mercato dell'arte tra Roma e Napoli nel Seicento*, Naples: Electa, 2006.

Lukehart, Peter. "Appendix." In *The Accademia Seminars. The Accademia di San Luca in Rome, c. 1590–1635*, edited by Peter Lukehart, 348–350. New Haven and London: Yale University Press, 2009.

Mahon, Denis. *Nicolas Poussin. Works from his First Years in Rome* (exh. cat). Jerusalem: Israel Museum, 1999.

Mazzetti di Pietralata, Cecilia. "Joachim von Sandrart e la Roma dei Barberini: Incisioni, disegni e spigolature d'archivio." In *I Barberini e la cultura europea del Seicento. Atti del convegno internazionale, Palazzo Barberini*, edited by L. Mochi Onori, S. Schütze, F. Solinas, 403–410. Rome: De Luca, 2007.

McPhee, Sarah. *Bernini's Beloved: A Portrait of Costanza Piccolomini*. New Haven and London: Yale University Press, 2012.

Missirini, Melchiorre. *Memorie per servire alla storia della Romana Accademia di San Luca fino alla morte di Antonio Canova*. Rome: Stamperia De Romanis, 1823.

Nessi, Silvestro. *Andrea Camassei: Un pittore del seicento tra Roma e l'Umbria*. Perugia: Quattroemme, 2005.

Nicolai, Fausto. *Mecenati a confronto: Committenza, collezionismo e mercato dell'arte nella Roma del primo Seicento. Le famiglie Massimo, Altemps, Naro e Colonna*. Rome: Campisano, 2008.

Nicolai, Fausto. "'Le molte pitture moderne buone' nella raccolta di Giovan Battista Mellini (1591–1627)." *Rivista d'arte: Periodico internazionale di storia dell'arte medievale e moderna* 2 (2012): 217–236.

Pampalone, Antonella. "Pittori fiorentini a Roma alla fine del Cinquecento: Vittorio Travagni e Nicola Cianchi." *Annali della Pontificia Insigne Accademia di Belle Arti e Lettere dei Virtuosi al Pantheon* 11 (2011): 415–442.

Pierguidi, Stefano. In *Bernini* (exh. cat., Galleria Borghese, Rome), edited by Andrea Bacchi and Anna Coliva, 86–87. Milan: Officina Libraria, 2017.

Pierguidi, Stefano. *Note sui dipinti di Poussin (e Vouet?) di provenienza Roccatagliata e dal Pozzo. Studi Piemontesi* 41, no. 1 (2012): 113–123.

Porzio, Giuseppe, and Domenico Antonio D'Alessandro. "Ribera between Rome and Naples: New Documentary Evidence." *The Burlington Magazine* 157 (2015): 682–683.

Poussin et dieu (exh. cat., Musée du Louvre), edited by Nicolas Milanovic and Mickaël Szanto. Paris: Hazan, 2015.

Rice, Louise. *The Altars and Altarpieces of New St. Peter's. Outfitting the Basilica 1621–1666*. Cambridge: Cambridge University Press, 1997.

Rice, Louise. "Poussin's Elephant." *Renaissance Quarterly* 20 (2017): 548–593.

Roma di Sisto V, Comitato Nazionale per le Celebrazioni del Pontificato di Sisto v (1585–1590), Centro di Studio sulla Cultura e l'Immagine di Roma Rome: De Luca, 1993.

Rosenberg, Pierre. *Le cardinal Fesch, Poussin et Midas*, Ajaccio: Musée Fesch-Ville d'Ajaccio, 2012.

Rosenberg, Pierre. *Nicolas Poussin. Les tableaux du Louvre. Catalogue raisonné*. Paris: Musée du Louvre; Somogy, 2015.

Rossi, Sergio. "La compagnia di San Luca nel Cinquecento e la sua evoluzione in accademia." *Ricerche per la storia religiosa di Roma* 5 (1984): 367–394.

Salvagni, Isabella. *Da* Universitas *ad* Academia. *II. La fondazione dell'Accademia de i pittori e scultori di Roma nella chiesa dei Santi Luca e Martina 1588–1705*. Rome: Società Romana di Storia Patria, 2021.

Sickel, Lothar. "Pietro Veri: ein Florentiner Künstler in Diensten des Herzogs von Bracciano Virginio Orsini." *Marburger Jarbuch für Kunstwissenschaft* 30 (2003): 183–209.

Sickel, Lothar. "The 'Madonna dei Cappuccini' of Giovan Domenico Angelini at Ferentillo." *Bollettino d'Arte* 94 (2009): 157–164.

Sickel, Lothar. "Anthonis Santvoort. Ein niederländischer Maler, Verleger und Kunstvermittler in Rom. Mit einem Anhang zum Testament Cornelis Corts." In *Ein privilegiertes Medium. Deutsche, Französische und Niederländische Kupferstecher und Graphikverleger in Rom von 1590 bis 1630*, edited by Eckhard Leuschner, 39–62. Munich: Hirmer, 2012.

Sparti, Donatella. "The dal Pozzo Collection again: The Inventories of 1689, 1695 and the Family Archive." *The Burlington magazine* 132 (1990): 551–570.

Spear, Richard, E. Philip Sohm. *Painting for Profit: The Economic Lives of Seventeenth-century Italian Painters*. New Haven: Yale University Press, 2010.

Sperindei, Simona. "Due pittori e 'bottegari' marchigiani nella Roma della prima metà del Seicento: Leonardo de Sanctis e Pier Francesco de Rossi." *Atti della giornata di studio Quesiti Caravaggeschi*, edited by Pierluigi Carofano, 149–169. Pontedera: Bandecchi & Vivaldi, 2014.

Standring, T. "A Lost Poussin Work on Copper." *The Burlington Magazine* 127 (1985): 615–617.

Standring, T. J. "Come fare l'inventario dei beni Dal Pozzo: Una disputa legale sul fedecommesso." In *I Segreti di un collezionista. Le straordinarie raccolte di Cassiano dal Pozzo 1588–1657* (exh. cat., Galleria Nazionale d'Arte Antica, Palazzo Barbarini), edited by Francesco Solinas, 200–224. Rome: De Luca, 2000.

Standring, Timothy. "*Another version of Christ's Agony in the Garden by Poussin.*" forthcoming.

Standring, Timothy J. "Poussin's erotica." *Apollo* 169 (2009): 82–88.

Standring, Timothy J. "Some pictures by Poussin in the dal Pozzo Collection: Three new inventories." *The Burlington Magazine* 130 (1988): 608–626.

Valentin de Boulogne. Beyond Caravaggio (exh. cat., The Metropolitan Museum of Art and Musée du Louvre), edited by Keith Christiansen and Annick Lemoine. New Haven and London: Yale University Press, 2016.

Vodret, Rossella. *Alla ricerca di "Ghiongrat." Studi sui libri parrocchiali romani (1600–1630)*. Rome: L'Erma di Bretschneider, 2011.

CHAPTER 10

Artists as Critics, and Critics as Artists: Collaboration and Inclination in Giulio Mancini's Taste Formation

Frances Gage

In ca. 1617–19, the Sienese physician and art critic Giulio Mancini (1559–1630), one of four doctors at the Hospital of Santo Spirito and personal doctor to several cardinals, drafted a treatise on one of his longstanding interests, the history and theory of painting. He declared in his *Discorso di pittura* [Discourse on Painting] that he was not writing in the tradition of earlier treatises on art, in which artists such as Albrecht Dürer (1471–1528), Leonardo da Vinci (1452–1519), Giorgio Vasari (1511–1574), Giovan Paolo Lomazzo (1538–1600) or Federico Zuccaro (1541–1609) had compiled precepts on art-making.[1] Mancini, as he would imply throughout what would become his expanded text, *Considerazioni sulla pittura* (1619–1625), was developing a new literary genre on art.[2] He identified his audience and his objectives in the opening paragraphs of his two texts, which closely parallel one another. In the *Discorso* he stated he was writing for the man of taste in the study of painting (later modified to *huomo di diletto*), explaining that this individual would engage in judging, acquiring, distributing and displaying pictures. Mancini declared he would set forth precepts by which the *huomo di gusto* could easily provide a true account or certain knowledge about a painting presented to him, employing those skills in the service of a prince who delighted in painting.[3] Over time, Mancini would conceive of an expanded audience that included any man who, either from genuine interest or a desire to leverage his cultural capital in the Eternal City, sought to cultivate his knowledge of the history and theory of painting.

1 Mancini, "Discorso di pittura," 291. See also the opening paragraph of *Considerazioni sulla pittura*, 5.

2 Gage, *Painting as Medicine*, 154.

3 Mancini, "Discorso," 29; Idem, *Considerazioni*, 5.

 | DOI:10.1163/9789004513938_012

1 Mancini's Principles of Connoisseurship

Mancini implicitly distinguished in this first paragraph of his *Discorso* between taste, on the one hand, and judgment, on the other, though they are associated in his thought, as evident when he instructed his elder brother Deifebo (1555–1632) in 1611 to acquire paintings "according to your taste and judgment."[4] For Mancini, the *huomo di gusto* was one who already possessed a heightened sense of pleasure in beholding a painting, and who, as a consequence, committed to further studying it. Judgment, on the other hand, could be divided into two modes requiring distinct skills. Evaluating color, perspective, or *affetti*, required no specialized knowledge, Mancini thought, and could be carried out by anyone with ordinary intelligence.[5] The second mode of judgment, distinguishing good paintings from bad, better from less good, entailed knowledge of the historical and theoretical aspects of painting, such as artists' hands, period or regional styles and composition, the natures of which Mancini was to articulate in his text.[6] Its principles could and should be taught.

Mancini is widely known for his important contributions to the development of connoisseurship *avant la lettre* and especially for his chapter of the *Considerazioni* on the arrangement and display of a collection of paintings within an extensive household of a wealthy man, whose residence contained distinct room types and users.[7] Although scholarly interest in Mancini to date is closely associated with his role as a collector, author and critic of painting, his cultural prominence in the Eternal City, following his arrival in 1592 until his death in 1630, lay principally in his profession of theoretical medicine.[8] His activities as literary figure and cultural broker, one who circulated objects

4 Maccherini, "Caravaggio nel carteggio familiare," 83, appendix, letter 19. For the concept of taste, see Gage, "Giulio Mancini's *Considerazioni*," 13–14, and relevant literature; Cropper and Dempsey, *Nicolas Poussin*, especially 88–91; Bourdieu, *Distinction: A Social Critique*.

5 Mancini, *Considerazioni*, 7.

6 Ibid., 217, writing about Agostino Carracci, whom Mancini remarks possessed "singolarissimo giudizio," because he immediately recognized every "minimo errore." In Mancini, "Alcune considerazioni del'honore fatte da Giulio Mancini per suo trattenimento," BAV, Barb. Lat., 4315, fol. 112r–v, Mancini describes judgment as "buona deliberatione," and "questo habito à giudicare et eleggere quello che convenga."

7 For Mancini and connoisseurship, see Paul, *The First Modern Museums*, 6; Frigo, "Can One Speak of Painting," 417–436; Pierguidi, "Giulio Mancini," 63–71; Sparti, "Novità su Giulio Mancini," 53–72. Within the now extensive bibliography on Mancini, see also Maccherini, "Novità su Manfredi," 131–41; idem, "Novità sulle *Considerazioni*," 123–28; idem, "Giulio Mancini: Committenza," 393–401. For Mancini and collecting, see Gage, "Exercise for Mind and Body," 1169–1207; idem, "Observing Order," 204–16.

8 Gage, *Painting as Medicine*, 19.

and knowledge within extensive social networks, are increasingly well-established.[9] What remains less clear is how Mancini the physician fashioned himself, by the 1620s, as a leading critic and judge of painting while pursuing polymathic interests.[10] In what way did Mancini navigate the Roman art world to position himself as cultural arbiter, imprint the artistic and intellectual culture of Barberini Rome and inform artistic culture in Rome and Siena over the seventeenth century? Reflecting on these processes will cast into greater relief early modern practices of taste-formation and the judgment of art.

Mancini articulated in both his *Discorso* and the *Considerazioni* that to cultivate skill in judging painting, one must both practice on one's own *and* hear the judgments of those who are more knowledgeable (*col giuditio di più intendenti*).[11] His development over the course of his life as an *intendente* exemplifies his stated advice. What we refer to as "taste formation," or the process of learning to discern qualitative artistic differences, was understood in early seventeenth-century Italy to be a fundamentally collaborative activity, but one that was also paralleled by the formation of personal inclinations.[12]

Mancini's interests in and knowledge of the visual arts developed in dialogue with those of Deifebo, whose engagement with these fields evidently predated his brother's. The role Deifebo played in Giulio's cultural achievements and the degree to which Giulio sometimes yielded to him, suggesting he recognized Deifebo's greater command of certain areas of knowledge, must be acknowledged, even if Deifebo's surviving letters and writings are scant.[13] According to Giulio's close friend, the apothecary Giovanni Battista Paolucci, Mancini repeatedly remarked that Deifebo was "adorned with various and delightful virtues as [in] engineering, antiquities, painting and histories."[14] "He [Deifebo] knows more than I in everything except medicine," Mancini allegedly declared.[15] This is borne out by Giulio's frequent solicitations of his brother's advice and opinions.

9 Ibid.

10 Ibid., especially chapter one.

11 Mancini, "Discorso," 292; idem, *Considerazioni*, 7.

12 Gage, "New Documents on Mancini," 654. See also n. 4.

13 Cesare Perini burned Deifebo's letters to Giulio. Archivio della Società di Esecutori di Pie Disposizioni (ASEPD), Carteggio Mancini (CXIX), 170, 23 August 1632, fol. 225r. All familial correspondence below is to this archive. Henceforth ASEPD and volume numbers alone will be given.

14 ASEPD, 170, 28 settembre 1630, Giovanni Battista Paolucci to [Deifebo Mancini], fol. 45r.

15 Ibid. For a slightly different interpretation of Deifebo, see Maccherini, "Ritratto di Mancini," 48.

2 Fashioning Taste and Developing Judgment

Giulio's first foray into the activities of a broker, acquiring paintings in Padua while he was a medical student to send to members of the Sienese elite, was almost certainly at Deifebo's behest.[16] He was not at this early date an *huomo di gusto* in painting, even if he was consulting Vasari's *Lives* and was developing a polemical relationship with the Florentine biographer.[17] In 1582, Giulio expressed frustration that Deifebo was evidently asking for drawings rather than books, for Giulio preferred the latter insofar as they were useful, while the former were, by implication, merely objects of pleasure.[18] Giulio's commitment to use-value above delight ran throughout his career; witness his remarks about the building of St. Peter's in 1613, that "Michelangelo had made a beautiful thing but without use," because of the difficulty of accommodating chapels, choir and sacristy in his open plan.[19] Giulio's attitudes to the visual arts changed significantly over time, but his preference for objects possessing didactic value as opposed to affording pleasure alone remained consistent throughout his career. By the second decade of the seventeenth century, when he drafted his *Considerazioni*, Giulio adumbrated his conceptions of the social, medical and ethical functions of painting.[20]

These exchanges between brothers confirm the indications in Giulio's early letters that Deifebo's predilections for architecture probably provided a significant component of Giulio's earliest artistic education, encouraging his interest in Sienese artists. In 1582, for unknown reasons, Giulio wrote to Deifebo requesting a drawing or model by Baldassare Peruzzi (1481–1536). Deifebo must have either already possessed such an object or have known where to acquire one easily; during the same decade Giulio sought architectural treatises and drawings by Sienese artists, such as Peruzzi, Francesco di Giorgio (1439–1501) and Giovanni da Siena (il Giannella; active 1384–1438).[21] Architecture was never to blossom into one of Giulio's primary theoretical interests, however.[22]

Intriguing evidence that Deifebo cultivated a specific delight in architecture emerges from the brothers' letters of 1624, the year after Giulio had been

16 For these activities, see Bartalini, *Le occasioni del Sodoma*, 21.

17 Gage, "Teaching Them to Serve," 79n.

18 ASEPD, 165, 21 March 1582, Padua, Giulio to Deifebo, fol. 861r.

19 ASEPD, 168, 8 February 1613, Padua, Giulio to Deifebo, fol. 42r.

20 Gage, *Painting as Medicine*.

21 ASEPD, 165, 21 March 1582, Padua, Giulio to Deifebo, fol. 861r; 165, 20 July 1582, Padua, Giulio to Deifebo, fol. 875r.

22 See Rice in n. 24 (341n 11) below, who suggests that Mancini may have been the author of a treatise on the vaulting of the portico of the Pantheon.

appointed personal physician to Pope Urban VIII and as he was still eagerly solidifying his cultural and intellectual prominence at court. While Pope Urban VIII (1568–1644) was reflecting upon the commission for the *Baldacchino* (fig. 10.1) in St. Peter's, Giulio wrote to his brother on 15 June 1624 and, without mentioning Gian Lorenzo Bernini (1598–1680), remarked that the Pope had requested that Giulio contribute to the deliberations over the drawings for the commission and the execution of the work.[23] Giulio had responded to the pope, writing that he would do whatever the pope commanded, but that his brother, "had a taste for these things." Giulio had been granted the opportunity to shape the designs for one of the most significant contemporary commissions in Rome, evidence of the recognition of Giulio's artistic judgment. Yet, in deference to his brother and in the hopes of promoting him and a Sienese artist, he passed the opportunity to Deifebo. A month later, Giulio explicitly solicited a design for the Choir of St. Peter's from his brother in Siena—an opportunity to enlist a Sienese artist for the commission—but the scheme failed. The drawing came too late, and Giulio judged it very poor; neither brother ultimately contributed. Yet Giulio henceforth took note of the *Baldacchino* and Bernini's work in the papal foundries, prompting Cesare Perini, the brothers' nephew, to report to Deifebo in November 1625 that the last bronze beams from the Pantheon had been removed for use "either in cannon for Castel Sant'Angelo or to put in San Pietro at the Altar of the Apostles."[24] This underscores how the brothers' tastes and knowledge in the arts developed together and informed each other, but nonetheless remained distinct. It was expected, even between brothers, that one yielded to whomever maintained the keener taste and better judgment in a field.

The move to Rome, which the brothers made together in 1592, but where Deifebo resided only temporarily, radically transformed Giulio's perceptions about painting, greatly expanding his knowledge to a global reach. He would mention in passing artistic production from Asia, Africa and the Americas: porcelain, carpets, metal inlay, "Indian" embroidery and feather painting from the "Indies."[25] Beyond numerous opportunities to observe public and private works, Giulio's interaction with collectors and artists provided the foundation whereby he became, of the two brothers, the more discerning critic of

23 For the drawings for St. Peter's see Maccherini, "Ritratto di Mancini," 53–54.

24 For Bernini see Mancini, "Alcune considerazioni del'honore," (as in note 6), fol. 96v. For Perini's letter, see 170, 8 November 1625, Cesare Perini to Deifebo, fol. 609v. On the bronze from the Pantheon, see Rice, "Bernini and the Pantheon," 337–352.

25 Mancini, "Discorso," 294.

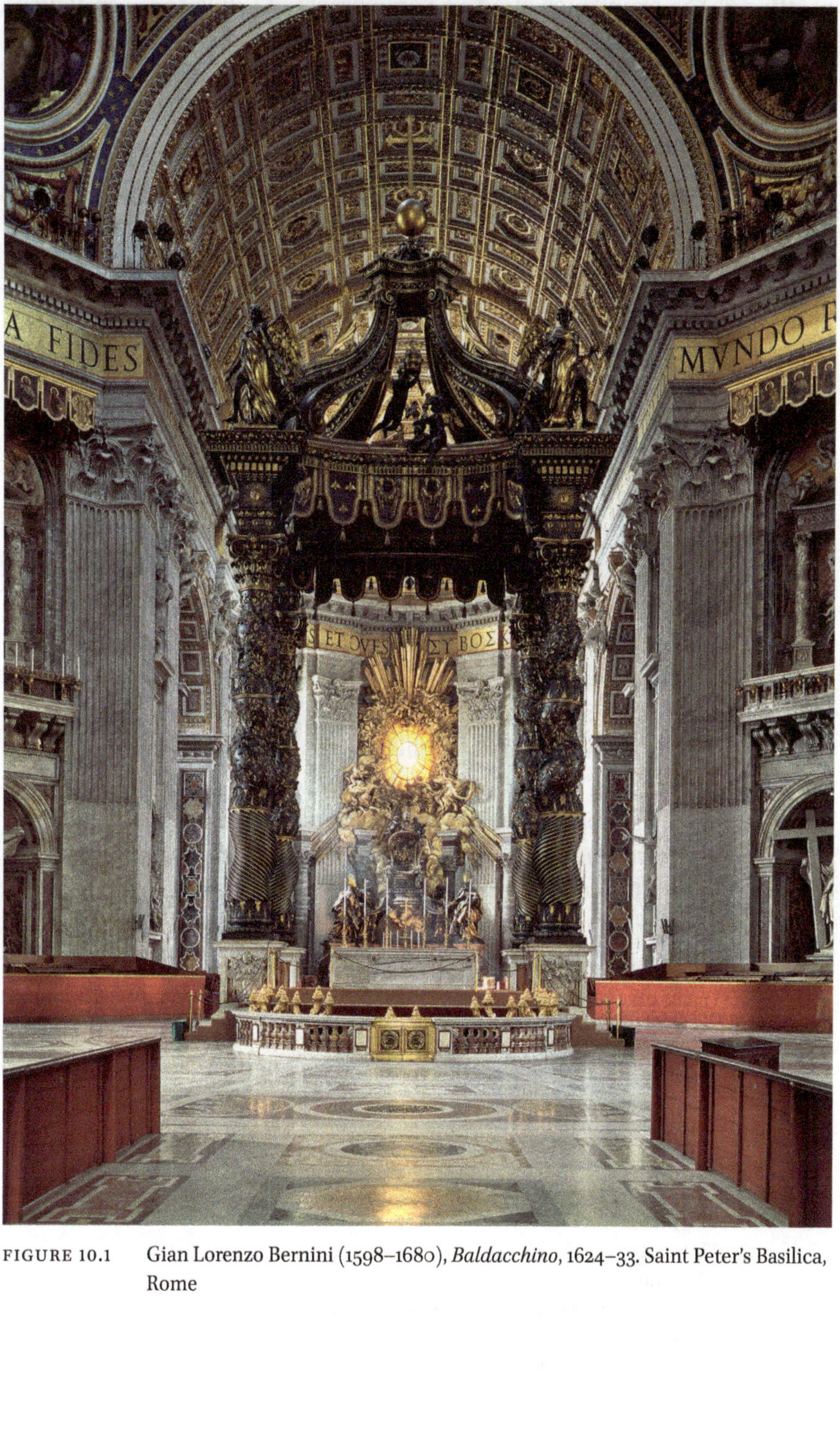

FIGURE 10.1 Gian Lorenzo Bernini (1598–1680), *Baldacchino*, 1624–33. Saint Peter's Basilica, Rome

painting.[26] The abundance of art in Rome prepared Giulio to coach Deifebo on how to cultivate skills of judgment, recognize hands and assemble their collection. In 1606, Giulio wrote to Deifebo that he should compile a volume of their drawings, organizing all "those by Carracci together ... those of Raphael [1483–1520], and so, hand by hand," adding that he did not doubt that Deifebo would thereby learn the various artists' styles.[27] Giulio's declarations suggest that Deifebo may have had a taste for painting, but did not yet fully possess the skills to judge paintings historically or to classify them stylistically according to individual, period and regional styles. It also suggests that Giulio had utilized similar methods, probably widely practiced in Rome, to acquire this knowledge himself, which he would eventually compile in his *Discorso* and *Considerazioni* for the sake of teaching others.[28]

By the first decade of the seventeenth century Giulio had successfully honed his skills as a critic. Whereas in Padua he had typically described pictures in no more detail than "beautiful," or "old," he now deployed a varied critical vocabulary and identified both positive and negative stylistic characteristics.[29] One of the earliest surviving instances of Giulio's evaluative skill arose in his well-known negotiations to acquire Caravaggio's (1571–1610) *Death of the Virgin* from the Carmelite fathers of Santa Maria della Scala. He found the picture to be "without decorum, invention and cleanness," but "well-made."[30] Three years later, Giulio provided a critical judgment of a *Flight into Egypt* by Francesco Vanni (1563–1610), noting both its aesthetic appeal and shortcomings: "somewhat lovely (*vaghetto*), but there is no solidity (*sodezza*)."[31] Giulio was already evaluating leading artists' styles in Rome in language that would make its way into his *Considerazioni*. He wrote to his brother in 1613 that "there is a painting by Giuseppe [Cesari d'Arpino] in the Campidoglio that succeeds well, [is] spirited, with invention and [in] his particular taste (*gusto*) and according to his *ingegno*, for being a battle with horses."[32]

Giulio's growing confidence as a critic was surely owing to his exposure to contemporary artistic production, but more significantly to his developing friendships with various artists working in Rome, including Domenico

26 Gage, "'It is not so easy'," 63–87.

27 Maccherini, "Caravaggio nel carteggio familiare," 81, appendix, letter no. 1. Gage, "'It is not so easy'," 73–4.

28 Gage, "'It is not so easy'."

29 Gage, "'Teaching them to serve'," 79n5.

30 Maccherini, "Caravaggio nel carteggio familiare," 81–2, appendix, letter no. 2. Gage, "Illness, Invention and Truth," 337.

31 Ibid., 83, appendix, letter no. 17.

32 ASEPD, 168, 9 Novembre, 1613, Rome, Giulio Mancini to Deifebo Mancini, fol. 107. Mancini, *Considerazioni*, 109.

Passignano (1559–1638), Ludovico Cigoli (1559–1613), Lavinia Fontana (1552–1614) and Annibale Carracci (1560–1609), as well as with major collectors, some of whom were patrons and patients.[33] The *Considerazioni* attests to the fundamental role in Mancini's theories played by the Carracci, whose voices emerge repeatedly. Mancini must have communicated with Ludovico (1555–1619), who remained in Bologna, outside of a brief Roman visit: "In speaking with signor Ludovico Carracci, I came to know that he esteemed him [Guercino] greatly," this painter admired by Deifebo as well.[34] Practices of sociability extended to occasions in which Giulio observed and evaluated paintings with artists, though his terse prose in his missives provided few details. On one occasion Lavinia Fontana had shown Giulio a painting that he had not been satisfied with and he informed her of this.[35]

Mancini developed his skills of judgment by soliciting opinions from collectors, *intendenti*, his brother and artists and by comparing them. For example, in 1608, he contrasted Deifebo's displeasure at a painting of a Madonna with the judgment of Cigoli, who had "lost his heart" to it.[36] He often indicated both general consensus and his own opinion. In 1615 he remarked that he had seen a tiny *Annunciation*, and "according to what they say, and I believe it, they say to be the hand of Simone [Martini; ca. 1284–1344]."[37] Reporting on the reception of Rutilio Manetti's (1571–1639) *Four Seasons* in 1620, Giulio compared the overall favorable reception in Rome, where it was held to be "a very beautiful thing," to his individual response: "and it pleases me."[38] Deifebo hosted Giulio's artist and collector friends whenever they passed through Siena and would have invited friends to admire objects in their collection. When Giulio anticipated in 1615 that Guido Reni (1575–1642) would pass through Siena, he instructed Deifebo to treat him well, reminding his brother that often friends would travel through, and their house and paintings should be ordered so that visitors could see something pleasing (*di garbo*).[39] But civility evidently dictated that one did not suggest to a visitor of elevated rank or a *huomo di gusto* that his judgment was underdeveloped or mistaken. When the educated and refined gentleman Sforza Sforzosi (to whom Deifebo sent some of Giulio's writings) was expected in Siena, Giulio instructed Deifebo to suggest to his visitor the name of the artist only since Sforzosi would discern what was good

33 Maccherini, "Ritratto di Giulio Mancini," 49.

34 Mancini, *Considerazioni*, 245.

35 Maccherini, "Caravaggio nel carteggio familiare," 82, appendix, no. 11. The author of the picture is unclear.

36 Ibid., 83, appendix, no. 13.

37 Ibid., 84, appendix, no. 28.

38 ASEPD, 169, 2 January 1621, Rome, Giulio Mancini to Deifebo Mancini, fol. 893v.

39 Maccherini, "Caravaggio nel carteggio familiare," 86, appendix, letter no. 33.

and bad on his own during their visit to the Duomo and when observing public works by Domenico Beccafumi (1484–1551) and Il Sodoma (Giovanni Antonio Bazzi, 1477–1549).[40]

Giulio even articulated concern that an artist see appropriate works to ensure or foster quality production, demonstrating the degree to which boundaries between roles of artist and critic were sometimes blurred or even inverted. On 25 January 1613, Giulio wrote to request that Deifebo send him drawings by Agostino Carracci (1557–1602), whom Giulio greatly admired, so that Giulio in turn could show these to Antonio Carracci (1592–1618) in order to enable him to "seize the good invention of his father."[41] Significantly, when Giulio wrote his short biography of Antonio in his *Considerazioni*, he praised him for his invention, a skill he must have attributed in part to his own cultivating role.[42]

3 Mancini in the Papal Court

Giulio's contributions to Rome's artistic culture underwent another profound transformation when he was named personal physician to Urban VIII in 1623, a position he had long coveted, and then in the following year made a Canon of St. Peter's, in which he was to shape court culture. His impact was to be felt in several ways, most thoroughly in his literary endeavors for which he was lauded and furnished with a scribe.[43] Giulio had always been parsimonious and that was not to change now that he was an old man; his view was that literary production, not a collection of paintings, constituted a worthy legacy and avenue to fame.[44] The documentary record attests to his patronage, collecting, gifting and activities as a critic, the latter of which, together with gifting, remained the most significant.

While continuing to respond to Deifebo's requests, Giulio employed a two-pronged approach in his late commissions and acquisitions in selecting work from established artists, on the one hand, thereby reinforcing broad cultural preferences, while promoting young artists of promise (especially Sienese ones), on the other. In 1624, Deifebo requested portraits of the papal family. Francesco Rustici, il Rustichino (ca. 1575–1626) was selected to paint likenesses

40 ASEPD, 169, 30 November 1614, Rome, Giulio to Deifebo Mancini, fol. 165r. Mancini, *Considerazioni*, 212, mentions Sforzoso as author of a treatise on art in Cremona.

41 ASEPD, 169, 25 January 1613, Rome, Giulio to Deifebo Mancini, fol. 40r.

42 Mancini, *Considerazioni*, 220.

43 Gage, *Painting as Medicine*, 28–29.

44 Maccherini, "Giulio Mancini: Committenza," 394. Gage, *Painting as Medicine*, 28–29.

of the pope and Carlo Barberini.[45] Perini soon reported that these were not appearing at all naturalistic, but Giulio expected the arrival of an unnamed young "intelligent" painter from Urbino "who works quickly and well" to execute the likeness of Costanza Magalotti Barberini (1575–1644).[46] Less than two weeks after reporting on the papal portraits, Perini communicated that Giulio was securing the leading painter Cavaliere Cesare d'Arpino (1568–1640) an audience with the pope (thereby encouraging Barberini support for the artist), for which the painter gifted him a *Deposition*.[47] This picture, in turn, became the object of particular interest to Francesco Barberini's *Maestro di Camera*, the collector Ascanio Filomarino (1583–1666), who "had fallen in love" with it and schemed to acquire it by any means at Giulio's death.[48]

Rustichino's portrait of the pope was sketched in by mid-January 1625.[49] The following month, Giulio remarked (through Perini) that he liked Rustichino's hands and Perini noted that Giulio would show the portrait to the pope in order to help the painter find work.[50] By summer, a member of Cardinal Francesco Barberini's entourage reported that Giulio and Marcello Sacchetti (1586–1629), the depository general and papal treasurer, were engaged in negotiations to favor Rustichino.[51] Mancini, Sacchetti and Filomarino formed a select group of *intendenti* who evidently conferred together upon paintings, evaluating objects collectively or trusting another to do so on their behalf. This evidently occurred when the *Moses* by Guercino (1591–1666) of ca. 1624 (Galleria Colonna, Palazzo Colonna), arrived as a gift to Giulio.[52] The fact that Giulio's *vita* of Pietro da Cortona (1596–1669) was drafted the following year suggests that Sacchetti was in turn soliciting the papal physician's opinion of his youthful protegé. This underscores the relationship between the practices of reception and judgment in the Barberini court and Mancini's *Considerazioni*. Here Giulio explicitly noted Cortona's *Triumph of Bacchus* (fig. 10.2) and a *Sacrifice*

45 ASEPD, 170, 22 June 1624, Cesare Perini to Deifebo Mancini, fol. 461.

46 Ibid. Portrait commissions, relatively economical, demonstrated attachment to the Barberini, and could have been easily circulated or sold in Siena.

47 Gage, *Painting as Medicine*, 30.

48 ASEPD, 170, Rome, 11 and 19 July 1631, Cesare Perini to Deifebo Mancini, fols. 138r, 140r. This painting is surely the picture listed in the 1685 Filomarino inventory. See Loredana Lorizzo, *La collezione del cardinale Filomarino*, 109, no. 51.

49 ASEPD, 170, 15 January 1625, Rome, Mattia Naldi to Deifebo Mancini, fol. 577r. Maccherini, "Giulio Mancini, committenza e commercio," 421, no. 6.11, notes that Giulio had already helped Rustichino in 1615.

50 ASEPD, 170, 8 February 1625, Rome, Cesare Perini to Deifebo Mancini, fol. 582r.

51 ASEPD, 169, 4 July 1625, Fontainebleau, Agostino Oliveti to Cesare Perini, fol. 995. The letter is not entirely legible.

52 Gage, "New Documents on Mancini," 654.

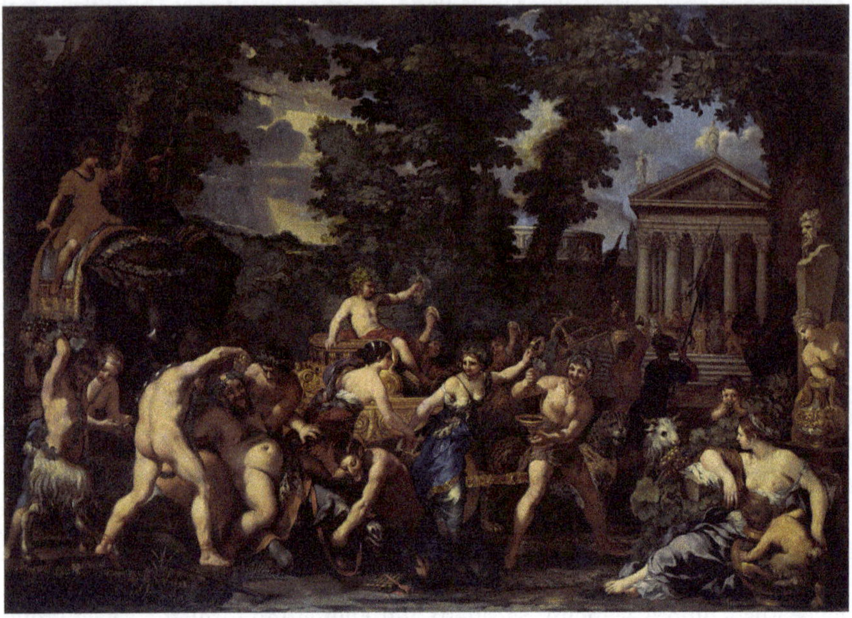

FIGURE 10.2 Pietro da Cortona (1596–1669), *The Triumph of Bacchus*, ca. 1625. Oil on canvas, 56.69 × 81.49 in.
PINACOTECA CAPITOLINA, ROME

(certainly the *Sacrifice of Polyxena*), which he must have observed on an occasion similar to the one in which Sacchetti evaluted Guercino's *Moses*.[53] In praising Cortona's drawing *al naturale* and representation of night scenes and antiquities, the Sienese physician responded to but also encouraged a cultural taste for the artist among the readers of his treatise, presumably doing so *viva voce* as well.

In February 1626, Perini reported that Rustichino's portrait of the pope was not succeeding and Perini, undoubtedly encouraged by Giulio, would provide Rustichino access to the pope so that the painter would produce a more accurate likeness.[54] Eventually it was acknowledged that, even though Giulio had made Rustichino produce this picture and the painter had spent hours with the pope, he painted an awkward (*goffo*) portrait, rendering the pope in the form of Bacchus. It did not please at all.[55] Probably to compensate

53 Guarino, "Con grandissima leggiadria," 68. Guarino cast doubt that Mancini had seen these paintings, but there is now no doubt.

54 ASEPD, 170, 21 February 1626, Rome, Cesare Perini to Deifebo Mancini, fol. 681r. And also the following note.

55 Ibid., and ASEPD, 170, 6 June 1626, Rome, Cesare Perini to Deifebo Mancini, fol 692r. This probably means that the pope unintentionally recalled Bacchus, not that it was a disguised portrait. Perini could have made this comparison to reiterate its inappropriateness.

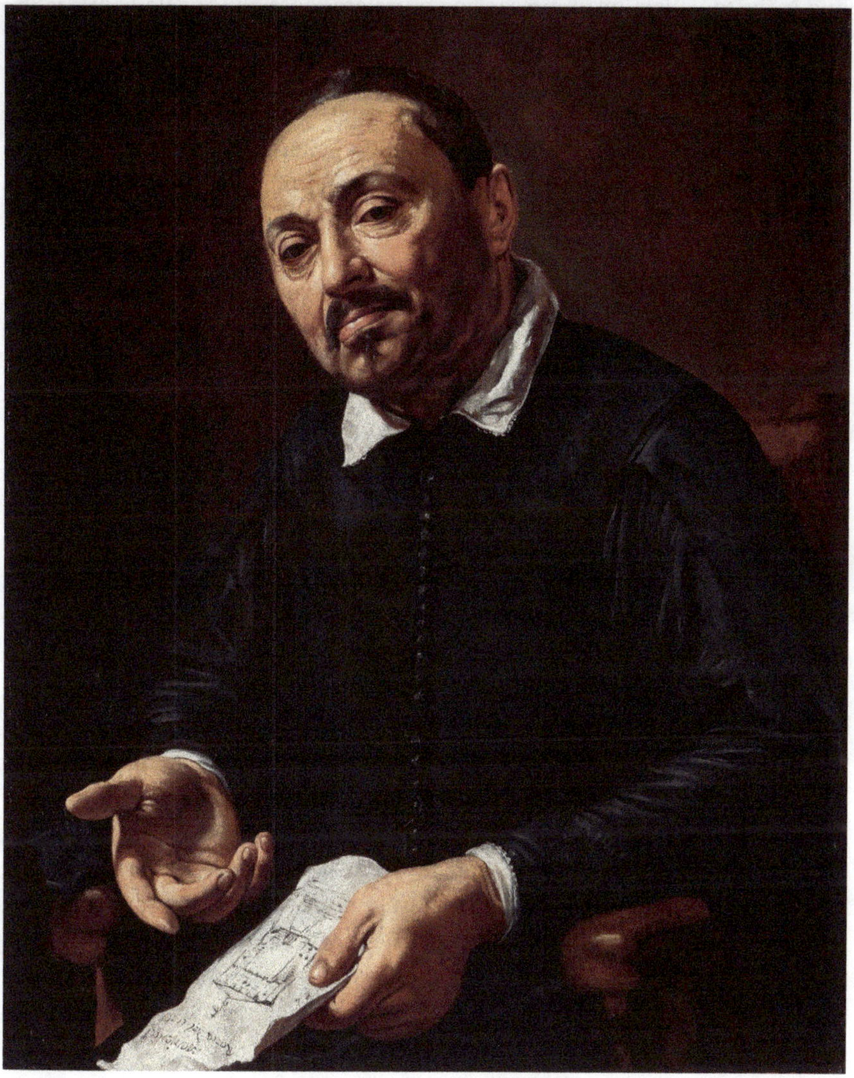

FIGURE 10.3 Valentin de Boulogne (1591–1632), *Portrait of Raffaello Menicucci*, ca. 1627–28. Oil on canvas, 31 ¾ × 25 7/8 in.
INDIANAPOLIS MUSEUM OF ART, INDIANAPOLI

for this, Giulio in 1627 took up the idea of another portrait commission, now suggesting an unnamed French artist for the task, probably Valentin de Boulogne (ca. 1591–1632), who not only worked within the Barberini orbit in these years but also produced court portraits such as of the jester Raffaello Menicucci (Indianapolis Museum of Art) (ca. 1627–28) (fig. 10.3) and another one (private collection) representing a prelate, possibly Angelo Giori (1586–1662), and others now lost.[56]

These examples shed light on Giulio's activities, but still do not demonstrate the full import of his role as taste-maker in Barberini Rome. For that we must turn to the career of Giovanni Lanfranco (1582–1647), from whom Giulio was also actively commissioning more significant pictures. Documentation is incomplete and postdates Giulio's death, when a dispute between Deifebo and the painter arose concerning payment for an unfinished and lost *Martyrdom of St. Bartholomew* (fig. 10.4) for the Mancini chapel in San Martino, Siena, for which Lanfranco was asking at least 500 scudi, while Deifebo thought a price of 300 to be high.[57] The dispute, which entailed numerous judgments of Lanfranco's altarpiece carried out by friends of the Mancini brothers, including artists such as Baccio Ciarpi da Barga (Cortona's master), shed light on important and hitherto unnoted contributions by Mancini to contemporary artistic culture.[58]

One of Lanfranco's justifications for an inflated fee was that he had tirelessly sought to please an overbearing Mancini, by "doing and undoing the painting repeatedly," a comment that again strongly suggests that the papal physician developed distinctive and forcefully held aesthetic ideas, which he exerted in commissions.[59] Lanfranco might have sought to portray Giulio as overweening when critiquing and thereby attempting to modify the picture in progress, but we have already seen that the latter intentionally set out to inform the style and appearance of paintings by Antonio Carracci and Rustichino. In the case of Lanfranco, it is unclear how Mancini directed the painter to alter his canvas, but according to Agostino Chigi, Rector of Santa Maria della Scala in Siena, the good and vivacious figures in the work were done while monsignor was alive, suggesting Giulio played a direct role in keeping their quality high.[60]

In this dispute, as each party sought to manipulate the price by interweaving arguments about the number of additional goods or services the other party

56 Lemoine, Christiansen, et al, *Valentin de Boulogne*, 193, cat. 41 and 128, ct. 18, painted a few years earlier. Valentin produced portraits of the Barberini, including Francesco, and members of the court including Cassiano dal Pozzo, Ascanio and Scipione Filomarino, suggesting Mancini participated in the development of this cultural taste at this moment. ASEPD, 170, 1 May, 1627, Rome, Cesare Perini to Deifebo Mancini, fol. 843r, reported Mancini selected the artist "for his excellence."

57 For the picture, its compositional study in Oxford and the dispute, see Maccherini, "Ritratto di Giulio Mancini," 51; Gage, "'It is not so easy'," 76–79; Schleier, *Giovanni Lanfranco*, 375–77.

58 ASEPD, 170, 11 July 1631, Rome, Cesare Perini to Deifebo Mancini, 139r. It's unclear when the Mancini brothers met Ciarpi.

59 Gage, "'It is not so easy'," 79.

60 ASEPD, 167, 4, month unknown, 1631, Rome, Agostino Chigi to Matteo Naldi, fol. 126v.

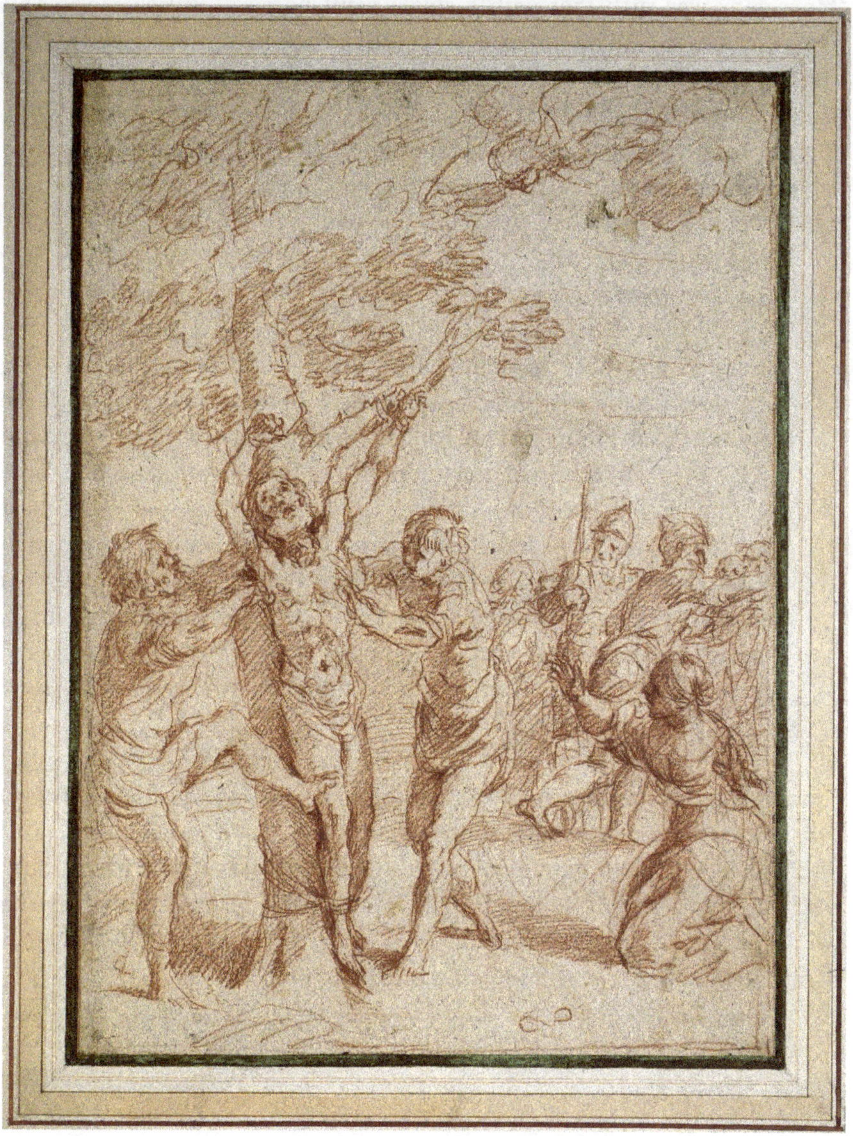

FIGURE 10.4 Giovanni Lanfranco (1582–1647), *Compositional Study for the Martyrdom of St. Bartholomew*. Red chalk on ivory white paper, 13.46 × 9.84 in.
CHRIST CHURCH PICTURE GALLERY, OXFORD

had received, Lanfranco not only asserted he had given paintings to Mancini—for which he must have received payment in kind, as had d'Arpino—but also made the strategic error of boasting of Giulio's power to promote him, thereby hoping to shame Deifebo into paying the full amount the artist demanded.

"Monsignor was such that with a single word he could enrich me."[61] This remark attests to Giulio's power to sway artistic culture on account of his elevated social rank as well as reputation as a critic. Lanfranco, however, quickly realized he had undermined his own position. Thinking better of it, he took the opposite tone the following day when he met Perini, insisting that Mancini had done nothing for him whatsoever. Perini immediately hit back with a withering rejoinder. He reported to Deifebo:

> It was necessary to respond to him as I responded, telling him that he lied, because, from the deceased Monsignor Uncle, he had received every kind of service [possible,] [Mancini] having dragged friends and patrons along to favor him to have work, as he had done with the work in San Paolo, the painting in San Pietro, and the Knighthood, and other medium sized and large works, which he had from more and diverse people and when there were none of them, they were there and followed him—I being most informed about this—and were there to make him known and give him satisfaction. And because he desired to serve him, he made *Nostro Signore* come to see his work in the Cupola of San Andrea della Valle [fig. 10.5]. Similar princes don't move to see paintings; there are other painters [who are] *valentuomini* and not inferior [to Lanfranco], who have not had such honors at the end of their work.[62]

Perini thought his diatribe was effective, for at the end of it, he said, Lanfranco "remained ashamed and didn't know [what to say] ... and he left mortified."[63] Although Perini could have exaggerated his uncle's sway in the papal court, Lanfranco himself had confirmed Giulio's influence—his power to enrich the painter with a mere word—in what was a powerful testimony of Mancini's significance as a taste-maker in Barberini Rome.

4 Conclusion

As a student, Mancini acted as a broker of art objects, but his personal preference remained for books that facilitated the acquisition of knowledge. His inclinations for and critical judgment of painting truly developed after his move to

61 ASEPD, 170, 27 December 1630, Rome, Giovanni Lanfranco to Deifebo Mancini, fol. 20r.

62 ASEPD, 170, 28 December 1630, Rome, Cesare Perini to Deifebo Mancini, fol. 103v. For the bitter competition in San Andrea between Lanfranco and Domenichino, see Cropper, *The Domenichino Affair*.

63 See Perini's letter of 28 December, 1630, as in previous note.

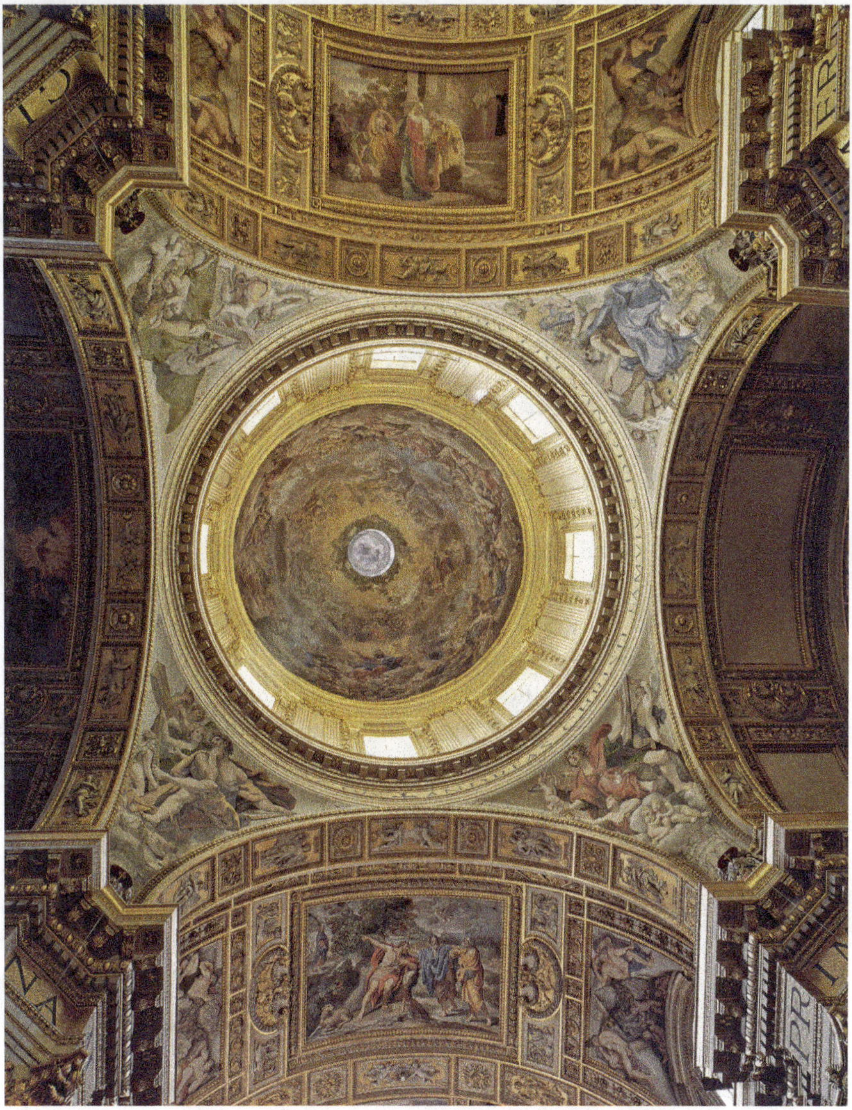

FIGURE 10.5 Giovanni Lanfranco (1582–1647), *Assumption of the* Virgin, 1625–27. Fresco, Cupola of San Andrea della Valle, Rome

the Eternal City, when he gained access to a broad history of art in Rome's churches as well as through his profession of medicine, in which he frequented men of all walks of life, including artists, elite patrons and art collectors, all of whom contributed to the formation of his conception of painting.[64] In the first

64 For Mancini's biography, see Gage, *Painting as Medicine*, 25–32.

two decades of the seventeenth century, Mancini's activities as agent and critic increasingly evolved together. Mancini sharpened his critical abilities through his conversations with artists, from whom he learned about techniques, terminology and artistic judgment.[65] The paintings he eventually evaluated in his *Considerazioni* often corresponded to those he had observed or acquired, whether to sell the latter immediately or to keep for a time and then pass on via the market or gifting.[66] Despite the direct link to personal experience, Mancini presented largely neutral descriptions or favorable critical judgments of the varied styles and manners of artists active in Rome within his *Considerazioni*, presenting potential patrons with a catalogue of artists for selection and underscoring their relative promise or availability.[67] With few exceptions, he suppressed negative criticism in his treatise, such as Rustichino's inability to produce a likeness. His overarching critical evaluations in this context therefore diverged from the personal opinions he sometimes articulated to Deifebo, Cesare Perini, or to fellow *intendenti*.

The final shift in Mancini's career occurred following his appointment to the rank of papal physician and then to monsignor, a juncture at which his acclaim on account of his literary activities and position as a taste-maker reached its zenith. Mancini sponsored young artists of promise within the papal court as well as artists well-known in Rome, if still awaiting Barberini support.[68] When he perceived that Lanfranco, who had seen his support from the Sacchetti and others decline, lacked patronage from those of Giulio's rank, he seized the opportunity; Lanfranco was an admired artist and former pupil of Annibale, the "great master" Mancini most admired.[69] Yet Lanfranco's *Martyrdom of St. Bartholomew*, Giulio's single most significant life-time commission, never reached its final destination. Following Giulio's death, Deifebo remained dissatisfied with the picture, which had apparently declined in quality without the supervision and insistence of Giulio to maintain it.[70] Ultimately then, Giulio's most important legacy in his patronage of this artist was ensuring Lanfranco's subsequent success with the Barberini, thereby imprinting cultural tastes and helping to maintain the canonical status of the Carracci and their pupils in Rome into the fourth decade of the seventeenth century.

Mancini negotiated the dialectical relationship between cultural taste and personal inclination in his artistic endeavors and throughout his

65 Gage, "Visual Evidence and Periodization," 259–60.

66 Gage, *Painting as Medicine*, 27.

67 Gage, "'It is not so easy'," 73.

68 Mochi Onori. "Giovanni Lanfranco e la famiglia Barberini," 77.

69 Mancini, *Considerazioni*, 247.

70 For the subsequent history of this picture, see Gage, "'It is not so easy'," 79.

Considerazioni. For instance, whereas Mancini's admiration for Annibale remained firmly imprinted on his treatise, Giulio recognized already in 1612 that Guido Reni "is held to be the best and better now than Annibale was during his convalescence," as he remarked to Deifebo.[71] Even after 1621, at a point when Mancini was an experienced critic and supported by ever more elite patrons, he deferred to those with "greater understanding" of Reni when writing about Paul v's commissions of the Annunciation and Pauline Chapels in the Quirinal Palace and S. Maria Maggiore respectively.[72] (Here deference to another's judgment corresponded as much to rank as anything.) Following Annibale's death, Giulio had little choice but to respond to the widespread proclivity for the Carracci pupils, but this no doubt reflected his personal preferences and his critical assessments. Assuming the position of principal patron of Lanfranco for a time brought him honor and influence. All the while Mancini stayed directly informed about Cortona and Bernini and other emerging artists through his own endeavors and his contacts with Sacchetti, Filomarino and the Barberini, and promoted young painters such as Rustichino and Valentin, consolidating his influence at court and across Rome.

Bibliography

Bartalini, Roberto. *Le occasioni del Sodoma: dalla Milano di Leonardo alla Roma di Raffaello*. Rome: Donzelli, 1996.

Bourdieu, Pierre. *Distinction: A Social Critique of the Judgement of Taste*. Translated by Richard Nice. Cambridge, MA: Harvard University Press, 1984.

Cropper, Elizabeth. *The Domenichino Affair: Novelty, Imitation, and Theft in Seventeenth-Century Rome*. New Haven: Yale University Press, 2005.

Cropper, Elizabeth, and Charles Dempsey. *Nicolas Poussin: Friendship and the Love of Painting*. Princeton: Princeton University Press, 1996.

Frigo, Alberto. "Can One Speak of Painting if One Cannot Hold a Brush?: Giulio Mancini, Medicine and the Birth of the Connoisseur." *Journal of the History of Ideas* 73, no. 3 (2012): 417–36.

Gage, Frances. "Giulio Mancini's *Considerazioni sulla pittura*: Recreation, Manners and Decorum in Seventeenth-Century Roman Picture Galleries." Ph.D. diss., Johns Hopkins University, 2000.

71 Maccherini, "Ritratto di Giulio Mancini," 50–1.

72 Mancini, *Considerazioni*, 241.

Gage, Frances. "Exercise for Mind and Body: Giulio Mancini, Collecting, and the Beholding of Landscape Painting in the Seventeenth Century." *Renaissance Quarterly* 61, no. 4 (2008): 1167–1207.

Gage, Frances. "Teaching Them to Serve and Obey: Giulio Mancini on Collecting Religious Art in Seventeenth-Century Rome." In *Sacred Possessions: Collecting Italian Religious Art, 1500–1900*, edited by Gail Feigenbaum and Sybille Ebert-Schifferer with the assistance of Galina Tirnanić, 68–82. Los Angeles: Getty Research Institute, 2011.

Gage, Frances. "Observing Order." *Display of Art in The Roman Palace, 1550–1750*, edited by Gail Feigenbaum with Francesco Freddolini, 204–16. Los Angeles: Getty Research Institute, 2014.

Gage, Frances. "Illness, Invention and Truth." In *Gifts in Return: Essays in Art in Honor of Charles Dempsey*, edited by Melinda Schlitt, 337–62. Toronto: Center for Reformation and Renaissance Studies, 2012.

Gage, Frances. "New Documents on Giulio Mancini and Guercino." *The Burlington Magazine* 156, no. 1339 (2014): 653–656.

Gage, Frances. "Visual Evidence and Periodization in Giulio Mancini's Observations on Early Christian and Medieval Art in Rome." In *Remembering the Middle Ages in Early Modern Italy*, edited by Lorenzo Pericolo and Jessica N. Richardson, 257–69. Turnhout: Brepols, 2015.

Gage, Frances. *Painting as Medicine in Early Modern Rome: Giulio Mancini and the Efficacy of Art*. University Park, PA: Pennsylvania State University Press, 2016.

Gage, Frances. "'It is not so easy to recognize the period and age of paintings': Visual and Textual Evidence in Giulio Mancini's *Considerazioni sulla pittura* and in Early Modern Connoisseurship." In *Zeigen – Überzeugen – Beweisen: Methoden der Wissensproduktion in Kunstliteratur, Kennerschaft und Sammlungspraxis der Frühen Neuzeit*, edited by Elisabeth Oy-Marra and Irina Schmiedel, 63–87. Merzhausen: ad picturam, 2020.

Guarino, Sergio. "'Con grandissima leggiadria et diletto dei riguardanti': Note su Pietro da Cortona e i Sacchetti." In *Pietro da Cortona (1597–1669)*, edited by Anna Lo Bianco, 67–72. Milan: Electa, 1997.

Lemoine, Annick, Keith Christiansen, Patrizia Cavazzini, Jean-Pierre Cuzin, Gianni Papi. *Valentin de Boulogne: Beyond Caravaggio*. New York: Metropolitan Museum of Art, 2016.

Lorizzo, Loredana. *La collezione del cardinale Ascanio Filomarino: Pittura, scultura e mercato dell'arte tra Roma e Napoli nel Seicento, con una nota sulla vendita dei beni del Cardinale del Monte*. Naples: Electa, 2006.

Maccherini, Michele. "Caravaggio nel carteggio familiare di Giulio Mancini." *Prospettiva* 86 (1997): 71–92.

Maccherini, Michele. "Novità su Bartolomeo Manfredi nel carteggio familiare di Giulio Mancini: Lo *Sdegno di Marte* e i quadri di Cosimo II granduca di Toscana." *Prospettiva* 93–94 (1999): 131–41.

Maccherini, Michele. "Novità sulle *Considerazioni* di Giulio Mancini." In *Caravaggio nel IV centenario della Cappella Contarelli: Convegno internazionale di studi*, edited by Caterina Volpi, 123–28. Città di Castello: Petruzzi, 2002.

Maccherini, Michele. "Ritratto di Giulo Mancini." In *Bernini dai Borghese ai Barberini: La cultura a Roma intorno agli anni venti*, edited by Olivier Bonfait and Anna Coliva, 47–57. Rome: De Luca, 2004.

Maccherini, Michele. "Giulio Mancini: Committenza e commercio di opere d'arte fra Siena e Roma." *Siena e Roma: Raffaello, Caravaggio e i protagonisti di un legame antico*, 393–401. Siena: Protagon Editore, 2005.

Mancini, Giulio. *Considerazioni sulla pittura.* Edited by Adriana Marucchi. 2 vols. Rome: Accademia Nazionale dei Lincei, 1956–57.

Mancini, Giulio. "Discorso di pittura." In *Considerazioni sulla pittura*, edited by Adriana Marucchi, vol. 1. Rome: Accademia Nazionale dei Lincei, 1956–57.

Mochi Onori, Lorenzo. "Giovanni Lanfranco e la famiglia Barberini." In *Giovanni Lanfranco: Un pittore barocco tra Parma, Roma e Napoli*, edited by Erich Schleier, 77–82. Milan: Electa, 2002.

Paul, Carole. *The First Modern Museums of Art: The Birth of an Institution in 18th- and Early-19th-Century Europe.* Los Angeles: The J. Paul Getty Museum, 2012.

Pierguidi, Stefano. "Giulio Mancini e la nascita della 'connoisseurship'." *Zeitschrift für Kunstgeschichte* 79 (2016): 63–71.

Rice, Louise. "Bernini and the Pantheon Bronze," *Sonderdruck aus Sankt Peter in Rome: 1506–2006.* Beiträge der internationalen Tagung vom 22–25 Februar 2006 in Bonn. Edited by George Satzinger and Sebastian Schütze, 337–352. Munich: Hirmer Verlag 2008.

Schleier, Erich. *Giovanni Lanfranco: Un pittore barocco tra Parma, Roma e Napoli.* Milan: Electa, 2002.

Sparti, Donatella. "Novità su Giulio Mancini: Medicina, arte e presunta 'connoisseurship.'" *Mitteilungen des Kunsthistorischen Institutes in Florenz* 52, no. 1 (2008): 53–72.

Index of Subjects

www.ingramcontent.com/pod-product-compliance
Lightning Source LLC
Chambersburg PA
CBHW071323230926
51849CB00002B/304